POLITICS AND
PUBLIC MORALITY

POLITICS AND PUBLIC MORALITY:
THE GREAT AMERICAN WELFARE REFORM DEBATE ★★★

GARY BRYNER

Brigham Young University

W · W · NORTON & COMPANY · NEW YORK · LONDON

The text of this book is composed in New Caledonia
with the display set in Berthold Waldbaum Book
Composition by PennSet, Inc.
Manufacturing by The Courier Companies, Inc.
Book design by Jack Meserole

Library of Congress Cataloging-in-Public Data
Bryner, Gary C., 1951–
    Politics and public morality : the great American welfare reform debate /
  Gary Bryner.
       p.   cm.
    Includes bibliographical references and index.
    ISBN 0-393-97173-2 (pbk.)
    1. Public welfare—United States.   2. Public welfare—Moral and
  ethical aspects.   I. Title.
  HV95.B74   1997
  362.5'8'0973—dc21   97-33693

W. W. Norton & Company, Inc., 500 Fifth Avenue, New York, N.Y. 10110
http://www.wwnorton.com
W. W. Norton & Company Ltd., 10 Coptic Street, London WC1A 1PU
1 2 3 4 5 6 7 8 9 0

To Larry and Virginia Stevens

Contents

Acknowledgments

My goal in writing this book is to lay out the history and evolution of welfare policy and reform efforts, explain how the law has changed, and explore the experience of states in reforming welfare. I hope this book will be useful to readers as a source of information about the debate and a framework for assessing the issues. My own conclusions naturally shape the discussion and analysis, but I offer them as part of the analysis and invite readers to examine the arguments and propose their own responses to the issues. I am convinced that welfare policy reform must go well beyond fixing welfare. Solutions to welfare problems will require an enormous amount of good will, hard work, and coordinated effort by all members of the community and cannot simply be imposed through a national program. Reforming welfare is only part of a much broader agenda of actions needed to improve prospects for those whose lives are stifled by a lack of opportunity for meaningful work and participation in social and economic life.

Just as important as examining the politics of welfare or any other policy is an inquiry into the consequences of policy making for our long-term, collective capacity to address and remedy important public problems. This book seeks to encourage discussion among citizens, interested groups, policy makers, and students of politics and public policy about the most promising ways of reforming the welfare system to deal with poverty among American families. It seeks to provide some of the information people need to participate in the debate, assess competing diagnoses and proposed remedies, and suggest public policies and voluntary actions that we should pursue.

In writing this book I have accumulated an enormous number of debts, and I am grateful for the opportunity to acknowledge them here. This project has required the collection and organization of a great deal of information, and several research assistants have made major contributions to the project. I greatly appreciate the work of Allison Wiltbank Brady, Jennifer Hogge, and Elizabeth Romney. During the last year, while writing the chapters, I had the great fortune to have Danille Christensen help me organize materials, identify key issues, and collect information from states and federal agencies. She also edited the manuscript and made major contributions to every chapter. The project could not have been completed without her. Funding for this research was generously provided by the Women's Research Institute, the Virginia Cutler lectureship, and the research committee of the College of Family, Home, and Social Sciences, all at Brigham Young University. Welfare agency officials in virtually every state have been most helpful in sending information about their welfare reform programs and answering questions. Officials in the Department of Health and Human Services, congressional committees with responsibility for welfare, and representatives of advocacy groups have also provided indispensable assistance. I have benefited greatly from participation in and attendance at panels organized by the Association for Public Policy Analysis and Management and the American Political Science Association on the topic of welfare reform. The citations in the endnotes and bibliography do not begin to acknowledge how much I have learned from scholars of welfare policy. David Stoesz provided many helpful suggestions in his review of the manuscript, and Barbara Gerr did a wonderful job copyediting it. Sarah Caldwell, Steve Dunn, Roby Harrington, and others at W. W. Norton have vastly improved the manuscript I first sent to them, and it has been a great pleasure to work with them.

Most important has been the support of my family and their patience as I have worked on this book. That support and interest reaches beyond my immediate family to my extended family, and I gratefully dedicate this book to Larry and Virginia Stevens for their kindness, support, and love.

Introduction

Welfare has been one of the United States' most intractable public policy challenges over the last thirty years. Debate over welfare "reform" regularly reappears in presidential elections; the promise to "end welfare as we know it" is the bipartisan creed of presidential and congressional candidates. For conservatives and liberals, welfare is a fundamentally important political issue, either representative of everything wrong with the American welfare state policy or one of the central collective obligations we all share and a primary responsibility of government. The symbolic importance of welfare in the American political system dwarfs its actual share (about 1 percent) of the Federal budget.

Welfare policy is intertwined with some of the most pressing public problems in the United States, ranging from poverty, racism, sexism, crime, and urban decline to the status of women, children, and the family. The debate over welfare reform is ultimately a debate over the public values to which Americans subscribe, the growing uneasiness more and more working Americans feel about their economic future, and the role of government and the future of the welfare state. Welfare itself is sometimes blamed for perpetuating an urban underclass—plagued by crime, drug use, out-of-wedlock childbirths, high unemployment, and racial hostility—by sending checks to single mothers.[1]

Welfare policy is particularly important because of its impact on those who are most vulnerable in our society—single-parent families, children, the poor, and residents of economically depressed urban areas. Welfare policy also has an important impact on the family as the central social unit of American society. Because it is so politically visible, an effective welfare policy is a critical component of the agenda for re-dressing poverty in America, but successful policies seem to elude us. There is widespread dissatisfaction with the current system and growing cynicism that it can ever be successful in reducing poverty and helping its intended beneficiaries to become self-sufficient. For some, welfare reflects the "feminization of poverty," where women and children have come to dominate the poverty rolls. For others, welfare traps women and children in a cycle of dependency and lack of economic and social opportunity.

The term *welfare* has many meanings: It has sometimes described the Aid to Families with Dependent Children (AFDC) program; other times it has represented all means-tested programs (those based on recipients' income) aimed at helping low-income Americans, such as Food Stamps, Medicaid, and Supplemental Social Insurance. Some-times it is used to describe federal programs, whereas other times peo-ple mean it to include both federal and state efforts. In contrast, AFDC has usually been an unambiguous reference to that one program. Some people use *welfare* to mean only the AFDC program; this is the source of some misunderstanding. Critics of welfare, for example, regularly cite the figure of some $5 trillion as the cost of welfare over the past forty years, and argue that the reduction or elimination of AFDC is an es-sential element of any balanced budget or spending-reduction plan. Others emphasize that AFDC only represents about 1 percent of the federal budget, so spending cuts would not provide a major source of budget savings. The discussion here generally uses *welfare* in the broader sense of describing AFDC (and the program created in 1996 to replace it, Temporary Assistance for Needy Families), Food Stamps, Medicaid, SSI, and other means-tested programs aimed at poor families because that is the way Congress and others generally used the term throughout the debate. But caution is required since the term's use can be confusing.

Welfare reform is sometimes equated with a virtual overhaul of the welfare state, reaching Food Stamps and nutrition programs, Medicaid, enforcement of child-support obligations, public housing, and funding for child care, but much of the attention has been directed toward remedying the long-term dependency of female-headed families on AFDC. The welfare system has undergone periodic legislative and ad-ministrative modifications in response to changes in society, culture, and economics, but has never been as complex as some other policy areas such as health care. Advocates for more generous benefits and programs have battled with those who resent that taxes paid by working people are going to those who are not working. Advocates for helping poor women and children bump up against those who fear the personal and social consequences of illegitimacy and teenage mothers.

The agenda for welfare reform has come to focus on a relatively small number of issues—how to reduce long-term dependency from one generation to the next, how to provide effective preparation for work, how to create incentives to encourage work and self-sufficiency, and how to provide child care, health insurance, and other support programs once welfare recipients begin to work. There is widespread agreement that welfare dependency harms women and children and that the solution is to help welfare mothers find jobs and to discourage the formation of new female-headed, low-income families. Although debate continues over the best way to help recipients become self-sufficient and move into the work force and discourage the creation of new welfare families, the issues are manageable and solutions seem possible. The costs of even the most ambitious reforms are relatively modest, in comparison with other social programs, but a significant increase in welfare spending, if that is what is required to reform welfare, is not likely.

Despite the characteristics of welfare policy that ought to make effective reform possible, we have largely failed to generate the political support to remedy the problems that plague welfare. Welfare reform has regularly fallen victim to politics. The Family Support Act of 1988, for example, passed with bipartisan support and much fanfare, promised to revolutionize welfare but failed to do so. Welfare reform has mostly been a set of exaggerated promises that have created unreasonable expectations and have resulted in more cynicism and skepticism when the next round of promises are made.

No politician has done more to raise expectations about welfare reform than Bill Clinton, whose 1992 presidential election campaign generated great support by promising to "end welfare as we know it." The Clinton administration's welfare reform task force and congressional initiatives in 1993 and 1994 promised welfare reform, but the Democratic Congress had failed to act by November 1994, when the Republicans gained control of Congress. The "Contract with America," proposed by the Republican leadership of the House of Representatives as a platform for candidates to run on and an agenda for the first days of the new Congress, included welfare reform as one of its primary goals. The Contract culminated in the bill passed by the House in March 1995, which dramatically reformulated welfare policy. The Senate passed its welfare reform bill with bipartisan support in 1995. By the end of 1995, however, welfare reform had fallen victim to the acrimonious budget process.

More promising was the welfare reform agenda of states. Throughout the 1980s and early 1990s, states had taken the lead in experimenting with welfare policy initiatives. These state programs have been widely copied throughout the nation and have served as the basis for national proposals. Governors have used welfare reform to build political reputations as policy innovators. Welfare reform has been used to cut state spending in many states, but in others it has led to expanded services to some poor women and children and improved the chance that they will become self-sufficient. States saw in welfare reform the opportunity to continue to receive federal funds but with many fewer strings attached.

In July 1996, political calculations were revised, and Congress once again passed a welfare reform bill. This time, after negotiations with Congress and within the Clinton administration, in August the president signed a historic welfare reform bill, the Personal Responsibility and Work Opportunity Reconciliation Act of 1996. (The term *reconciliation* is included in the title to reflect another purpose of the law, to help reconcile government revenues and expenditures in pursuing the goal of a balanced budget.) Although the new welfare law was hailed as reform, it would be more accurately described as welfare devolution— welfare policy has largely been delegated to states. It ends welfare as a Federal entitlement, where benefits are assured to all persons who meet the qualifications, and converts it to block grants that can be used by states to devise whatever kind of welfare program they choose. It gave AFDC a new name, Temporary Assistance to Needy Families (TANF). States are free to devise comprehensive programs to help welfare recipients or to save money by cutting programs; welfare can include a mix of social services or be primarily a job-finding program. States may contract with religious, charitable, and private organizations to provide services to recipients. With the law now enacted, states have continued to experiment in order to devise the kind of welfare system that is most compatible with their political, social, and economic values and constraints.

Although states have broad discretion in devising their own welfare programs, federal funds can be spent only in certain ways. Recipients are eligible for assistance only for up to two years at a time, with a five-year lifetime cap for receiving benefits. States cannot use federal funds to provide cash benefits to children born to women already on welfare, to noncitizens, or to single, teenage mothers who do not live with their parents. In order to receive their full grants, states must ensure that a certain percentage of recipients are participating in work activities. And states must spend on their new assistance program at least 80 percent of what they spent on welfare in 1994.

The passage of the new welfare law in 1996 has not ended the great American debate over welfare reform. During the 1996 presidential campaign, President Clinton promised to reform the reforms and seek new funding to restore some of the $35 billion worth of cuts that had little to do with reforming welfare, but that affected other social programs. Some conservatives complained that welfare had not been changed enough and promised to push for more; some liberals warned that the changes had gone too far and promised to restore some provisions. In 1997, Congress again took up welfare issues in a budget reconciliation bill, and provided $13 billion in new grants to states to provide Supplemental Social Insurance benefits to legal immigrants who were in the United States on August 22, 1996 (when the new law was enacted), give Medicaid benefits for disabled children who lost SSI benefits under the new law, and extend benefits to 15 percent of the able-bodied and childless adults between 18 and 50 who had been denied eligibility for Food Stamps in 1996. An additional $3 billion was allocated to spend on moving welfare recipients who were poorly prepared for work into jobs. The 1997 changes also prohibited states from contracting to private entities decisions concerning eligibility for Food Stamps and Medicaid and expanded Medicaid benefits to reach an additional five million poor children. Congress upheld regulations issued in May 1997 by the Department of Labor that ordered employers to comply with the Fair Labor Standards Act and other federal requirements in programs moving recipients from welfare to work. Republicans in Congress and many governors warned that requiring employers to pay the minimum wage and comply with other Labor Department mandates would make it too expensive to hire welfare recipients. But Democrats vigorously defended the minimum wage and insisted that welfare recipients be treated as others, and armed with the threat of a presidential veto, the Democrats prevailed. While the Republicans largely got the kind of welfare reform legislation they wanted in 1996, President Clinton achieved most of the changes he promised to pursue when he signed the new welfare law.

The welfare reform debate will continue for years as part of our public discussion of how to reduce poverty in America. America's most pressing social problem is to find solutions to the poverty that has enveloped many urban neighborhoods. At least for the next few years, that debate will increasingly take place in the states and communities, and less in Washington. Solutions to poverty and options for making welfare a program that promotes self-sufficiency, work, and strong families require our best public efforts. Welfare and poverty pose tremendous challenges to states, cities, counties, and communities, particularly in areas where welfare has contributed to and sustains a cycle of lost opportunity, despair, and dependency.[2] But they will also continue to require some national decisions about federal funding and goals.

In the past, the debate over welfare reform has in part served as an excuse to avoid the broader issues. Politicians have competed with each other to see who could be most critical of welfare mothers. Attacks on the poor and on the welfare system on which they are dependent have substituted for the more troublesome debate over how to improve the prospects of low-income Americans and increase equality of opportunity. Although the devolution of responsibility for welfare to the states means that we will continue to struggle with difficult issues of helping welfare recipients, the passage of the new law can also free us to focus on improved education and training, improved child care and access to health care, and, ultimately, the goal of ensuring that every person who is able to work will have a job. But devolution also carries the risk that in passing the welfare law we will feel we have done all that needs to be done to address poverty and can comfortably go on to other issues and concerns.

A FRAMEWORK FOR ASSESSING WELFARE REFORM

The welfare reform debate can be examined from a variety of perspectives. The politics of welfare policy provides a unique occasion to study in detail the interaction of Congress and the White House in the legislative process, the differences in how the Senate and House operate, the role of organized interests, public opinion, and the other elements of the political process. It is a particularly useful vehicle to examine federalism and the growing interest in rethinking the responsibilities of state and national governments. Perhaps no other issue is so heavily influenced by a debate over values and public morality than is welfare. The debate points up the sharp contrast between liberal and conservative political philosophy and goes to the heart of questions about what is the appropriate role of government and what are the limits of public policies. Because it is so important and politically visible, welfare policy has consequences for the political system that go beyond changes in welfare programs themselves to the future of the welfare state and our expectations about what government can accomplish and what tasks it should undertake.

The conventional model of the policy-making process typically includes five general steps: (1) problem identification; (2) getting on the policy agenda; (3) policy formulation; (4) policy implementation; and (5) evaluation and redefinition of the problem. These steps are not discrete events, but are inextricably intertwined; they are not sequential, but form a spiral of interactive efforts. The policy process, for most policies, is never completed, but is a continual attempt to understand problems, devise policies, execute plans, and make adjustments. Welfare and other policies are further complicated by the interaction of different levels of government during each phase of the process. Most important, implementation of policies is critical: Without the prerequisites for effective implementation the entire policy effort is compromised.

This model of the policy-making process provides a structure for describing the major events in the evolution of public policies. However, this framework does not help explain *why* policies evolve the way they do, the consequences of the process for attaining policy goals, or the cumulative capacity of the political system to accomplish public purposes. The debate over policy options to reform welfare poses daunting challenges for policy analysis, and provides an excellent opportunity for exploring how public policies that implicate strongly held normative values can be assessed.[3]

The analysis takes place at four levels. At the heart of any policy assessment is a common-sense inquiry: What are the goals, and how well are they likely to be achieved? These are questions we should ask of all public policies. Answers are difficult, being affected by our predispositions, but they are inescapable. The traditional model of policy analysis centers on one key question: Does the policy at issue accomplish the objectives established for it? Policy analysis here is understood as part of a rational enterprise of identifying a problem, formulating remedial goals, identifying possible consequences and assigning a value to each, and selecting the optimal alternative. Cost-benefit analysis and other analytic tools are used to assess the extent to which policy interventions have caused or will cause the desired outcome.[4]

A second analytic approach places the policy effort in a broader context and asks to what extent the policy goal is relevant to the problem at which it is aimed: Will the promised policy actually solve the problem? How appropriate are the goals, given the nature of the problems? Policies may accomplish their goals rather efficiently and effectively, but if the goals are misdirected or fail to center on the problems to be solved, the policy effort will ultimately fail. This approach also focuses attention on the conflicting policy objectives we pursue and how efforts aimed at one set of goals may conflict with others.[5]

A third framework for policy analysis focuses on the impact of the policy effort on the broader society. To what extent do policy goals affect or contribute to societal values? Are the policy goals consistent with fundamental societal commitments to free markets, equality, justice, fairness, individual rights, and other essential beliefs of the polity? However, there may be little agreement over core public values, or at least over how they come together in assessing public policies such as welfare. Since these fundamental social commitments are themselves to some extent inconsistent, successful policies will require a careful balancing of competing public concerns.[6]

The final set of questions explores the consequences of specific policy efforts for the long-range capacity of politics and government. The cumulative impact of public policies shapes the prospects for future policy efforts and the long-term ability of government to accomplish the important purposes we have for it. Reforms may temporarily reduce some frustrations with the limits of public policies, but the consequences over time or in other policy areas of these reforms may be quite damaging to effective governance. From this perspective, public policies are ultimately judged by their compatibility with self-government, political participation, community, and the other political values that promote democratic citizenship.[7]

The current welfare system, as well as welfare reform proposals, can be assessed on all four levels of analysis. The framework of questions focuses on the political forces that shape expectations of, demands for, and assessments about welfare. It also includes the institutions that create and manage the welfare system and the legal and bureaucratic structures in which the welfare system operates. The following discussion provides an overview of the arguments I explore in the chapters that follow.

AN OVERVIEW OF THE ISSUES AND ARGUMENTS

The new welfare law promises to make some improvements over the old welfare system. The most promising changes are those that require recipients who can work to move quickly into private-sector jobs and that provide the support services, such as child support, necessary for recipients to be able to work. It is difficult to predict the consequences of the new law. The number of people on welfare fell by 1.9 million between January 1993 and August 1996, when the new welfare law was passed, and by an additional 1.45 million between August 1996 and

May 1997. Although politicians were quick to claim that the new law produced the reduction, the new law did not take effect until July 1, 1997. The rise and fall in the welfare rolls is largely a function of the strength of the economy and to a lesser extent of tax policies affecting low-income Americans, enforcement of child support, state welfare policies affecting eligibility and work requirements, and other factors. There is considerable evidence that as states began requiring work and warning recipients of time limits in the early-to-mid 1990s, many potential recipients were discouraged from applying for welfare. Work requirements also affected the expectations of some of those on welfare who began looking for alternatives. However, there is little information available concerning what happened to families dropped from welfare rolls. The real test of welfare reform will come during the next economic downturn, when unemployment rises and it becomes more difficult to find jobs for people on welfare. The ultimate concern is whether more families become self-sufficient and fewer children live in poverty, rather than what happens to welfare rolls.

Reforming welfare—making it more effective in achieving its goal of reducing poverty—is difficult for several reasons. In order to help recipients who are most disadvantaged, most dependent on AFDC, and least likely to be able to leave welfare soon, the training, counseling, and other programs are expensive. It is cheaper to issue a welfare check than to provide the services that might be helpful. We do not know very much about how to prevent welfare dependency and how to end it. Reducing the behaviors that contribute to welfare dependency is difficult: How do we discourage out-of-wedlock teenage pregnancy, for example? It is difficult to ensure that children do not suffer when their parents are irresponsible. Policies aimed at punishing parents or changing their behavior may adversely affect children. Welfare is a highly charged political issue and provides an attractive vehicle for political posturing and gamesmanship that make compromise difficult. Even when welfare programs are successful in helping recipients become self-sufficient, welfare still cannot solve the problems of crime, economic isolation, poor education, discrimination, and lack of jobs confronting many people. Welfare programs depend on these other public policy pursuits, and policy shortcomings in one area will affect efforts in the other areas.

Congress has largely turned the problem of reforming welfare over to the states. The experience of states in experimenting with their own welfare programs varies greatly. States are given great discretion under the new welfare law to devise their own welfare systems. But much of what states will do will build on their experience with pilot programs and other experiments they engaged in during the past ten to fifteen years. In general, the experience of these state programs has been that it is relatively easy to get most recipients a job; the challenge is in providing mentoring and helping them keep their job. The top third of welfare recipients can move rather easily into work once they find jobs. The middle third are not ready for work, but they can be helped with education and training programs and work support like child care and transportation assistance. The bottom third face major barriers to moving into the world of work, such as poor health, children with special needs, domestic violence, drug and alcohol dependency, poor education, and lack of personal skills and discipline. Remedial programs have had only limited success with those most dependent on assistance.

Devolution of welfare policy to states is attractive for several reasons. Welfare policy can be tailored to local concerns, conditions, and priorities even more that the old federal-state partnership permitted. States can work out different ways of helping recipients become self-sufficient; successes can be copied and failures avoided. Perhaps most important, welfare policy can become more of a state and local enterprise, where state policy makers work with nongovernmental organizations, businesses, and private citizens to figure out how best to help welfare families.

However, devolution poses its own set of challenges. We need to find ways to accumulate and share the lessons learned by states and communities over next decade of experimentation. Welfare recipients can still serve as convenient scapegoats for people frustrated with a weak economy or ineffective, unpopular government. Budget pressures can encourage state legislators and governors to cut spending on such programs as welfare that have few influential supporters. States can "race to the bottom" in spending on welfare in order to encourage welfare seekers to go elsewhere and in order to spend public funds on more popular programs. During the first year of the new law, states were more generous with benefits than many expected. Block grants are allocated based on the size of states' caseload in earlier years, when levels were much higher. The dramatic drop in welfare rolls of nearly 24 percent between March 1994 and May 1997 and increased federal spending on child care have given states much more money to spend on welfare under the new law than they received under the old law. That promise of a welfare windfall prompted many governors to enthusiastically support block grants. States have used the funds for child care, transportation subsidies, and health insurance to help in the transition from welfare to work. Restoring cuts to the SSI and Medicaid programs has also softened the impact of the new law. And an economy more robust than projected has made welfare reform appear much easier than expected.

How states have used waivers from the provisions of the national program during the past fifteen years is sobering. Although some states have sought waivers in order to develop more effective welfare-to-work programs, many others have used them to cut benefits, tighten eligibility, and reduce spending. The cheapest way for states to meet the goals of encouraging work is to tighten eligibility requirements. The political incentives to cut spending on welfare and use the funds for programs that constituents support, such as education, will be too strong for many to resist. During an economic downturn, states simply cannot afford to be known as being much more generous with welfare benefits and programs than their neighbors.[8]

States that are committed to helping welfare recipients become self-sufficient face major challenges but only receive modest help under the new law. One of the key elements of the original Clinton welfare reform proposals was that the federal government would serve as the employer of last resort, but that provision was abandoned because of cost. Public employee unions and others fear that moving welfare recipients into work will further depress wages and increase competition for low-skill and entry-level jobs. In some economically depressed areas, there are simply not enough jobs for welfare recipients. In other areas, jobs may be available, but recipients may be so lacking in education, job skills, and experience that they are unemployable. The law allows states to exempt 20 percent of their caseloads from the work requirements and time limits. This means that many families will continue to be dependent on assistance. Little money is available for the intensive, expensive programs necessary for these families become self-sufficient. The new welfare law does not significantly alter the problems faced by families whose breadwinners receive only minimum-wage earnings. Without major increases in the minimum wage, child care subsidies, housing assistance, health insurance, and other benefits, it will still be more of a financial burden on single mothers to work than to stay at home with their children.[9]

The impact of the new law on children is similarly difficult to assess. Some will be better off as their families become more integrated into the world of work and self-sufficiency. Others will bear the brunt of the shortcomings of their parents and the efforts of governments to change behavior. A central element of the old welfare system was a national commitment to provide a social safety net for children; that commitment has now disappeared. Many state reforms developed even before the new law was enacted were heralded as "tough love"—doing what is best for parents by imposing and enforcing strict requirements on resistant adults. But poor children are caught in the middle of that struggle to reform their parents, and part of the price of changing the behavior of parents is to increase the suffering of children. Democrats favored including in the new welfare law vouchers to be given to families for the needs of children, but Republicans removed them because they feared vouchers would maintain dependency. Perhaps states will step in to provide new forms of assistance to children, and we may return as a nation in the near future to the need for a national safety net for children.[10]

The goals of the welfare reform law enacted in 1996 are straightforward and largely consistent with widespread public values: require welfare recipients to work, make parents responsible for their children, reduce pregnancy among single teenage girls, give states flexibility in administering their welfare programs, and reduce federal spending on and responsibility for assistance to poor families. But part of the challenge of welfare reform is the lack of consensus over these goals. For some, reducing out-of-wedlock pregnancy must be a national priority because it undermines key moral values. Anything that makes the lives of single mothers and their children easier is a mistake because it will just encourage that behavior. For others, divorce and single motherhood makes a great deal of sense in certain situations. It is far better to be dependent on government assistance than on an abusive husband. The next rounds of welfare reform debates will need to address these broader issues of the vulnerability of women and children.[11]

Underlying all these goals, although not often expressly addressed in the debate over welfare reform, is the goal of reducing poverty in America. But much of the debate over welfare reform, and the provisions of the law enacted, has focused on the narrower goals and provisions of the welfare system.

The broader policy context in which welfare reform must take place in order to accomplish its overall goal of reducing poverty has largely been ignored in the recent debate. Even if welfare reforms achieves the same specific objectives as the current system, with some of the inconsistencies removed so that the emphasis is primarily on moving recipients into the work force and discouraging single young women from having children and going on welfare, it will not accomplish the broader goal. Welfare recipients will still be battered by the host of problems that confront poor Americans.

In order to end welfare as we know it, we have two broad policy choices: cut back the program drastically and hope that recipients will be able to find ways to meet their needs, or replace welfare with a commitment to finding a job for everyone who wants one. Those who can work should be ensured the opportunity to do so. A commitment to securing work opportunities and providing support for those who work, to include child care, health insurance, Food Stamps and other nutrition programs, and educational opportunities for those who are working to improve their skills, is much more consistent with American public values than simply cutting back on the welfare state. These commitments are challenging but not impossible. They can be achieved by state and local governments with the federal government facilitating the sharing of information and financial assistance. Some people in our society cannot work; we should continue to offer them support through SSI and other programs that permits them to live lives of modest dignity.

More difficult is the agenda surrounding the broader context of poverty in America. In order to pay for the cost of a full-employment policy, other social policies such as middle-class entitlements may have to be revised so benefits are limited to low-income recipients. State and local governments and communities will need to provide minimal food and shelter for those who choose not to work. State and local governments and communities will need to realize more clearly that prevention of social problems is much superior to treating them, and that prevention begins with helping children in families that cannot provide for their basic needs. The host of other collective tasks such as improving public safety, education, housing, transportation, and urban infrastructure are also part of the solution to reducing poverty and creating a more sustainable society.

Welfare reform can address only a small part of the social problems plaguing the nation. We need reasonable expectations about what it can and cannot accomplish. But despite the narrowness of the welfare reform agenda, if its goals are accomplished, it will be a considerable achievement. Welfare reform efforts that require recipients to engage in constructive, contributing activities may help bridge the political chasm separating proponents and opponents of the welfare state. If we can get welfare reform right, we may be able to tackle more complex problems, and we can give a boost to democratic politics and government and to our collective capacity to try to solve the pressing public problems we face. Modest success in welfare policy may encourage us to take on some of the other issues that must be addressed if we are seriously to reduce the poverty and bleak prospects and opportunities that burden so many of our neighbors.

AN OVERVIEW OF THE BOOK

Chapter 1 briefly reviews the history of welfare policy from its creation in the 1930s to its expansion in the 1960s. It describes the major characteristics of welfare recipients, discusses how the old welfare system worked, and explains how welfare fits within the broader system of agencies and policies that make up the welfare state. It concludes with an overview of the challenges welfare policy poses for would-be reformers.

Chapter 2 examines how well welfare policy has achieved its goal of reducing poverty among single-headed families and the broader public policy challenges posed by poverty in America. The chapter also assesses the broader goals of welfare policy, how appropriate these goals are given the nature of poverty in America, and how consistent the goals of welfare are with the public values underlying American political culture.

Chapter 3 briefly traces the evolution of the politics of welfare reform and the substantive issues raised during the past twenty-five years. Throughout these years, debate has focused on the same issues. However, the proposals for reform have changed dramatically: Early reforms emphasized job training and education, whereas the recent round of reforms centered on time limits. The chapter examines how early reform efforts established a pattern of included ambitious promises and limited funding, a pattern that continued through 1996.

Chapter 4 examines welfare reform in the 1994 congressional election and its role in the "Contract with America," the bills passed in 1995, and the efforts to find a White House–congressional compromise in 1996 that culminated in passage of the new welfare law in August.

Chapter 5 assesses the latest welfare reform effort, the Personal Responsibility and Work Opportunity Reconciliation Act of 1996. The chapter includes an overview of the major provisions of the new law, an assessment of the competing and contradictory goals of its proponents, a brief review of the experience of states in reforming welfare, and an examination of some of the difficulties involved in assessing welfare reform efforts.

The next three chapters examine three of the most important issues that states will be grappling with as they devise their own approaches to welfare reform. These chapters lay out the mandates given to the states under the new law in these three areas. The chapters highlight the difficult challenges confronting states as they devise their own approaches to the perplexing problems of welfare and review the experience states had gained as of the end of 1996. While some of the programs described in these chapters may be eliminated by states, the experimentation with such programs illustrates the challenges states face as they take over welfare policy making responsibility.

Chapter 6 explores the debate over work requirements for welfare recipients, including job training and educational programs, work, and other obligations, and what time limits should be placed on participation in welfare programs.

Chapter 7 looks at the debate over eligibility for welfare benefits, including ideas on limiting the eligibility of teenage mothers who live away from their parents, legal immigrants, children born to mothers on welfare, and ideas on placing time limits on participation in welfare programs. This chapter also explores the consequences of reducing eligibility on teen pregnancy, abortion, the formation of families, and breaking the cycle of welfare participation.

Chapter 8 examines the administrative changes that are implicated in welfare reform. One of the greatest challenges is changing the way in which welfare offices operate and reorienting them away from traditional welfare programs and toward work preparation, placement, and empowerment of recipients. Welfare reform also suggests the integration of welfare and welfare-related services such as Medicaid, Food Stamps, and other assistance. Reforms also recognize that it is not enough to simply require work; welfare programs must also provide assistance in the transition to work through child care, transitional health care, transportation vouchers, and other benefits.

The final chapter discusses the major challenges confronting states in implementing the new law, including the timetable for implementation, the difficulties in changing behavior through sanctions and incentives, imposing time limits and creating exemptions from them, creating jobs, and reducing teenage pregnancy and promoting fatherhood. The chapter then turns to a broader discussion of welfare, poverty, and social policy. The contentious arguments over welfare are far from over, but are an enduring element of the debate over how to address inequality in America.

REFERENCES

[1] "Clinton's Secret Weapon," *The New Republic* (June 20, 1994): 7.

[2] "Sign It," *The New Republic* (August 12, 1996): 7–8, at 7.

[3] The framework outlined here is based on Frank Fischer, *Evaluating Public Policy* (Chicago: Nelson Hall, 1995).

[4] For a discussion of these and related issues, see Edith Stokey and Richard Zeckhauser, *A Primer for Policy Analysis* (New York: Norton, 1978).

[5] For a useful examination of assessing the impact of policies, see Lawrence B. Mohr, *Impact Analysis for Program Evaluation* (Pacific Grove, Calif.: Brooks Cole, 1988).

[6] See Robert A. Heineman, William T. Bluhm, Steven A. Peterson, and Edward N. Kearny, *The World of the Policy Analyst: Rationality, Values, and Politics* (Chatham, N.J.: Chatham House, 1990) for a study of how philosophical and ethical issues might be addressed in policy analysis.

[7] See Helen Ingram and Steven Rathgeb Smith, eds., *Public Policy for Democracy* (Washington, D.C.: Brookings Institution, 1993).

[8] For a helpful overview of these issues, see Mary Jo Bane, "Welfare As We Might Know It," *The American Prospect* (January–February 1997): 47–53.

[9] For more on this issue, see Christopher Jencks, "The Hidden Paradox of Welfare Reform," *The American Prospect* (May–June 1997): 33–40.

[10] Bane, "Welfare As We Might Know It," 52–53.

[11] Jencks, "The Hidden Paradox of Welfare Reform," 40.

1

The Old American Welfare System

Aid to Families with Dependent Children, or AFDC, was part of a sixty-year-old package of federal programs aimed at helping poor children, low-income families, and the elderly. Some of the programs that make up the welfare state, such as Medicare and Social Security, have become extremely popular. Others, such as Food Stamps and Medicaid, have developed strong constituencies. In contrast, AFDC was often singled out as the weakest portion of the social safety net. Myths abound about how welfare works and who benefits from it. This chapter outlines the main provisions of welfare policy in the United States, describes the characteristics of welfare recipients, and places welfare policy within the broader context of the other policies that comprise the welfare state.

NEW DEAL FOUNDATIONS

Title IV of the Social Security Act of 1935 created the Aid to Dependent Children (ADC) program. The purpose of the program was to assist states, through matching federal funds, to "broaden and supervise existing mothers' aid programs." ADC was primarily aimed at helping widows care for their children; it has evolved into a program that largely helps divorced, deserted, and never-married mothers and their children.

ADC was created when societal values called for mothers to be at home with their young children. It began in the 1910s when states passed mothers' pensions laws that permitted widows to stay at home with their children, rather than send them to orphanages. Unlike other

1

countries that created a paternalist welfare state, aimed at providing social insurance and assistance to industrial workers, the United States opted for a maternalist welfare state, aimed at women and children. Progressive reformers sought but failed to expand Civil War pensions into social programs for working men and their families. It was not until the Great Depression and the New Deal that government would create a social safety net for both men and women. But states had already established welfare for single mothers. The Social Security Act of 1935 federalized the program.[1]

The Social Security Act of 1935 was also part of the revolutionary response of the New Deal to the problems of poverty and unemployment that plagued the United States during the Great Depression. No longer was poverty seen as the result of individual character flaws but as a social problem that could affect anyone. The fear of social unrest and populist remedies led the Roosevelt administration to draft an income security bill within a year of Roosevelt's 1933 inauguration. Congress passed the bill with few changes and by overwhelming margins, but not until 1935. The Social Security Act became the framework for the American welfare state. Although specific programs have evolved considerably and have grown dramatically in size, the basic structure of the law and its underlying assumptions and values have not changed from what was enacted more than sixty years ago.[2]

The Social Security Act contained eleven titles that created seven new programs. Two programs were insurance programs: Old Age and Survivors or Social Security, and unemployment insurance. The former was a national program, the latter state run. Six public-assistance programs were created to give grants to states, each aimed at a different problem or disability: Old-age Assistance, Aid to Dependent Children (ADC), Aid to the Blind; Maternal and Child Welfare (hospital, nursing, and public-health services for mothers and children), Vocational Rehabilitation, and Public Health. ADC was aimed at providing help to children who had been deprived of support because of the death or absence of a parent and to help keep families that had lost their primary breadwinner together. Each program had relatively specific standards for determining eligibility that were to be strictly enforced. Minimum benefit standards were set by the law that provided only meager assistance, but states could be more generous if they chose to.

The dramatic expansion in the role of the federal government in creating a national welfare, regulatory state constituted a constitutional revolution of profound importance. In 1941 Franklin Delano Roosevelt issued a call for the worldwide recognition of the "Four Freedoms"—

freedom of speech and expression, freedom of worship, freedom from want, and freedom from fear.[3] Although the speech was primarily aimed at world affairs and the growing threat of the fascist powers, it also signaled an expansion of the role of government at home. Three years later, as victory in the war appeared inevitable, Roosevelt returned to this theme:

> This Republic had its beginning, and grew to its present strength, under the protection of certain inalienable political rights—among them the right of free speech, free press, free worship, trial by jury, freedom from unreasonable searches and seizures. They were our rights to life and liberty.
>
> As our Nation has grown in size and stature, however—as our industrial economy expanded—these political rights proved inadequate to assure us equality in the pursuit of happiness.
>
> We have come to a clear realization of the fact that true individual freedom can't exist without economic security and independence. . . . In our day these economic truths have become accepted as self-evident. We have accepted, so to speak, a second Bill of Rights under which a new basis of security and prosperity can be established for all—regardless of station, race, or creed.

New, positive rights were needed:

> The right to a useful and remunerative job in the industries or shops or farms or mines of the Nation;
> The right to earn enough to provide adequate food and clothing and recreation;
> The right of every farmer to raise and sell his products at a return which will give him and his family a decent living;
> The right of every businessman, large and small, to trade in an atmosphere of freedom from unfair competition and domination by monopolies at home or abroad;
> The right of every family to a decent home;
> The right to adequate medical care and the opportunity to achieve and enjoy good health;
> The right to adequate protection from the economic fears of old age, sickness, accident, and unemployment;
> The right to a good education . . .[4]

Although the New Deal fell far short of establishing programs that ensured the enjoyment of these rights, it created a new realm of expectations for government intervention in social and political affairs. Intervention was defended as being consistent with individual freedom, as a way to guarantee that individuals enjoyed real equality of opportunity. That goal of equality of opportunity was not new; Roosevelt's contribution was in arguing that government had a much expanded role to play so that all citizens would enjoy the preconditions for that opportunity.[5]

Legislation establishing Social Security, unemployment compensation, the Federal Housing Administration, the Civilian Conservation Corps, and a host of regulatory agencies reflected the idea that new rights had been recognized and government had a duty to make sure that those rights were realized. This constitutional revolution engendered vociferous criticism as a violation of the old order, which it surely was. However, it was just as aggressively defended as an essential response to the failure of a free market economy, a response regulated by the common law system of liability, contracts, and torts, so that all Americans would have an equal opportunity to make meaningful life choices.

AFDC AND HOW IT WORKED

The cash welfare program was renamed Aid to Families with Dependent Children in a 1962 amendment to the Social Security Act that also provided increased benefits to help reduce poverty, funded more vocational training for welfare recipients, and permitted states to apply for waivers from federal rules for experimental, pilot, or demonstration projects. Under this amendment, states could require unemployed adults to join community work and training programs in order to be eligible for AFDC benefits.[6]

The change in the law reflected the change in welfare clients. AFDC mothers were required to assign to the state child-support payments they received and to cooperate with officials to establish the paternity of children born outside of marriage. AFDC was an entitlement: States had to give AFDC benefits to all persons whose income and resources were below the state-defined limit. Decisions of federal courts expanded welfare coverage and benefits beyond the provisions of the law.[7]

Every state—as well as the District of Columbia, Guam, Puerto Rico and the Virgin Islands—operated an AFDC program and determined benefit levels. The Federal government paid 50 percent of administrative costs and about 55 percent of all benefits given, although the percentage paid by the federal government varied inversely with the state's per capita income. The actual federal share ranged from 50 to 80 percent of the total benefits different states offered. States were not required to adjust benefit levels in response to inflation. However, the

Federal government provided a modest check on states that sought to cut benefits: If states reduced benefit levels below those provided on May 1, 1988, the Department of Health and Human Services could not approve the state's Medicaid plan.[8]

In 1967, Congress created the Work Incentive (WIN) program, which required states to offer work and training programs to AFDC recipients; in 1971, the WIN program was amended to require all able-bodied recipients to register for the program. Ten years later, Congress gave states more freedom to impose work requirements on recipients, and so states began to experiment with welfare-to-work programs. These efforts culminated in passage of the 1988 Family Support Act. The Job Opportunities and Basic Skills (JOBS) program was created as part of that legislation's goal to "lead to lasting emancipation from welfare dependency." The act required states to establish a JOBS program by October 1, 1990. States were given discretion to design and implement their own JOBS programs but they also had to ensure, to the extent resources permitted, that all able-bodied recipients participated in the JOBS program if they had no children under three. States were required to enroll at least 7 percent of their AFDC families in JOBS in 1991 and 11 percent thereafter.[9] Each state was to match between 17 and 40 percent of Federal funds with its own spending, depending on the state's poverty rate. Although most states met the 1990 deadline for creating a JOBS program, many had problems raising sufficient funds to meet the matching requirement, and by 1993 states had requested only about 70 percent of the matching funds available.

AFDC RECIPIENTS

During the 1970s and 1980s the number of families receiving AFDC remained fairly constant, at about 3.5 million families. However, between 1989 and 1991 the number of families on AFDC grew to 4.6 million, an increase of more than 24 percent. Only a small part of that overall increase can be attributed to changes in Federal and state law; most of the increase was the result of the 1990–1992 recession. Welfare rolls increased by nearly 30 percent between 1989 and 1994 (see Figure 1.1). In 1994, AFDC rolls included more than 14.2 million persons; 67 percent of recipients, nearly 10 million, were children. Five million families received welfare benefits, representing more than 5 percent of the total population.[10] The number of families on welfare peaked at 5.083 million in March 1994, then fell to 4.963 million in

FIGURE 1.1
THE RISE IN THE WELFARE ROLLS, 1960–1994

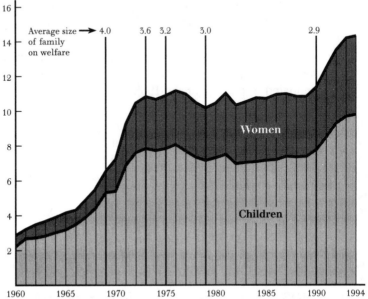

Source: "Welfare as We've Known It," *The New York Times*, June 19, 1994, p. E4.

January, 1996.[11] The rapid growth in the welfare rolls in the early 1990s raised concern about the growing number of people who had become dependent on assistance and, most important, fueled demands in the states to change welfare in ways that would reduce the financial pressure on the states. However, by the beginning of 1996, AFDC caseloads in many states had fallen, as Table 1.1 indicates, and they have continued to decline through 1997.

The White House, governors, and members of Congress all clamored for credit for the decline in welfare rolls. The decrease appeared to be the result of a stronger economy, state welfare initiatives approved by the Clinton administration, and changes in the attitudes and behaviors of recipients. The increase in job availability may be the most important factor, since some reforms have occurred too recently to have had much of an impact. Douglas Besharov of the American Enterprise Institute concluded that "the answer is the economy." State-by-state comparisons showed that declines in welfare rolls are affected by the health of state

TABLE 1.1
TOTAL AFDC RECEIPTS BY STATE, 1993–1996

State	Jan. 1993	Jan. 1996	Percent Change
Alabama	141,746	108,100	−24
Alaska	34,951	35,400	+1
Arizona	194,119	171,600	−12
Arkansas	73,982	59,100	−20
California	2,415,121	2,645,100	+10
Colorado	123,308	99,700	−19
Connecticut	160,102	161,600	+1
Delaware	27,652	23,200	−16
Dist. of Col.	65,860	70,100	+6
Florida	701,842	575,600	−18
Georgia	402,228	366,600	−9
Hawaii	54,511	66,700	+22
Idaho	21,116	23,600	+12
Illinois	685,508	664,700	−3
Indiana	209,882	146,300	−30
Iowa	100,943	91,500	−9
Kansas	87,525	70,800	−19
Kentucky	227,879	174,900	−23
Louisiana	263,338	238,800	−9
Maine	67,836	56,200	−17
Maryland	221,338	207,800	−6
Massachusetts	332,044	236,400	−29
Michigan	686,356	534,700	−22
Minnesota	191,526	158,200	−17
Mississippi	174,093	132,300	−24
Missouri	259,039	238,100	−8
Montana	34,848	32,500	−7
Nebraska	48,055	38,600	−20
Nevada	34,943	40,200	+15
New Hampshire	28,972	24,500	−15
New Jersey	349,902	293,900	−16
New Mexico	94,836	102,600	+8
New York	1,179,522	1,205,500	+2
North Carolina	331,633	281,000	−15
North Dakota	18,774	13,600	−27
Ohio	720,476	552,300	−23
Oklahoma	146,454	110,200	−25
Oregon	117,656	92,200	−22
Pennsylvania	604,701	552,600	−9
Rhode Island	61,116	58,500	−4
South Carolina	151,026	121,100	−20
South Dakota	20,254	16,800	−17
Tennessee	320,709	246,500	−23
Texas	785,271	713,200	−9
Utah	53,172	41,100	−23
Vermont	28,961	25,800	−11
Virginia	194,212	165,900	−14
Washington	286,258	276,000	−3
West Virginia	119,916	98,100	−18
Wisconsin	241,098	184,200	−24
Wyoming	18,271	13,500	−26

Department of Health and Human Services, Administration for Children and Families, personal correspondence (6 June 1996).

economies. Welfare rolls declined during economic upswings, but then grew when the boom ended; the challenge, as Tom Corbett, from the Institute for Research on Poverty at the University of Wisconsin puts it, "is sustaining those declines over time." A Congressional Budget Office study attributed one-fourth of the increase in welfare in the early 1990s to the recession; about one-half was the result of an increase in fatherless families. A 1997 report by the Council of Economic Advisers found that 44 percent of the decline in the welfare rolls between 1993 and 1996 was due to an improved economy. However, some welfare recipients are so removed from the labor market because of poor education and lack of job-relevant skills and motivation that economic swings will not likely affect their ability to work.[12]

Welfare recipients can be described a number of ways. Their key demographic characteristics have changed over time and are briefly summarized below. Because about three-fourths of the AFDC caseload was made up of single women, most of the figures, unless otherwise indicated, represent the characteristics of this group. The remaining balance of the welfare population includes two-parent families and single-male-headed families.[13]

AVERAGE FAMILY SIZE AND NUMBER OF CHILD RECIPIENTS

One popular myth is that welfare families are large and getting larger as recipients seek more benefits. In reality, the average AFDC family size fell from 4.0 to 2.9 persons between 1969 and 1993 (see Table 1.2). From 1969 to 1983, the percent of families with no more than two children increased from 49.6 percent to 72.7 percent.

TABLE 1.2
AVERAGE FAMILY SIZE AND NUMBER OF CHILDREN IN AFDC FAMILIES

		Number of Child Recipients (% of AFDC Cases)			
Year	Average Family Size	One Child	Two Children	Three Children	Four or More Children
1969	4.0	26.6	23.0	17.7	32.5
1975	3.2	37.9	26.0	16.1	20.0
1983	3.0	43.4	29.8	15.2	10.1
1993	2.9	na	na	na	na

Source: U.S. House of Representatives, Ways and Means Committee, *Overview of Entitlement Programs, 1994* (Washington, D.C.: U.S. Government Printing Office, 1994), 325.

REASONS FOR ENROLLMENT IN WELFARE

Divorce or separation is the primary reason why families have ended up on welfare; the second most common reason has been out-of-wedlock childbirth. Other factors have also contributed to the need for assistance. Marriage was the most common cause of leaving welfare (see Table 1.3).

TABLE 1.3
REASONS FOR ENROLLMENT IN AFDC

Reasons for Participating in AFDC	Distribution
Divorce or Separation	45%
Unmarried woman gives birth	30
Drop in income	16
Other or unidentified reasons	10
Reasons for Leaving AFDC	
Marriage	35%
Increased earnings	26
Increase in transfer income other than AFDC	14
Children leave home	11
Other or unidentified reasons	14

Source: Sar A. Levitan, *Programs in Aid of the Poor* (Baltimore: The Johns Hopkins University Press, 1986), 157.

AGE OF SINGLE WELFARE MOTHERS

The average age of single women receiving welfare decreased from 34 years in 1976 to 31 years in 1992. In 1992, about 25 percent of single women receiving AFDC were under twenty-five; 10 percent of all single mothers were under twenty-five during that year.[14] Most welfare mothers, about 47 percent of the total, were between the ages of 20 and 29. More than half of all welfare spending went to families headed by women who first gave birth as teenagers.[15] Teenage mothers have represented only a small percentage of total recipients, but much of the criticism of welfare has focused on the incentives that some believe welfare creates for teenage girls to get pregnant, drop out of school, and thus start a life of welfare dependency.

Contrary to myth, the growth in never-married welfare mothers was not due to a major increase in AFDC enrollment by teenage mothers.

Although former teenage mothers made up a large proportion of the increase in never-married women on welfare, never-married women who did not give birth until they were twenty or older produced an even greater proportion of the increase in never-married AFDC mothers. This group grew from 9 percent of all single AFDC mothers in 1976 to 26 percent in 1992.[16]

The growth of never-married mothers on welfare is not just a problem affecting teenagers. In fact, never-married women on welfare were more likely in recent years than in the past to be twenty-five or older. In 1976, 48 percent of the never-married women on AFDC were twenty-five or older; by 1992, that number had grown to 62 percent.[17]

AGE OF CHILDREN

The number of children on welfare at different ages has been distributed fairly evenly across the age brackets, but the trend has been for more and more children on welfare to be younger (see Table 1.4). Child care for younger children has been even more important to welfare mothers recently than in the past.

TABLE 1.4
AGE OF CHILDREN ON WELFARE (% OF TOTAL CHILDREN)

Year	Under 3	3–5	6–11	12+	Unknown
1969	14.9	17.6	36.5	31.0	na
1975	16.5	18.1	33.7	30.9	0.8
1983	22.5	20.1	31.5	25.5	0.3

Source: U.S. House of Representatives, Ways and Means Committee, *Overview of Entitlement Programs, 1994* (Washington, D.C.: U.S. Government Printing Office, 1994), 401–02.

EDUCATION OF AFDC MOTHERS

In 1969, most welfare mothers had relatively little educational background, having only completed high school or less. By 1991 the educational attainment of all recipients had risen considerably; more than 12 percent had completed some college (see Table 1.5).

In spite of this increase, dealing with the lack of educational achievement of mothers receiving AFDC has been one of the most difficult challenges in welfare policy because education and work experience are linked. Single working women receiving AFDC were more likely to have at least a high school education than those who did not work.

TABLE 1.5
EDUCATION LEVEL OF WELFARE RECIPIENTS

Year	8th Grade or Less	1–3 Years of High School	High School Diploma	Some College	College Graduate	Unknown
1969	29.4	30.7	16.0	2.0	0.2	21.6
1975	16.7	31.7	23.7	3.9	0.7	23.3
1991	11.2	35.1	40.7	12.1	0.8	

Source: U.S. House of Representatives, Ways and Means Committee, *Overview of Entitlement Programs, 1994* (Washington, D.C.: U.S. Government Printing Office, 1994), 401–02.

Work experience, in turn, affects other parameters of welfare policy. For instance, AFDC women who worked were more likely to have smaller families than nonworking recipients.[18]

EMPLOYMENT STATUS OF MOTHER AND EARNINGS OF AFDC FAMILIES

Almost all welfare mothers have been unemployed (see Table 1.6). Between 1969 and 1993 the percentage of welfare recipients who worked fell from 14.5 to 6.4 percent.[19]

The averaged earned income reported by female-headed welfare families, including wages and salaries earned by all household members 15 and older, fell by 34 percent, in real dollars, between 1976 and 1992. During nearly the same time period, AFDC benefits declined (by 43 percent between 1970 and 1992). The total average income for these families declined by 37 percent between 1976 and 1992. These figures do not include the value of noncash benefits such as Medicaid and Food Stamps. The proportion of female-headed AFDC families receiving incomes of less than 50 percent of the poverty level doubled between 1976 and 1992.[20]

TABLE 1.6
PERCENTAGE OF WELFARE RECIPIENTS WHO WORKED

Year	Full-Time Job	Part-Time Job
1969	8.2	6.3
1975	10.4	5.7
1983	1.5	3.4
1993	2.2	4.2

Source: U.S. House of Representatives, Ways and Means Committee, *Overview of Entitlement Programs, 1994* (Washington, D.C.: U.S. Government Printing Office, 1994), 401–02.

TABLE 1.7
PERCENTAGE BY RACE OF ALL WELFARE RECIPIENTS

Year	White	Black	Hispanic	Native American	Asian	Other and Unknown
1969	48.7	45.2	NA	1.3	NA	4.8
1975	39.9	44.3	12.2	1.1	0.5	2.0
1983	41.8	43.8	12.0	1.0	1.5	NA°
1991	38.1	38.8	17.4	2.8	1.3	1.6
1994	37.0	36.0	20.0	1.0	3.0	3.0

° For 1983, 12.6 percent of recipients where race was unknown was allocated proportionately across all categories.

Source: U.S. House of Representatives, Ways and Means Committee, *Overview of Entitlement Programs, 1994* (Washington, D.C.: U.S. Government Printing Office, 1994), 401–02.

RACE OF WELFARE RECIPIENTS

Welfare recipients have been just as likely to be white as black; the percentage of all welfare recipients who are black has declined since the late 1960s, as Table 1.7 shows.

In 1992, white women made up about 39 percent of the single-woman AFDC caseload; black women accounted for about 44 percent; Hispanics, about 15 percent; and others, about 2 percent (see Table 1.8).

TABLE 1.8
PERCENTAGE BY RACE OF SINGLE WOMEN RECEIVING AFDC
(1992 DATA)

Race	Receiving AFDC	All Single Mothers
White	38.7	58.5
Black	43.6	30.4
Hispanic	15.5	11.1
Other	2.2	NA

Source: U.S. General Accounting Office, "Families on Welfare: Sharp Rise in Never-Married Women Reflects Social Trend" (May 1994), 19–20.

Most never-married mothers on welfare have been black, but that figure fell from 71 percent in 1976 to 57 percent in 1992; in contrast, the percentage of white never-married AFDC mothers grew from

TABLE 1.9
PERCENTAGE BY RACE OF NEVER-MARRIED WOMEN
RECEIVING AFDC AND ALL NEVER-MARRIED MOTHERS,
1992

Race	Never-Married Women Receiving AFDC	All Never-Married Mothers
White	27.2	34.6
Black	56.9	49.9
Other	15.9	15.4

Source: U.S. General Accounting Office, "Families on Welfare: Sharp Rise in Never-Married Women Reflects Social Trend" (May 1994), 48.

19 percent to 27 percent (see Table 1.9). Black children have been more than five times more likely to be on welfare than are white children (see Table 1.10).

TABLE 1.10
RACE OF CHILDREN ON WELFARE

Year	White	Black
1973	6.5	42.7
1992	6.2	35.1

Source: U.S. House of Representatives, Ways and Means Committee, *Overview of Entitlement Programs, 1994* (Washington, D.C.: U.S. Government Printing Office, 1994), 401–02.

NEVER-MARRIED WOMEN ON WELFARE

Much of the concern with welfare has focused on never-married women who become mothers and go on welfare. Their children often go on welfare as well, creating a cycle of dependency. The number of out-of-wedlock births in America grew from 400,000 in 1970 to more than 1.2 million in 1991. The proportion of single women on welfare who have never been married quadrupled between 1976 and 1992, from 380,000 to over 1.5 million; this population made up more than half of all female-headed AFDC families. However, the increase in never-married women who receive AFDC was not primarily due to more teenage mothers going on welfare; women 20 years old or older have accounted for most of the increase.[21] The decline of the two-parent family, the rise of female-headed households, and the increase in out-of-wedlock births have all contributed to the rise of the feminization of poverty in general and more specifically in welfare rolls.

Several problems have traditionally been at the root of poverty among female-headed families. One set of factors has been adolescent out-of-wedlock pregnancy and childbearing, and divorce. A second complicating set of contributing factors is that the problems of many poor black women are intertwined with those of black men. The overall prospects for black men in the labor market have important implications for female-headed poverty among black families: Employment figures show that blacks and women of all races are much less successful than white males in competing in the labor market, and this disparity has been rather stable during the last three decades (see Chapter 2).

Duration of Welfare

A significant proportion of AFDC families have become long-term dependents: In 1991, the median length of time on welfare was 22 months. About one-third of welfare families received support for one year or less; about one-fifth received support for more than five years. In 1991, 40 percent of the families on AFDC had been on the welfare rolls before. Dependency is not concentrated in one age group: In 1993, the median age of adults was 28.9 years (women) and 34 years (men). Eight percent of the total AFDC female adult population was 16 to 19 years old; 12 percent was 40 or older. Long-term dependency is concentrated among those who do not complete high school and those who first receive welfare payments as teenagers.[22]

Almost 50 percent of the people on AFDC left the program within two years, but long-term clients accounted for much of AFDC's costs. The debate over welfare has therefore focused on welfare recipients who seem permanently dependent on assistance, particularly those who enter the system as young teenagers. Fewer than one in five people in the welfare system received assistance for more than five consecutive years, but, counting repeat spells, an estimated one-half of the current caseload has accumulated a total of at least five years. Most recipients who were likely to be on welfare long term were able-bodied mothers under age 24 who were never married and who lacked a high school diploma or work history.[23]

INTERGENERATIONAL WELFARE DEPENDENCY

A 1984 study found that most daughters in welfare families did not receive welfare when they became young adults. Only 19 percent of black daughters and 25 percent of white daughters in "highly dependent" welfare families (families receiving at least 25 percent of average family income as cash welfare payments) became "highly dependent" themselves. Some 42 percent of black daughters and 27 percent of white daughters who were raised in "highly dependent" families did not receive any welfare as adults. However, "young women who grew up in welfare families were more than twice as likely to receive welfare themselves as young adults whose parents received no welfare assistance" (55 versus 27 percent)[24]. The failure of noncustodial parents, primarily fathers, to pay child support also contributed to welfare dependency. Among low-income women with children:

57 percent had not received a child-support award
25 percent had received some child support
18 percent had been awarded support but not received it.[25]

WELFARE HOUSEHOLDS' PARTICIPATION IN OTHER SOCIAL SERVICES

The data available on welfare recipients show great variety in the circumstances surrounding participation in welfare and the characteristics of welfare recipients. The number of welfare recipients grew dramatically between 1990 and 1994. The size of welfare families has declined, although welfare mothers are likely to have more children than those not on welfare. Unmarried teenage mothers have made up a small percentage of total recipients, but the number of welfare mothers who had their first child as teenagers has formed a sizable part of the entire welfare caseload. Most welfare mothers have been between the ages of 20 and 29, just as likely to be white as black, and more likely than not to have a high school diploma. Those who have been most likely to be on welfare for a long period of time have been under age 24 and have neither work experience nor a high school diploma.

Many questions remain about welfare and welfare recipients: What impact have different reform approaches had on the more disadvantaged part of the AFDC population? on women with young children? on people with low educational achievement? on people who report specific problems that appear likely to limit or minimize their partici-pation in JOBS? on people whose motivation to participate is low? Is there a threshold of disadvantagedness below which different programs and services are not effective?[26]

The different needs among welfare recipients require different kinds of welfare policy provisions tailored to the needs of recipients. Women on welfare because they have been recently divorced, for example, may be able to participate in the labor market fairly soon, perhaps with some training or retooling. Some women cannot find work that pays enough to cover child care, medical, and other expenses, or simply cannot find work at all. Some women will need a great deal of assistance in pre-paring to become economically self-sufficient as they try to overcome a lack of education or work experience.

TYPES OF WELFARE BENEFITS

AFDC recipients were eligible for Medicaid, free school lunches, Food Stamps, and other programs such as the Low-Income Energy Assistance Program, and public housing or subsidized rent. Food Stamps are avail-able for households with incomes below 130 percent of the poverty line; child nutrition programs help those with incomes below 185 percent of the poverty line.[27]

The welfare state includes two major kinds of programs: contributory programs, which require participants to pay part of the the cost of the benefits they receive, and noncontributory programs, which do not. So-cial welfare policies are also divided into those that provide cash benefits and those that provide in-kind assistance (see Box 1.1).

AFDC was one of about seventy-seven programs aimed at low in-come persons that are either means tested (based on recipients' income) or categorical grants that are aimed at economically distressed com-munities or areas with a high percentage of low-income residents. In-kind assistance programs are available to working and nonworking women and their children who meet low-income requirements. The problems of women and children who were dependent on AFDC are particularly acute, but poor working women face daunting challenges as well. The Food Stamps program serves about twice as many people as welfare; supplemental social insurance, or SSI, serves less than one-half the number of people served by AFDC.

AFDC benefits varied widely from state to state. In January 1996, average AFDC benefits for a family of three ranged from $120 in Mis-sissippi to $923 in Alaska. Even when Food Stamps were added to cash benefits, the average income among recipients fell below the national poverty level in every state. The nationwide monthly average cash benefit was $378 per family; the average AFDC family of three was eligible for a maximum of $415 a month, or $4,980 a year. Combined AFDC and Food Stamp benefits for the average recipient family totaled $664 a month, or $8,000 a year. When AFDC and Food Stamps are combined, the maximum monthly benefit for a family of three varied from $424 in Mississippi to $1,223 in Alaska. In 1994, the median state AFDC maximum benefit for a family of three fell to $366 per month; the median AFDC benefit was 36 percent of the poverty threshold.[28] The poverty threshold in 1994 was as follows:[29]

Size of family	Poverty threshold, 1994
1 person	$ 7,551
3 persons	11,817
4 persons	15,141

Benefits ranged from 13 percent of the poverty threshold in Mississippi to 75 percent in New York. Figure 1.2 shows the variation in welfare

FIGURE 1.2
VARIATION IN STATE AFDC AND FOOD STAMP BENEFITS

Maximum monthly AFDC and Food Stamp benefit for a family of three, 1995

☐ Below $600 ▨ $600 to $699 ▩ $700 to $799 ■ $800 and above

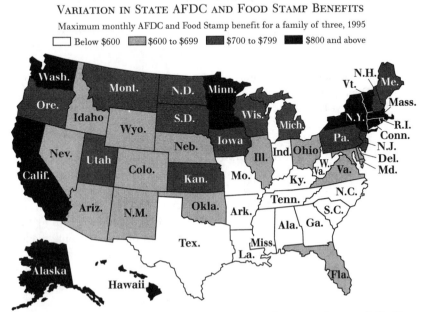

Source: Sam Howe Verhovek, "Welfare in Transition: the National Picture," *The New York Times*, September 21, 1995, p. A1.

Box 1.1
THE AMERICAN WELFARE STATE

Types of Government Assistance Programs

Type of Program	Year Enacted
Contributory	
Old Age, Survivors, and Disability Insurance	1935
Unemployment Compensation	1935
Medicare	1965
Noncontributory	
Aid to Families with Dependent Children	1935
Housing Assistance to Low-Income Families	1937
School Lunch Program	1946
Food Stamps	1964
Medicaid	1965
Supplemental Security Income	1974
Job Training and Partnership Act	1982

Major Government Programs That Assist Low-Income Families

Program	Aid Provided	Target Groups
CASH ASSISTANCE		
Aid to Families with Dependent Children (AFDC)	Cash grants	Low-income, single-parent, and some two-parent, families with children
IN-KIND ASSISTANCE		
Medicaid	Free or low-cost medical care	All AFDC recipients and most recipients of Supplemental Security income; pregnant women and children up to age six in families with incomes up to 133 percent of poverty; some medically needy families who have lost AFDC coverage for specific reasons (coverage limited in duration)

Program	Aid Provided	Target Groups
Food Stamps	Food vouchers	Most low-income families and individuals
Housing Assistance	Subsidized housing units of rent subsidies	Familiese and elderly and handicapped individuals with low incomes
Special Supplemental Food Program for Women, Infants, and Children (WIC)	Food supplements, nutritional screening	Low-income pregnant and postpartum women, their infants, and children up to age 5 who are at risk nutritionally
Child Support Enforcement	Location of absent parents, and help establishing and collecting child support	All AFDC recipients and all other who request assistance
Job Training Partnership Act (JTPA)	Work-related training and services	Economically disadvantaged individuals, including youth and welfare recipients
Social Services Block Grant	Child care, child welfare, adoption, foster care, family planning information and referral services, and other social services	Determined by the states
Maternal and Child Health Block Grant	Health services	Determined by the states

Source: U.S. Congress Congressional Budget Office, "Sources of Support for Adolescent Mothers" (Washington, D.C.: U.S. Government Printing Office, 1990), 36–37.

benefits across the country. Figure 1.3 shows the percent of poverty those benefits represented for a family of three. Benefits were lowest in the southern states, followed by some mountain and Midwest states. Benefits were highest in California, Washington State, Minnesota, New York, Vermont, Rhode Island, and Connecticut. Food Stamp and AFDC benefits approached the poverty line most closely in Alaska and New York, but were furthest from bringing recipients up to the poverty level in Mississippi, Alabama, Tennessee, and Texas.

Although spending has increased dramatically for social welfare programs in general, AFDC expenditures did not keep pace. After adjusting for inflation, AFDC benefits declined by nearly 50 percent from 1970 to 1994.[30] The real value of AFDC and Food Stamp benefits in 1994 was about the same as AFDC benefits in 1960. About 75 percent of AFDC families did not live in subsidized housing.[31] Most AFDC families received Medicaid benefits, and many received benefits through the Special Supplemental Nutrition Program for Women, Infants, and Children (WIC) and the Low-Income Home Energy Assistance Program. The number of recipients increased by 91 percent from 1970 to 1993 (from 7.4 million to 14.1 million). During that same period, the number of families grew 163 percent, from 1.9 million to 5.0 million. Expenditures for AFDC benefits only grew 44 percent, from $15.5 to 22.3 billion, after adjusting for inflation. The maximum monthly benefit for a four-person family, measured in constant dollars, fell from $840 in 1970 to $450 in 1994 in the median state, a reduction in purchasing power of 46.5 percent. Despite increases in Food Stamp benefits, the real value of AFDC and Food Stamps fell 20 percent between 1971 and 1994.[32] Federal and state spending on AFDC, in real dollars, declined by 9 percent between 1987 and 1994.[33] Administrative costs remained constant at about $3.0 billion a year; they represented 19 percent of AFDC benefits in 1970 and 13 percent in 1993.[34] In 1994, Federal and state AFDC benefits reached $22.7 billion; an additional $3.1 billion was spent on administration and $1.1 billion on job training.[35]

In contrast, Social Security, widely viewed as an insurance or investment program for the aged, along with other programs aimed at the general public, have been politically very popular. Programs aimed at poor women and children have simply not enjoyed the same level of support. Social Security payments to the elderly and to disabled workers and the survivors of deceased workers have eliminated much more poverty than AFDC payments have. Social Security benefits prevent poverty among some 70 percent of the aged; AFDC payments result in removing only about 4 percent of recipients from poverty.[36]

FIGURE 1.3

MAXIMUM MONTHLY AFDC AND FOOD STAMP BENEFITS
AS A PERCENT OF POVERTY FOR A FAMILY OF
THREE PERSONS, JULY 1996*

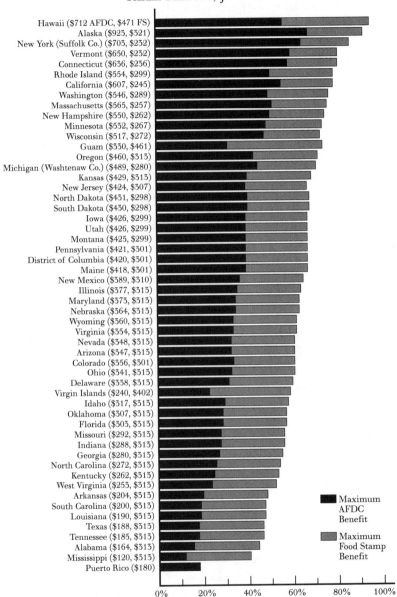

* Based on the 1996 federal poverty guideline for a family of three persons, $12,980, converted to a monthly rate of $1,082. For Alaska, this amount was increased by 25 percent; for Hawaii, by 15 percent; following the practice of the Department of Health and Human Services in issuing federal poverty guidelines. *Note:* Food Stamps are not available in Puerto Rico (which has a "nutritional assistance" program).

AFDC represented about 1 percent of the Federal budget and 2 percent of the average state budget. In contrast, 48 percent of the federal budget goes to direct benefits payments for individuals, for Social Security, and for other programs that are not means tested, as well as benefits to low-income people.

Still another way to understand the welfare state is to focus on the relationship between the federal government and the states. Some programs, such as Social Security, Medicare, and Food Stamps, are federal programs; AFDC and Medicaid are jointly funded and administered. Until the Great Depression, federal aid to states was primarily aimed at funding land-grant colleges, agriculture, roads, vocational education and rehabilitation, forestry, and public health. During the 1930s, aid was extended for income security and other social concerns. By the mid-1970s, social programs had become the dominant component of federal assistance; by the late 1980s, health care became the primary program funded, and the percentage of aid to individuals increased by 86 percent between 1980 and 1995.

WELFARE AND TAX POLICY

The welfare state and its programs aimed at helping the poor are largely grants to individuals and to state and local governments. One exception is the Earned Income Tax Credit, a tax policy aimed at low-income working families. The EITC was created in 1975 to achieve two goals: to encourage welfare recipients to leave welfare and go to work without suffering any financial penalty from low-paying jobs; and to help low-income families earn enough to avoid going on welfare. Families at the lowest end of the income range (less than $23,050 in 1996) can receive a refund on their taxes as a tax credit.

The Omnibus Budget Reconciliation Act of 1993, signed in August of that year, expanded the EITC; the maximum credit was increased and the program now covers (as of 1996) low-income workers without children.[37] The EITC program is not fully adjusted for family size; the goal of the EITC program is to end poverty for a family of *four* if a parent works full time at the minimum wage or higher and receives the tax credit and food stamps.[38]

EITC used to be a very popular, bipartisan-supported program that rewarded work and avoided welfare. President Reagan called it "the best anti-poverty, the best pro-family, the best job-creation measure to come out of Congress."[39] It has expanded over the years as a way to counter the increase in the Social Security payroll tax, which disproportionately affects low-income workers, and the failure of Congress to adjust the minimum wage for inflation. The EITC became embroiled in the debate over the tax cuts proposed by the Republicans in Congress in 1995 and 1996. In 1995, Republicans targeted the EITC for changes, arguing that it failed to target low-income families and was riddled with fraud and error. They included in their balanced-budget plans a proposal to reduce the number of families eligible for benefits. Democrats charged that, as a result of reducing the tax credit, overall taxes would increase for working families in order to help pay for the tax cuts for wealthy families that the Republicans are seeking. The Clinton administration, they argued, had already instituted reforms to deal with fraud and errors.

The budget impasse in 1995 and 1996 protected the EITC, but the efforts by Republicans to reduce the program was evidence that, except for Social Security, virtually every program of the welfare state was under attack, even those aimed at low-income working families. The politics surrounding Social Security may be unique, but the experience of Social Security shows that if we are serious about reducing poverty for certain groups of people we can do so.

THE POLITICS OF WELFARE REFORM

Critics of the welfare state have argued that its programs are too expensive, and too ineffective, to continue. The programs are blamed, along with government regulation, for macroeconomic problems as well as for encouraging recipients to be less productive. One figure popularized by the conservative Heritage Foundation is that the United States has spent more than $5.3 trillion on "welfare programs" since the onset of the War on Poverty in the mid-1960s. During the same period of time, the study argues, the poverty rate has "remained unchanged."[40] Republicans used that figure and the accompanying conclusion repeatedly in Congress during the welfare debate of 1995 and 1996: We have spent trillions but have accomplished nothing, and so should abandon the effort. It is a remarkably misleading argument. The $5.3 trillion cited overstates tremendously the money actually spent on helping poor families. As indicated above, AFDC has only constituted a tiny fraction of the entire Federal budget. Between 1964 and 1973, the poverty level fell from 19 to 11 percent, largely due to a growing economy. Since 1973, and especially since 1990, the increases in the poverty rate have been linked to economic problems such as the decline in wages (see Chapter 2). As the Heritage Foundation figures themselves show, most of the increased spending for social programs has been for in-kind programs such as health care. These benefits are not counted in measuring poverty, so cannot be criticized for having failed to reduce poverty.[41]

The Congressional Research Service estimated that federal spending aimed at low-income Americans totaled $208 billion in 1992, and that estimate included many programs benefitting families above the poverty line. All governments—federal, state, and local—only spent $290 billion in all on these programs. Social Security, Medicare, and Medicaid are the elements of the welfare state that represent the real growth in entitlement spending. These entitlements are crucial elements of any plan to balance the budget; nonmedical, means-tested programs such as AFDC are not nearly so important in achieving that goal.

CHALLENGES IN REFORMING WELFARE

The primary goal of welfare policy has been to reduce poverty in single-parent families, but it had only limited success. The percentage of Americans who are considered poor has hovered around 15 percent; more than 20 percent of children are poor; and more than one-third of families headed by single females live in poverty.[42] The value of AFDC payments, in real dollars, fell 43 percent between 1970 and 1992. The proportion of female-headed AFDC families receiving incomes less than 50 percent of the poverty level doubled between 1976 and 1992.[43] Chronic underfunding and limited participation in education, training, and job placement programs have contributed to policy failure, as has the lack of available jobs for those who try to leave welfare. Other changes in American society have increased the challenges confronting welfare policy making: the tripling of out-of-wedlock births since 1972 and the doubling since 1976 of single women on welfare who have never been married are just two of these changes.

The overall goal of reducing poverty has spawned a number of more specific objectives, such as providing short-term assistance to people between jobs or otherwise temporarily in need; allowing mothers of young children to stay at home with them and encouraging poor mothers and children to stay together as families (without perpetuating a cycle of dependency across generations); discouraging out-of-wedlock childbearing; and encouraging women to become more self-sufficient and integrating them into the workplace (and requiring them to find others to care for their children). These objectives must also satisfy demands for reducing welfare expenditures or at least not increasing them. Accomplishing all these objectives seems impossible. Cutting welfare spending, for instance, means that fewer services aimed at promoting self-sufficiency will be available.

Not only have we failed to achieve the goals of welfare, but the goals themselves are flawed. Requirements aimed at providing assistance may discourage men from assuming child support and other responsibilities; improving the child-support system will increase income to women and children and make them less likely to need help from welfare. Welfare policies can be assessed in terms of the number of participants who leave the program, for example, but if they take dead-end jobs that prevent them from supporting their family and that last for only a few weeks, then little progress has occurred. Economic downturns or upturns may have a greater effect on the need for welfare than any programmatic changes. We may have effective educational and training programs, for example, that move people off welfare rolls, but if they have only a small number of participants, their impact on the welfare population will be uncertain. Welfare recipients living in economically depressed or isolated areas may have few options besides welfare. Reducing welfare benefits may decrease the likelihood that teenage girls will get pregnant so they can go on welfare and get away from dysfunctional family situations or have the independence that comes from setting up their own households, but abortions may increase.

Welfare policy is ultimately limited by much broader phenomena such as the economic forces that determine levels of unemployment and economic opportunity and their geographic distribution, the performance of educational institutions, and cultural values and practices that help shape the preparation of future workers. Shifts in the global economy have left many urban areas economically devastated and isolated, and have increased the demand for welfare and other social services. For African-American men and women, the missing cohort of marriageable males—because of employment discrimination, poor education, victimization by crime, unemployment, imprisonment, military service, and other factors that disproportionately affect them—places severe constraints on the formation of families.[44] Discrimination against women in the work force produces fewer opportunities for employment or promotion; a wage gap also contributes to their economic vulnerability. Changes in divorce law that make splitting families easier have contributed to the formation of female-headed households, as have changes in sexual behavior among nonmarried women and men. The declining quality of education, the loss of public order and the rise of crime in some neighborhoods, and other characteristics of certain urban areas reinforce the problems that welfare can neither escape from nor solve.

Welfare has never been effectively integrated with other efforts to remedy poverty in America. It has treated more or less successfully some of the symptoms, but not the underlying problems and root causes. Welfare has also failed to deal with the consequences of racism and discrimination that have led to poverty rates and unemployment among blacks that have been three times as high as those for whites. The United States has never included in its labor policy a major public commitment to developing the capacity of its workers. Educational and training programs have been piecemeal, poorly funded, aimed at helping specific groups such as AFDC recipients or disabled persons. We have never had a proactive policy aimed at long-term capacity building, rooted in a comprehensive approach to employment-related services.[45]

Welfare policy also conflicts with strongly held social values. Many expect government to play an affirmative role in expanding opportunities for all persons. Others believe that role of government should be limited to those who make an effort to become contributing members of society. Giving welfare without requiring work in exchange denigrates those who work for low wages and struggle to get by on their own. The rise of a culture of poverty, rooted in discrimination, economic isolation, and hopelessness, challenges traditional American values of hard work, individualism, independence, and faith in equality of opportunity. Dissatisfaction with bureaucratic government in general and the demands for reinventing government also account for part of the frustration surrounding welfare policy. Chapter 2 examines in more detail the broader goals of welfare policy and how they interact with the values underlying American political culture.

REFERENCES

[1] See Theda Skocpol, *Protecting Soldiers and Mothers: The Political Origins of Social Policy in the United States* (Cambridge, Mass.: Harvard University Press, 1992).

[2] See Theodore J. Lowi, *The End of Liberalism* (New York: Norton, 1979), Ch. 8.

[3] Franklin Delano Roosevelt, "Message to the Congress on the State of the Union," 1941, *The Public Papers and Addresses of Franklin D. Roosevelt*, volume 9 (1969), 663–72.

[4] Franklin Delano Roosevelt, "Message to the Congress on the State of the Union," 1944, *The Public Papers and Addresses of Franklin D. Roosevelt*, vol. 13 (1969), 41.

[5] See, generally, James MacGregor Burns and Stewart Burns, *A People's Charter: The Pursuit of Rights in America* (New York: Knopf, 1991), 237–67.

[6] For an overview of AFDC, see Susan Kellam, "Welfare Experiments: Are States Leading the Way Toward National Reform?" *CQ Researcher* 4:34 September 16, 1994): 795–815.

[7] See R. Shep Melnick, *Welfare Rights* (Washington, D.C.: Brookings Institution, 1994).

[8] In 1992, the Bush administration waived this provision for California. Jennifer A. Neisner, "State Welfare Initiatives," CRS Report for Congress (Washington, D.C.: Congressional Research Service, January 24, 1995).

[9] U.S. House of Representatives, Ways and Means Committee, *Overview of Entitlement Programs: 1994 Green Book* (Washington, D.C.: U.S. Government Printing Office, 1994).

[10] Ibid., 395.

[11] U.S. Department of Health and Human Services, Administration for Children and Families, personal correspondence (June 6, 1996).

[12] Judith Havemann and Barbara Vobejda, "As Welfare Cases Drop, Politicians Fight for Credit; But Experts Say Reasons For Decline Are Unclear," *The Washington Post*, May 13, 1996, p. A1. Council of Economic Advisers, "Technical Report: Explaining the Decline in Welfare Receipt, 1993–1996" (Washington, D.C.: Council of Economic Advisers, May 1997).

[13] Data before 1979 come from surveys of agency case files; data after that year come from cases within the National Integrated Quality Control System monthly sample of cases. U.S. House of Representatives, Committee on Ways and Means, *Overview of Entitlement Programs: 1994 Green Book*, 401. See also Robert Pear, "Debate in House on Welfare Splits GOP," *The New York Times*, March 23, 1995, p. A11.

[14] U.S. General Accounting Office, "Families on Welfare: Sharp Rise in Never-Married Women Reflects Social Trend" (Washington, D.C.: General Accounting Office, May 1994), 25.

[15] Evelyn Ganzglass, "Research Findings on the Effectiveness of State Welfare-to-Work Programs" (Washington, D.C.: Center for Policy Research, National Governors' Association, 1994).

[16] U.S. General Accounting Office, "Families on Welfare: Sharp Rise in Never-Married Women Reflects Social Trend," 62.

[17] Ibid., 50.

[18] Ibid., 33.

[19] Ibid., 32.

[20] Ibid., 34, 36, 38.

[21] Ibid., 4, 62.

[22] Ganzglass, "Research Findings on the Effectiveness of State Welfare-to-Work Programs," 2.

[23] Jennifer A. Neisner, "State Welfare Initiatives," CRS Report for Congress (Congressional Research Service, January 24, 1995).

[24] House Ways and Means Committee, *Overview of Entitlement Programs: 1994 Green Book*, 448.

[25] *Budget of the United States Government Fiscal Year 1996* (Washington, D.C.: U.S. Government Printing Office, 1995), 28.

[26] Manpower Demonstration Research Corporation, "Overview of the JOBS Evaluation," working document (New York: Manpower Demonstration Research Corporation, November 1991).

[27] Vee Burke, "Clinton Welfare Reform Proposal: Issue Summary" (Washington, D.C.: Congressional Research Service, September 3, 1993).

[28] Carmen Solomon-Fears, "Aid to Families with Dependent Children (AFDC): A Fact Sheet" (Washington, D.C.: Congressional Research Service, Library of Congress, June 28, 1996).

[29] U.S. Department of Commerce, Bureau of the Census, personal correspondence (January 12, 1995).

[30] Carmen D. Solomon, "Aid to Families With Dependent Children (AFDC): A Fact Sheet," CRS Report for Congress (Washington, D.C.: Congressional Research Service, December 9, 1994).

[31] Sharon Parrott, "How Much Do We Spend on 'Welfare'?" (Washington, D.C.: Center on Budget and Policy Priorities, 4 August 1995), 3.

[32] Neisner, "State Welfare Initiatives" (January 24, 1995), 7.

[33] Robert H. Haveman and John Karl Schloz, "The Clinton Welfare Reform Plan: Will It End Poverty as We Know It?" (Madison, Wisc.: Institute for Research on Poverty Discussion Paper no. 1037-95, revised July 1994).

[34] House Ways and Means Committee, *Overview of Entitlement Programs: 1994 Green Book*, 325.

[35] Jennifer A. Neisner, "State Welfare Initiatives," CRS Report for Congress (Washington, D.C.: Congressional Research Service, September 1, 1995): 1.

[36] Theodore R. Marmor, Jerry L. Mashaw, and Philip L. Harvey, *America's Misunderstood Welfare State: Persistent Myths, Enduring Realities*, (New York: Basic Books, 1990), 84–85.

[37] PL 103-66. See Vee Burke, "Clinton Welfare Proposal: Issue Summary" CRS Report for Congress (Washington, DC: Congressional Research Service, September 3, 1993).

[38] Burke, "Clinton Welfare Proposal: Issue Summary."

[39] Rep. Bill Archer, "Let's Return Tax Credit Program to Its Original, Useful Intent . . ." and Rep. Sander M. Levin, ". . . Wrongheaded Republicans Ought to Leave the EITC Alone," *Deseret News*, October 28, 1995.

[40] Robert Rector and William F. Lauber, *America's Failed $5.4 Trillion War on Poverty* (Washington, D.C.: The Heritage Foundation, 1994).

[41] Parrott, "How Much Do We Spend on 'Welfare'?" 3.

[42] "Only High-Income Households Have Recovered Fully from the Recession" (Washington, D.C.: Center on Budget and Policy Priorities, October 24, 1995), 8.

[43] General Accounting Office, "Families on Welfare: Sharp Rise in Never-Married Women Reflects Societal Trends," 36, 38.

[44] See William Julius Wilson, *The Truly Disadvantaged: The Inner City, the Underclass, and Public Policy* (Chicago: University of Chicago Press, 1987).

[45] Desmond King, *Actively Seeking Work: The Politics of Welfare and Unemployment Policy in the U.S. and Great Britain* (Chicago: University of Chicago Press, 1995).

2

Welfare Policy: Goals, Values, and Results

The primary goal of welfare has been to reduce poverty among female-headed families. The great growth in female-headed families that are poor and the persistence of poverty among children in America, however, are evidence that welfare has not achieved its primary goal. AFDC, Food Stamps, and other benefits have increased the income of families that need help and have slightly improved their very nominal standard of living. If we were really serious about reducing poverty, we could simply increase the level of cash and noncash benefits we provide until poverty is reduced. Social Security is a clear example of our ability to identify a segment of our population and provide transfer payments to alleviate poverty.

If reducing poverty were the only goal of welfare, then criticism would zero in on the low level of payments, the failure to index them for inflation, their variation among states, or other similar concerns. But the breadth and depth of dissatisfaction with welfare points to a wider set of expectations that welfare policy has failed to satisfy, for a number of reasons.

This chapter focuses on three principal criticisms aimed at welfare: that welfare policy is plagued by inconsistent goals; that these goals clash with important public values: and that welfare has failed significantly to reduce poverty in America. All of these shortcomings have plagued welfare for decades and continue to challenge policy making as it has devolved to states.

ASSESSING THE GOALS OF WELFARE POLICY

A great number of studies and surveys demonstrated clearly that the old welfare system was dysfunctional, but diagnoses of the causes of the problems differed. They fall along two dimensions, both of which claim that welfare policies are inconsistent with their goals.

First, some argue that the welfare system itself is the problem, One perspective, welfare is a powerful force in the lives of disadvantaged women that undermines their character, discipline, and esteem.[1] Welfare encourages and contributes to an intergenerational cycle of dependency, discourages women from integrating themselves into the work force and the larger society, and hinders self-sufficiency. Welfare encourages other socially dysfunctional behavior such as illegitimacy, divorce or desertion, and the failure to form families.

Other critics counter that welfare is too weak to solve the problems that confront poor families. Welfare does little to help prepare women for meaningful work. Training programs are of poor quality and underfunded. Neither child care nor good jobs are available. What jobs there are do not pay enough to meet the basic needs of poor families. In an urban environment riddled with crime, poor public services, and other problems, welfare is simply inadequate.[2]

A second dimension of the debate over welfare focuses on the cause of poverty. Again, one view is that welfare-dependent and other low-income families live in economically depressed areas with few employment opportunities. The poor are particularly vulnerable to the global economic trends that are affecting even middle-class workers, let alone those with limited education and experience.[3] Others see a culture of poverty that promotes dependency, discouragement, and unwillingness to work. The solution to poverty is to encourage or force people to change the way they think and act.[4]

These two theoretical dimensions are not mutually exclusive and even overlap. Welfare policy falls short in addressing all of these goals. Some of these goals are well beyond the scope of welfare policy itself; others are central to the core values and assumptions underlying the system, and are discussed later in this chapter. Chapter 1 demonstrated significant differences among welfare recipients. Many are recently divorced women who need short-term, transitional assistance. Divorce almost always results in diminished economic resources and opportunities for women, and welfare serves as a critical bridge as they move toward economic independence. Many recipients have little education, little work experience, and little preparation for self-sufficiency and need a great deal of assistance. Contrary to popular belief, only a small percentage of women on welfare are teenage mothers, but they will also need a great deal of help to avoid becoming long-term welfare recipients.

More broadly, welfare cannot be understood apart from changes in the U.S. and global economy. The recent decline in levels of economic growth, the stagnation of worker wages, the flight of industry from the Rust Belt's urban centers, and other structural changes make it extremely difficult for people living in economically depressed areas with limited education to be successful in the labor market. Welfare reform efforts will ultimately be limited by the ability of recipients to find jobs, and the trends are not encouraging. Many communities and regions simply lack job opportunities. States with high unemployment, stagnant economies, and other problems will be unable to reduce their welfare rolls unless they simply cut back on benefits or eligibility.

Work is often hailed as a panacea for poverty, but there are not enough jobs for the unskilled and undereducated to end poverty or even welfare dependence. Many job markets are depressed because of plant closures, foreign competition, and technological obsolescence. Most of the new jobs are located in the suburbs, far from centers of poverty. Employers increasingly rely on subcontracted, part-time, and temporary work. Many jobs, such as those in the lower-paid service industries, do not pay enough to support a family. They are not very secure, offer few fringe benefits such as health insurance, are subject to frequent layoffs, and offer little chance for promotion. Minorities and women are often discriminated against in hiring, promotion, and salary decisions.[5]

Welfare reform is also a function of broad social and cultural developments. The challenges of designing and implementing welfare policies raise the problem of contradictory demands. How can states help poor children without encouraging irresponsible behavior by their parents? How can we get tough on parents without increasing their children's suffering? Increased benefits for children may make welfare more attractive; sanctions against women may harm children. Family caps and no benefits for teen mothers will probably put children at risk; taking children away from parents and placing them in orphanages may not make children better off. Similarly, how can we help poor families without creating incentives for welfare dependency? How can we increase benefits, services, effectiveness without encouraging more people to come on welfare? Or can we increase sanctions against deadbeat dads without making it more difficult for them to meet payments? Does it do any good to take away their driver's licenses or put them in jail? Other risky incentives could also have perverse outcomes: Will family caps and teenage-mother exclusions lead to more abortions? The assumptions underlying AFDC have been questioned: Middle-class women work and struggle to help support their families; shouldn't mothers on welfare do the same? Finally, can welfare be prevented? Can education be improved, work made more renumerative, and job creation made more effective?

The debate over welfare policy is also intertwined with issues of federalism, the decline of support for federal agencies, and the growing demand for devolution of programs and authority to state governments and agencies. Welfare is a national concern, given the mobility of the population and the regional disparities in economic wealth, but there is strong pressure to give states more autonomy to develop welfare programs that work. Since current welfare policy is widely viewed as unsuccessful in promoting strong, self-sufficient families, there is great interest in letting states experiment with alternative approaches. However, some of those approaches will be objectionable. There has already been a "race to the bottom," or at least to the edge, among some states. How can we balance that with a federal role of setting a minimum standard so states don't compete with each other to export poor families?

Welfare is also interwoven with race. Given the concerns about the persistence of racism and the critical role the federal government has played in protecting minority rights, can we dispense with a strong federal presence? We need to look for any cases of discrimination and vulnerability suffered by those who are least able to protect themselves politically or economically.

Effective welfare policy efforts at the state level have been difficult politically. They require careful negotiation between advocates of women and children and advocates of traditional or religious values, but that has been a difficult coalition to fashion. Some coalitions have been built because the dissatisfaction with current programs is so great, but policy failure is common because of the many sensitive issues that surround welfare reform.

Public Opinion and Welfare

A 1996 survey by the Public Agenda Foundation concluded that "an overwhelming percentage of Americans believe welfare is badly flawed and in need of overhaul." Their primary concern is not fraud or the cost of welfare; 65 percent of respondents said that the most trouble-some part of welfare is that "it encourages people to adopt the wrong lifestyles and values." Sixty percent of respondents favored a complete overhaul of welfare, while one-third said it should be "adjusted some-what." Only 3 percent said it did not need change.[6]

The general public is not the only group unhappy with the welfare system. Welfare recipients themselves think the program could use some revision. A May 1995 *Wall Street Journal*/NBC News Poll, for example, asked the following questions:

Do you think the welfare system does more good than harm, be-cause it provides assistance and training for those who are without jobs and live in poverty, or does more harm than good because it encourages the breakup of the family and discourages the work ethic?

	Blacks	Welfare Recipients*	Whites
Does more good than harm	36%	33%	21%
Does more harm than good	52	57	72

Which proposals do you think would be effective in improving the welfare system?

	All Adults	Welfare Recipients*
Requiring recipients to work for benefits	84%	75%
Provide job training for recipients	84	90
Provide subsidized child care for poor mothers who leave welfare for work	77	84
Allow recipients who leave welfare for work to keep getting health benefits	43	50
Make unmarried mothers under 18 ineligible	42	38

* Past and current recipients

Source: Joe Davidson, "Welfare Mothers Stress Importance of Building Self-Esteem if Aid System Is to Be Restructured," *The Wall Street Journal*, May 12, 1995, p. A14.

In interviews, welfare recipients emphasized that one of the most important changes to be made is for welfare bureaucracies to encourage self-respect and self-confidence; for many recipients, the current system is a profound attack on self-esteem.[7] The surveys show that support for welfare is widespread; only 4 percent of the respondents said it should be scrapped. The authors of the study offered this conclusion: "Americans attach a simple moral corollary to helping the needy. 'We will support your efforts to regroup and re-enter the mainstream, but in exchange, we expect you to give something back to the community.' "[8]

Public opinion polls find criticism of the welfare system to be overwhelming, but it has never been the dominant domestic issue. In January 1994, only 6 percent of respondents in a Gallup poll said welfare was the most important problem facing the nation. In January 1995, that number had doubled to 12 percent, the highest level of support for welfare reform Gallup polls had ever measured. But Americans have been ambivalent about what exactly what should be changed in welfare policy: Majorities favored strict efforts to force adults off welfare but opposed initiatives that would harm poor children. There was strong support, 64 percent, for shifting welfare responsibility to states and for cuts in welfare spending; only 30 percent supported smaller cuts and continued federal responsibility. A December 1994 Gallup poll found 58 percent of respondents agreeing with the position that recipients who had not found a job after two years be denied benefits; 62 percent favored limiting lifetime benefits to a total of five years, but 78 percent said their children should continue to receive benefits. Other issues split respondents. Fifty-six percent favored denying benefits to legal immigrants until they have lived in the country for five years; 46 percent favored prohibiting benefits to children born to mothers on welfare. About half of the Gallup respondents, 54 percent, believed that government should provide jobs for welfare recipients if none are available in the private sector.[9]

Public opinion on welfare spending has changed. In 1972, 71 percent of respondents said welfare spending should be maintained or increased; by 1994, that figure fell to 48 percent. Perhaps most interesting was a 1994 Gallup poll that found strong support for an effective welfare-to-work effort, even if it cost more money:

*Would you favor or oppose replacing the current welfare system
with a completely new system to help poor people get off welfare,
if that new system cost the government more money in the next
few years than the current system?*

Favor	68%
Oppose	27
No opinion	5

Source: Michael Golay, "America's Welfare System: A Hand Up or a Hand Out?"
in Michael Golay and Carl Rollyson, *Where America Stands 1996* (New York: John
Wiley and Sons, 1996), 69–87, at 69, 84.

A 1996 *New York Times* poll reported the following:

*Do you favor or oppose limiting how long mothers with young
children can receive welfare benefits?*

Favor:	78%
Oppose:	14
Don't know:	7

Source: Peter T. Kilborn and Sam Howe Verhovek, "Clinton's Welfare Shift Reflects
New Democrat," *The New York Times*, August 2, 1996, p. A1.

Hostility toward welfare is "remarkably democratic," wrote Linda
Gordon,

> "Welfare" is hated by the prosperous and the poor, by the women who
> receive it and by those who feel they are paying for it. It stigmatizes its
> recipients, not least because they are so often suspected of cheating, claiming
> "welfare" when they could be working or paying their own way. It humiliates
> its recipients by subjecting them to demeaning supervision and invasions of
> privacy. Yet it does nothing to move poor women and their children out of
> poverty and often places obstacles in the paths of women's own attempts to
> do so.[10]

These problems with welfare have been widely discussed in public.
Several books have documented in vivid terms the violence, crime, fear,
and the discouragement and resignation that pervade poor urban neighborhoods.[11] Many policy analysts have focused on the problems with
the welfare system itself and compared it with alternative systems.[12]
Charles Murray's influential study depicted the perverse incentives created by welfare.[13] Lawrence Mead argued that the real problem is the
permissiveness of welfare and its failure to compel any obligation on
the part of recipients to take responsibility for their lives.[14] Mary Jo

Bane and David T. Ellwood's study of welfare dependency examined the results of welfare-to-work experiments and explained how difficult it is to help welfare recipients make such a transition.[15]

Desmond King, in his study of welfare and work assistance in the United States and Great Britain, argues that programs in both countries have sought to stigmatize recipients and make assistance unattractive, but have not helped equip recipients with the skills they need to participate in the labor force. Welfare is a traditionally "liberal" program in the sense that it is based on notions of individual freedom, a preference for markets over governments in economic activity, and a safety net for the poor. However, there has been little commitment to help workers develop their capacity to compete in the marketplace, no major investment in human capital as a way to ensure people can be self sufficient.[16]

Journalists have been just as critical. *Newsweek*'s Joe Klein described the welfare system as "an abomination . . . inflexible, bureaucratic, heartless." He claimed two problems were central. First, welfare is "incompetent to deal with a new sort of poverty—cross-generational dependency, poverty that has its roots in behavior more than economics —that began to manifest itself in the 1990s." Second, welfare is based on the mistaken assumption that social work is a profession, but Klein argues that "it is a *calling*. The work of caring for the poor is best done by inspired individuals and institutions, not career government workers."[17] Robert Rector, a welfare analyst at the Heritage Foundation, summed up welfare this way: "In welfare, you get what you pay for. We paid for nonwork and nonmarriage and we've gotten dramatic increases in both."[18]

PUBLIC VALUES AND WELFARE POLICY

Given the nature of the problem of poverty, does welfare rest on the right policy goals? There is no easy answer to such a question, nor are the methodologies to be used clear. How do we decide what the goals of a policy like welfare should be? Part of the answer is to explore carefully the problem's context. We can also try to make sense of the values at the heart of the policy issue. We can evaluate the existing policy in terms of its impact on society: Does it have instrumental or contributive value to society? Is the goal of the policy consistent with societal values? Likewise, we can also assess proposed policies in terms of the extent to which they contribute to these core values.[19]

The challenge is in determining what those values are and how policy goals interact with them. Society has competing goals: We want to promote work and responsibility from adults, but we don't want their children to suffer. We want to promote two-parent families, but we also want to protect women and children from harmful home situations. The values of key institutions, stakeholders, and policy makers are particularly important in understanding the overall value context. Public policies are constrained by ideological commitments. Policy options, in order to be successful, may need to be consistent with our core public commitments. But this ideology may also be difficult to make concrete. We may have major disagreements over our core public philosophy, or at least over the policy implications of that ideology. The ultimate test of welfare or any other policy may be its contribution to our hopes and dreams for economic growth, equality of opportunity, justice, and fairness.

Public policies are often criticized because they fail to accomplish purposes identified for them. But most policies, particularly important and challenging ones, have multiple goals that cannot all be achieved simultaneously. Policies are bundles of compromises. They include contradictions that are responses to political demands, interests, and preferences.[20] We seek to help people who are poor as well as help prevent people from becoming poor. We try to eliminate the causes of poverty, so that transfer payments designed to alleviate poverty eventually will not be needed. But payments may serve to reward the existing conditions and create disincentives for the changes necessary to become independent of assistance.

Analysis of welfare policy (as well as of many other public policies) cannot escape an assessment in light of the public values that shape problems and possible policy options, since the public concern with values has become so central to the policy debate. Teenage pregnancy, for example, is a result of a number of factors related to changes in our culture's norms and values. Does welfare make these kinds of problems worse?[21]

Agreement is widespread that social policy should be aimed at strengthening two-parent families, because that is the best environment in which to nurture and prepare children. But we expect government to strengthen families, given the nature of the family and the kinds of relationships that are central to family life? Can other institutions of our civil society strengthen families? How can public policy interact with the role of churches, voluntary groups, and others in strengthening the family? There is some tension between keeping certain kinds of families together and helping women to be self-sufficient and empowered. Facilitating divorce so women can escape abusive and other debilitating relationships is important, but it obviously affects the viability of two-parent families. Mothers who are working or in training programs have less time to nurture their children.[22]

David Ellwood argues that four values underlie welfare policy: (1) our respect for the autonomy of the individual; (2) the virtue of work and our expectation that everyone engage in it; (3) the privacy and autonomy of the family; and (4) our commitment to community, to connectedness and compassion. These values combine in a set of social policy conundrums. We seek to provide a sense of security for all members of our community, but we also want to enforce work expectations, and we fear that welfare will weaken commitment to work. We aim assistance primarily at single-female-headed families, because we believe the need is greatest there, but in the process we may also encourage divorce and single parenthood. We focus on those with the greatest needs, but in targeting them we may also be isolating them and decreasing the likelihood that they will become integrated into the work force and the broader society.[23]

Part of the failure of welfare is the failure to account for differences among recipients. Different policies are required to address different problems, but welfare policy has lumped all recipients together. One set of welfare mothers are unmarried, under 18, and have usually dropped out of school. They need some kind of parental instruction and assistance, which might be best provided through a group home that can provide child care, control alcohol and drug use, and help mothers complete high school. A second group are single women 18 and older who have children. They may need a wide range of services, from basic education to job training, from parent-training to other forms of counseling, to prepare them for work, but they may be able to live independently. A third group of recipients are single women who have been deserted, divorced, or widowed and who need temporary assistance until they can find jobs. Welfare may include job training and work preparation or be limited to child care, Medicaid, and other forms of assistance. A fourth group might be women who are themselves disabled or must care for those who are and cannot be expected to work.

A second category are the fathers of the children who are on welfare. The primary task is to ensure they pay child support. That may mean offering education, job training, and other programs to help them. Identification of these men should be a prerequisite for the mothers' participation in welfare.

A third group are two-parent families where both adults lack the training to find a job or need temporary assistance in finding work.[24]

Perhaps the ultimate conundrum of welfare is its comparison with other social policies. Welfare's position in the welfare state has always been tenuous. It has never been part of the social insurance system. The 1935 Social Security Act of 1935 created nine different programs. The social insurance programs, Linda Gordon argues, "were superior both in payments and in reputation, while public assistance was inferior—not just comparatively second-rate, but deeply stigmatized." The Supplemental Security Income program, established in 1974, brought aid to the blind, disabled, and the aged within the social insurance program; only AFDC remained outside. Much of the popularity of the contributory programs lies in the belief of recipients that they have paid into the system, but in many cases recipients receive much more back than they put in, and the balance is provided by other workers or the general taxpayers.[25] Welfare has never been able to overcome its origins.

The New Deal work programs and those that were created as part of the Social Security Act all reinforced the idea of work—except the AFDC program. The WPA public works programs, Social Security, unemployment compensation, and other programs continue to be popular because they were limited to those who worked. Supplemental aid to the elderly and disabled was just as widely accepted, because those recipients were unable to work. Only AFDC has become widely unpopular.

THE POLITICS OF WELFARE AND PUBLIC VALUES

The criticism surrounding welfare policy is symptomatic of the broader uneasiness Americans feel about their economic and political future. Theodore J. Lowi's *End of Liberalism*, first published more than twenty-five years ago, argued that government is incapable of achieving social justice. Pluralist politics—a politics built by interest groups that compete for power and thereby produce the public interest—is deeply flawed. It has produced a crisis of authority, unlimited government and political power without purpose; it is a politics that lacks constitutional formality, discipline, legitimacy, and the ability to achieve justice and other important public purposes. Liberalism's passion for justice was dissipated as it tried to accommodate every interest and delegate governmental power indiscriminately. Pluralist politics produces government "where there is no formal specification of means or of ends . . . therefore, no substance."[26]

Politics has become increasingly demoralized as the crisis of public authority Lowi identified has deepened. Our politics is now dominated by individuals' search for security—political isolation, physical protection, and political exit. The urban poor's problems are pushed to the local level, but race and localism mean that those problems will not be solved. A moral and political corrosion has produced distrust and discouragement.[27]

The liberalism that aimed at regulating the excesses of the market and evening out the peaks and troughs of economic cycles seems to be floundering. Support for government regulation and services has eroded. Globalization, technological change, low wages, acceleration of trade, and other economic developments have severely weakened government's ability to play the role prescribed by liberalism. Businesses roam the globe for profits while governments are powerless to regulate capital flight. Tax laws encourage offshore investment and provide insurance for investments in politically high risk areas. Tax cuts and budget constraints mean government cannot afford to do many things. Government is no longer able to pursue the liberal agenda.

Liberalism spawned the welfare-regulatory state, and the liberal idea still holds some popularity. People still support such liberal solutions as environmental protection, Social Security, Medicare, and other policies. Even though conservative politicians have argued that Washington does not work, the public endorses an active government role in job training, in regulation, and other areas. Civil rights is perhaps the ultimate liberal issue, where people support interests beyond their own, in contrast to a conservatism that seeks only to harness self-interest. But even conservatives acknowledge the success of that liberal enterprise as they call for an end to affirmative action in order to realize the civil rights ideal of a color-blind society.

The political equality plank of liberalism continues to be popular; however, the social and economic justice planks are much less secure. Part of the agenda has been achieved, and liberalism is exhausted by its success. Part of the agenda remains, and it seems just as exhausted by its shortcomings. The rise of conservatism in the 1980s and 1990s challenges the expectations created by liberalism. Conservatism may preserve some of the accomplishments of liberalism, but still it undermines them through unrelenting criticism of the role of government and an unshakable faith in business and markets.

In the debate over the welfare state, both Democrats and Republicans have emphasized individualism. Opponents charge that forcing taxpayers to pay for welfare is coerced charity that violates individual freedom. Proponents champion these programs because minimum standards of income, housing, education, and health care are prerequisites for personal autonomy and choice.[28] Liberals seek to ensure that individuals are free to choose for themselves whatever ends they wish to pursue. Government's role is to facilitate those choices, even if it plays a minimal role and apart from providing some public goods, leaves people alone. Or government may play a much more activist role in contributing to the capacity of individuals to make what they will of their lives. Either way, government remains neutral over the choices individuals pursue and seeks to ensure that everyone respects the choices made by others. Civic republicans, in contrast, believe that self-rule involves more than ensuring individual autonomy, but requires participation, deliberation, and collective action to shape the community in which people live. Self-government requires people to possess a public character that makes collective life possible.

In the past, these two approaches have competed for a place in our public philosophy.[29] For instance, during the Progressive Era, people came to fear the power of big corporations but were divided over how to respond. The Progressives believed that decentralizing economic power would allow communities to retain control over economic activity. Supreme Court Justice Louis D. Brandeis, for example, championed trust-busting and the breaking up of large corporations as a way to ensure democratic control over business. Industrial democracy promised to strengthen workers' commitment and capacity to engage in politics and self-government. Others argued that the power of large corporations could best be countered by expanding the reach of the national government. President Theodore Roosevelt, for example, believed that big business was an inevitable consequence of capitalism and industrialization and could only be countered by a strong spirit of nationalism. For both camps, democratic government was the goal: They differed on how to pursue that goal in the face of the economic power of large corporations.[30]

The debate continued during the New Deal. Some reformers demanded a new round of antitrust and other measures to increase competition and reduce the concentration of power. Others saw comprehensive national planning as the best way for government to counter corporate power. Franklin D. Roosevelt experimented with both approaches in response to the Great Depression. The economic imperatives of mobilizing for and fighting World War II clearly tipped the scale in favor of expanding the national government. But with victory in sight, the focus shifted from preserving democracy to ensuring economic growth. We had come to accept a large national government in exchange for a commitment to a national policy of economic expansion.

We also came to embrace a procedural republic that emphasized individual rights and prerogatives more than civic participation and responsibilities. The public agenda no longer included moral character; the task was to stimulate economic growth and foster free, independent persons. Liberalism thus became a politically attractive public philosophy: "The image of persons as free and independent selves, unbound by moral or communal ties they have not chosen, is a liberating, even exhilarating ideal."[31]

The expansion of the welfare state in the Great Society of the 1960s was not constructed on the idea of community or shared obligation but on a preference for individual rights and enabling people to make their own life choices. Freedom was the goal; welfare was the means. Work requirements, job training, family planning and other conditions that might have been imposed on recipients were rejected as inconsistent with the goal of freedom for all persons to decide how they would live their lives, even the poor. For liberals, community was often the problem: Racism, sexism, intolerance, and other problems were a result of the power of communities that could be countered only by a strong, interventionist national government to protect individual rights against the tyranny of local majorities.[32]

The trauma of the late 1960s and 1970s shook Americans' faith in themselves and in their government and in the collective ability to deal with the changes confronting them. Candidates from both parties began to run against government, against Washington bureaucrats. Ronald Reagan was the most successful protest candidate. His New Federalism sought to weaken the concentration of federal political power and to strengthen states and local governments. But he did nothing to counter the power of large, multinational corporations whose actions could devastate communities and leave workers more vulnerable than ever before to forces beyond their control. Nor did the "Reagan revolution" target the institutions of civil society for renewal or seek to protect them in the face of the overwhelming power of capitalism.[33]

For fifty years, criticism of the welfare state rested on libertarian grounds. By the mid-1980s the focus had shifted to the consequences of welfare, the dependency and irresponsibility it fostered in recipients. Bill Clinton embraced such criticisms in his 1992 campaign and subsequent speeches, calling for the end of "welfare as we know" it in order to promote discipline, self-reliance, and other virtues. The flimsy legs on which the welfare state now rests is, in part, a result of all these developments. The nationalization of policy did not include a nationalization of purpose. It relied on a commitment to fair procedures and individual rights rather than on common commitments and shared purposes.[34]

ASSESSING THE IMPACT OF WELFARE ON POVERTY

Even though welfare is inconsistent with strongly held public values, if it had effectively reduced poverty, perhaps it could have been salvaged. But it has not.

Poverty can be described in a variety of ways and from a variety of perspectives. Perhaps nothing is more powerful, aside from experiencing poverty directly, than to read accounts of the pain and suffering that accompany the poverty in novels, plays, and personal accounts. Contemporary writers such as Ruth Sidel have poignantly described what it is like to be poor in America. In *Women and Children Last*, she writes of the women and children who make up the vast majority of poor people in America. One mother and her child in Maine about five years ago, for example, lived on $376 a month; after fixed expenses, they had $56 a month for food, clothing, laundry, transportation, and medical costs. As the mother explained:

> I am badly in need of dental work, my daughter needs new shoes but there is no money left for these things. And I know of women who are in situations worse than mine—who have more children than I do, who pay more rent, who are not able to stretch their food stamps and pennies as far as I can, whose children have their only real meal at noon at the day care center or the baby-sitter's.[35]

Poverty can also be described in more "general," "objective" terms by focusing on numbers, statistics, and trends. This approach reflects little of the immediacy and intensity of the personal accounts of poverty, but it nevertheless help describe the magnitude of the problem.

Poverty is a function of several factors. The way the economy works, including problems of low wages, lack of opportunities, and discrimination, is one set of the ingredients of poverty. Poverty often comes as part of the decline of an entire community or region and its isolation from economic activity. A lack of work-related values, attitudes, and background are another part. Poor education contributes a significant share, as do crime and disorder. The decline of two-parent families and responsible fathers and the growth in out-of-wedlock births and female-headed families contribute to the challenge in overcoming poverty.[36] All the news is not bad, however. Poverty has been dramatically reduced among the elderly, demonstrating that government policies can remedy the problem, but poverty has been persistent among women and children, and the rise of fatherless families has greatly aggravated the problem.

The literature on poverty in America is enormous; many issues deserve attention. The discussion here looks at a small slice of the problem by reviewing some of the available data on poverty in America. This will provide a perspective for thinking about why welfare policy has seemingly had such a limited impact on reducing poverty. Poverty in this country is inextricably intertwined with race and marital status as well as education and geographic location. Poverty is also closely intertwined with economic conditions and the state of the economy.

DEMOGRAPHICS AND POVERTY

The percentage of Americans who are classified as poor has varied considerably during the past half-century. Poverty declined in the 1960s and 1970s then began increasing slightly in the late 1980s and into the 1990s. More striking than the trends in poverty is the stark difference in the rate of poverty among blacks, Hispanics, and whites (see Table 2.1). Poverty is associated with certain demographic characteristics such as race, gender, age, ethnicity, and marital status. Just as striking is the relationship between marital status and poverty.

Families headed by single females are six times as likely to be poor as are two-parent families. About half of all black and Hispanic families headed by single women are living in poverty (see Table 2.2). Poverty rates for fatherless families have always been high. They have not appreciably increased during the past few decades. But the number of these families has dramatically grown during the last thirty years.[37]

From one view, poverty is viewed as the inevitable consequence of a dynamic economic system. Winners and losers are the necessary result of a system that promotes efficiency and liberty. Differences in talents, abilities, motivation, and efforts are likely to produce both successes and failures. Even the poor should be left alone to work out their problems: Giving assistance to them will only prolong their dependence, and the sooner they are left on their own the sooner they will muster the motivation to end their poverty. Government interference with the operation of the economy will only make it less efficient and productive.[38]

TABLE 2.1
PERSONS BELOW THE POVERTY LEVEL
BY RACE AND HISPANIC ORIGIN, IN THOUSANDS

| Year | All Persons | | White Percent | Black Percent | Hispanic Percent |
	Percent	Number			
1960	22.2	39,851	18.1	NA	NA
1965	17.3	33,185	13.3	NA	NA
1970	12.6	25,420	9.9	33.5	NA
1975	12.3	25.877	9.7	31.3	26.9
1980	13.0	29,272	10.2	32.5	25.7
1985	14.0	33,064	11.4	31.3	29.0
1990	13.5	33,585	10.7	31.9	28.1
1993	15.1	39,265	12.2	33.1	30.6
1994	14.5	38,059	11.7	30.6	30.7
1980–1994 average	14.1	34,063	11.2	32.7	28.2
1970–1979 average	11.8	24,792	9.1	31.6	NA

Source: U.S. Bureau of the Census, Current Population Reports, compiled in "Poverty and Income Trends: 1994" (Washington, D.C.: Center on Budget and Policy Priorities, March 1996), 11.

TABLE 2.2
FEMALE-HEADED FAMILIES BELOW THE POVERTY LEVEL
BY RACE AND HISPANIC ORIGIN, IN THOUSANDS

| Year | All Families | | White Percent | Black Percent | Hispanic Percent |
	Percent	Number			
1970	32.5	1,952	25.0	54.3	NA
1975	32.5	2,430	25.9	50.1	53.6
1980	32.7	2,972	25.7	49.4	51.3
1985	34.0	3,474	27.4	50.5	53.1
1990	33.4	3,768	26.8	48.1	48.3
1993	35.6	4,424	29.2	49.9	51.6
1994	34.6	4,232	29.0	46.2	52.1
1980–1994 average	34.5	3,703	27.5	50.5	51.4
1970–1979 average	32.2	2,361	24.6	51.9	NA

Source: U.S. Bureau of the Census, Current Population Reports, compiled in "Poverty and Income Trends: 1994" (Washington, D.C.: Center on Budget and Policy Priorities, March 1996), 15.

TABLE 2.3
NUMBER AND PROPORTION OF POOR FAMILIES HEADED BY A FEMALE
BY RACE AND HISPANIC ORIGIN, IN THOUSANDS

Year	Number of Poor Female- Headed Families	As % of All Poor Families	As % of All Poor White Families	As % of All Poor Black Families	As % of All Poor Hispanic Families
1970	1,952	37.1%	29.7%	56.3%	NA
1975	2,430	44.6	36.3	66.4	44.5
1980	2,972	47.8	38.4	71.2	48.2
1985	3,474	48.1	39.1	73.2	48.5
1990	3,768	53.1	43.5	75.1	46.1
1993	4,424	52.7	43.6	76.4	47.5
1994	4,232	52.6	43.8	77.5	44.8
Change					
1980–1994	52.2%	9.9%	14.3%	8.8%	–7.0%
1970–1979	35.5	30.5	26.8	27.3	NA

Source: U.S. Bureau of the Census, Current Population Reports, compiled in "Poverty and Income Trends: 1994" (Washington, D.C.: Center on Budget and Policy Priorities, March 1996), 16.

For others, a major problem with our economic system is that it "allows the big winners to feed their pets better than the losers can feed their children."[39] Poverty is a human tragedy of great proportions, a violation of human solidarity, of our shared commitments as human beings. Our common humanity requires that we be sensitive to the pain and distress of others, do all we can to reduce suffering, and make our economic and social institutions and practices more just and less cruel.[40]

Even if poverty is viewed as a natural consequence of our economic system, the fact that women and minorities are disproportionately poor is problematic. Poverty is not randomly distributed throughout the population. Nor is it a natural and fair outcome of competitive market relationships among economically rational individuals. Blacks and other minorities and women are overrepresented in most categories of poverty and related disadvantagement. Race and sex ought to be irrelevant in a free-market system, since discrimination on the basis of criteria unrelated to performance is by definition inefficient. The loss of human potential reflected in poverty among women and children is, even from an economic perspective, a problem of great proportions. The distribution of poverty among women and minorities makes it even more compelling to help low-income families. More than three-quarters of

TABLE 2.4
CHILDREN (ALL PERSONS UNDER 18) BELOW THE POVERTY LEVEL
BY RACE AND HISPANIC ORIGIN

Year	All Children		White Percent	Black Percent	Hispanic Percent
	Percent	Number			
1976	16.0	10,273	11.6	40.6	30.2
1980	18.3	11,543	13.9	42.3	33.2
1985	20.7	13,010	16.2	43.6	40.3
1990	20.6	13,431	15.9	44.8	38.4
1993	22.7	15,727	17.8	46.1	40.9
1994	21.8	15,289	16.9	43.8	41.5

Source: U.S. Bureau of the Census, Current Population Reports, compiled in 'Poverty and Income Trends: 1994" (Washington, D.C.: Center on Budget and Policy Priorities, March 1996), 21.

black families living in poverty are headed by females, as are nearly half of poor white and Hispanic families (see Table 2.3).

In Table 2.3, "all families" does not include unrelated subfamilies. As of 1979, the term "total poor" does not include a small number of people living in what the Census Bureau calls related subfamilies— boarders, live-in employees, and other families not related to the primary family in the household. Poor persons living in female-headed households would be a higher proportion of total poor if persons in related subfamilies were included.

Estimates of poverty rates for different groups vary for a number of reasons, from differences in sampling techniques to variations in definitions and assumptions. Nevertheless, it is clear that being black, female, and a parent are associated with extremely high rates of poverty, and that children are the primary group of poor people in America.

CHILDREN AND POVERTY

Poverty is increasingly concentrated in families headed by younger parents and the impact on children and the opportunities they have is profound. Over 40 percent of all black children living in the richest country in the world are poor (see Table 2.4). The poverty rate of children in the United States is the highest among Western nations as is the gap between youth and adult poverty rates.[41] The Luxembourg Income Study examined the United States and seventeen other countries and found that the general status of poor children in the United States is worse than in most other countries in the study. Even though the United States has the second-highest economic output per person, poverty among children is more severe here than in other countries, for several reasons. Unlike other countries, American households with children are less affluent than households without children, and mothers are less likely to return to work after childbirth as quickly as European mothers. The U.S. also has the widest gap between rich and poor and the least generous social programs of any of the countries studied.[42]

The socio-economic situation of black children is particularly alarming. According to the Children's Defense Fund, black children are twice as likely to die in the first year of life, be born prematurely, live in substandard housing, and have unemployed parents as are their white counterparts. Black children are three times as likely to be poor, live in a female-headed family, be in foster care, and die of known child abuse; four times as likely to live with neither parent and be under the direction of a welfare agency, be murdered before the age of one or as a teenager, and be incarcerated between the ages of 15 and 19. Black children are five times as likely to be on welfare.[43]

In the 1960s and 1970s, relatively little attention was given to the emerging problems of black families. The one prominent exception was Daniel Patrick Moynihan's 1965 report on race in America, which argued that a disproportionate number of black children were being raised in the "disorder of welfare dependency" and were not prepared to take advantage of the opportunities that the civil rights movement was securing for them. Moynihan's warning triggered a backlash that discouraged others from examining the distress of black families. Those who returned to that subject in the 1980s were struck by the deterioration in conditions in black families. Some argue that the current crisis is a result of past welfare programs that have profoundly harmed their intended beneficiaries. Others blamed a shift in focus toward welfare rights, toward a "policy focus on services and welfare" that lost sight of the central imperative of "getting blacks into the labor market." Some placed the blame on a culture of poverty and dependency, on communities for failing to foster values and work habits required for successful participation in the work force, and on government programs that excluded the poor from economic opportunities and created dependency on transfer payments.[44]

Much attention has been focused on the urban "underclass." Although there is no consensus about how to define the underclass, these families are usually described as being headed by females who are permanently unemployed, persistently poor, dependent on welfare, giving birth out of wedlock, predominantly black or Hispanic, poorly educated, and living in blighted urban areas overwhelmed with crime, pollution, drugs, and other social problems. Women and children in the underclass suffer enormous deprivation and represent a tremendous waste of human potential. The cycle of despair and lack of opportunity feeds on itself, and the problem is growing. Estimates range from 2 million persistently poor people, who are neither disabled nor elderly and who live in urban areas, to nearly 6 million poor people who live in census tracts where the poverty rate is greater than 40 percent. The number of people living in census tracts with high concentrations of female-headed families, school dropouts, welfare dependents, and permanently unemployed men grew by 230 percent between 1970 and 1980.[45]

Poor children are concentrated in urban areas: Although cities include 30 percent of American children, they are home to 45 percent of poor children. One third of all children living in central cities are in families whose income is below the poverty level. In 1994, 15.3 million children were poor; 6.9 million lived in city centers—3.3 million whites, 3.1 million blacks, and 2.1 million Hispanics and those of other races. Almost one half of black and Hispanic children in central cities are poor; one-fourth of white children are poor. Nearly 36 percent of city children are raised in fatherless homes, compared with 23 percent of children nationwide. More than 70 percent of Hispanic children, 65 percent of black children, and more than 50 percent of white children who live in fatherless families in city centers are poor. For children in married families, the figures are 34 percent for Hispanics, 17 percent for blacks, and 15 percent for whites. More than one of every seven children on AFDC live in New York City, Los Angeles County, and Cook County (Chicago area).[46]

WOMEN AND POVERTY

The urban underclass is the most intense manifestation of poverty, but female-headed families include a much wider range of characteristics. They include women who work full time, women who work part time because full-time work is not available, disabled and retired persons, and mothers at home with young children. The causes of poverty among female-headed families are intricately intertwined. Some women work at or near minimum wages, but fail to earn enough to bring their families out of poverty. (A family of four needs a full-time wage of about $6.00 an hour for the entire year to reach the poverty level, much higher than the minimum wage.) Others seek full-time work but can only work part-time, given child-care responsibilities.[47]

Women are disproportionately concentrated in occupations that pay much less than others requiring similar education and experience but that are dominated by male workers. Women and blacks continue to be disproportionately represented in the lowest-paying occupations and underrepresented in professional jobs even after controlling for age, educational attainment, region, and marital status, although there has been some improvement in some categories such as law and medicine. The percentage of women in professional, technical, and similar positions has increased considerably. Black, college-educated women have reached parity with their white counterparts, although not with men.[48] The median weekly earnings for women continue to hover around 70 percent of those for males.[49]

Poverty among these women is complicated by additional factors, from lack of education and experience to poor health. The presence of children is particularly important. Many women who have had out-of-wedlock children as adolescents drop out of school and never gain the kind of educational and work experience necessary for successful job competition.[50] Divorce often leaves women economically devastated, and few receive child support.[51]

AFRICAN-AMERICAN MEN

A complicating factor is that the problems of many poor black women are intertwined with those of black males. The overall prospects for black men in the labor market have important implications for female-headed poverty among black families: Employment figures show that blacks and women are much less successful than white males in competing in the labor market, a disparity that has been rather stable during the last three decades. Nonwhite men during the peak years of employment (25 to 54 years of age) have been unemployed at two and one half times the rate of white males of the same age. Unemployment rates fall during periods of economic expansion and increase during economic downturns for blacks and women as they do for white males. But unemployment rates for blacks are even more influenced by overall economic health than are rates for whites. Blacks make more gains than whites during periods of economic expansion but lose more than whites during recessions.

Black men are significantly less likely to be working or actively seeking jobs than their white counterparts. The percentage of black men in the labor force has steadily declined since 1960, while overall participation in the labor force increased during that time, primarily due to greater participation by women—black women in particular. These figures are especially significant because they demonstrate declining participation in work among black males and reflect a rise in discouraged workers—those without current employment but who are not actively seeking work and are not reflected in unemployment rates. In proportion to their percentage of the total population, there are some 2 million fewer blacks in the labor force than there are whites. This alone might account for almost 25 percent of the black–white per capita earnings gap.[52]

The consequence of these labor market problems is that a large group of black males is missing from the labor force: For whites, there are 9.2 males for every 10 females; for blacks, there are only about 8.2 males for every 10 females. Increasing numbers of black women continue to enter the labor force, while the participation rate of black men continues to fall. The increase in black single mothers and black female-headed families, and their tremendously high rates of poverty, may be to a significant extent due to the lack of young black employed males who are marriageable. As the number of black males able to support a family decreases, black women may find that having children will be possible only if they go on welfare. The number of employed black men compared with the number of employed white men is much lower for every age group, but is particularly low for younger blacks. The number of employed black males between the ages of 25 and 34 is about 25 percent less than for white males of the same age. For blacks from 20 to 24, the difference is more than 20 percent.[53]

The group that has the most difficulties in the labor market and appears to suffer the most from employment discrimination is young black males, even though much of the emphasis on affirmative action is aimed at opening up job opportunities for young blacks. Affirmative action may have helped create new opportunities for black workers and may be responsible for some of the progress made in occupational advancement, although significant numbers of blacks have not been placed in senior management positions. Affirmative action has been most effective in opening up opportunities for blacks who have the background and preparation to compete in the labor market. It will only benefit blacks who can meet job qualifications; few affirmative action plans require that unqualified persons be hired to meet hiring goals.[54]

Despite its successes, affirmative action is widely under attack and its future role in helping to reduce poverty in America is uncertain.[55] One important criticism of affirmative action is that it promotes racial segregation and divisiveness and fails to help poor blacks. Those who do take advantage of preferential treatment are often the children of successful black families who receive an advantage they really do not need—an advantage that seems unfair in comparison with the plight of disadvantaged white children. Far better, some argue, would be a class-based approach that would identify people who are disadvantaged and devise programs to give them a chance to be successful. Parental income, education, and occupation; the quality of education; neighborhood influences and family structure; and other measures could be devised to indicate when young people are likely to be disadvantaged and in need of additional assistance. Critics of the class-based approach, and defenders of affirmative action, argue that racism and discrimination are still serious problems in America and we are unfortunately not ready for color blindness in public policy. Class-based criteria are difficult to formulate and may be just as stigmatizing as racial categories. Others argue that we simply need better education, nutrition programs, and other collective benefits for everyone, regardless of race or class. But with limited public resources we will likely have to make choices about where the greatest needs are.[56]

Affirmative action rests on the belief that once blacks are hired or promoted into new positions, they will be able to compete with others. "Although affirmative action programs do create opportunities for some less advantaged minority individuals," William Julius Wilson has written,

> ghetto underclass individuals are severely underrepresented among those who have actually benefitted from such programs. In other words, what we really see is a "creaming" process in the sense that those with the greatest economic, educational, and social resources among the less advantaged individuals are the ones who are actually tapped for higher paying jobs and higher education through affirmative action.[57]

Other limitations on employment opportunities for blacks may be beyond the reach of affirmative action. Some argue that welfare benefits are so attractive that incentives to work are reduced. Others believe that the federal minimum wage prevents employers from hiring young blacks with few skills and paying them wages lower than the federal standard. Social factors may be impediments to employment as well. The flight of black middle-class families from urban ghetto neighborhoods has resulted in a loss of jobs, role models, and social stability. Employers may believe that they will have more problems with young blacks than with other employees, that young black males are more likely to be absent from work more often, more likely to use drugs and alcohol on the job, more crime-prone, and less able to write clearly and effectively and make basic mathematical calculations.[58]

TABLE 2.5
ELDERLY PERSONS BELOW THE POVERTY LEVEL
BY RACE AND HISPANIC ORIGIN, IN THOUSANDS

| Year | All Persons | | White Percent | Black Percent | Hispanic Percent |
	Percent	Number			
1966	28.5	5,114	26.4	55.1	NA
1970	24.5	4,793	22.6	48.0	NA
1975	15.3	3,317	13.4	36.3	32.6
1980	15.7	3,871	13.6	38.1	30.8
1985	12.6	3,456	11.0	31.5	23.9
1990	12.2	3,658	10.1	33.8	22.5
1993	12.2	3,755	10.7	28.0	21.4
1994	11.7	3,663	10.2	27.4	22.6

Source: U.S. Bureau of the Census, Current Population Reports, compiled in "Poverty and Income Trends: 1994" (Washington, D.C.: Center on Budget and Policy Priorities, March 1996), 27.

THE ELDERLY

As previously mentioned, the percentage of elderly persons who are poor has declined significantly since the 1950s and early 1960s through the expansion of welfare benefits. But race is still a factor here: despite those efforts, black seniors are still almost three times as likely to be poor as whites of the same age (see Table 2.5). Since Social Security benefits are, to some extent, a function of wages earned, and since blacks earn less than whites over their working lives, that would explain at least part of the disparity. Social security payments to the elderly and to disabled workers and the survivors of deceased workers have eliminate much more poverty than AFDC payments have. Social Security benefits prevent poverty among some 70 percent of the aged; AFDC payments result in lifting only about 4 percent of recipients above poverty.

Just as difficult as race is the generational gap: Public spending for Medicare and Social Security, particularly the transfer payments from working to retired persons, raises important questions about how to reduce poverty among children. Social Security has for the past several decades paid beneficiaries several times the amount of money they contributed to the system. The decision in 1972 to increase benefits by 20 percent and to index future benefits to the Consumer Price Index, coupled with the high inflation of the late 1970s, contributed to the fiscal problems facing Social Security. A new benefit formula inadvertently resulted in a double indexing that gave windfall benefits to a number of recipients before it was discovered and repaired in 1977, giving rise to the "Notch Baby" movement of recipients who complained because the windfall was not extended to them. In the late 1970s the formula was altered further so that benefits rose along with real wage increases. The Social Security system faced a crisis in 1983 that resulted in increased payroll taxes, taxation of benefits, and the phasing in of a higher retirement age.

During the 1970s benefits grew, in real terms, ten times faster than did the number of Americans who were 65 and older. By the 1980s, the average Social Security couple received four times its payroll contribution to the system (in 1993 dollars, the average payroll contribution was $50,000 and the payout was $210,000). The regressive nature of the tax (it is imposed only on the first $62,700 of earnings each year) is countered by the structure of benefits, which gives lower-wage workers a higher percentage of their preretirement pay. But the overall impact is still regressive, since high-income earners get a lower percentage of a much higher wage. Spouses get 50 percent of the worker's benefits, so larger payments go to higher-income families. Despite the changes, Social Security is not sustainable for very far into the future. Under the current system, $60 billion in benefits goes to retired households with an income of at least $50,000; $15 billion goes to those with incomes over $100,000. In 1950, seven workers were paying into the system for every beneficiary; in 1990, five workers; by 2030 there will be fewer than three. Life expectancy has increased by fourteen years since Social Security was created. Although contributions currently exceed payouts by about $30 billion a year, the surplus is invested in Treasury bills, loaned to the Federal government to finance the budget deficit. This funding scheme cannot continue without a combination of further tax increases, benefit cuts, and increases in the retirement age. But Social Security taxes have already increased 3 percent per decade since the 1950s and hit low- and middle-income families the hardest. The combined worker/employer rate of 15.3 percent is higher than the income tax rate paid by most Americans. By 2030, Social Security and Medicare payroll contributions are estimated to be from 33 to 40 percent of total payroll costs.

Fixing Social Security and Medicare may be our most pressing social policy concern. Focusing attention on this problem deflects attention from problems facing children. But not addressing it also threatens younger Americans. As spending on Social Security and other entitlements increases, and cash assistance to poor families becomes a discretionary expenditure, the needs of poor children will not be addressed.

And questions about the future solvency of the Social Security Trust Fund may mean that the future of today's children (and their parents) will be much less secure than that of their grandparents. The July 1997 budget agreement passed by Congress cut taxes for children and capital gains, raised taxes for tobacco, increased spending for poor children's health and for assistance to legal immigrants, and promised to balance the federal budget by 2002. All of those measures served as further evidence that neither Congress nor the Clinton administration was interested in addressing the long-term problem of funding entitlements like Medicare and Social Security even when the economy was booming and government revenues were higher than expected.

From the beginning, Social Security has been built on a tradeoff between the needs of the elderly and other social needs. As a transfer program from young, working Americans to older, retired ones, it helps reduce poverty among the aged while reducing the standard of living of the rest of society. Federal spending on the elderly is currently eleven times greater than what is spent on children under eighteen. Even moderate reforms such as taxing benefits so that retired families with the same income as young families pay the same taxes, or imposing limits on benefits and cost of living adjustments for wealthier seniors (and permitting laborers who cannot work so long as others to be able to retire earlier) seem beyond political feasibility. Neither raising taxes nor cutting benefits appears to be acceptable to leading candidates of either party. However, a range of modest steps is possible, such as raising the earnings subject to the Social Security tax, raising the retirement age, or increasing the tax on Social Security benefits for better-off recipients or reducing their benefits. Proposals for more fundamental changes include privatizing the system and permitting young workers to create their own personal retirement accounts. But the current pay-as-you-go system would require current workers to continue to contribute to the current system as well as building their own.

Changes in Social Security are inevitable; or as Herb Stein, former Council of Economic Advisors put it, "the only thing comforting about an unsustainable trend is that it can't go on forever."[59] Social Security is the most successful social program in America. Its benefits go beyond reducing poverty among the poor to being a key element of the social contract and a central part of whatever level of communitarianism exists in America. The loss of this shared commitment to social insurance and assistance to the elderly might affect the entire commitment to the welfare state. One of our challenges is to not lose sight of ways to reduce poverty among children even as we try to solve problems that are more politically salient.

PROBLEMS IN MEASURING POVERTY

The poverty rate has become an important measure of economic well-being and a critical indicator for social policy. The Social Security Administration created it at the beginning of the Johnson administration as a quickly devised index to use in designing the Great Society's War on Poverty. The index measures the proportion of the population with an annual income that falls below a poverty threshold that varies according to household type and size.

Critics have argued that the poverty index fails to take into account geographic variation in the cost of living, inaccurately adjusts for cost of living increases over time, does not include the real value of government assistance programs to low-income households, does not fully reflect actual earnings, and fails to differentiate between those who own homes and those who pay rent. Over time, the Bureau of the Census has tried to respond to these criticisms.[60]

More fundamental are the criticisms that the index is quite misleading because poverty should be measured by consumption rather than income. The Department of Labor's annual Consumer Expenditure Survey, for example, finds that low-income Americans spend more money than they report earning. In 1994, for example, the lowest fifth of the respondents reported an average pretax income of under $6,800 but an average total spending of more than $14,000. In order to maintain their consumption during periods when income falls, these consumers draw on their savings, borrow money, receive help from friends and relatives, and take other actions.[61] So the index likely overstates poverty.

Other indicators of consumption raise questions about the level of poverty in America. A Census Bureau report found that poor Americans have access to appliances at levels that exceed the average of all European residents: Sixty percent of poor Americans have VCRs, 60 percent have microwave ovens, 20 percent have dishwashers, and 50 percent have clothes dryers. In contrast, the percent of all residents of ten European countries surveyed range from 25 to 65 percent for VCRs, 6 to 48 percent for microwaves, 11 to 34 percent for dishwashers, and 5 to 39 percent for dryers.[62]

Other questions have been raised about how we measure poverty and the policies we fashion in response. A large percentage of the poor (37 percent of the households in the bottom fifth of income) are elderly; much of this population owns houses and other resources that soften the impact of low income: Forty-one percent of Americans in the bottom fifth of income own their own homes, and 75 percent of these households own their home free and clear of any mortgage payments.[63] So although the official poverty rate in 1993 was about the same as it was in 1966 at the beginning of the War on Poverty, levels of consumption have increased substantially during this period. Based on household expenditure levels, one study estimates the poverty rate at 31 percent in 1949, 13 percent in 1965, and 2 percent in 1989. Even then, the study does not account for noncash benefits such as Medicaid, public housing, and other services. Since food and housing are two of the largest expenditures of poor families, those who receive Food Stamps and government housing may have even higher consumption than reported.[64]

A commission of economists chaired by Michael Boskin, the former chair of President Bush's Council of Economic Advisers, concluded that the Consumer Price Index, or CPI, which is used to calculate changes in the cost of living, has overstated the rise in the cost of living by some 1.5 percent a year. The commission argues that the index fails to recognize that people substitute cheaper food and goods for more expensive ones, shop in discount stores, and buy goods whose quality and energy efficiency have increased. The cumulative impact of these inaccuracies has significant consequences for our understanding of poverty. According to the commission's estimate, the median weekly earnings for full-time male workers did not fall by 12 percent from 1979 to 1994 but actually rose 14 percent. If the CPI has overstated the cost of living by 1.5 percent since 1967, then there are 15 million, rather than 38 million, poor Americans today.[65]

Has poverty actually dramatically declined during the past thirty years? Which measure should we use to assess changes in poverty: income or consumption? Proponents of the welfare state might use consumption figures to argue that we have indeed made progress in improving the conditions of the poor and that we should continue our efforts. Opponents can use the same figures to argue that there is no compelling need for these programs since consumption is much higher than we believed. Despite the limitations of the way in which poverty is estimated, official government figures do provide useful information about trends in income. They are also widely cited by policy makers in defending proposals and evaluating existing or opposing programs. A brief review of the figures on poverty will help provide the context in which the welfare reform debate has taken place, and provides some indication of whether welfare has helped reduce poverty in America.

POVERTY AND THE ECONOMY

The commitment to the welfare state cannot be pursued without acknowledging the increasing fear on the part of many Americans that their economic future is insecure. The optimism that has traditionally fueled Americans' views on the economy—that the standard of living will continually increase—has been shaken by the decline in real wages for an increasing number of people. From the 1950s to the early 1970s, the economy and wages grew steadily. Most Americans expected that their standard of living would continue to grow and that their children would be better off financially than they were. That optimism began to wane in the mid-1970s when wages began to stagnate. For example, the Bureau of Labor Statistics includes 80 percent of American workers in the category of production and nonsupervisory workers, who are below the managerial, executive, and technical level. The average weekly earnings for production and nonsupervisory workers, after adjusting for inflation, fell by 18 percent between 1973 and 1995. In contrast, the real annual pay of executives rose by 19 percent between 1979 and 1989. Despite increases in productivity, real hourly wages have not increased during a recovery for the first time since World War II.[66] The pay ratio of chief executives to average workers, according to one survey, has grown from 41:1 in the 1970s to 187:1 in 1995. During those same years, the average pay of workers in companies with more than twenty-five thousand employees, in actual dollars, rose from $8,000 to $20,000 (in real dollars, earnings actually declined); for CEOs in the same companies, salaries grew from $326,000 to $3.7 million a year.[67]

According to calculations made by Robert H. Havemann and John Karl Schloz, the earnings of workers with low levels of education have fallen dramatically, placing additional pressure on antipoverty programs. The median income of men 25 years old and older who completed only one to three years of high school fell, in terms of 1989 dollars, from $24,079 in 1972 to $14,439 in 1989. During those same years, their earnings as a percentage of income of men with college degrees fell from 59 to 38 percent.[68]

Economists and others argue that workers' wages are falling for a number of reasons. One argument is that workers cannot resist efforts by employers to cut wages and benefits through *outsourcing*—contracting out part of their manufacturing to other firms that are not unionized or that operate in areas where low wages predominate. For example, GM workers earn an average of $18.58 an hour and receive another $16 an hour in benefits; however, GM can outsource the manufacturing of component parts to companies that pay $13.15 an hour and $3.68 in benefits. More extreme disparities occur when U.S. business outsource to even lower-cost areas in the less-developed world (average wages in Mexico are $2.61 an hour, for example). The decline in the power of unions and the difficulties in organizing nonunion factories, the failure of Congress and the president to enact national health insurance that would remove health benefits from bargaining agreements, and global competitiveness blamed for exporting jobs to the less-developed world all combine to put downward pressure on wages and benefits.[69]

Another cause of the widening gap between high- and low-paid workers is development in technology that results in a premium to skilled workers. Computerization has eliminated millions of jobs and transformed millions more; workers who have technical expertise flourish, those who don't languish. Federal Reserve Chairman Alan Greenspan observed that "human skills are subject to obsolescence at a rate perhaps unprecedented in American history."[70] Higher-paying jobs are increasingly reserved for workers with higher education and computer skills. The challenge is balancing those consequences of technological innovation that have adverse impacts on wages and jobs for the unskilled with increasing productivity, competitiveness, and wealth without inflation. The benefits of innovation include new jobs, but it is not clear that the new jobs will be created fast enough and pay high enough wages to offset those lost. Many argue that these benefits have not occurred.

These and other forces have come together to make inequality in America even more pronounced. The bottom end of the poverty population is falling farther and farther behind, and the challenges confronting policy makers in addressing poverty seem more and more difficult. The bullish stock market and low unemployment in 1996 and 1997 deflected attention from the problem of inequality in America.

THE MINIMUM WAGE AND POVERTY

Finally, the value of the minimum wage, adjusted for inflation, is near a forty-year low.[71] In 1996, the minimum wage became the subject of a battle between Democrats and Republicans. Proponents of the minimum wage prevailed in August 1996, when Congress passed and the president signed a law that increased the federal minimum wage from $4.25 to $4.75 an hour beginning October 1, 1996, and to $5.15 on

September 1, 1997. Republicans included in the package $10 billion in tax cuts for businesses over five years. The final vote (the House vote was 354–72; the Senate vote was 76–22) disguised the bitterness and partisanship of the minimum wage debate. But it became difficult to vote against increasing the minimum wage as the welfare reform debate centered on making sure that welfare recipients went to work.[72]

Proponents argued that boosting the minimum wage would assist the more than 12 million workers who earn from $4.25 and $5.15 an hour. Of these 12.3 million workers, 53 percent work part time, 25 percent are 16 to 19 years old and are spread evenly across household income levels, and fewer than 9 percent support a family as the sole breadwinner. Minimum wage increases appear to reduce employee turnover and increase employer recruitment and training efforts. Many proponents of the minimum wage increase recognize that employment will be reduced but that that cost is outweighed by the benefit to those already working. Critics argue that in weak labor markets, where wages are low, wage increases would cause employers to lay off workers and would be particularly harmful for the least experienced and educated workers, especially minority teenagers.[73]

House Republicans proposed an alternative package of benefits for workers with children that would also have eliminated the earned income tax credit for workers with no children so that wages would, in effect, rise without requiring employers to pay more.[74] But some opponents argue that the real cost of increasing the minimum wage would be in the loss of jobs, because employers could not afford to give marginal workers higher pay. Opponents of the minimum wage hike also argue that the Earned Income Tax Credit is a better vehicle to help poor workers because it can be targeted to needy families, unlike the minimum wage, which might benefit teenagers from well-to-do families as much as it would heads of households. However, the GOP attacks on the EITC, which Republicans characterized as cuts in "corporate welfare," have reduced that option for helping low-income workers.[75]

The cost of the minimum wage hike of $.90 for the 13 million workers who earn between $4.25 and $5.15, and a wage increase for the 10 million who earn from $5.15 to $6.15, would total $33 billion a year, 6 percent of the 1995 corporate profits of $550 billion. Corporate executives whose pay has grown from forty times the average worker's salary to 150 times are not in a strong position to complain about spending more on the lowest-income workers.[76]

Business groups have recognized that the decline in the real value of the minimum wage is only one of the problems facing low-income Americans and the companies that hire them. A number of large corporations formed the Empower Group to help address employee problems that contributed to high turnover. Some companies have already established their own welfare-to-work programs to provide new employees with basic job skills. Other companies have instituted employee hotlines that provide assistance with child care, immigration, and other concerns; tied maternity benefits to good prenatal care; subsidized child care for employees; and created other collaborative efforts between employers, employees, and government that reduce turnover. J. W. Marriott, Jr., one of the leading corporate executives in this effort, believes that the objective is to "pay a competitive wage and to do everything we can to help people help themselves."[77]

Polls reported in 1996 showed that from 70 to 80 percent of Americans favored an increase in the minimum wage. Eleven states and the District of Columbia already require minimum wages above the Federal minimum. Unlike public opinion, however, expert opinion is divided over the appropriateness of having a minimum wage at all, let alone increasing it. One economist recently wrote that "most economists are quite skeptical of the research claiming that minimum wages either raise employment or do not reduce employment"; another wrote that "most economists may now accept recent studies that found that raising the minimum wages caused little or no reduction in employment, and in some cases apparently increased it."[78]

CRITICISM OF WELFARE AND THE AGENDA OF WELFARE REFORM

Although the traditional AFDC system may have made a lot of sense when it was designed in the 1930s, conceptually it seems obsolete today. Economic, cultural, societal changes have been so significant that they challenge the underlying assumptions of the 1930s. Public policy has been rather slow to respond to this change. The traditional belief was that single mothers should be supported while they stay home to raise their children; we no longer see that as a tenable option. Despite some interest in providing income to help single mothers stay at home, the importance of integrating them and their children into the work force and the larger society in order to avoid the problems of dependency have become compelling.

We expect welfare policy to help recipients become self-sufficient. We expect it to contribute to broader social goals that seek to nurture children, encourage two-parent families, and generate jobs that pay wages sufficient for families to live. But requirements aimed at providing assistance may discourage men from assuming child support and other responsibilities; improving the child-support system will increase income to women and children and make them less likely to need help from welfare. A primary complaint about the current welfare system is that it has failed to change the behavior of the women who receive welfare checks; but the behavior we most want to change is that of the men who father children, commit crimes, and terrorize neighborhoods with drugs.[79]

Much of the dissatisfaction with welfare is rooted in the unrealistic goals we have set for welfare alone to achieve. The public policies of which welfare is a part are exceedingly ambitious. Alone, welfare cannot reduce poverty and help families become self sufficient. Welfare alone cannot create parents who are dedicated to raising healthy, productive children, but our future depends on that. Welfare cannot remedy the loss of industrial jobs in urban areas, the decline in real wages, economic uncertainty, job discrimination, changes in the global economy, poor or limited education, and other factors that have combined to reduce the opportunities available to many people.

Welfare policy implicates strongly held values that are politically powerful and susceptible to political demagoguery. The debate over these values transcends the debate over specific policy options and taps into fundamental public values and concerns. These values are the ultimate criteria by which current welfare policy must be judged; they also help generate options for reforming welfare, which are discussed in the chapters that follow.

REFERENCES

[1] See Charles Murray, *Losing Ground: American Social Policy, 1950–1980* (New York: Basic Books, 1984).

[2] Herbert J. Gans, *The War Against the Poor: The Underclass and Antipoverty Policy* (New York: Basic Books, 1995).

[3] See William Julius Williams, *The Truly Disadvantaged: The Inner City, the Underclass, and Public Policy* (Chicago: University of Chicago Press, 1987).

[4] See Lawrence M. Mead, *The New Politics of Poverty: The Nonworking Poor in America* (New York: Basic Books, 1992).

[5] Sarah K. Gideonse and William R. Meyers, "Why the Family Support Act Will Fail," *Challenge* (September–October 1989): 33–39, at 34.

[6] Richard Morin, "Fed Up With Welfare," *The Washington Post*, National Weekly Edition, April 29–May 5, 1996, p. 37.

[7] Joe Davidson, "Welfare Mothers Stress Importance of Building Self-Esteem if Aid System Is to Be Restructured," *The Wall Street Journal*, May 12, 1995, p. A14.

[8] Morin, "Fed Up With Welfare."

[9] Michael Golay, "America's Welfare System: A Hand Up or a Hand Out?" in Michael Golay and Carl Rollyson, *Where America Stands 1996* (New York: John Wiley and Sons, 1996), 70, 81, 84, 86.

[10] Linda Gordon, *Pitied But Not Entitled: Single Mothers and the History of Welfare* (New York: The Free Press, 1994), 3.

[11] Alex Kotlowitz, *There Are No Children Here: The Story of Two Boys Growing Up in the Other America* (New York: Doubleday, 1991).

[12] Theresa Funiciello, *Tyranny of Kindness: Dismantling the Welfare System to End Poverty in America* (New York: Atlantic Press, 1993); Marvin Olasky, *The Tragedy of American Compassion* (New York: Regnery Gateway, 1992).

[13] Murray, *Losing Ground*.

[14] Lawrence M. Mead, *Beyond Entitlement: The Social Obligations of Citizenship* (New York: Free Press, 1986).

[15] Mary Jo Bane and David T. Ellwood, *Welfare Realities: From Rhetoric to Reform* (Cambridge, Mass.: Harvard University Press, 1994).

[16] Desmond King, *Actively Seeking Work?* (Chicago: University of Chicago Press, 1995).

[17] Joe Klein, "Monumental Callousness," *Newsweek* (August 12, 1996): 45.

[18] Quoted in Golay, "America's Welfare System, A Hand Up or a Hand Out?," 69–87, at 73.

[19] See Frank Fischer, *Evaluating Public Policy* (Chicago: Nelson-Hall, 1995).

[20] Theodore Marmor, Jerry L. Mashaw and Philip L. Harvey, *America's Misunderstood Welfare State: Persistent Myths, Enduring Realities* (New York: Basic Books, 1991), 222–23.

[21] See Sharon Parrott and Robert Greenstein, "Welfare, Out-Of-Wedlock Childbearing, and Poverty: What is the Connection?" (Washington, D.C.: Center on Budget and Policy Priorities, January 1995); "Welfare, Out-Of-Wedlock Childbearing, and Poverty: What is the Connection?" (Washington, D.C.: Center on Budget and Policy Priorities, revised March 7, 1995); and Patrick F. Fagan, "Rising Illegitimacy: America's Social Catastrophe" (Washington, D.C.: The Heritage Foundation, June 29, 1994).

[22] For a review of the current debate, see Rob Gurwitt, "The Politics of Divorce," *Governing* (May 1996): 34–40; William A. Galston, "Braking Divorce: For the Sake of Children," *The American Enterprise* (May/June 1996): 36; and Karl Zinsmeister, "Divorce's Toll on Children," *The American Enterprise* (May/June 1996): 39.

[23] David Ellwood, *Poor Support: Poverty in the American Family* (New York: Basic Books, 1988).

[24] See James Q. Wilson, "Welfare: Where Do We Go from Here? In an Ideal World," *The New Republic* (August 12, 1996): 21.

[25] Gordon, *Pitied But Not Entitled*, 5.

[26] Theodore J. Lowi, *The End of Liberalism*, 2d ed. (New York: Norton, 1979), 63.

[27] Margaret Weir, Comments at a roundtable on "The End of Liberalism" (American Political Science Association, September 1995).

[28] Michael J. Sandel, "America's Search for a New Public Philosophy," *The Atlantic Monthly* 277 (March 1996): 57–74, at 58.

[29] Ibid.

[30] Ibid., at 59–63.

[31] Ibid., at 66.

[32] Ibid., at 67–69.

[33] Ibid., at 68–69.

[34] Ibid., at 74.

[35] Ruth Sidel, *Women and Children Last* (New York: Penguin, 1986), 88.

[36] For a review of the factors leading to poverty see the essays in Michael R. Darby, ed., *Reducing Poverty in America: Views and Approaches* (Thousand Oaks, Calif.: Sage Publications, 1996).

[37] For further discussion of these issues, see Harrell Rodgers, Jr., *Poor Women Poor Children* (Armonk, N.Y.: M. E. Sharpe, 1996).

[38] See Murray, *Losing Ground*.

[39] Arthur Okun, *Equality and Efficiency: The Big Tradeoff* (Washington, D.C.: Brookings Institution, 1976), 1.

[40] For a thoughtful examination of this issue, see Richard Rorty, *Contingency, Irony, and Solidarity* (Cambridge: Cambridge University Press, 1989).

[41] David Ensign, *State Government News* (April 1994), 14–15, at 14.

[42] The study was funded in part by the National Science Foundation and reported in *Frontiers: Newsletter of the National Science Foundation* (March 1996): 7.

[43] Marian Wright Edelman, *Families in Peril: An Agenda for Social Change*, (Cambridge, Mass.: Harvard University Press, 1987), 2–3.

[44] See, for example, Daniel Patrick Moynihan, *Family and Nation* (San Diego: Harcourt Brace Jovanovich, 1986); William Julius Wilson, *The Truly Disadvantaged* Charles V. Hamilton and Dona C. Hamilton, "Social Policies, Civil Rights, and Poverty," in Sheldon H. Danziger and Daniel H. Weinberg, eds., *Fighting Poverty: What Works and What Doesn't* (Cambridge, Mass.: Harvard University Press, 1986); Thomas Sowell, *Civil Rights: Rhetoric or Reality?* (New York: William Morrow, 1984); and Walter E. Williams, *The State Against Blacks* (New York: McGraw-Hill, 1982).

[45] U.S. General Accounting Office, "The Urban Underclass" (Washington, D.C.: General Accounting Office, 1990), 6.

[46] Vee Burke, "Poverty and Welfare Among Urban Children: A Fact Sheet," CRS Report to Congress (Washington, D.C.: Congressional Research Service, June 28, 1996).

[47] Victor R. Fuchs, *Women's Quest for Economic Equality* (Cambridge, Mass.: Harvard University Press, 1988), 84–89.

[48] Reynolds Farley and Walter R. Allen, *The Color Line and the Quality of Life in America* (New York: Russell Sage Foundation, 1983), 281.

[49] U.S. Department of Commerce, *Statistical Abstract of the United States: 1995* (Washington, D.C.: U.S. Bureau of the Census, 1995), 433.

[50] Parrott and Greenstein, "Welfare, Out-Of-Wedlock Childbearing, and Poverty" (January 1995); "Welfare, Out-Of-Wedlock Childbearing, and Poverty" (revised March 7, 1995); Fagan, "Rising Illegitimacy."

[51] Gurwitt, "The Politics of Divorce," 34–40; Galston, "Braking Divorce," 36; Zinsmeister, "Divorce's Toll on Children," 39.

[52] David Swinton, "Economic Status of Blacks 1986," in National Urban League, *The State of Black America 1987* (Washington, D.C.: National Urban League, 1987), 56–57.

[53] Wilson, *The Truly Disadvantaged*, 84–89.

[54] Gary Bryner, "Affirmative Action: Minority Rights or Reverse Discrimination?" in Raymond Tatalovich and Byron Daynes, eds., *Social Regulatory Policy* (Boulder, Colo.: Westview Press, 1988), 142–76.

[55] See Barbara Bergmann, *In Defense of Affirmative Action* (New York: Basic Books, 1996).

[56] For a concise summary of this debate, see Richard Kahlenberg, "Class, Not Race," *The New Republic* (April 3, 1995): 21–27.

[57] Wilson, *The Truly Disadvantaged*, 115.

[58] Jewelle Taylor Gibbs, ed., *Young, Black, and Male in America* (Dover, Mass.: Auburn Publishing, 1988).

[59] Quoted in Miller, "Uh-Oh," 25.

[60] Nicholas Eberstadt, "A Poor Measurement," *The Wall Street Journal*, April 22, 1996, p. A16.

[61] Ibid., p. A16.

[62] The countries include Belgium, Denmark, France, Germany, Italy, Netherlands, Spain, Sweden, Switzerland, and the United Kingdom. Data are reported in Bruce Bartlett, "How Poor are the Poor?" *The American Enterprise*, vol. 7 (January–February 1996): 58.

[63] Ibid., 59.

[64] Eberstadt, "A Poor Measurement," p. A16.

[65] "Blue-Ribbon Commission Suggests Poverty in America is Over-Estimated," *The American Enterprise*, vol. 7 (January–February 1996): 58–59.

[66] These issues are well summarized in Simon Head, "The New, Ruthless Economy," *The New York Review of Books* (February 29, 1996): 47–52, at 47.

[67] Richard Reeves, "Jobs! Jobs! Jobs!" *The Washington Monthly* (January/February 1996): 12–22.

[68] Robert H. Havemann and John Karl Scholz, "The Clinton Welfare Reform Plan: Will It End Poverty As We Know It?" (Madison, Wisc.: Institute for Research on Poverty Discussion Paper no. 1037-95, revised July 1994).

[69] John B. Judis, "Oracle at Delphi," *The New Republic* (April 15, 1996): 6.

[70] Quoted in G. Pascal Zachary, "High Tech Explains Widening Wage Gaps," *The Wall Street Journal*, April 22, 1996, p. A1.

[71] See "Minimum Wage Drops to Second Lowest Level Since 1955, Report Finds" (Washington, D.C.: Center on Budget and Policy Priorities, January 11, 1995); Isaac Shapiro, "Four Years and Still Falling: The Decline in the Value of the Minimum Wage" (Washington, D.C.: Center on Budget and Policy Priorities, January 11, 1995): Isaac Shapiro, "Assessing an $5.15-An-Hour Minimum Wage" (Washington, D.C.: Center on Budget and Policy Priorities, February 3, 1995).

[72] H. R. 3448; Conference report: H. Rept. 104-737. See Alissa J. Rubin, "Congress Clears Wage Increase With Tax Breaks for Business," *Congressional Quarterly Weekly Report* (August 3, 1996): 2175–2177.

[73] Bernard Wysocki, Jr., "A Hot Potato: A Popeyes Chain Frets Over How to Handle A Minimum-Pay Rise," *The Wall Street Journal*, April 24, 1996, p. A1.

[74] Jackie Calmes and Christopher Georges, "House GOP Members Plan Alternative To Democrats' Minimum-Wage Boost," *The Wall Street Journal*, April 24, 1996, p. A8.

[75] Matthew Miller, "Econ 2," *The New Republic* (April 29, 1996): 6.

[76] Ibid.

[77] Sue Shellenbarger, "Several Large Employers Join Forces To Solve Problems of Low-Wage Workers." *The Wall Street Journal*, April 26, 1996, p. A7.

[78] Quotes are, respectively, from David Newmark and Robert Eisner, in "Minimum Wage vs. Supply and Demand," *The Wall Street Journal*, April 24, 1996, p. A14.

[79] Paul Offner, "Welfare Dads," *The New Republic* (February 13, 1995): 12–13.

3

The Politics of Welfare Reform

As Chapter 1 argued, welfare policy tries to fulfill difficult and sometimes contradictory purposes. As a result, welfare reform has been a major political issue for twenty-five years. It has been a major theme of presidents from Nixon to Clinton, but earlier presidents also targeted welfare for reform. This chapter looks at the origins of welfare reform and then turns to a review of reform efforts from the 1970s to the 1990s in Washington, as presidents took the lead in criticizing welfare and in proposing alternatives. The discussion then shifts to the states to focus on efforts of governors and legislators to develop their own welfare policy. The chapter traces the evolution of welfare reform proposals as well as the politics of reform and the political forces that pushed for changes as well as those that kept major reform from occurring.

One of the reasons that the evolution of welfare policy has been so interesting is the interaction of federal and state policy makers. Since the mid-1960s, the federal government has come to dominate policy making. In many aspects, states have played subservient roles in the policy making process, uninvolved in policy formation and responsible only for policy implementation. Congress and presidents often appeared uninterested in the states' perspectives, content to fashion new federal policies and instruct states what to do to achieve the policy goals.

In contrast, the relationship between the federal government and states for welfare policy has been more interactive. Governors and other state policy makers have played major roles in devising welfare reform proposals, with a significant impact on national policy. But the experience of states in reforming welfare also demonstrates some of the problems with state-level policy making in a national economy.

Welfare reform also raises questions about how a federal system can deal with strongly held values. From one view, federalism defuses tension and conflict over fundamental values by permitting residents in different states to devise different approaches to welfare. From another view, federalism increases tension because of the disparities it produces in the way citizens are treated, thereby challenging the formulation of rights and privileges to be enjoyed by all citizens. Those two views of federalism are at the heart of much of the criticism over welfare policy and alternatives to reform it.

THE EVOLUTION OF WELFARE REFORM

The basic framework of welfare and the larger federal welfare state did not change for nearly thirty years after its creation in 1935, although state programs evolved considerably. Despite the hope that public assistance would eventually no longer be needed, Aid to Dependent Children (ADC) payments grew. Support for Social Security and related programs aimed at reducing poverty among the elderly grew in popularity, but Republicans and Democrats came to see welfare as more and more of a problem. By 1960 one of four children on welfare had been born out of wedlock; half lived in families split by divorce or abandonment; and half were black.

The Kennedy administration was the first to promise a war on poverty and new programs were created across the executive branch to help low-income people. Welfare was renamed Aid to Families with Dependent Children in 1961 to focus attention on poverty among children. Benefits were expanded to two-parent families in response to criticism that welfare was causing families to split up in order to get payments (AFDC-U was created for unemployed, two-parent families). In 1962, John F. Kennedy proposed and Congress enacted modest changes in the welfare system to give states more discretion in creating and administering rehabilitation programs. States were permitted to petition the federal government for waivers from federal standards as they experimented with their own programs. Amendments emphasized welfare as part of the problem of poverty in America and offered counseling and other assistance to get at the root causes of poverty. But Kennedy's goal was more ambitious than the provisions he proposed, reflecting the chronic mismatch between welfare reform rhetoric and the specific changes made:

> The steps I recommend to you today to alleviate these problems will not come cheaply. They will cost more money when first enacted. But they will restore human dignity; and in the long run, they will save money. . . . Our objective is to prevent or reduce dependency and to encourage self-care and self-support—to maintain family life where it is adequate and to restore it where it is deficient.[1]

THE EXPANSION OF WELFARE AND THE WELFARE STATE

The revolution begun by Franklin D. Roosevelt was reborn when Lyndon B. Johnson launched the Great Society, another effort to realize economic and social rights for all Americans. Welfare and health care programs were created or expanded. Public housing, urban renewal, the funding of public education, the guaranteeing of adequate food, and the protection of civil rights became central responsibilities of the national government. The revolution was secured when a Republican president, Richard Nixon, embraced these programs and supported Congress in recognizing even more rights—the rights of workers to a healthy and safe workplace, the rights of consumers to safe products, the rights of all Americans to clean air and water, the reproductive and workplace rights of women, and the rights of those accused of crimes.

This extraordinary revolution in the role of government was widely viewed as consistent with individual rights and often defended as promoting equality of opportunity. A narrow view of equality of opportunity might minimize governmental intervention in society, but a richer notion of equality of opportunity requires governmental intervention. Individuals need to have some minimum level of resources before they can effectively make choices and pursue opportunities. A commitment to equal rights for all Americans required that government intervene aggressively to limit the exercise of private power that interfered with individual rights and to provide the material preconditions for the exercise of individual choice. Government was to ensure that individuals were given the resources necessary to live meaningful, self-determined, self-directed lives. Welfare was reformed by broadening its goals and benefits.[2]

Although poverty was a target of many of the Great Society programs, the lack of opportunity that women and people of color suffered from was an even more pressing problem. Affirmative action programs required active government intervention in private organizations to ensure that the effects of past discrimination were overcome, that victims of past discrimination were put in the place they would have been had discrimination not occurred, and that traditional barriers limiting the life choices of women and people of color be eliminated. Affirmative action and nondiscrimination regulations, as much as any other government policy, recognized the need for government to take positive steps to ensure the rights of all persons and reinforced the idea that aggressive government programs are consistent with individual rights.[3]

Antipoverty efforts were uncoordinated, prompting the Johnson administration to create "Community Action Programs" that were to involve recipients of assistance in administering programs and provide a comprehensive attack on poverty. These community programs were aimed at revitalizing local government antipoverty efforts but did not materially change the existing programs. Unlike the 1935 framework, the new law provided few standards or criteria; it simply delegated broad new powers to local governments to solve poverty somehow.[4]

The 1964 Economic Opportunity Act established the Community Action Programs as well as created new programs—the Job Corps and Volunteers in Service to America or VISTA, among others. When signing the law, Johnson promised to end welfare dependency:

> Our American answer to poverty is not to make the poor more secure in their poverty but to reach down and to help them lift themselves out of the ruts of poverty and move with the large majority along the high road of hope and prosperity. The days of the dole in our country are numbered.[5]

Congress amended AFDC in 1967 to encourage work by permitting states, when determining eligibility, to ignore part of the money that recipients earned from working. The Work Incentives Program, also created in 1967, required that adult recipients register for work with state employment offices. (The program was first known as WIP, but that acronym was problematic for a compulsory work requirement and so was changed to WIN.) In theory, eligibility was contingent on willingness to work or participate in job training, but in practice, welfare became a guaranteed-income program for female-headed families. Benefits continued to vary widely among states; children were still given assistance only if their parents complied with program requirements. Food Stamps and Medicaid were added to the arsenal of the War on Poverty. Eligibility for these two in-kind programs were tied to AFDC standards. Food Stamps were aimed at any household whose income was low enough that members might not be able to obtain a nutritionally adequate diet. Eligibility was determined by federal agency officials and was not limited to welfare recipients. Medicaid benefits were also extended to low-income families, but many states linked eligibility for Medicaid with welfare. When recipients left the AFDC program their Medicaid were terminated, giving them an incentive to stay on welfare.

Programs proliferated. Eligibility requirements and benefit levels varied widely among the states. Caseloads increased by 36 percent between 1962 and 1967 as eligibility requirements were loosened. Reformers in the late 1960s found social workers too meddlesome and subjective, and called for uniformity and strict accountability in dispensing welfare benefits. As one Massachusetts welfare official put it, "We've been trying to get the people who think like social workers out and the people who think like bank tellers in."[6] Only a fraction of welfare recipients in the Work Incentive Program actually enrolled in work and training programs.

THE REPUBLICAN RESPONSE TO WELFARE

The tremendous expansion of the welfare state and public assistance programs in particular under Lyndon Johnson's War on Poverty triggered a major effort at welfare reform under Richard Nixon. By 1969, Democrats and Republicans alike were criticizing the War on Poverty but for different reasons. Some felt it was too costly and caused recipients to become permanently dependent on assistance rather than using it for temporary relief. Others felt that the levels of benefits varied widely and that most of the money never really reached the poor. Nixon sought a major welfare reform by replacing welfare with an income-maintenance or negative income tax program that promised to reduce poverty by guaranteeing poor families—those working as well as those on welfare—an annual grant of $1,600. Recipients who were not working would be required to participate in job-training programs to keep their benefits. In introducing his proposal in 1969, Nixon summarized his view of welfare:

> The present welfare system has failed us—it has fostered breakup, has provided very little help in many States and has even deepened dependency by all-too-often making it more attractive to go on welfare than to go to work. . . . I propose a new approach that will make it more attractive to go on work than to go on welfare.[7]

The House passed the Nixon plan in 1970 but it died in the Senate. It was the White House's top priority in 1971 and passed the House again, only to be blocked one more time in the Senate. Nixon's proposal was killed both by conservatives who feared federal payments as a disincentive to work and by liberals who found the benefits too stingy and the requirements too onerous. Congress stopped action before the 1972 election. Nixon abandoned his legislative effort and pursued administrative changes. However, Nixon was successful in consolidating assistance programs for the elderly, blind, and disabled into one program, Supplemental Security Income or SSI, in 1972. Needy recipients could receive SSI in addition to Social Security and other benefits. But AFDC remain unreformed, and Nixon moved on to other issues and problems. The debate over welfare reform shifted to alternatives for providing services to poor families. Incremental reform efforts included mandatory job searches, efforts to provide work experience, training programs, and an incentives approach that sought to increase the earnings welfare recipients could keep from part-time work that arose in the 1990s.[8] Perhaps Nixon's main impact on welfare reform was his questioning of the presence of the federal government in areas where it had come to play a dominant policy role. His New Federalism, a proposal to shift power from the federal government to the states, helped shape the subsequent debate over welfare and other policies.

THE CARTER WELFARE REFORM INITIATIVE

Jimmy Carter campaigned against Washington, pushing for devolution of welfare. In announcing his welfare reform initiative in 1977, he also promised to end "welfare as we know it":

> Shortly after I became President, I announced that a comprehensive reform of the Nation's welfare system would be one of our first priorities. . . . I would like to point out that the most important conclusion is that the present welfare system should be scrapped entirely and a totally new system should be implemented.[9]

Carter proposed the Program for Better Jobs and Income, which would have replaced AFDC, SSI, and Food Stamps with a cash payment to poor families and would have created 1.4 million public service jobs.[10] His efforts collapsed under the weight of tremendous controversies concerning race, class, sexual morality, and federalism. The political pressures generated by vocal interests and strong public sentiments have whipsawed politicians for decades; they have prompted one would-be reformer, Jimmy Carter's secretary of health, education, and welfare, Joseph Califano, to describe welfare politics as the Middle East of domestic politics, dominated by warring factions and seemingly irreconcilable demands.[11]

The "Reagan Revolution" and Welfare Reform

Ronald Reagan gave the "New Federalism" and welfare reform new life in the early 1980s. The Reagan administration sought to delegate more discretion to states through block grants, giving states permission (in the form of "waivers") to place new restrictions on recipients. States began to experiment with "welfare to work" proposals. Arkansas, for example, developed an innovative program under Governors Frank White and Bill Clinton that required welfare recipients to take job search classes, look for jobs under the supervision of a caseworker, and, do unpaid work for public and private employers for up to three months.

More important, Reagan took on the entire welfare state. Although many presidential elections focus on economic policy, Americans became increasingly concerned with values, culture and society, and the causes of the problems that many of them feared. No one addressed that nagging concern more effectively than Ronald Reagan. During his administrations, tax cuts, the resulting deficits, and pressure to keep the red ink in check also kept the welfare state from expanding. No radical restructuring of income-support policies occurred; most programs offered only minimal benefits. Squeezing significant cutbacks from these programs was no easy task, since efforts to reduce those programs made the administration vulnerable to accusations of unfairness and heartlessness.[12] Reagan and others challenged the very existence of welfare, but debate largely focused on how programs could be maintained without discouraging work.[13] Efforts to cut middle-class programs such as Social Security and Medicare were also undertaken, but their popularity insulated them from attack.

The one exception to retrenchment in the welfare state during the 1980s was the expansion of the Earned Income Tax Credit. The EITC was attractive to Reagan Republicans and Congressional Democrats alike because it clearly targets the "deserving" poor, fosters work incentives; is simple and market oriented, is "off budget" (does not contribute directly to deficit spending), and could remedy other problems such as regressive taxation, low wages, and the cost of child care. Particularly after Republicans were damaged by the "fairness issue" in the early 1980s, expansion of the EITC gained widespread, bipartisan support.[14]

The overall effects of the "Reagan Revolution" were limited, in one sense. Expenditures on social programs remained relatively constant.[15] Cuts were greater in housing programs and unemployment benefits, whereas other income transfer and health programs largely escaped cuts. Retrenchment occurred largely where advocacy groups were weak.[16]

Reagan's ambitious attempt to scale back the welfare state ultimately failed because of public opposition. But his efforts helped lay the foundation for the Republican assault of 1995. His impact on the Federal government's long-term capacity to fund social programs was profound. The budget deficits that resulted from the tax cuts of the 1980s have made it exceedingly difficult for advocates of the welfare state to expand its programs.[17]

Reagan was no more successful in revolutionizing the AFDC program, which he had complained was "expensive, intrusive, bureaucratic, fraud-ridden, and discouraged individual initiative."[18] The administration initially cut spending by reducing benefits and imposing higher eligibility rules, but ran into opposition when it tried to impose a major shift of responsibility for welfare to the states. States were unenthusiastic about, and Congress was hostile to, the "New Federalism" idea of turning over full responsibility for AFDC and Food Stamps to the states.[19]

Some progress was made in transforming welfare into a work program. Liberals saw "workfare" rhetoric as a way to help recipients and to encourage moderate program expansion. But those changes were more expensive than the existing program and were resisted by conservatives, who saw workfare as a way to deter potential welfare recipients. Workfare could result in reducing welfare spending.[20] That tension remains: Liberals and conservatives can both favor workfare, but for very different reasons. That tension underlay the drafting and passage of the Family Support Act of 1988.

THE FAMILY SUPPORT ACT OF 1988

Through the mid-1980s, AFDC caseloads and spending continued to rise, prompting the focus of welfare reform to shift from providing cash benefits to giving recipients education and job-training opportunities. President Reagan called on Congress in 1986 to enact "real welfare reform—reform that will lead to lasting emancipation from welfare dependency."[21] Governors, led by Bill Clinton (Democrat of Arkansas) and Michael N. Castle (Republican of Delaware), played key roles in keeping welfare reform on the agenda and pushing Congress to pass the law. The Reagan administration argued for no new spending, and encouraged states to experiment with welfare reforms. Conservatives in Congress pushed for requirements that states enroll a minimum of recipients in job and training programs, and that at least one parent in two-parent families work at least sixteen hours a week. Liberals argued that the work requirement was punitive and too costly to administer, but compromised on these two positions in exchange for requiring states to offer benefits to poor two-parent families and to provide a year of Medicaid and child care for parents moving from welfare to work.

The one area of strong, bipartisan consensus called for stronger measures to enforce child support. A 1984 law had required automatic withholding of court-ordered child support payments whenever the parent fell behind by an equivalent of thirty days of benefits, and ordered states to collect past-due payments from income-tax refunds. The 1988 act required states to withhold court-ordered child support from errant parents' paychecks without waiting for the thirty-day shortfall and to increase efforts to establish the paternity of children on welfare. It also required judges to use the guidelines created in the 1984 act to ensure more consistency across the nation in child-support obligations.[22]

One of the most contentious issues was the House and Senate demand to require all states to extend AFDC to unemployed parents (AFDC-UP). The Reagan administration opposed the expansion. A 1961 law authorized states to establish AFDC-UP if they so chose; by 1987, twenty-seven states offered assistance to these two-parent families. But AFDC-UP families only represented about 6 percent of the caseloads in the participating states: It also included other restrictions such as a "one hundred rule" (prohibiting benefits to families where the principal wage earner worked more than ninety-nine hours a month) and the requirement that the principal wage earner worked, collected unemployment, or was involved in a training program in at least six of the thirteen calendar quarters before applying for benefits. Similar proposals had been made in 1978 and had been attached to two budget reconciliation bills, in 1986 and 1987; the White House threatened a veto and the provision was removed both times. Finally, the White House could not sustain its opposition as critics attacked its pro-family rhetoric and its support for the existing law's incentive for family breakup. The Family Support Act of 1988 required all states to operate AFDC-UP programs by October 1990.[23] Welfare reform was passed with overwhelming support: the House passed the final measure by a vote of 347–53; the Senate, by 96–1.[24]

Like other welfare reform proposals, the 1988 Family Support Act promised to do much, much more than it was actually designed to do. According to its leading sponsor, Senator Moynihan, it was going to "turn the welfare program upside down." In signing the bill, Ronald Reagan was similarly ambitious:

> I am pleased to sign into law today a major reform of our nation's welfare system. . . . This bill responds to the call for real welfare reform—reform that will lead to lasting emancipation from welfare dependency.[25]

However, the act itself included only modest provisions. It established the Job Opportunities and Basic Skills (JOBS) program, which required states to provide education, training opportunities, and child care assistance for recipients. JOBS sought to reorient welfare toward reaching women with younger children, targeting more difficult-to-serve people, involving a greater share of the AFDC caseload in work, and providing basic education and other intensive activities. The emphasis was on providing participants with the long-term training necessary to achieve self-sufficiency and become productive members of society.[26]

Teenage parents from 16 to 19 were required to attend school or participate in education or employment activity. Additional federal funding was made available for other efforts to assist recipients in moving from welfare to work.[27] The act, however, excused about half of recipients from this requirement, primarily mothers with young children. Of those who are eligible for participation, the act required only that 20 percent be "participating" in some job-preparation activity by 1995.[28] Governors emphasized that participation rates should be kept low so that limited resources would not be spread too thinly.[29]

States were obligated to strengthen and expand their child-support collection programs by withholding payments from paychecks and establishing an automated tracking and monitoring system. They were also to develop uniform child support payments, create paternity-establishment programs, implement JOBS programs in every political subdivision, and use only licensed day care for children of parents in programs. The Federal government agreed to help states locate absent parents.

Congress never adequately funded the JOBS program to ensure that all recipients could participate, nor have states provided their share of matching funds for these programs. States applied for only part of the $1 billion available in annual federal matching funds. Though states were authorized to require some kind of work or community service in exchange for welfare benefits, only a few did so because of the expense of JOBS programs—the training and education, the assistance to employers, and the costs of managing public jobs and service activities. The great increases in number of recipients overwhelmed available resources.[30]

The 1988 act also extended the mandatory AFDC-UP program for unemployed two-parent families; the twenty-three states that had to create an AFDC-UP program were permitted to implement it on a time-limited basis (as little as six months within any given year). These families were also required to participate in the JOBS program. States could count full-time attendance in an educational program as work. Some limits were placed on innovative programs: Experiments in education and job training were limited to no more than eight sites; each innovation could last no longer than five years; and states were required to provide an evaluation to the federal government of the experiment. Welfare reform, for several years after 1988, became largely a state activity. The Bush administration continued to encourage state experimentation. It sought to streamline the waiver process so that approval was granted within four weeks—no small task, since the review involved officials from several agencies in the Department of Health and Human Services (the Administration for Children and Families, the Office of the Assistant Secretary for Planning and Evaluation, and the Health Care Finance Administration), the Food and Nutrition Service of the Department of Agriculture, and the Department of Housing and Urban Development.[31]

WELFARE REFORM, 1992–1994

The Bush administration's emphasis on conservative values included an attack on the "culture" of welfare. For the president and for Vice-President Dan Quayle, welfare represented much that was wrong with liberals and the welfare state they had created. The vice-president in particular sought a bully pulpit to draw attention to "family values" and the decline in those values that resulted from the welfare state. He blamed welfare and other government handouts (as well as Hollywood) for encouraging dependency and illegitimacy and contributing to the economic and moral decline of urban communities.

Critics of the Bush administration, including Democratic presidential candidate Bill Clinton, blasted the Bush administration for its lack of interest in welfare policy, the economy, and other domestic policy issues. For Bush, welfare reform was largely a state issue. In his 1992

State of the Union address, the president promised to support state experimentation on welfare:

> States throughout the country are beginning to operate with new assumptions: that when able-bodied people receive government assistance, they have responsibilities to the taxpayer, a responsibility to seek work, education or job training; a responsibility to get their lives in order; a responsibility to hold their families together and refrain from having children out of wedlock—and a responsibility to obey the law. We are going to help this movement. Often, state reform requires waiving certain federal regulations. I will act to make that process easier and quicker for every state that asks our help.[32]

The Department of Health and Human Services granted nine waivers for state experiments during the year.[33]

In February 1992, Senate Democrats took the offensive. Daniel Patrick Moynihan (D.-N.Y.) introduced a bill that would have quadrupled funding for the Family Support Act's program to train welfare recipients for employment. Moynihan charged that President Bush's and Vice-President Quayle's frequent references to welfare dependency in recent campaign speeches and television advertisements amounted to using the issue "as a focus of resentment and a code word for you-know-what."[34] The next month, Senators David Boren (D.-Okla.) and Paul Simon (Dem.-Ill.) proposed that welfare recipients other than women with young children to take public-service jobs unless they were already enrolled in education or training programs.

Bill Clinton's 1992 presidential campaign chose as one of its major planks the pledge to "end welfare as we know it." Part of his claim to fame was that as governor of Arkansas he had led governors' efforts to reform welfare. He proposed a new approach to welfare that would provide health care and job training to welfare recipients and, after two years, require work of those who are capable. If private employment was not available, community jobs would be provided:

> We will scrap the current welfare system and make welfare a second chance, not a way of life. We will empower people on welfare with the education, training, and child care they need for up to two years so they can break the cycle of dependency. After that, those who can work will have to go to work, either by taking a job in the private sector or through community service.[35]

Welfare reform was an important element of Clinton's electoral strategy. His focus on breaking the "culture of dependence" for the 20 to 25 percent of recipients who were enmeshed in a cycle of poverty and dependency was significant: Finally, a Democrat was willing to take on the problem of the urban underclass, one of the most persistent and difficult public policy problems in America. His proposal was a combination of conservative toughness and activist government to ensure that young women could not decide to become single mothers and then live on welfare checks but would make better choices such as staying in school, getting married, or working. Perhaps more than any other issue, welfare reform was evidence of Bill Clinton's "New" Democratic credentials—a willingness to rethink traditional Democratic positions and find common ground between liberals and conservatives.[36]

The president was intimately involved in the formation of his administration's welfare reform proposals, given his long involvement with the issue as a governor. He created an interagency welfare task force—the Working Group on Welfare Reform, Family Support and Independence—co-chaired by Bruce Reed, a White House domestic policy adviser, and David T. Ellwood, assistant secretary of Health and Human Services and an influential welfare policy scholar. This task force took primary responsibility for developing the welfare reform plan.[37] In a February 1993 speech to the National Governors' Association, President Clinton announced six principles that would guide his welfare reform proposals:[38]

- Education, employment and training government programs
- Time-limited benefits
- Mandated work
- Tougher child-support enforcement
- Making work pay
- Flexibility for state experimentation

By February 1993, however, Health and Human Services Secretary Donna E. Shalala signaled that welfare reform might be more complicated than the campaign had promised. President Clinton's welfare reforms would build on existing programs and that any plan to "end welfare as we know it" would require extensive support services to help recipients move off public assistance into jobs. She emphasized that Clinton's announced plan to require welfare recipients to take jobs after two years had been interpreted "too narrowly." Ending welfare would not simply reduce benefits, but would require additional spending on education, job training, child care, and other benefits to aid in the transition from welfare to work.[39]

Congress did not sit back and wait for the president's welfare reform bill. In January 1993, Senator Daniel Patrick Moynihan (D.-N. Y.) again introduced a bill that would authorize "full" funding for the JOBS program.[40] But congressional Democrats were divided over welfare reform as it evolved in 1993. In October, the Democratic Mainstream Forum "applauded" President Clinton's efforts in welfare reform in a letter signed by seventy-seven representatives, but Democrats were split over giving priority to job placement or training and education.[41] In November, Representative Patsy Mink (D.-Hawaii) and eighty-eight other Democrats who formed the Progressive Caucus wrote a letter to the president that found the time limit in his preliminary proposal on welfare reform to be "unacceptably arbitrary." By December, House Speaker Thomas Foley (D.-Wash.), and Majority Leader Richard Gephardt (D.-Mo.) suggested Clinton hold off on welfare legislation in order to focus on health care reform.[42] Thirty-four of the forty members of the Congressional Black Caucus told the president in a March 1994 letter that they were "very troubled" by the direction the president seemed to be taking in welfare reform. They also complained that they had not been "directly consulted on the direction and details of the administration's initiative."

Republicans were more united. In February 1993, House Ways and Means Committee Republicans introduced a plan that would place two-year time limits on welfare benefits and require thirty-five hours of work per week for those who have been on AFDC for over two years.[43] In November, House Minority Leader Robert Michel (R.-Ill.) introduced the Empowerment Support Program Providing Employment, Child Care, and Training Act (cosponsored by 162 of the 176 House Republicans), which became the leading Republican welfare reform bill that significantly shaped future Republican proposals. It would have converted AFDC into a two-year transitional program in which able-bodied recipients would be required to participate in at least ten hours of education, training, job search, or related activities each week. (Exemptions include the incapacitated, mothers of new babies, parents of children returned after removal from the home, persons who provide full-time care for a disabled dependent, and, at states' discretion, substance abusers who are making progress toward recovery). After two years benefits would be cut off (except for Medicaid) unless recipients participated in a work program of public or subsidized jobs for at least thirty-five hours per week. States could limit participation to three years. The bill would also:

Limit federal funding for AFDC, SSI, Food Stamps, public housing, and the refundable part of Earned Income Tax Credit to a base level adjusted for inflation, plus 2 percent

Authorize states to make many AFDC changes such as converting

AFDC into a block grant, denying benefits to the child of a minor, denying benefits to additional children, and paying new residents the benefit of their former state (when lower)

Allow states to adopt a permanent and more liberal earnings disregard—up to the first $200 in monthly earnings plus one-half remaining earnings

Establish an Interagency Waiver Request Board (to make obtaining waivers for reform easier)

End welfare for most noncitizens (estimated by CBO to save $21.7 billion over 5 years)

Require teenage recipients to live at home.[44]

Welfare reform languished in 1994, despite efforts by Senator Moynihan, who was against postponing welfare legislation in order to focus on health care: "That won't work. We don't have a health care crisis in this country. We do have a welfare crisis. And we can do both."[45] Clinton responded in his 1994 State of the Union address that the White House would send Congress a welfare proposal in the spring that would meet his campaign pledge. But he stressed the importance of reforming health care along with welfare: "Millions of people on welfare today are there because it's the only way they can get health care coverage for their families," Clinton said. "Until we solve the health care problem, we will not solve the welfare problem."[46]

In January 1994 Senate Republicans introduced a welfare reform bill written by Senator Hank Brown (Colo.) and cosponsored by seventeen other Republican Senators, including Bob Dole, that was similar to the 1993 House Republican initiative. Their proposal would have established a two-year time limit for JOBS, after which a family's benefits would be reduced by the parent's share unless the parent then worked; required states to establish "employment voucher" programs under which AFDC and Food Stamps would subsidize a job for up to one year; authorized states to deny benefits for additional children, liberalize treatment of stepparent families, pay interstate immigrants lower benefits, and deny AFDC to unmarried parents; required the Immigration and Naturalization Service to treat legal aliens as a public charge after they receive certain welfare benefits for more than one year; established an interagency board to expedite action of requests for waivers; and required AFDC teenagers to live at home.[47]

Other Senate bills were introduced in the spring of 1994. Senator Nancy Kassebaum (R.-Kans.) proposed that the Federal government assume Medicaid costs; in return states would be required to fully fund AFDC, Food Stamps, and WIC.[48] Senator Joseph I. Lieberman, (D.-Conn.) proposed legislation that would ease requirements for granting states waivers. Current rules require state projects to be budget neutral to the federal government; Lieberman's proposal would provide additional funding to states for their experiments. Although none of these proposals went very far in the legislative process, they helped to develop some agreement over key elements of welfare reform.

By February 1994, the White House task force on welfare reform had decided to recommend gradually phasing in its planned two-year limit on welfare benefits, starting with only the newest and youngest recipients (those born after 1972). Administration officials said that the proposal would reduce the costs of expensive educational and vocational services at the outset of the program, when the administration would be struggling to make budget cuts to pay not only for welfare reform but for health care reform as well. In addition to the phase-in was a recommendation that teenage mothers on welfare be required to live with their parents.[49]

The task force had also agreed on measures to prod former recipients to leave subsidized or community service jobs and get work in the private sector as soon as possible. The task force proposed to cut off welfare benefits to young adults after two years and force them to work—and the overall proposal envisioned subsidized jobs if no private positions were available. The task force proposed that refusal to accept a private-sector job if one was available should result in termination of benefits under the planned "work for wages" part of welfare reform. A final disincentive would gradually reduce federal reimbursement to the states the longer people continued receiving benefits under the subsidized-work program. This was designed to encourage the states to move people into private-sector employment.[50]

After discussions within the administration the task force expanded its recommendations. In March 1994, the task force recommended to President Clinton the following proposals for welfare reform: requiring a two-year time limit on welfare for those born after 1972; requiring states to establish a program called WORK for those without jobs after the two-year limit (federal funds would be provided so that states could create a minimum number of work assignments for at least fifteen hours and a maximum of thirty-five hours per week for each recipient); permitting states to deny benefits for an extra child; offering AFDC to needy two-parent families without regard to their work history; repealing the exemption from required JOBS participation for mothers with children younger than age three; expanding funds for child care; require "up-front" job searches for most applicants; and requiring minor mothers to live at home in order to receive AFDC.[51]

The plan called for $15 billion in new spending over five years for day care, education and training, expanded coverage to two-parent families, and projected that at the end of five years, only 130,000 recipients, or 3 percent of those on AFDC, would have exhausted their benefits and be required to work.[52] The task force released its proposal in March after it had been leaked by some of the group's members, who found the proposal to be too aggressive.

In March 1994, the Mainstream Forum, ninety moderate and conservative House Democrats, joined with Republicans in urging that welfare benefits for most noncitizens be eliminated to pay for welfare reform. Taken together, the members of the forum and Republicans held a majority in the House.[53] But the president indicated in a March 24 news conference that he was unwilling to finance the welfare changes solely through cuts in aid to immigrants. By April he had ruled out any new taxes to pay for welfare reform and had decided to support a leaner $9.5 billion package focused on training, education and public-service jobs. Clinton also decided against a federal gambling tax that could have raised an estimated $3 billion over five years that would have been used to provide child care for poor workers, as well as additional small projects and experiments.[54] Instead, Clinton would attempt to fund the welfare initiative through a "well-balanced financing package" composed of cuts from other federal programs, including subsidies for "wealthy farmers." The result would be $9.5 billion in new money spread over five years, a considerable reduction from the $12.5 billion to $15 billion anticipated by Clinton's thirty-two-member welfare reform working group as recently as one month earlier.[55]

On April 28, 1994, a small group of conservative Republicans, led by freshmen Representative James M. Talent (Mo.) and Senator Lauch Faircloth (N.C.), introduced a much more restrictive plan to compete with the original GOP proposal. William Bennett, a leading Republican proponent of welfare reform, attended the Capitol Hill announcement of the Talent-Faircloth proposal, dubbed "The Real Welfare Reform Act of 1994," and urged congressional Republicans to scrap their original plan, which he called "several years" out of date.[56] The bill that was eventually introduced in May proposed to prohibit AFDC, Food Stamps and housing for children of unmarried mothers under 21; ban benefits for new babies to AFDC mothers; and prohibit noncitizens from receiving benefits from fifty-eight programs.[57]

In May, Representative Mink and other liberal Democrats in the

House responded with their own bill that would target for JOBS services those recipients who could move into jobs quickly, extend eligibility for aid (cash, Food Stamps, housing) for two years after the start of a job, increase the minimum wage, expand the EITC, and increase funding for child care.[58] Rep. Mink stated "I'm concerned about the two-year limit, and they have not backed off that at all. But those positions hardened long before we [liberals] ever got to the scene."[59]

In May, President Clinton suggested that his welfare reform plan would include a proposal to allow states to deny additional benefits to women who have children while they are on welfare. Immediately, a broad coalition of eighty-five civil rights and religious organizations, including abortion rights and antiabortion groups, said it would challenge the "child exclusion" policy in federal courts. Civil rights activists complained that the policy would "punish innocent children," antiabortion advocates said it would encourage abortions, and abortion rights supporters said it would punish welfare mothers who exercise a personal choice.[60]

On June 14, 1994, President Clinton introduced his welfare plan, the Work and Responsibility Act, which included a version of virtually every experiment states had considered in their efforts to reform welfare. It also reflected most of the issues raised in congressional bills: By this time, over twenty major welfare reform proposals had been introduced in the 103rd Congress. The Clinton plan proposed the following:

Time limits: A two-year time limit on welfare benefits (starting after age 18, and suspended for periods of part-time work and sickness) would be followed by a transition into the workplace or community jobs (the WORK program).

Work: Recipients would be required to develop a personal employment plan identifying the education, training, and job placement services they would need in order to hasten their transition into the work force. If offered a job, they would be required to take it.

Child care: Child care would be provided during education and work programs, and for one year after recipients left AFDC for employment.

Job training: Job training would be provided; JOBS would be linked to JTPA, the school-to-work initiative, Pell Grants, and other programs that help prepare recipients for work.

Sanctions: Those who refused to stay in school, look for work, or receive job training would be sanctioned, usually by losing their share of AFDC.

Exemptions: Even those who cannot work must meet certain expectations. Those with disabilities or those caring for disabled children would be exempt from the two-year time limit; however, they would be required to develop a work plan.

Earnings disregard: To reward work, AFDC benefits would not have to be reduced dollar-for-dollar for work; recipients would be allowed to save more without a reduction in benefits.

Identifying fathers: AFDC applicants would be required to identify the father at the birth of a child, and to help find him.

Child support: Child-support payments would increase as the father's income rises. Those who refused to pay child support would have wages withheld and professional, occupational and/or drivers' licenses suspended. A national child-support clearinghouse would be established.

Noncustodial parents: Grants would be provided to states for demonstration projects that provided mediation, counseling, education, and visitation enforcement for noncustodial parents in order to encourage ongoing involvement in their childrens' lives.

Two-parent families: States could choose to lift the special-eligibility requirement for two-parent families in order to encourage families to stay together.

Family cap: States would be allowed to limit benefits to children who were conceived while their parents were on welfare.

Legal immigrants: States would be required to verify alien status and Social Security numbers, and to assign national identification numbers. The national clearinghouse would use the numbers to monitor compliance with time limits and work.

Administration: AFDC and Food Stamp regulations would be simplified in order to reduce paperwork. States would be encouraged to move from welfare checks and Food Stamps to electronic benefits transfer (EBT), using an ATM card.

Teenage pregnancy: A national campaign to reduce teenage pregnancy would be launched; teenage mothers would be required to identify fathers and to live at home or with a responsible adult.

The plan was estimated to cost $9.3 billion over five years. In order to finance the plan, President Clinton proposed restricting the eligibility of noncitizens for AFDC, SSI, and Food Stamps (five-year savings: $3.7 billion); a ceiling on state spending in the emergency assistance program ($1.6 billion savings); an extension of the corporate tax for the superfund hazardous waste cleanup plan (five-year revenues: $1.6 billion); restricting the SSI benefits for alcoholics and drug addicts ($800 million savings); limiting farm subsidies for those with incomes over $100,000 ($500 million savings); restricting certain subsidies for meals provided to family day care homes ($500 million savings); denial of EITC for nonresident aliens ($300 million savings); reducing the proportion of money that states are allowed to keep when they discover Food Stamp overpayments that resulted from violations ($100 million savings); and an extension of railroad fees that are used to conduct safety inspections ($200 million savings). The Clinton proposal also assumed that his universal health care coverage plan would pass, thus ensuring that all welfare recipients would have health care, and also proposed an expansion of the Earned Income Tax Credit.[61]

Republicans criticized the Clinton welfare proposal for not delivering what was promised in campaign speeches. Newt Gingrich complained, "The president is brilliant at describing a Ferrari, but his staff continue to deliver a Yugo." Bob Dole said that Clinton's proposal might only represent "the end of welfare reform as we know it." Others complained that the bills failed to deal effectively with teenage pregnancy and would not push enough welfare recipients into the work force.[62]

Under pressure from Democratic leaders, in July the House Ways and Means Committee began working on a welfare reform bill containing the broad outlines of President Clinton's welfare reform package.[63] But time ran out. The Clinton welfare bill was never brought to the floor of either house. That summer, Senate Republicans used the filibuster to kill presidential nominations, legislation, and anything else the Congressional Democrats and President Clinton tried to pass. So intent were the Republicans on obstructing Congress that they even filibustered bills they had helped write.[64] Their strategy was successful: In ensuring that the 103rd Congress was ineffective, they paved the way for the Republican takeover of both the House and Senate after the 1994 congressional election.

ASSESSING THE FAILURE OF WELFARE REFORM IN 1994

The mid-1990s saw more of a consensus on what to do about welfare than at any earlier time. Thinking about welfare had also evolved tremendously during the past decade: In 1984 Charles Murray was castigated for arguing that welfare encourages the formation of the underclass; by 1994 his views had become widely accepted. Characterizations of welfare recipients had also changed. In the past, recipients were described as willing to work; all they lacked was a job. Now it was argued that many recipients—a fourth or a third, perhaps—are incapable of work, that disadvantagement has become so entrenched that creating work opportunities would not be enough.[65]

By 1992 recognition was widespread that welfare reform efforts had suffered from a number of flaws: Work requirements must be combined with adequate funding for child care; creation of public-sector jobs is required; counseling, food, shelter, and child care needs to be provided for those who fail to take or keep jobs or otherwise drop out of the system; and, perhaps most important, real welfare reform is more costly than maintaining the current system. Compromise seemed quite possible.

Bill Clinton's welfare reform ideas, sketched out broadly in the 1992 campaign, triggered a congressional Republican response in 1993 and 1994 that called for even more spending on jobs and child support. Democrats in Congress voiced their support for time limits. But the Clinton administration argued that health care reform must come before welfare reform, for two reasons. First, welfare recipients may fail to take jobs for fear they would lose their Medicaid benefits (under the old system, they could keep Medicaid benefits for one year after leaving AFDC). Second, in order to get the support of the liberal wing of the Democratic party for his health care reform package, Clinton had to be sure he did not offend them by taking a tough stand on welfare reform.

The first issue could have been overcome through extending the transition period or other relatively minor changes until national health care legislation was enacted. The second barrier was more difficult: The Children's Defense Fund (chaired in the past by Hillary Rodham Clinton and Health and Human Services Secretary Donna Shalala) opposed time limits. Public-employee unions continued to fear the competition to their members from welfare recipients who were forced to work and also tried to slow down the reform process as the first step in defeating it.[66] One Republican House leader argued that Clinton was afraid of angering the "left wing of his party" through welfare reform, thus endangering the support he would need for health care policy.[67]

Some White House officials believed that both health and welfare reform legislation could not pass through the same congressional committees at the same time, and priority should be given to health legislation. They were joined by Speaker Tom Foley and House Majority Leader Richard Gephardt in urging the administration to not pursue welfare reform until health legislation was enacted. Others, however, urged a joint venture, because health and welfare are closely interrelated, and there was some political momentum for action on both fronts.

Senator Daniel P. Moynihan, chair of the Senate Finance Committee and a leading scholar of welfare policy, threatened to hold the Clinton health care initiative hostage unless welfare reform proceeded.[68]

When the Clinton plan was released, it was naturally attacked by partisans. But it was also criticized for substantive reasons. One problem with the plan was the failure to provide the funds necessary to impose the work requirements on all able-bodied recipients. Raising taxes to expand welfare would be a tough sell for anyone. But the administration did not have a strong commitment to ensure funding of public-sector jobs for all recipients. At the same time, the administration could not be seen as leaving welfare families with no assistance after their two years of eligibility expired. In order to save money, the two-year time limit would only apply to the 1.8 million AFDC recipients born after 1971. The administration believed that getting younger recipients into the job market would have a greater impact on the long-term dependency problem.[69]

The Clinton plan also included sanctions in the form of reduced grants to those who failed to show up for work or training sessions or other obligations. After two years, those who were offered jobs but failed to work would have all benefits cut. (In contrast to Clinton's workfare proposal, in which the welfare agency would send the checks and monitor attendance and work performance, under the work for wages program, welfare recipients, like any other workers, would be paid directly by the employer.)

The Clinton plan expanded coverage of two-parent families to counter the incentive created in the current welfare system for single-parent families.[70] But critics feared that the expansion of coverage might create an incentive for families to go on welfare for two years and then worry about work; at least the current system created an incentive for families that wanted to stay together to join the work force and apply for Food Stamps if they needed help. This expansion of coverage alone was projected to cost $1 billion, nearly one-sixth of the additional spending on welfare.

Another criticism was that the two-year training period might encourage low-income workers to take two years off and go on welfare, although the proposal also required recipients to search for jobs immediately on entering the system. The reforms would also have permitted recipients who worked part-time to keep more of their earnings and still receive benefits as an incentive for work. Under the current system, benefits are reduced as earnings increase. The change might encourage full-time workers to work part time and go on welfare.

The Clinton proposal also included several exemptions. Mothers were excused from training or work during the first year of their child's life, unless conception occurred while they were on welfare, extending the deadline to three years. Recipients who could show they had a "serious barrier to work" were also given additional time. The plan called for limiting these exemptions to 25 percent of the caseload, but since the caseload changes constantly, it could affect millions of recipients. Nor did the plan contain provisions to help the unemployed women and children who might lose welfare benefits after two years and become homeless.[71]

The Congressional Budget Office said that President Clinton's welfare reform proposal would cost $2.5 billion more than the $9.3 billion the administration had calculated. In a preliminary cost analysis, the CBO said the proposal would not reduce the welfare caseload as much as the administration expected. The CBO also calculated that the financing provisions in the Clinton bill would bring in $2.4 billion less than administration estimates. The discrepancies in cost and financing would add more than $4.9 billion to the federal budget deficit.[72]

The failure of the Clinton welfare reform bill was partly the fault of liberal Democrats, who failed to present a united front in the face of the Republicans' attacks. The Coalition on Human Needs, supported by eighty-eight House members, opposed work requirements and time limits in recommendations issued in 1993. The Congressional Hispanic Caucus wanted funding for welfare recipients to go to college. Others supported the reforms in theory but feared they would force welfare mothers into low-wage, dead-end jobs. These Democrats tried to load the proposals with restriction such as a minimum wage of $9 per hour for public-service jobs, or called for more spending on job-training programs rather than imposing work requirements. The Children's Defense Fund and others warned that budget constraints made only harsh, punitive proposals possible, and proposed that reforms should wait.[73]

The National Organization for Women's Legal Defense Fund and others took aim at the family cap, or child exclusion rule, as racist and sexist. The family cap was particularly controversial. Welfare mothers who have been raped or are unable to afford contraceptives have not made an independent decision to have another child. Studies estimating that in New Jersey, the birth rate of welfare mothers dropped by nearly 9 percent after the state imposed a family cap were criticized by those who believed the rule simply caused women not to report childbirth. But they would still have some incentive to report new children, since Medicaid and Food Stamp benefits increase.[74]

The ACLU, Legal Services, and the NOW Legal Defense and Education Fund in New Jersey sued the state and the federal government, challenging the child exclusion rule as harmful research on human subjects—welfare recipients—that was being conducted without their consent. Since 1974, every human services appropriations bills has included a requirement that subjects of any risky federally funded research give their consent. In 1994, the Ninth Circuit Court invalidated a waiver given by the Health and Human Services Department to California because it did not consider the harm that would result from benefit cuts. The complaint was not so much about the imposition of regulations but the idea of "withholding benefits to see if you can alter human behavior." The litigation raised fears that the waiver process would become bogged down in judicial review, state experimentation would be curtailed, and support would grow in Congress to eliminate HHS's supervision of welfare reform efforts to ensure they are not too harsh.[75]

As 1994 wore on, common ground for welfare reform appeared to center on requiring work, though there was less agreement on actually paying for it. Less consensus existed over the difficult things left—denying benefits to teenage mothers under 18, creating alternatives such as orphanages or residential schools for children, and letting states experiment with different ways of accomplishing the goal of ending welfare dependency. Other issues also remained: cutting benefits to legal aliens as a way to save money, time-limiting public service jobs, increasing benefits to welfare mothers who have more children. But the White House and the Republicans in Congress were close to a compromise. The differences dividing them were not great, and strong public support for action was obvious.[76]

By June 1994, Clinton was taking a passive stance toward welfare reform, hoping that it might "catch fire" in Congress but doing little to fan the flames. He failed to list it as one of his priorities when asked. His Harris poll approval rate was 42 percent, even though a *Los Angeles Times* poll found that 90 percent of respondents supported his welfare reform plan; even 60 percent supported it after being told it would cost $50 billion over ten years. The plan had been scaled back from $15 to $10 billion a year over the next five years, but the core of the program—that when the two-year time limit expired, recipients would be offered community jobs, and if they did not work they would not get paid—seemed extremely popular.

Bill Clinton's and the congressional Democrats' failure to reform welfare, while at the same time leading the criticisms of welfare, left the door open for Republicans. They set loose the forces for welfare reform but then lost control of the process. When the Republicans had their turn, they looked to the states for new ideas about how to reform welfare.

WELFARE REFORM IN THE STATES

Governors have played a major role in welfare reform for the last decade. A 1986 task force in New York State presented to Governor Mario Cuomo a proposal for converting AFDC into a transitional program with time limits on participation. For some, 1988 marked a significant departure in policy making for welfare reform: "This is an indication of the new federalism," said then-Governor Michael N. Castle (R-Del.), co-chair of the National Governors Association working group on welfare reform and now a member of Congress. "It's a policy that actually began at the state level and then bubbled up to the federal level, as opposed to almost any health and social service policy in the last sixty years, which started at the federal level and went back down."[77] Senator Daniel Patrick Moynihan said that without the work of the governors, "there would be no [welfare reform] legislation. The experimental mode of the states and their enthusiasm is what brought [Congress] to the debate."[78] Then-Governor Bill Clinton argued that "this was a very unusual thing both at the level of involvement of the governors with the Congress and the level of bipartisan involvement from the states and federal government crossing together."[79]

In 1988 governors played key roles in generating bipartisan support for welfare reform and in getting Congress to enact reforms that made sense to the states in their role as implementers of the law. They found common ground between conservatives, who came to accept that federal and state governments have a responsibility to provide education, training, and support services to help AFDC recipients obtain and keep jobs, and liberals, who came to see that mothers of even small children should work. Conservatives got requirements for set percentages of enrolled welfare recipients to join work and training programs and a requirement that at least one parent in two-parent families work part time at community service or another job. (This affected only a small percentage of families but had a much larger, symbolic importance in emphasizing work.) Liberals ensured that federal and state governments would share education and job training costs for seven years and provide transitional Medicaid and child care for twelve months after recipients left welfare. Other gains for liberals were that parents would not be required to accept job reducing net cash income, and that all states would be required to pay some benefits to poor two-parent families.

But this level of involvement by governors in Federal policy making is unusual. Despite the interdependence of federal and state government in most areas of domestic policy, the relationship has not been one of partnership. States play a largely subordinate role. Welfare and other policies (with the notable exceptions of Medicare and Social Security, which are purely national programs) require a great deal of interaction between federal and state agencies. But Congress has, until recently, viewed states not as equal partners or independent sovereigns but as subservient administrative units. Broad grants with few strings attached have given way to unfunded mandates, in which states are required to provide and pay for important public services and regulate industry and commerce. Federal courts have similarly expanded the tasks and obligations of state governments without providing the resources to accomplish those tasks.[80]

As a result, states have spent much of their time trying to gain funds to meet their mandates, and persuading the same members of Congress who enacted the laws to find loopholes to help with funding. Governors sometimes appear to be another lobbying group seeking federal benefits. But the role of the National Governors Association in the creation of the Family Support Act in 1988, and in the welfare reform proposals in 1995 and 1996, was much different. House and Senate Republican leaders welcomed governors as partners in achieving the Republican revolution. Governors played major roles in the development of welfare and Medicaid proposals. Their power was a function of the alignment of governors who sought more flexibility and fewer mandates with Republicans in Congress who were in favor of a smaller national government. Republican governors also had some experience as welfare reformers and knew more than members of Congress about how to remedy welfare's defects. State successes with reducing welfare through work programs, time limits, and caps on benefits to children born to mothers on welfare were exactly the kinds of solutions members of Congress were looking for. Republican governors from Wisconsin, Massachusetts, and other states with welfare reform programs in place worked closely with Congress. In 1996, after the budget breakdown stymied welfare reform, governors developed a bipartisan proposal for welfare reform that seemed for a time to re-energize the federal debate.[81]

The debates over welfare reform and Medicaid may have an important impact on federalism. Members of Congress have traditionally been sensitive to state and local constituencies that are important in elections, but have been much less interested in the problems states face in implementing public policies. Republicans, because devolution was an important part of their agenda, opened the doors to governors. If the governors continue to be successful in developing pragmatic, bipartisan solutions to policy problems, their policy-making partnerships with Congress may grow. The election of Republican, welfare reform–minded governors in several states also contributed greatly to welfare reform. Tommy Thompson of Wisconsin, John Engler in Michigan, and William Weld of Massachusetts played key roles as policy entrepreneurs.

STATE WAIVERS FROM FEDERAL WELFARE POLICY

The Department of Health and Human Services was authorized to waive Federal requirements for AFDC programs so that states could carry out experimental or demonstration projects that promoted the objectives in the Social Security Act, which created AFDC. States did not begin seeking waivers for their welfare programs in large numbers until the 1980s. State welfare programs could diverge from the federal requirements if (1) states received permission (in the form of a waiver) from the secretary of Health and Human Services; (2) the change was "cost neutral" to the federal government; (3) the state submitted to rigorous evaluations; and (4) the program conformed to the general AFDC objectives.

Limited evaluation funds have provided little incentive for states to follow through with quality evaluations, but the waiver process and the resulting evaluations have served as important sources of information about the strengths and weaknesses of alternative approaches to changing welfare.[82] States had some incentive to be careful in proposing demonstrations because they would bear the full burden of any cost overruns. Most were reluctant to invest money in long-term programs because they might not appear to be "cost neutral" when the evaluation period ended. States were encouraged to combine innovative operations with benefit cuts in order to ensure that federal costs would not increase. Evaluation focused on the impact of the total program on the total caseload; that, in turn, focused attention on experiments that produced that outcome.[83]

By 1996, forty-three states had received welfare reform waivers; only Alaska, Idaho, Kansas, Kentucky, Nevada, New Mexico, Rhode Island, and the District of Columbia had not.[84]

STATE APPROACHES TO WELFARE REFORM

State experiments in the 1980s and early 1990s imposed time limits and work requirements, tightened child-support enforcement, allowed working families to keep more of their income, eliminated benefit increases for mothers on welfare who have additional children, and coordinated welfare and other services.[85] Most waivers seem to reflect common assumptions: AFDC rules are a disincentive to work and encourage long-term dependency, they discourage marriage and encourage out-of-wedlock births, and they perpetuate a cycle of hopelessness and dependency that is passed on from one generation to the next.[86] States' experiences with waivers are discussed in detail in Chapters 6 through 8.

States have taken different approaches to welfare reform. For some it has entailed building a new system from the bottom up through pilot or model projects. Others have built a new system from the top down by redefining agency missions, changing administrative structures, and redrawing agency boundaries. A third strategy has been to make incremental changes in the way welfare systems operate.[87]

A second dimension of reform centers on the portion of the caseload on which states focus. One option is to operate a low-cost program that reaches a substantial portion of the caseload. Another approach provides more intensive, higher-cost services to a smaller, more specific group. A third possibility is a program that includes both general low-cost services and specific, higher-cost programs for much smaller groups.[88]

A third set of choices focus on the goals of the welfare program. For some, the objective is to reduce poverty, including long-term efforts, where necessary, to help recipients gain basic education and job training and skills. For others, the goal is to emphasize job placement and to move recipients as quickly as possible into the work force. This second goal can also be tied to reducing spending on welfare.[89] Research on the impact of these different approaches to welfare reform can illuminate some of the choices would-be reformers face (see Chapters 6 through 8).

The idea that welfare recipients should work or provide some community service in exchange for the benefits they receive has become the current general goal of virtually every reform package. But when specific proposals are made, they generate considerable controversy. Programs that offer subsidies for employers to hire unemployed workers have been criticized, because many employers resist hiring people who have been so stigmatized. Proposals for creating public-sector jobs have been attacked by unions, which fear that the lower wages to be paid to these workers will undercut their own pay scales. Unions have demanded that if jobs are to be created, their wages be set at prevailing levels; opponents claim those demands will render any such program economically unfeasible. Low-paid workers' jobs will be threatened by a major effort to employ welfare recipients.[90] Public-sector job creation efforts have been derided as make-work that wastes public funds on dead-end jobs. Others fear that in an economy with 8 million unemployed persons, and millions of others discouraged or otherwise not actively seeking work, welfare recipients will have few opportunities to find jobs.[91]

One of the essential elements of the welfare reform debate is to recognize that the most innovative options for helping people become self-sufficient are generally much more expensive than simply providing a welfare check. Clinton administration officials have promised, or perhaps warned, that welfare reforms will be made with "deficit-neutral funding."[92] According to one estimate, it costs at least $5,000 a year (in addition to the cash payments) to provide educational and training opportunities, including child care and other services, to each welfare mother. Subsidizing employment costs about $4,000 a year for day care, transportation, and supervision. Creating public-sector jobs costs much more. Some 1.5 million such jobs might be required if welfare recipients are obliged to work after two years in the program. A 1992 estimate projected that it would cost $5 billion to fund the work requirement, and perhaps another $10 billion for the training program. Under the Comprehensive Employment and Training Act of 1973, only about half that many jobs were created each year; the program became mired in charges of fraud and make-work and was terminated eight years later.[93]

The story of welfare reform in the states is complex, the conclusions are mixed, and as will be discussed later, states have not all been great laboratories of social experimentation. The impact of some quite recent reforms will not be known for several years. It will naturally take some time to bring about a real, permanent change in the behavior of or work opportunities for welfare recipients. But welfare reform in states has largely been driven by two forces. One is budgetary constraints and the demand to check the growth of welfare rolls in the late 1980s and early 1990s. The second is conservative attacks on welfare as inconsistent with the public values of work, self-reliance, responsibility, and maintenance of the traditional family structure as opposed to illegitimacy and the cycle of poverty. Wisconsin has given more attention to reforming welfare than any other state. Its efforts were particularly influential in shaping thinking about welfare. Wisconsin's experience with welfare reform is briefly reviewed below.

WELFARE REFORM, WISCONSIN STYLE Wisconsin Governor Tommy Thompson was a leader in early reform efforts. A Republican, Thompson first used welfare in the 1980s to defeat an incumbent Democratic governor.[94] The governor's welfare reform initiatives evolved over a decade. In 1987 Governor Thompson was the lone dissenter against a welfare reform plan proposed by the nation's governors that called for every able-bodied recipient to work or get training. He rejected it on the grounds that Wisconsin already had a program he was proud of, and a national program might hamper his state's efforts.[95] In 1988 the state implemented its Learnfare program, a "tough love" measure aimed at increasing school attendance among teenagers (ages 13–19) by reducing their families' welfare benefits if they did not attend school. A "Children First" program was approved in 1988 to increase child-support payments by requiring noncustodial parents to receive on-the-job training to prepare for employment. A 1992 initiative, the "Parental and Family Responsibility Initiative," often called "Bridefare," tried to remove disincentives to marriage in the AFDC program and discouraged minors from having children.[96] Welfare benefits would be partially capped after the first child was born, so a mother would receive only half of the increase she might otherwise receive if she had a second child. She would receive no additional benefits beyond that more modest increase for a second child, no matter how many more children were born.[97]

An assessment of Wisconsin's Learnfare program by the state Legislative Audit Bureau concluded that cutting families' benefits if their children missed too many days of school "had no detectable effect on school participation." But the program had some impact: because of faulty bookkeeping, hundreds of people in Milwaukee lost their benefits.[98] In May 1993, Governor Thompson issued a challenge to President Clinton by unveiling a welfare-reform plan requiring work from able-bodied recipients and cutting their benefits after two years. This was the first welfare-reform program to mandate work and place a limit on how long people could receive welfare payments. "President Clinton bragged about 'work, not welfare'" during the campaign, Thompson said. "Well, we're going to implement it here in Wisconsin." Dubbed "Work Not Welfare," Wisconsin's pilot program, to be implemented in two selected counties, required that:

Every able-bodied person applying for welfare sign a contract promising to work for benefits. Recipients would begin work or training
for work within thirty days, and after one year all recipients must
be working.

Some recipients might also be required to undertake motivational
workshops, parenting education, counseling for drug and alcohol
abuse, or other programs to overcome barriers to employment.

The number of hours recipients worked would be determined by
dividing the cash value of the Food Stamps and AFDC grants they
received by the federal minimum wage of $4.25 an hour. No one
would have to work more than forty hours per week.

Money earned by recipients would offset reductions in state welfare
payments.[99]

Welfare advocacy groups lobbied officials in the Department of
Health and Humans Services to reject the waiver, but senior White
House officials supported the state as did the President, since it was
difficult for them to oppose the kind of changes they promised to make
themselves. In November 1993 the Clinton Administration gave Wisconsin the go-ahead for its Work, Not Welfare program.[100]

In Madison, however, Democratic legislators charged that the governor was just trying to grab headlines as a social reformer and so attached to his bill a provision that would abolish the current program.
"Some members in our caucus wanted to embarrass [the Governor],"
one legislator said. "They wanted a headline that said, 'Governor vetoes
Democratic plan to end welfare.'"[101] The Democrats assumed that he
would then veto the bill; instead, Thompson vetoed the Democratic
proposals (governors have the line item veto in Wisconsin), including
the provision that public-sector jobs be provided for those who could
not find jobs themselves. He argued instead that incentives should be
given to private employers to hire former welfare recipients.[102]

In December 1993 Governor Thompson signed into law a measure
that would end AFDC by December 31, 1998, making Wisconsin the
first state to try doing so.[103] The Wisconsin law was signed after months
of careful maneuvering by Thompson, a conservative Republican, and
Democratic legislators, "who pushed through the radical measure in
part as a political dare, doubting the Governor would affix his name to
it."[104] In signing the law, Governor Thompson said: "We think the best
thing to do is to start over afresh, rather than tinker around the
edges."[105] Wisconsin's plan provided no options for people who reached
the two-year time limit and could not find a job. Clinton administration

officials reportedly did not like the plan, but they feared they would be cast as backtracking on the issue of time limits if they blocked it, and granted the waiver.[106]

In June 1994, Wisconsin was permitted to give welfare recipients from other states the same benefit level as they received in the previous state for their first six months in Wisconsin in order to see if high benefit levels attracted recipients.[107] In July, the state began the Parental and Family Responsibility Demonstration Project in six counties, which limited benefits for additional children born to welfare families. In January 1995, Work, Not Welfare was instituted in Pierce and Fond du Lac counties (which have approximately one thousand recipients) to help clients find full-time work or enter a job-training program within thirty days of signing up for assistance. It also limited cash benefits to no more than twenty-four months over a four-year period; cash assistance would then be denied for the next three years. Child care was provided while parents worked or received training.[108] The pilot was developed by the Hudson Institute to replace the state's AFDC program. The new program, nicknamed W-2, emphasized employment as its primary goal. Clients with meager work histories were to develop more substantial job records in government-subsidized jobs. Those lacking basic job skills and work habits would work for a time in community-service jobs. Each participant would work with a "personal planner" before and during their job experience.[109] W-2 also provided extended health care for families and allows custodial parents to collect all child-support payments directly. In addition, the W-2 plan provided child care subsidies to *all* low-income working families.[110]

Wisconsin officials report that their welfare caseload fell dramatically between 1987 and 1995. Spending increased in some areas: The cost of training programs grew from $1 million in 1986 to $57 million in 1995. Some 54 percent of recipients participated in education and job search activities, compared with 11 percent of recipients nationwide. Nearly 20 percent of recipients were working, in contrast to the 1 percent, on average, of recipients who work. The state found that by 1995 its reforms resulted in a monthly savings of $16 million.[111]

In April 1996 Thompson signed another welfare law that expanded W-2, promising to abolish welfare statewide by 1997 and replace it with strict work requirements. The program was expected to cost $340 million a year, $40 million more than the current cost of the state's welfare program. About 30 percent of welfare recipients were expected to find jobs in the private sector; the balance would work at subsidized private-sector jobs or community-service jobs. Extensive benefits would be offered for child care and transportation expenses. Wisconsin's approach was the most radical of any state welfare initiative, and it is not clear what will happen to the children of those who fail to show up for their jobs and as a result don't get paid.[112]

The plan requires recipients to immediately participate in job-related programs (unless they are mothers with children under twelve weeks of age). Recipients receive $518 a month in cash assistance, regardless of the size of their family, and Food Stamps. Subsidized child care and health care are available for all low-income families. A new category of caregivers is authorized to provide child care at one-half the current rate. Recipients must pay a copayment for child care and health insurance. The plan cuts benefits to recipients who miss job interviews or caseworker appointments. The state plans to create some thirty-thousand community-service positions; fathers who live with their families would be eligible for the jobs. The plan is projected to cost the state $119 million, or 13 percent more than the current welfare program.[113]

The state requested eighty-eight waivers dealing with its AFDC, Medicaid, and Food Stamp provisions. Federal officials found several provisions problematic: The state would have been allowed to replace workers with welfare recipients, for example. When federal officials objected, this was described as a clerical error. Recipients had to do forty hours a week of on-the-job training at $3.20 an hour, well below the minimum wage. People who were cut off from welfare could not appeal their cases.[114] W-2 took effect on September 1, 1997.

Ruth Conniff's assessment of W-2 concluded the reforms would "drive most participants deeper into poverty. . . . More than half of them will be making less than the minimum wage at state-subsidized, make-work jobs, and they will have the extra burden of co-payments for child care and health care." The goal of W-2 is to get people off welfare, "not to get people out of welfare." She described the challenge facing a typical recipient:

> A single mother who makes $5 an hour in Madison (about $800 a month) and has two children currently qualifies for fully subsidized child care. Under W-2 she will have to pay a $62 monthly co-payment for child care and a $20 a month co-payment for health insurance. She can expect to pay $620 a month for a two-bedroom apartment (there is an 18 to 24 month waiting-list for subsidized housing). Even if she obtained the maximum $225 monthly allotment of Food Stamps, she would have less than $100 a month for transportation, clothing and everything else for herself and her children.[115]

Judith Havemann, a *Washington Post* reporter, interviewed recipients in a Milwaukee pilot project of the W-2 program. She described the result as "administrative chaos . . . [a] "culture of people who have lived at home in poverty, often on the margins of society and in isolation from the world of work, [who] now must contend with a highly regimented computerized system of strict work requirements."A major challenge was moving the state welfare bureaucracy into the equivalent of the state labor department overnight, producing backlogs and other administrative problems.[116]

Archbishop Rembert G. Weakland of Milwaukee focused on W-2's terms, which provided that no state resident was entitled to W-2 services, even if they were eligible. The Archbishop described W-2 as welfare repeal, not reform: "Catholic social teaching holds that the poor, especially children, have a moral claim on the resources of the community to secure the necessities of life." He also argued that W-2's provisions would not ensure that working families could meet their needs: "According to [the] state's own projections, 75 percent of the families now on AFDC will be assigned to W-2 work slots that provide less than a full-time worker earns at the minimum wage. Accordingly, the responsibility of these parents to care for their children must be supported when necessary by a safety net adequate to meet the family's basic needs."[117]

The archbishop's complaint drew an angry response from Governor Thompson, who insisted, "People are going to be better off."[118] The journalist Mickey Kaus defended the denial of an entitlement in W-2 as the state's response to a Supreme Court decision that held that once a state creates an entitlement, it creates a right in the benefit that can be withdrawn only after a due-process proceeding.[119] Mark Greenberg of the Center for Law and Social Policy argued that Wisconsin's latest welfare reform initiative does not ensure that welfare recipients will be able to find work: The state does not guarantee a job, nor does it guarantee child or health care. In seeking to control costs, Wisconsin's plan reduces aid to a broad range of families: Low-income working families will have to make copayments for child care, for example, and benefits will be reduced for disabled parents and for grandparents or other non-parents providing child care.[120]

Kaus defended the Wisconsin plan as the long-sought for compromise between liberals and conservatives "in which the left would agree that welfare recipients should work, while the right agreed to spend the money to provide the necessary public jobs and child care." Paying recipients at below minimum wage rates ensures that people will not leave private jobs for public ones. Paying the same rate to families regardless of their size is consistent with the way the private-sector labor market works—workers generally don't get a pay raise just because they have another child. The state does not guarantee assistance beyond the time limits; officials argue that recipients will find private sector jobs more quickly if they know public benefits are time limited. That, Kaus argues, is not implausible and should be tested.[121]

Wisconsin had clearly achieved its goal of reducing welfare. Between 1986 and 1994, the welfare caseload in Wisconsin fell by 51 percent; between March 1994 and May 1997, the caseload declined by 46 percent. In the rural counties, it fell by 73 percent, and in Milwaukee, with the largest and most persistent caseload, it declined by 25 percent. Between 1989 and 1994, states averaged a 34 percent increase in AFDC participation, but Wisconsin (and three other states) saw their welfare rolls decline. Welfare benefits in Wisconsin had been among the highest in the nation. The decline in the caseload resulted from a number of factors. The state had a strong economy and low unemployment (below 3 percent in many counties). The state has one of the most effective systems for enforcing child-support payments, which has reduced the need for welfare in some families. The state cut benefits in 1987, falling from offering the fifth-highest benefits in 1987 to the twelfth-highest in 1996. The state's aggressive efforts to train recipients for jobs and its strong emphasis on work also helped produce lower welfare rolls.[122]

Wisconsin clearly has found the answer to reducing welfare. Part of that success is a result of a significant shift in welfare policy. Welfare reform has emphasized the enforcement of values, a decidedly conservative approach, but is also willing to provide assistance to recipients, as liberals have urged, to go beyond short-term job placement and develop skills for long-term employment prospects. Wisconsin has spent much more money on each welfare recipient than is spent elsewhere in traditional programs. Perhaps the most important asset in Wisconsin has been its highly professional and competent welfare bureaucracy, which has been able to change welfare policy effectively. But part of the Wisconsin experience is ambiguous: Is reducing welfare rolls the ultimate goal? Are former welfare recipients better off now that they are off welfare? Are they more self-sufficient? Are those who have been discouraged from joining the welfare system because of its strict work requirements better off than those who are part of the system? Research is underway that looks at the impact of welfare reductions on poor families in Wisconsin. The ultimate test of any welfare reform is its impact not just on the size of the rolls but on how well it promotes self-sufficiency and contributes to the well-being of families in need.[123]

THE POLITICS OF STATE WELFARE POLICY MAKING

In most states, welfare reform has been driven by the twin concerns of getting control of state budgets and ending a program whose values are at odds with those of most Americans. Only a few states, such as Wisconsin, have been real policy innovators; most have tinkered with program provisions based on what they have seen or heard happening in other states. There have been some successes but few dramatic breakthroughs in dealing with the most difficult dilemmas of welfare policy. But in most states, welfare reform has been good politics. It has usually enjoyed bipartisan support and has helped build the careers of many politicians. Governors have promoted their efforts and helped create expectations for reforming the system that went well beyond what was actually happening. States continued to explore welfare reform in the mid-1990s even as they watched Washington to see what the Clinton administration and Congress would do. In turn, congressional and White House reformers looked to the states for ideas. The perception that states were engaged in creative, successful policy innovation gave tremendous impetus to national efforts. Does the politics of welfare reform in the states inspire more confidence than the debate in Washington since 1994?

REFERENCES

[1] John F. Kennedy, comments on signing the Public Welfare Amendments Bill, July 26, 1962.

[2] For an elaboration of these arguments, see Cass R. Sunstein, *After the Rights Revolution: Reconceiving the Regulatory State* (Cambridge, Mass.: Harvard University Press, 1990), especially Chapter 1.

[3] For useful debates on affirmative action and equal opportunity, see Norman E. Bowie, ed., *Equal Opportunity* (Boulder, Colo.: Westview Press, 1988); Ellen Frankel Paul, Fred D. Miller, Jr., and Jeffrey Paul, *Reassessing Civil Rights* (Cambridge, Mass: Blackwell, 1991); and Russell Nieli, *Racial Preference and Racial Justice* (Washington, D.C.: Ethics and Public Policy Center, 1991).

[4] Theodore Lowi, *The End of Liberalism (Second Edition)* (New York: Norton, 1979), 210–16.

[5] Lyndon B. Johnson, remarks on signing War on Poverty legislation, "The Economic Opportunity Act of 1964," August 20, 1964.

[6] Quoted in Mary Jo Bane and David T. Ellwood, *Welfare Realities: From Rhetoric to Reform* (Cambridge, Mass.: Harvard University Press, 1994), 16.

[7] Richard M. Nixon, Special Message to Congress on Reform of the Nation's Welfare System, August 11, 1969.

[8] David H. Greenberg, Charles Michalopoulos, and Philip K. Robins, "Making Work Pay: Testing the Use of Financial Incentives to Reduce Welfare Dependency in the United States and Canada" (paper presented at the annual meetings of the Association for Public Policy and Management, Chicago, October 29, 1994).

[9] Jimmy Carter, remarks at press conference announcing his comprehensive welfare reform initiative, May 2, 1977.

[10] "After Years of Debate, Welfare Reform Clears," *Congressional Quarterly Almanac 1988* (Washington, DC: Congressional Quarterly, 1989): 349–64, at 349–50.

[11] Jason De Parle, "The Difficult Math of Welfare Reform," *The New York Times*, December 5, 1993, p. 130.

[12] Paul Pierson, *Dismantling the Welfare State? Reagan, Thatcher, and the Politics of Retrenchment* (New York: Cambridge University Press, 1994), 105, 127.

[13] Ibid., 103.

[14] Ibid., 126.

[15] Ibid., 4–5.

[16] Ibid., 6.

[17] Ibid., 131, 158–61.

[18] Ibid., 105.

[19] Ibid., 120–22.

[20] Ibid., 122–25.

[21] "After Years of Debate, Welfare Reform Clears": 349–50.

[22] Ibid., 350–51.

[23] Ibid., 355–56.

[24] Ibid., 349.

[25] President Ronald Reagan, remarks at the signing ceremony of the Family Support Act, October 13, 1988.

[26] Daniel Friedlander and Judith M. Gueron, "Are High-Cost Services More Effective than Low-Cost Services? Evidence from Experimental Evaluations of Welfare-to-Work Programs" (New York: Manpower Demonstration Research Corporation, 1990).

[27] Jennifer A. Neisner, "State Welfare Initiatives," CRS Report for Congress (Washington, D.C.: Congressional Research Service, May 24, 1994).

[28] Mickey Kaus, *The End of Equality* (New York: Basic Books, 1992), 10.

[29] Julie Rovner, "Welfare Reform: The Issue that Bubbled Up from the States to Capitol Hill," *Governing* (December 1988): 17–21, at 19.

[30] Vee Burke, "Clinton Welfare Proposal: Issue Summary," CRS Report for Congress (Washington, D.C.: Congressional Research Service, September 3, 1993): 1.

[31] Michael Wiseman, "New State Welfare Initiatives" (Madison: La Follette Institute of Public Affairs, University of Wisconsin–Madison, August 1992).

[32] Susan Kellam, "Welfare Experiments: Are States Leading the Way Toward National Reform?" *CQ Researcher* 4:34 (September 16, 1994): 795–815, at 805.

[33] To Georgia and Maryland (preschool immunization projects); Michigan (to make it easier to work and receive benefits); Missouri (to expand JOBS program and to mandate school attendance); New Jersey (for a family cap); Oregon (to expand the JOBS program); Utah (single-parent employment project); and two for California (to cut benefits and to block benefits to new residents; the latter was blocked by the Supreme Court).

[34] Paul Taylor, "Moynihan Urges Training for Welfare Recipients; Bill Offered as Challenge to Administration" *The Washington Post*, February 29, 1992, p. A14.

[35] William Clinton, *Putting People First* (New York: Times Books, 1992).

[36] Gerald F. Seib, "Clinton Aides Debate Whether Welfare Reform Will Interfere With Legislation on Health Care," *The Wall Street Journal*, December 28, 1993, p. A12.

[37] The White House, "Working Group on Welfare Reform, Family Support and Independence" (June 11, 1993).

[38] Sheri Steisel, "Presidential Words Ignite New Round of Welfare Debate," *State Legislatures* (May 1993): 25.

[39] Barbara Vobejda, "Shalala: Welfare Overhaul to Spring From Family Support Act," *The Washington Post*, February 4, 1993, p. A10.

[40] 103rd Congress, S. 16.

[41] Jeffrey L. Katz, "Clinton Plans Major Shift in Lives of Poor People," *Congressional Quarterly Weekly Report*, January 22, 1994): 117–22, at 121.

[42] Ibid., 119.

[43] 103rd Congress, H.R. 741. See *State Legislatures* (May 1993): 25.

[44] 103rd Congress, H.R. 3500.

[45] Katz, "Clinton Plans Major Shift in Lives of Poor People," 119.

[46] Ann Devroy, "President Insists Congress Enact Reforms in Welfare, Health Care; Veto Threatened If All Americans Are Not Covered," *The Washington Post*, January 26, 1994, p. A1.

[47] *Welfare Reform Act of 1994*, 103rd Congress, S. 1795.

[48] 103rd Congress, S. 1891.

[49] William Claiborne, "White House Panel Backs Phased-in Welfare Cutoffs," *The Washington Post*, February 25, 1994, p. A1.

[50] William Claiborne, "Clinton Welfare Task Force Proposes Time Limitations for Subsidized Jobs," *The Washington Post*, March 10, 1994, p. A12.

[51] Vee Burke, "Time-Limited Welfare Proposals," CRS Report for Congress (Washington, D.C.: Congressional Research Service, May 31, 1994): 5.

[52] Mickey Kaus, "Tough Enough," *The New Republic* (April 25, 1994): 22–25.

[53] William Claiborne, "Immigrants' Benefits at Risk; House Alliance Wants Funds for Welfare Reform," *The Washington Post*, March 24, 1994, p. A1.

[54] Guy Gugliotta, "Clinton to Support No-Tax Welfare Reform," *The Washington Post*, April 26, 1994, p. A6.

[55] Ibid.

[56] Eric Pianin, "Formerly United House Republicans Split Over Welfare Reform Package," *The Washington Post*, April 29, 1994, p. A37.

[57] 103rd Congress, S. 2134, H.R. 4473.

[58] 103rd Congress, H.R. 4498.

[59] Jeffrey L. Katz, "Welfare Overhaul Forces Ready to Start Without Clinton," *Congressional Quarterly Weekly Report* (April 2, 1994): 800–803, at 803.

[60] William Claiborne, "Reluctant Allies Oppose Clinton 'Family Cap' Welfare Proposal," *The Washington Post*, May 27, 1994, p. A1.

[61] 104th Congress, S. 2224, H.R. 4605. See *Taylor's World of Politics* (September 1994): 8–9.

[62] Jeffery Katz, "Long-Awaited Welfare Proposal Would Make Gradual Changes," *CQ Guide to Current American Government* (Fall 1994): 94.

[63] Eric Pianin, "Ways and Means Tries to Mold Welfare Reform Before August Recess," *The Washington Post*, July 31, 1994, p. A4.

[64] "The October Massacre," *The New Republic* (October 24, 1995): 7.

[65] "What Works," *The New Republic* (January 3, 1994): 7.

[66] "Welfare First," *The New Republic* (February 7, 1994): 9.

[67] Jason De Parle, "Clinton Puzzle: How to Delay Welfare Reform Yet Seem to Pursue It," *The New York Times*, January 5, 1994, p. A13.

[68] Richard L. Berke, "Professor Moynihan and His Presidential Pupil," *The New York Times*, January 14, 1994.

[69] Kaus, "Tough Enough," 22–25.

[70] Ibid.

[71] Ibid.

[72] Barbara Vobejda, "CBO, Clinton Differ on Welfare Reform Cost," *The Washington Post*, December 3, 1994, p. A14.

[73] Dante Ramos, "Kvetch, Kvetch," *The New Republic* (April 25, 1994): 24.

[74] Dante Ramos, "Rats," *The New Republic* (August 8, 1994): 16–17.

[75] Ibid.

[76] "Clinton's Secret Weapon," *The New Republic* (June 20, 1994): 7.

[77] Rovner, "Welfare Reform," 17.

[78] Ibid.

[79] Ibid., 21.

[80] Martha Derthick, "New Players: The Governors and Welfare Reform," *The Brookings Review* 14 (Spring 1996): 43–45.

[81] Martha Derthick, *Policymaking for Social Security* (Washington, D.C.: The Brookings Institution, 1979), 45.

[82] Matthew Birnbaum, "Policy, Planning and Social Experimentation: The Sad Case of the Wisconsin 100-hour Rule Experiment" (Madison: Department of Urban and Regional Planning, University of Wisconsin–Madison, November 1995): 12.

[83] Wiseman, "New State Welfare Initiatives."

[84] Robert Pear, "Changes in How Welfare Is Operated, While Sweeping, Will Be Taking Shape Slowly," *The New York Times*, August 6, 1996, p. A11.

[85] Deborah L. Cohen, "Governors Tout State Welfare Reforms," *Education Week* (9 February 1994): 15.

[86] Neisner, "State Welfare Initiatives," 1.

[87] Jane Waldfogel, "Integrating Child and Family Services: Lessons from Arkansas, Colorado, and Maryland" (Cambridge, Mass.: Malcolm Wiener Center for Social Policy, Kennedy School of Government, Harvard University, October 1994), 2.

[88] Friedlander and Gueron, "Are High-Cost Services More Effective than Low-Cost Services?"

[89] Ibid.

[90] "Welfare Reform in the Making," *New York Times*, December 13, 1993, p. A16.

[91] William Claiborne, "Clinton Welfare Task Force Proposes Time Limitations for Subsidized Jobs," *The Washington Post*, March 10, 1994, p. A12.

[92] Ibid.

[93] Paul Offner, "Target the Kids," *The New Republic* (January 24, 1994): 9–11, at 10.

[94] Donald F. Norris and Lyke Thompson, eds., *The Politics of Welfare Reform* (Thousand Oaks, Calif.: Sage Publications, 1995), 23–26.

[95] Kellam, "Welfare Experiments," 811.

[96] Carol Innerst, "Clinton Gets a Victory, By a Whisker; Wisconsin Chief Challenges Clinton on Welfare Reform," *The Washington Times*, May 28, 1993, p. A1.

[97] "Wisconsin: Gets Federal Waiver to Implement Welfare Reforms," *Abortion Report* (April 13, 1992).

[98] Ruth Conniff, "Wisconsin Doesn't Work: The State's Welfare 'Reforms' Are a Model—For What Not to Do," *The Washington Post*, July 28, 1996, p. C2.

[99] Jason DeParle, "Wisconsin to Impose 2-Year Limit on Welfare," *The Louisville Courier Journal*, November 2, 1993).

[100] Spencer Rich, "Wisconsin Gets Approval for Welfare Reform Test," *Los Angeles Times*, November 2, 1993, p. A15.

[101] Jason De Parle, "Wisconsin Pledges to Take Own Path on Welfare by '99," *The New York Times*, December 14, 1993, p. A1.

[102] Ibid.

[103] Kellam, "Welfare Experiments," 806.

[104] De Parle, "Wisconsin Pledges to Take Own Path on Welfare by '99,"

[105] Ibid.

[106] Ibid.

[107] Kellam, "Welfare Experiments," 807.

[108] Ibid., 806.

[109] Rochelle L. Stanfield, "Will Wisconsin Show the Way?" *National Journal* (September 23, 1995): 2382.

[110] Ibid.

[111] Michael Golay, "America's Welfare System: A Hand Up or a Hand Out?" in Michael Golay and Carl Rollyson, *Where America Stands 1996* (New York: Wiley, 1996): 69–87, at 80.

[112] Dirk Johnson, "Wisconsin Law Seeks to End Welfare," *The New York Times* April 26, 1996, p. C18.

[113] Mickey Kaus, "Adopt the Wisconsin Plan," *The Washington Post*, July 9, 1996, p. A15; Vee Burke, "Welfare Reform" (Washington, DC: Congressional Research Service, August 2, 1996).

[114] Conniff, "Wisconsin Doesn't Work," p. C2.

[115] Ibid.

[116] Judith Havemann, "Welfare Reform Drama Auditions in Milwaukee," *The Washington Post*, July 14, 1996, p. A12.

[117] Rembert G. Weakland, O.S.B., " 'Wisconsin Works': Breaking a Covenant," *The Washington Post*, July 4, 1996, p. A29.

[118] Havemann, "Welfare Reform Drama Auditions in Milwaukee."

[119] Kaus, "Adopt the Wisconsin Plan."

[120] Mark Greenberg, "Wisconsin Cheese" (letter to the editor), *The New Republic* (August 5, 1996): 5.

[121] Kaus, "Adopt the Wisconsin Plan."

[122] Lawrence M. Mead, "The Decline of Welfare in Wisconsin" (Milwaukee: The Wisconsin Policy Research Institute, Inc., March 1996).

[123] Lawrence M. Mead, "The Decline of Welfare in Wisconsin" (paper presented at the annual conference of the Midwest Political Science Association, Chicago, April 1997).

4

Welfare Reform Returns
to Washington, 1995–1996

The emergence of state welfare reform efforts, along with increasing challenges to the liberal welfare state, prompted serious debate about welfare in Washington. By 1993, welfare reform seemed like a sure bet. Democrats more than Republicans were in a position to generate the kind of political support needed for changing social policy; especially such "New" Democrats as Bill Clinton who wanted to save the welfare state by improving it. By the end of 1995, however, welfare reform had fallen victim to gridlock. It was then dramatically resuscitated in the summer of 1996 and a new welfare law was passed in August. Why was welfare reform, a wildly popular enterprise, so difficult to consummate? Part of the answer is that welfare reform meant different things to different people: It was a way to make welfare less attractive and thereby save money, and it was a way to ensure that welfare recipients were prepared to work and able to find a job, which would require welfare spending to increase. Some reformers lost their enthusiasm for change when welfare reform as budget cuts came to dominate. Others lost their zeal when they saw a political backlash develop against changes that appeared mean spirited and punitive.

This chapter examines the rise and fall of welfare reform in 1995 and 1996 at the national level and focuses on the evolution of welfare policy proposals as well as on how politics prevented Congress and the president from rewriting welfare law. The welfare law that Congress and the president eventually agreed on was a major shift in policy that ended sixty years of the federal entitlement for poor families. But the new law largely delegated to states the difficult task of "reforming" welfare—

transforming it into an effective policy for fostering self-sufficiency and independence among recipients, providing the assistance required for those with little job experience to move into the work force, reducing teen pregnancy and strengthening families, and reducing poverty. Congress and the president were quick to claim success in policy reform and just as quick to turn most of the problem over to the states. Given the nature of the debate over welfare reform in 1995 and 1996 in Washington, the decision by Congress and the president to turn the responsibility for welfare reform to the States may have been the best thing that could have happened.

THE REPUBLICAN REVOLUTION
MEETS WELFARE REFORM

In September 1994, congressional Republicans released their "Contract with America," a campaign manifesto to which virtually all Republicans running for the House swore allegiance. Among the proposals was a promise to reform welfare. Republicans effectively used the Contract to focus attention on the failures of the Democratic Congress and swept to an astounding victory in November. Revelation of what kind of welfare reform the Republicans had in mind started immediately. On November 13, 1994, the Speaker of the House–elect Newt Gingrich said that Congress should consider cutting off welfare recipients after sixty days and turning over further care for the destitute to private charities and orphanages.[1]

One of the most important characteristics of the welfare reform debate was that the major divisions were not just partisan ones; Democrats and Republicans were divided among themselves over how to proceed. But since the Republicans controlled the Congress, their intraparty battles were the most significant and shaped the law that was eventually enacted. Representative Clay Shaw (R.-Fla.), who became the chair of the Ways and Means subcommittee that would handle much of the welfare bill, initially expressed doubts about the welfare plan in the GOP contract.[2] However, after a meeting with Bill Archer (R.-Tex.), the incoming chair of the Ways and Means Committee, Shaw announced that the GOP contract proposal "will be the basis for our deliberations."[3] But Republican unanimity was short lived.

One of the issues that divided Republicans was illegitimacy. Republicans had shifted their focus from the time limits and work requirements that were central to their 1993 bill, to preventing teenage pregnancies.[4] This was due, at least in part, to the new position of strength in which such conservative Republicans as James Talent (Mo.) found themselves since the Republican victory.[5] More important was the question of federal-state relations.

In early December, the GOP leadership expected their welfare bill to be sent to the floor without amendments, when the new Congress convened in January.[6] The GOP leadership then had a critical meeting with the governors of many states where they discussed the GOP welfare proposal and the option of replacing some welfare programs with grants that would give states discretion over their use. Some GOP governors expressed a willingness to accept reduced federal aid in these programs by 10 percent or more in exchange for greater flexibility. As a result, GOP leaders said they would be willing to consider alterations in the Contract proposal, such as replacing welfare and other programs with block grants.[7]

In January 1995, Republican congressional leaders announced their welfare proposal. They would replace hundreds of federal programs with direct cash payments to the states, which would allow states to create their own welfare systems with little direction from Washington. Although states would still be required to follow minimal federal standards, they could make many of their own decisions about who qualified for welfare assistance and how long they would receive it. In exchange for the broad latitude they would be granted under the legislation, states would agree to no funding increases from the federal government for at least five years. The GOP proposal would end the entitlement status of AFDC and several other programs, meaning that poor Americans who meet certain eligibility criteria would no longer be guaranteed benefits. "The reduction in federal personnel and federal bureaucracy is simply staggering when we start talking about collapsing some 336 programs down into roughly eight block grants," said John Engler of Michigan, who headed a task force of four Republican governors negotiating with members of Congress on the details of the proposal. "The discussion today is very, very encouraging . . . from a state perspective." The proposal replaced the welfare reform bill initially prepared by the Republicans, demonstrating the influence governors were able to have in the new Congress.[8]

In January Gingrich indicated that Republicans might drop a plan to deny benefits to legal immigrants who have not become citizens. "I think we're going to revisit the question of eliminating legal aliens from ever getting access to government services after some length of time of being here and paying taxes and . . . participating," Gingrich said at a news conference. As proposed, the Republican legislation would bar most legal immigrants from sixty federal programs, prohibiting them from receiving free childhood immunizations, housing assistance, Medicaid, subsidized school lunches and many other federal benefits. Gingrich said that because thirty Republican governors are willing to accept a five-year freeze on growth in federal welfare payments in exchange for wider latitude to experiment, the government would save $40 billion and eliminate the "necessity" of cutting off aid to legal immigrants.[9]

Although Republicans in Congress had given great emphasis to consultations with governors, they made it clear they were not ready to hand over huge cash payments to the states without federal guidelines, despite pleas from governors for broad flexibility to design their own welfare programs. As he opened hearings on welfare reform in January, Representative Shaw called for legislation that would eliminate most federal welfare programs and replace them with block grants to the states. But such a plan must require states to follow certain rules, he said, including limiting the number of years welfare recipients could receive benefits, cutting off cash aid to unwed teenage mothers, denying additional benefits to welfare mothers who have more babies and ending welfare for legal immigrants who have not become citizens.[10]

The politics of welfare reform and abortion became intertwined. In a January Capitol Hill meeting, representatives of the U.S. Catholic bishops, Catholic Charities, and Feminists for Life joined the National Right to Life Committee in saying that certain changes in welfare proposed in the GOP contract would not deter low-income women from getting pregnant, but would discourage them from carrying those pregnancies to full term. In particular, they criticized the "child exclusion" and "family cap" proposals, which would disqualify pregnant women for benefits if they were under 18, already had a child on welfare, did not legally establish the child's paternity, or had been on welfare themselves for more than two years. Concern about abortion created an uncomfortable dilemma for some legislators. Freshman representative Jim Bunn (R.-Ore.) said that because of his convictions about abortion he had refused to sign the Contract. After talking with welfare mothers, he said he realized "it is very very clear the contract does not realistically meet their needs."[11]

On January 28, 1995, Republican leaders had a "working session" with President Clinton on welfare reform. Clinton hosted more than two dozen officials from both parties, including governors, members of Congress and local officials, for a nearly five-hour session. At a news conference after the meeting, Democrats and Republicans said they were in agreement on several points: The welfare system needed to be replaced, states should be given more flexibility, welfare recipients should be moved into jobs, child support collection should be stepped up, and teenage pregnancy should be curbed. But they said major disagreements remained, not only between the parties, but also among governors and members of Congress. Key issues of disagreement include how much discretion should be given to states in running their welfare programs and whether new programs would end the current entitlement to welfare. At the same time, Republican officials, emboldened by the November elections and their basic agreement on the shape of a legislative proposal, played down the importance of other actors, including the Clinton administration, which had introduced a welfare bill in 1994.[12]

While the White House and the House of Representatives were engaged in bipartisan talks, Democrats responded to the Republican welfare reform bill with a proposal to raise the minimum wage by 90 cents, to $5.15, over two years.[13] House Democrats offered a welfare reform plan in which adults applying for welfare would immediately have to find a job, accept a public-service job, or enter a training or job placement program. Those who refused would be denied aid, but they could not be cut off the rolls if they were willing to work but unable to find a job. The plan was not introduced as a bill, but Democrats vowed to offer amendments as the Republican bill worked its way through the House.

THE HOUSE STRIKES FIRST

The House Ways and Means subcommittee marked up its welfare reform bill in February. The White House, in a letter to Representative Shaw, chair of the subcommittee, strongly denounced the Republican proposal to turn over much of the responsibility for welfare to the states as a "failure to enact serious work-based reform. . . . The administration believes that no adult who is able to work should receive welfare for an unlimited time without working." Work, or efforts to get it, should begin on the "first day someone comes onto welfare." The GOP bill—which required 2 percent of all recipients to work in 1996 and 20 percent by the year 2003—raised "serious concerns." It included only "minimal and unenforceable requirements" that recipients work. It allowed " 'work activities,' loosely defined by the state welfare bureaucracy, rather than real work requirements" and "fail[ed] to provide allowances for potential growth in the need for cash assistance because of economic downturn, population growth or unpredictable emergencies." House Democrats joined the attack, calling the work requirements in the bill a "sham" that would require fewer welfare recipients to work than are required to get jobs under current law. The Republicans "don't want to pay for what it would take to have more meaningful work requirements," said Sander M. Levin (D.-Mich.). "Essentially their argument is you can do it on the cheap." Responding to Democratic pressure, the subcommittee passed on a voice vote an amendment to punish states by reducing a state's share of the block grant by 3 percent if it failed to meet the work participation standards. And in the most impassioned debate of the subcommittee's meeting, Republicans voted unanimously to prohibit states from making cash welfare payments to unwed mothers under eighteen. The issue, said Mac Collins (R.-Ga.), is the taxpayer who "accepts responsibility for his actions, works, pays taxes and has the government deduct from his paycheck money to be given to others who don't accept the same responsibility." Said Representative Jennifer Dunn (R.-Wash.), "It's time to use the theory of tough love. We've got to stop [subsidizing illegitimacy]. Now is the time." The subcommittee also voted to ban states from using their block grant funds to increase payments to welfare families who have additional children while receiving aid.[14]

The subcommittee's bill, as reported out, would have eliminated the main federal welfare program, Aid to Families with Dependent Children, and replaced it with a block grant to the states that could be used to provide cash assistance for up to five years. States would have been required to place half of their welfare caseloads in "work or related programs" by 2003. Unmarried teenage mothers and their children would have been denied welfare benefits until the mothers turned eighteen in an effort to discourage out-of-wedlock births. The bill would have dismantled federal foster care and adoption programs and turn the money over to the states with supervision by citizen review panels; the panels would be appointed by state officials, meet quarterly, and produce public reports after each meeting. It would have eliminated immigrants who have not become citizens from some welfare programs, and denied payments under the Supplemental Security Income (SSI) program to drug addicts and alcoholics who are disabled because of their addictions, and restricted the number of children eligible for cash assistance to those with severe impairments.[15]

A shouting match in the House Ways and Means Committee blocked final passage of the Republican welfare plan. As Republicans prepared to push through their plan to eliminate the guarantee of welfare benefits to every eligible American, Representative Jim McDermott (D.-Wash.) invoked House rules allowing a member to demand polished legislative language before voting. When Chairman Bill Archer (R.-Tex.) ruled the motion out of order, Democrats erupted. Representative Bill Thomas (R.-Calif.) summoned the sergeant-at-arms. Representative Fortney "Pete" Stark (D.-Calif.) invoked Nazi Germany. The nastiness of the debate made compromise virtually impossible, but because of the way the House operates, no compromise with congressional Democrats was necessary.

Continuing divisions among conservatives reflected the difficulty of fashioning a plan to reconcile the competing objectives Republicans had for welfare reform. Robert Rector, senior policy analyst for welfare at the Heritage Foundation and a leading Republican welfare expert, attacked the Republican plan as "extremely weak on work requirements" that needed to be "vastly toughened." He added that the subcommittee's proposal to turn welfare over to the states as "in some respects no better than the status quo." Rector focused on an aspect of the proposal that came under fire from Democrats as well: the requirement that 2 percent of recipients engage in "work activities" in 1996, increasing to 20 percent by the year 2003: "The most important weakness is that there is no definition of work. If a guy shows up one day for a job orientation class it could be counted. This enables states to pull the trick of pretending they have a lot of people working." He also characterized as a "sham" the provision that would dock recipients' checks for up to six months if they have not legally established the paternity of their children: It "just repeats the status quo by allowing the mother to wiggle out of responsibility for tracking down the father by claiming she has made a 'good faith effort,' " he said. Shaw responded that "work activities" were not spelled out because the governors did not want a definition in the bill. "We are going to put one in," he said.[16]

In March, House Republicans stripped from their welfare reform bill a provision that would have denied driver's and professional licenses to parents who fail to pay child support and other language that would have made it easier to track down deadbeat parents.[17] President Clinton countered with the announcement of a public campaign to make parents who fail to meet their child-support obligations ineligible for driver's licenses. He called the Republican proposal "budget-cutting . . . wrapped in the cloak of welfare reform."[18]

On March 14, 1995, House Republican leaders unveiled their revised welfare reform bill. They decided to allow noncitizen legal immigrants much greater access to federal assistance than they originally proposed. Noncitizens still would be barred from receiving aid under the five largest federal programs: Medicaid, Food Stamps, disability aid, the revamped Aid to Families with Dependent Children, and social service programs known as "Title XX." But unlike legislation approved in committee, the new bill would not bar legal aliens from receiving aid under dozens of other federal programs, including education and training, lead screening and elderly assistance. The revised bill was a consolidated form of legislation that three committees—Ways and Means, Economic and Educational Opportunities, and Agriculture—had approved in recent weeks. Congressional aides said the changes were made in part to allow immigrants access to programs—such as employment and training—that would help them improve their status. But immigrant advocacy groups said the change has done little to soften their opposition to the welfare reform.[19] Objections from Agriculture Committee Chairman Pat Roberts (R.-Kans.) and other farm state legislators scuttled the proposal to roll Food Stamps into a block grant. Eligibility changes would reduce benefits for almost all of the 27 million recipients of food stamps.

The House began debate on the revised bill on March 21. Republicans led off with figures prepared by the Congressional Budget Office that their bill would cost $66.4 billion over five years. The debate on the House floor became very heated. "Will you get these highly paid members to sit down and shut up?" Sam Gibbons (D.-Fla.) roared at the presiding officer at one point. Jim McCrery (R.-La.) interrupted, asking, "Is petulance a proper form of behavior for a member of Congress?" "I will be as petulant as I want to be," Gibbons boomed back, then complained that the legislation was mean to children. Republicans booed. "Boo if you want to, make asses out of yourselves if you want to," retorted Gibbons.[20]

At other times, the debate turned even nastier: "Generation after generation, we have enslaved these people," said House Economic and Educational Opportunities Committee Chairman William F. Goodling (R.-Pa.). "Unless we make a change, they will never get an opportunity to achieve the American dream." Ways and Means Committee Chairman Bill Archer (R.-Tex.) said that the welfare overhaul would "reverse the decades-long federal policy of rewarding unacceptable and self-destructive behavior. We will no longer reward people for doing the wrong thing." But Sam Gibbons, the top Democrat on Ways and Means, said, "This is a cruel piece of legislation. It punishes the children—the innocent children—because of the errors of the parent or parents. It would deprive them of the basic necessities of food, of housing, of education, of love." Harold E. Ford (D.-Tenn.) said that the federal government had "offered a financial security commitment to poor children with a sixty-year commitment to welfare, and they're taking it away." The partisan rancor on the floor reached a height when John Lewis (D.-Ga.) referred to Nazism in describing Republican ideas, whereupon Representative Shaw denounced the comparison as an "absolute outrage."[21]

The House approved amendments that would allow the savings from welfare reform (an estimated $66 billion) to be used for tax cuts; prohibited federal welfare funds from being used on abortions (proposed by Henry Hyde, R.-Ill.); tempered a ban on cash aid to unmarried teenage mothers and to children born to women on welfare by allowing them to buy diapers and other necessities; and added $160 million per year for child care through the year 2000. Amendments that were barred from consideration by House leaders included one by Harold Volkmer (D.-Mo.) and Pete Stark (D.-Calif.) that would have dropped a provision that rewarded states for reducing out-of-wedlock births.[22] The House also voted down a Democratic version of a welfare reform bill that would have preserved the entitlement status of cash welfare. It had similar work requirements to those in the Republican bill, but it guaranteed training, education, and a job, and would have limited AFDC benefits to four years as opposed to two.[23]

On March 24, 1995, the House approved the Republican welfare bill, the Personal Responsibility Act, by a 234–199 vote. Nine Democrats joined all but five Republicans in supporting the bill. President Clinton responded that the bill was not "real" welfare reform and was "weak on work and tough on children." Republicans countered by saying that Democrats were defenders of the status quo, and that the welfare bill freed the poor from a system that bred dependency. "Don't feed the bureaucrats, feed the children," said William Goodling (R.-Pa.). "Everybody agrees the current system has failed millions of Americans and enslaved them."[24] Cynthia McKinney (D.-Ga.), a black lawmaker, read into the record a hate letter that she said her office received from Texas. In racially demeaning terms, the anonymous letter compared African-American women on welfare to "monkeys" who bear too many children. "The spirit of GOP welfare reform lives in these words," McKinney charged. Later, two GOP lawmakers, John L. Mica (R.-Fla.) and the freshman Barbara Cubin (R.-Wyo.), compared welfare recipients with wild animals who become dependent on the care of humans—remarks that drew hisses, boos, and denunciations from Democrats. Referring to Mica's sign, which read "Don't Feed the Alligators," District Delegate Eleanor Holmes Norton (D) commented, "Don't feed the alligators, but please feed the children." "We have a millionaire from Florida comparing children to alligators, and we have the gentlelady in red over here comparing children to wolves," Sam Gibbons (D.-Fla.) said. "That tops it all."[25]

In sum, the House welfare bill permitted states to take over the Food Stamp program if they had a statewide system for delivering benefits electronically. It banned SSI payments to drug addicts and alcoholics; cut cash payments to some children with behavioral or mental disabilities; replaced cash with medical benefits for other disabled children; and allowed only the most severely disabled children to continue to receive cash. It replaced AFDC with a block grant to the states. Cash aid to women and children who qualified would no longer be guaranteed; benefits would end after five years, and unmarried parents under age 18 would not be allowed to receive cash assistance. Women who had additional children while on welfare would receive no additional benefits. Federal funding (with states paying additional money) was set at current levels of $15.4 billion annually. School breakfast and lunch programs were combined into a block grant to the states, as was funding for several nutrition programs, including the Women, Infants and Children supplemental feeding program. Nine child care programs were also made into a block grant. Most legal immigrants were barred from receiving Food Stamps, nonemergency health care, and some social services; exceptions would be made for refugees, the elderly, veterans, and the military. The bill also established state and national registries of child-support orders; each state would set up a computerized "State Directory of New Hires," indexed by the Social Security numbers of new employees; employers would withhold child support from the paychecks of delinquent parents, and the IRS and Social Security Administration would also use the system to track violators. Finally, the bill would create a limited rainy-day fund that states could borrow from to meet short-term welfare needs in times of budget constraints. In all, forty-five social programs would be consolidated or eliminated.[26]

The House welfare bill was an uneasy compromise between those who had acquiesced to Republican governors' calls for devolution of policy and those who sought to change the behavior of welfare recipients. The rancor made bipartisan compromise difficult, but in the end, widespread opposition to the current welfare system and the perception that welfare reform was good politics prevailed.

SHIFT TO THE SENATE

In April, a group of Republican governors and senators—Senate Majority Leader Bob Dole, Finance Committee Chairman Bob Packwood (Ore.), Senator John H. Chafee (R.I., a moderate member of the Finance Committee), Michigan governor John Engler, Wisconsin governor Tommy G. Thompson, and Massachusetts governor William F. Weld—began meeting. They were considering a welfare reform plan, proposed by the governors, that would reject many of the central and most contentious issues in legislation adopted by the House, such as provisions that would deny cash aid to unmarried mothers under age 18 and to most noncitizens. Their plan, like the House bill, would replace the AFDC program with a lump-sum payment to the states. But unlike the House Republican bill, whose program of block grants contained numerous restrictions, the proposal would hand the money over to the states with few strings attached.[27]

The governors' and senators' plan would eliminate the teenage-mother cutoff and the "family cap"; modify the language that would end eligibility for the major welfare programs to most noncitizen legal immigrants; reject the five-year time limitation on welfare benefits in the House version; give states the discretion to bar aliens from some welfare programs but would not order them to do so, as the House legislation did; not force states to refuse additional benefits to welfare mothers who give birth to additional children; retain the federal school lunch program, which was converted into direct payments to the states in the House bill; and turn the Food Stamps program over directly to the states.[28]

President Clinton rejected this proposal as unfair to states with large and growing welfare populations. Clinton emphasized that welfare reform was an area in which he hoped to find common ground with the Republican Congress, saying, "I am for much, much, much, much more flexibility to the states . . . but we have to do it in a way that is fair." Clinton said the governors' proposal did make some improvements over the version adopted the previous month by the House, which he had summarily dismissed. "Do you want to see a veto?" he threatened. "If the Senate passes the House bill, I'd be happy to veto."[29] He argued that "all the proposals [before Congress] are still too weak on [requiring] work and on helping people to move from welfare to work" and repeated his threat to veto the House bill.[30]

The Senate Republican welfare reform bill required states to put 45 percent of welfare recipients into jobs by the year 2000. Doubts about the Senate bill were kindled in a May Senate Finance Committee hearing on welfare reform when a Congressional Budget Office analyst warned members of Congress that the cost of such a requirement would be $10 billion a year, and that most states would probably opt out of the work requirement. They would most likely prefer the sanction (a 5 percent reduction in their block grant, a total loss of 5 percent of $16.7 billion, or $835 million) than pay the $10 billion for jobs.[31] The Republicans were stuck between softening their work requirement or cutting less from welfare reform than they had promised. Some governors suggested the work requirement be dropped and Congress simply trust states to require work. But states vary greatly in unemployment rates; they also therefore vary in the prospect of finding private-sector jobs for welfare recipients and the need to create public jobs as a last resort in making the welfare-to-work transition possible.[32]

The Senate passed its welfare reform bill in September within the context of the Republican presidential primary. Four Senators were running for the Republican nomination, particularly Senate Majority Leader Bob Dole and Phil Gramm (R.-Tex.). The majority leader had one eye on the conservative wing of the party, its influence in the primaries, and Gramm's position in that camp, and the other eye on the Republican moderates and moderate Democrats. But unlike the House bill, the Senate bill passed with strong bipartisan support (87–12) and differed from the House version in several ways. States could choose to convert Food Stamps to a block grant, but not child nutrition programs; states would be required to spend at least 80 percent of their 1994 spending on welfare; federal spending on Food Stamps and welfare would be reduced by $66 billion over seven years from what would otherwise be spent (the House would reduce spending by $102 billion); and states could decide whether to give aid to children of unmarried mothers under eighteen and children born to welfare mothers. In September, the Clinton administration hailed the Senate bill, threatening to veto the final bill if it included the House provisions. A conference committee was formed and began the effort to craft a compromise bill.

By the end of the summer of 1995, Clinton was ready to sign the Republican bill. His own welfare reform proposal was dead and he was willing to accept the Republican plan with more money for child care, a limit on how much states could cut their welfare spending, and additional funds to be set aside in the event of an increase in caseloads due to a recession. In exchange, he agreed to ending a sixty-year federal obligation to help poor children, a freeze on spending for welfare, and a five-year lifetime limit on welfare benefits. The Republican governors and members of Congress had largely gotten what they had wanted. The Senate overcame the nasty, partisan rancor in the House, and welfare reform seemed certain. But the coalition was fragile, and soon began to unravel as critics of the two bills mobilized and exploited the differences within Congress.

WELFARE REFORM MEETS THE BALANCED BUDGET BILL

The Republicans were slow to hammer a compromise in the House-Senate conference committee, and by the time the bill was reported out, it faced a much different political climate. Democrats in Congress began criticizing as punitive and harmful to children and families essentially the same bill that they had voted for a few months earlier. The Democrats focused on cuts in day care funding, a requirement that states maintain at least 75 percent of their welfare spending instead of the Senate bill's 80 percent guarantee, and a cap on benefits to children born to welfare mothers unless the governor and state legislature voted otherwise (the Senate bill just left it up to the states).[33]

A Health and Human Services Department report indicating that the welfare bill might move more than 2 million children into poverty, as Marian Wright Edelman and Pat Moynihan had been saying, helped generate opposition.[34] The leaking of the report; the realization that a $60 billion cut in AFDC, Food Stamps, and Medicaid would hurt low-income people; and the political fortune gained from standing tall against Republican congressional extremism all contributed to Democratic resistance to the welfare reform bill in Congress and to the president's veto of the bill. But the Democrats' charges were not persuasive given their earlier embrace of the Republican bill. The Democrats in Congress and the White House were able to keep the Republicans from reforming welfare, but had no plan of their own to improve welfare. The Clinton administration had shifted its position of welfare reform. Clinton had raised expectations with his promise to end "welfare as we know it" but then ignored the issue for two years. Moderate Republicans such as Kassebaum and Chafee complained about the harshness of the Republican bill but ended up voting for it, so the Democrats got little help from the other side of the aisle.[35]

In November 1995, welfare reform was sidetracked in the budget process and in the controversy surrounding the shutdown of federal agencies because of the failure of Congress to pass some appropriations bills and because of the president's vetos of other bills. By November 14, of the thirteen appropriations bills, three had been passed, one had been vetoed and four had been signed. The first Continuing Resolution, a stopgap measure to keep federal agencies operating, ran out on November 13. A new stopgap bill was vetoed because it included a Medicare Part B premium rise.[36]

In some respects, this was politics as usual. Congress has enacted fifty-five continuing resolutions since 1977; the entire fiscal year 1992 was governed by one as the Democratic Congress and the Bush administration could not pass appropriations bills. The government shut down for a couple of days in 1981, 1984, 1986, and 1990.[37] But welfare reform and almost every other issue fell victim to budget gridlock. Even uncontroversial issues were difficult to pass in 1996.

Congress had passed a nonbinding resolution in June 1995 calling for a balanced budget in seven years; the Clinton administration countered with a nine-year plan.[38] In the fall Congress passed a reconciliation bill to change tax and spending laws to conform with its June balanced budget plan.[39] Republican leaders in Congress attached their welfare reform bill to this measure to ensure passage. But Clinton vetoed the reconciliation bill in December because of its spending cuts and the tax cuts.[40] House and Senate leaders then decided to pass the welfare bill as a stand-alone measure in order to put pressure on the president. They restored provisions removed by the Senate[41] and roughly split the difference between the House and Senate spending reductions ($64 billion in seven years). The conference bill weakened the state maintenance-of-effort requirement and permitted states to divert up to 30 percent of their welfare block grant to other social programs, raising fears of a "race to the bottom" by states.[42] H.R. 4 was sent to the president, who vetoed the freestanding welfare bill on January 9, 1996.[43] In his veto message, Clinton explained his position:

> The current welfare system is broken and must be replaced, for the sake of the taxpayers who pay for it, and the people who are trapped by it. But H.R. 4 does too little to move people from welfare to work. It is burdened with deep budget cuts and structural changes that fall short of real reform. I urge the Congress to work with me in good faith to produce a bipartisan welfare reform agreement that is tough on work and responsibility, but not tough on children and on parents who are responsible and want to work.[44]

Table 4.1 charts the evolution of welfare policy in 1995, culminating with the bill that the president vetoed in January 1996. There were a number of important changes made from the original March 1995 House bill. The main framework of AFDC devolution did not change much; the issues that did see a shift were important, in terms of funding

TABLE 4.1
SUMMARY OF WELFARE REFORM PROPOSALS, 1995

Issue	HR 4[a] House-passed Personal Responsibility Act (March 24, 1995)	HR[6] Senate-passed Work Opportunity Act (September 19, 1995)	"Personal Responsibility and Work Opportunity Act of 1995" (H.R. 4, H. Rept 104–430 (December 22, 1995)[c]
Projected savings	$62.1 billion over five years; $102 billion over seven years	$38.6 billion over five years; $65.8 billion over seven years	$64.1 billion over seven years; ($4 billion in Medicaid)[d]
Program structure and funding	Entitlement eliminated; $15.4 billion annual block grant replaced AFDC and three related programs	Entitlement eliminated; block grants for cash welfare and job training	Entitlement eliminated; block grants for a variety of social aid programs
State maintenance of effort/distribution options	No maintenance of effort required; state option to transfer up to 30% of block grant to other social services programs and set aside some money for emergencies (reserved funds over 20% of federal grant could be used as general revenue)	States must pay at least 80% of 1994 benefit levels and funds must be used for specified social services such as cash assistance or child care; up to 30% of cash grant could be diverted to the child care block grant; some funds used to operate employment placement programs; 15% cap on administrative spending	States must pay at least 75% of 1994 benefit levels; up to 30% of grant could be diverted for other social services programs; some funds used to operate employment placement programs; 15% cap on administrative spending (exempts expenses for case-tracking technology)
Additional funding sources	$1 billion fund for interest-bearing loans to states with unemployment rates of over 6.5% over three months; $100 mil-	$1.7 billion fund for interest-bearing loans to states; 2.5% increase in block grant for states with growing pop-	$1.7 billion fund for interest-bearing loans to states; $800 million for states with growing populations; $1 billion

TABLE 4.1 (*cont.*)
SUMMARY OF WELFARE REFORM PROPOSALS, 1995

Issue	HR 4[a] House-passed Personal Responsibility Act (March 24, 1995)	HR[6] Senate-passed Work Opportunity Act (September 19, 1995)	"Personal Responsibility and Work Opportunity Act of 1995" (H.R. 4, H. Rept 104–430 (December 22, 1995)[c]
Additional funding sources (cont.)	lion annually for states with growing populations	ulation and low benefits; $1 billion contigency fund for 100% matching grants to states with high unemployment	contingency fund for states with high unemployment levels
Time limits	Five-year lifetime cash benefit limit; 10% of caseload exempted for hardship	Five-year lifetime cash benefit limit (less at state option); 20% of caseload exempted for hardship [e]	Five-year lifetime benefit limit; 15% of caseload exempted for hardship[f]
Work requirements	Mandatory participation in work activities within two years; 10% of single-parent caseload working by 1996, 50% by 2003; 50% of two-parent caseload working by 1996, 90% in 1998; no personal responsibility contract	Mandatory participation in work activities after three months; 25% of single-parent caseload working by 1996, 50% working by 2000; 60% of two-parent families working by 1996, 90% by 1999; mandatory personal responsibility contract	Mandatory participation in work activities within two years; 15% of single-parent caseload working by 1996, 50% by 2002; 50% of two-parent families working by 1996, 90% by 1999; no personal reponsibility contract
Work definition	Private- or public-sector employment, employment-related training or OJT; education activities if under 20 without a diploma; job search acceptable for four weeks; for single-parents, 35	Private- or public-sector employment, training (twelve months only), or community service; job search acceptable for four weeks; only 25% engaged in training; hourly requirements same	Private- or public-sector employment, training (twelve months only), or community service; job search acceptable for four weeks; only 20% engaged in training; all mothers, regard-

TABLE 4.1 (cont.)
SUMMARY OF WELFARE REFORM PROPOSALS, 1995

Issue	HR 4[a] House-passed Personal Responsibility Act (March 24, 1995)	HR[6] Senate-passed Work Opportunity Act (September 19, 1995)	"Personal Responsibility and Work Opportunity Act of 1995" (H.R. 4, H. Rept 104–430 (December 22, 1995)[c]
Work definition (cont.)	hours a week by 2002; for two-parent families, 35 hrs./wk. by 1996	as House; state option for single mothers with child(ren) under 6 to work 20 hours a week	less of age of child, required to work 35 hours a week by 2002
Work exemptions	No exemptions	Exemptions for mothers with children under 1 (children under 6 if unable to find child care); battered women	Exemptions for mothers with children under 1 (children under 6 if unable to find child care)
Incentives to meeting work requirements	Reductions in caseload unrelated to time limits reduce job-placement requirements	Job placement performance bonuses in 1998 (3% of block grant) and 1999 (4%); "high performance" bonuses	Employment quotas reduced if caseload is reduced; no job placement performance bonus; states most successful or improved in moving families from welfare to work could reduce 75% maintenance of effort requirement by up to 8%
Incentives to reducing illegitimacy	Bonuses for reducing illegitimate births without increasing abortions: 5% grant increase for 1% reduction, 10% for over 2% reduction compared with 1995	If abortion rates do not increase, $25/per child for states reducing illegitimacy rates by 1% compared with 1995 levels; $50 for 2% reduction	Same as House provisions

TABLE 4.1 *(cont.)*
SUMMARY OF WELFARE REFORM PROPOSALS, 1995

Issue	HR 4[a] House-passed Personal Responsibility Act (March 24, 1995)	HR[6] Senate-passed Work Opportunity Act (September 19, 1995)	"Personal Responsibility and Work Opportunity Act of 1995" (H.R. 4, H. Rept 104–430 (December 22, 1995)[c]
Teenage parents	Except in cases of rape or incest, aid denied to unwed teen mothers	Teens required to live in a supervised setting; must attend school unless mothers have a child less than 12 weeks old	Same as Senate provisions
Funding for children	Except for cases of rape or incest, no cash aid for children of unwed mothers under 18 or of mothers already on welfare for ten months; baby care vouchers given at state option	At state option, benefits denied to children of unwed mothers under 18 or of mothers already on welfare[g]	States must pass additional legislation in order to provide benefits for children born on welfare
Other eligibility restrictions	Out-of-state families to receive previous state benefit levels for up to twelve months; except in cases of rape or incest, monthly benefit penalty of up to 15% for not establishing paternity; noncooperating adults denied benefits; no aid for fugitive felons or those who break parole	"Interstate immigration" provision similar to House; recipients must help establish paternity	"Interstate immigration" provision similar to House and Senate; state option to deny full or partial payments if recipients fail to help establish paternity; no aid for fugitive felons or those who break parole

TABLE 4.1 *(cont.)*
SUMMARY OF WELFARE REFORM PROPOSALS, 1995

Issue	HR 4[a] House-passed Personal Responsibility Act (March 24, 1995)	HR[b] Senate-passed Work Opportunity Act (September 19, 1995)	"Personal Responsibility and Work Opportunity Act of 1995" (H.R. 4, H. Rept 104–430 (December 22, 1995)[c]
Child support enforcement	State and federal registries created; "new-hire" registries and Social Security numbers on all licenses required; recovered payments given to families	Same as House provisions; passports could be denied if unpaid support payments exceed $5,000; grandparents could be prosecuted	Same as Senate provisions
Legal and illegal aliens	Most legal immigrants ineligible for SSI, cash welfare, social services block grant funds, Medicaid and Food Stamps (one-year exemption for noncitizens currently receiving benefits; five-year exemption for refugees and those over 75; exemptions for the disabled and those with military service; sponsors legally bound to provide assistance	Most current noncitizens ineligible for SSI; ineligible for cash assistance and Food Stamps at state option; new immigrants ineligible for most low-income social services for five years; sponsor income deemed for a longer period; exceptions similar to House bill (battered women also exempted); eligibility restricted for new citizens	$15–22 billion saved in restrictions on aid; most noncitizens ineligible for SSI and Food Stamps; after Jan. 1, 1997, state option to provide block grant assistance to current legal immigrants; new immigrants ineligible for five years; exceptions for refugees, asylees, veterans and active duty military, and aliens who have worked at least forty calendar quarters; new citizens receive aid

TABLE 4.1 *(cont.)*
SUMMARY OF WELFARE REFORM PROPOSALS, 1995

Issue	HR 4[a] House-passed Personal Responsibility Act (March 24, 1995)	HR[6] Senate-passed Work Opportunity Act (September 19, 1995)	"Personal Responsibility and Work Opportunity Act of 1995" (H.R. 4, H. Rept 104–430 (December 22, 1995)[c]
Child welfare	Child Protection Block Grant replaced twenty-three programs including foster care, adoption assistance and child abuse prevention/treatment; mandatory maintenance of effort; up to 30% of funds could be transferred	Child Abuse Prevention and Treatment Act reauthorized; no block grants for child welfare services, foster care and adoption assistance	Child abuse prevention and treatment as well as adoption and foster care administration and funding folded in Child Protection Block Grant
Child care	Nine programs folded into capped Child Care and Development Block Grant; states could transfer up to 20% of this grant to other social services; no additional child care funds; federal health and safety regulations for child care repealed; no mandate to provide child care for AFDC recipients	Child Care and Development Block Grant totaling $11 billion; 100% maintenance of effort required; no transfers of grant funds; additional $3 billion in matching funds for child care over five years; health and safety standards retained	Child Care and Development Block Grant funded at $18 billion over seven years ($11 billion assured); no transfer of grant funds; additional $2 billion child care over five years; health and safety standards eliminated

TABLE 4.1 (cont.)
SUMMARY OF WELFARE REFORM PROPOSALS, 1995

Issue	HR 4[a] House-passed Personal Responsibility Act (March 24, 1995)	HR[6] Senate-passed Work Opportunity Act (September 19, 1995)	"Personal Responsibility and Work Opportunity Act of 1995" (H.R. 4, H. Rept 104–430 (December 22, 1995)[c]
Supplemental Security Income	Aid for children with behavioral disorders restricted, made into a block grant; future child recipients of SSI would have to require 24-hour care and might be given services only; impairment caused by drug or alcohol addiction no longer considered a disability	Aid for children with behavioral disorders restricted, but no block grant; future child recipients eligible for cash aid; impairment caused by drug or alcohol addiction no longer considered a disability; eligibility age for elderly raised to 67	$14 billion saved in cuts to aid for disabled children; eligibility for disabled children restricted; two levels of child benefits based on severity of injury; eligibility age for elderly raised to 67
Food Stamp benefits	Capped entitlement; benefits not indexed to inflation; benefits cashed out at state option; states with electronic benefit transfer systems have optional block grant	$24 billion saved in Food Stamp cuts; block grant at state option (revoked if hunger rate increases); state operation authority expanded; states could reserve up 10% annually; 6% cap on administrative spending	$26.2 billion saved in Food Stamp cuts (including cuts in immigrant aid, $31.6 billion over seven years); optional block grants for some states; states could reserve up to 10% annually; 6% cap on administrative spending
Food stamp eligibility	All able-bodied recipients aged 18–50 without dependents must find work or enroll in a training program within 90 days; penalties doubled for fraud	Able-bodied recipients aged 18–50 with no depen; dents lose benefits if unemployed for six months; penalties for fraud; battered women exempted; minors	Able-bodied recipients aged 18–50 with no dependents lose benefits if unemployed for four months; penalties for fraud

TABLE 4.1 *(cont.)*
SUMMARY OF WELFARE REFORM PROPOSALS, 1995

Issue	HR 4[a] House-passed Personal Responsibility Act (March 24, 1995)	HR[6] Senate-passed Work Opportunity Act (September 19, 1995)	"Personal Responsibility and Work Opportunity Act of 1995" (H.R. 4, H. Rept 104–430 (December 22, 1995)[c]
Food stamp eligibility *(cont.)*		living at home must apply for Food Stamps with their parents	
Nutrition and social services	Family Nutrition Block Grant and School-Based Nutrition Block Grant replace many programs, including school lunch, that provide nutritional assistance for pregnant women, infants, and children	School lunch program left intact (no block grant); food subsidies reduced; social services block grant reduced by 20%	Cuts in child nutrition programs; seven state demonstration project for a school lunch block grant; social services block grant reduced by 10%
Medicaid	Medicaid eligibility frozen to current AFDC rules	Medicaid coverage maintained for pregnant women and children under 13; twelve-month transitional coverage	Medicaid coverage not guaranteed for welfare recipients; states permitted to determine eligibility; no guarantee of twelve-month transitional Medicaid[h]
Earned Income Tax Credit	Repeals mandatory EITC disregard; EITC reduced by $23 billion	Repeals mandatory EITC disregard; EITC reduced by $43 billion	Repeals mandatory EITC disregard[i]
Status	Passed 234–199 March 24, 1995	Passed 87–12 September 19, 1995[j]	Passed the Senate 52–47 December 22, 1995; vetoed January 9, 1996[k]

[a] Originally designated H.R. 1214. The House bill sought to "restore the American family, reduce illegitimacy, control welfare spending and reduce welfare dependence."

[b] Formerly designated S. Report 104-96. The Senate sought "to enhance support and work opportunities for families with children, reduce welfare dependence, and control welfare spending."

[c] Congress included its first attempt to enact welfare reform in the budget reconciliation bill (H.R. 2491) it passed on November 17, 1995. This bill was vetoed by Clinton on December 6, 1995. Congress revised the welfare provisions of the bill slightly and sent a stand-alone welfare overhaul (H.R. 4, H. Rep. 104-430) to the White House in late December 1995. That bill was vetoed on January 9, 1996. The conference agreement listed the following as its goals: "To restore the American family, enhance support and work opportunities for families with children, reduce out-of-wedlock pregnancies, reduce welfare dependence, and control welfare spending."

[d] Provisions in the budget reconciliation bill called for an $81.5 billion reduction over five years.

[e] Those who received benefits as minors could apply for benefits as heads of households and not be penalized in terms of the time limit.

[f] Battered women could qualify for exemption at state option.

[g] The Senate bill also attempted to address illegitimate births by including funds for "abstinence education."

[h] The budget reconciliation bill Medicaid provisions were intended to save $170 billion over seven years by making Medicaid a block grant that guaranteed medical coverage only for pregnant women and those under thirteen. The Administration's proposal differed by $80 billion in Medicare/Medicaid proposals; Clinton opposed ending the health care entitlement.

[i] The November budget reconciliation bill would have reduced the EITC by $32 billion over seven years. The Administration was opposed to such a cut.

[j] Subsequent Health and Human Services analysis indicated that the five-year limit would impoverish 1.5 million children; future bills with similar provisions had fewer Democratic supporters.

[k] Clinton objected to deep budget cuts; cuts in programs for foster care and adoption assistance; decreased aid to disabled children, legal immigrants, and food stamp recipients; and tampering with the school lunch program.

Sources: "Welfare Side by Side," 141 *Cong. Rec.* S. 19156 (December 22, 1995); "Conference Report on H.R. 4, Personal Responsibility and Work Opportunity Act of 1995," 141 *Cong. Rec.* H. 15317 (December 21, 1995).

levels and requirements placed on states, but they did not alter the basic framework. The Republican largely kept control of the agenda. The Republican governors had played a major role in getting policy devolution. President Clinton focused on funding levels and used his veto to push for modest changes, but the process was dominated by the Republican congressional leaders.[45]

WELFARE REFORM REBORN

In January 1996, welfare reform appeared dead after the second Clinton veto. The president's strategy of continuing to support the idea of welfare reform while rejecting Republican efforts as extremist was to most observers' surprise politically successful. As 1996 began, President Clinton was bold and confident, Republicans discouraged and withdrawn. It was a remarkable political comeback for the president, and Republicans were particularly frustrated with their failure to enact the agenda outlined in the "Contract with America."

All fifty governors tried to resurrect welfare in February 1996 by issuing a welfare reform proposal based on three principles: Welfare must be temporary and linked to work, both parents must support their children, and child care must be available to enable low-income families with children to work. Their proposal started with the conference bill that Clinton had vetoed in January and made a few modest changes. It reaffirmed block grants with broad discretion and supplemental funds for emergencies. The proposal also suggested an additional $4 billion in child care funds, cash bonuses to states that met employment targets, a family cap, and a hardship exception for 20 percent of the caseload from the five-year limit in participation.[46] Critics of the governors' proposal argued that it would increase federal funds going to states but would allow states to spend less of their own resources on welfare and allow states to transfer up to 30 percent of their welfare block grants to other programs. The proposal would also cut other benefits such as Food Stamps.[47] President Clinton, in turn, endorsed the governors' welfare ideas but indicated additional changes were required before he would support the bill.

In the spring of 1996, Republicans were caught in a dilemma. The fall of Speaker Gingrich from his dominant position of agenda setter and the selection of Bob Dole as Republican presidential candidate put the Senate majority leader in charge. Dole could refuse to send a welfare bill to Clinton, then criticize him for having vetoed the two bills the Congress sent to him. Or he could get Congress to pass a bill that Clinton would likely veto, take credit for gaining passage, and then use the veto to highlight differences. Could Dole show that he was a get-things-done kind of leader and also stand up to Clinton? He and other Republican leaders began work in the spring of 1996 on a new welfare bill based on the governors' February proposal, but Clinton was not their only challenge. All the governors demanded that Medicaid and welfare reform proceed in tandem, raising fears of public backlash against cuts in health care.[48] Welfare reform was also folded into efforts to raise the minimum wage. Republican leaders, facing strong support for raising the minimum wage from the White House, congressional Democrats, moderate Republicans, and the public, explored adding Medicaid and welfare reform to the proposal.[49] In the meantime, President Clinton ordered the Federal government to end welfare payments to teenage mothers who quit school or refused to live with their parents. Although twenty states already had such a policy in effect, it was a politically potent way to reinforce the president's interest in reforming welfare.[50]

Welfare policy proposals proceeded in fits and starts through the spring of 1996 and the beginning of the 1996 presidential election season. One week there would be a flurry of proposals launched, followed by weeks of inaction. On May 18, 1996, in his weekly radio broadcast, the president praised the Wisconsin welfare reform initiative. The Wisconsin initiative required about forty waivers from existing federal requirements, and the president promised that his administration would quickly review them. The waivers would be reviewed during a thirty-day public comment period that began in mid-June; an administration official predicted that they would be granted "shortly" thereafter.[51] But the president did not promise to grant the waiver, he only said that he was "encouraged by what I've seen so far" and promised to work with Wisconsin "to make an effective transition to a new vision of welfare based on work, that protects children and does right by working people and their families." This prompted Bob Dole to complain that the president "didn't say he would actually grant the waiver," that it was simply another attempt to claim credit for supporting welfare reform without actually approving any real changes. Bickering over the waiver process continued. Clinton boasted of the waivers granted to 38 states while Dole objected that "every time it's had the opportunity in other states, the Clinton Administration has blocked firm time limits on welfare, the heart of the Wisconsin plan, and of any serious plan to end welfare as we know it." Mark H. Greenberg, a senior staff attorney with the Center for Law and Social Policy, argued that the administration had approved waivers for virtually everything the states had asked for; it insisted only that states continue to provide assistance to recipients who had complied with all requirements and had tried to find a job but were unable to do so.[52]

The White House and Congress traded volleys for two weeks, demonstrating the critical importance of welfare policy in presidential politics, but also the difficulty in knowing how it would play out in the minds of voters. The president's May 18 radio address was planned to divert attention from a speech to be given three days later by Bob Dole in which he promised to outline his position on welfare reform. Dole's May 21 speech called for state discretion to require work after two years or sooner, to deny benefits to unwed teenage parents, to deny all but emergency assistance to immigrants, and to set a five-year lifetime limit on benefits, with few exemptions. Two days later, Clinton challenged Dole to pass his welfare proposal before he retired from the Senate to pursue the presidency full-time.[53]

On May 22, the House Republicans announced their new welfare bill, which was coupled with their Medicaid proposal. The issues were the same, but new compromises between the factions within the party had been struck: The bill would replace AFDC with a block grant, require states to spend on welfare at least 75 percent of what they had spent in the past, allowed states to deny benefits to children born to mothers on welfare, require work within two years, and require states to place in jobs at least 50 percent of their caseload by 2002. A number of related provisions were included in the welfare reform bill, such as tightening eligibility for children applying for Supplemental Security Income, requiring states to create a tracking system for child-support orders and suspending the driver's license of deadbeat parents, and making legal immigrants ineligible for SSI and Food Stamps until they became citizens or had worked for at least ten years. Medicaid would be transformed under the bill into a block grant to states that would permit them to develop their own health insurance program for low-income persons; spending on Medicaid would be reduced by $72 billion from projected spending levels in 1997 to 2002. Welfare spending would be cut $53 billion.[54]

The day after the new Republican bill was introduced, President Clinton praised the House leaders for introducing a bill that "abandoned most of their extreme positions" and promised to signed a bill that included such provisions.[55] On June 5, the House Ways and Means Subcommittee passed its welfare-Medicaid reform bill. On June 6, the House tried to embarrass the president by passing a measure by a 288–136 vote (including yea votes by sixty Democrats) that ordered the administration to approve the Wisconsin waiver requests.

Once Bob Dole resigned from the Senate to devote full time to his presidential bid, the new majority leader, Trent Lott (R.-Miss.), began pushing conferees to complete their work. He and other Republican leaders sought a hard-line bill that remained close to the House version. Bob Dole's campaign also urged an aggressive bill that would permit Republicans to claim that they either forced the president to sign their bill or to veto it, giving Dole a strong campaign issue. In July, congressional leaders bowed to pressure from members and dropped Medicaid provisions from the welfare reform bill. Clinton hailed the bill as close to gaining his support, but opposed several measures: the ban on aid to legal immigrants, cuts in food stamp benefits, and ineligibility for aid for individuals convicted of a drug-related felony.[56] On July 31, the House passed the conference bill, and Clinton announced that he would sign it; the Senate passed the bill on August 1. Table 4.2 summarizes the evolution of welfare reform legislation in 1996.[57]

TABLE 4.2
SUMMARY OF WELFARE REFORM PROPOSALS, 1996

Issue	National Governors' Association Proposal (February 1996)[a]	HR 3734 (July 18, 1996)[b]	Senate bill (July 23, 1996)[c]	"Personal Responsibility and Work Opportunity Reconciliation Act of 1996" (HR 3734-H Report 104-725) (August 1, 1996)[d]
Projected Savings	$43.3 billion over seven years	$60 billion over six years	$56.3 billion over six years (before amendments)	$55 billion over six years
Program structure and funding	Entitlement ended; money dispersed in block grants	Entitlement ended; money dispersed to states in capped block grants	Entitlement ended; money dispersed to states in block grants	Entitlement ended; $16.4 billion annual block grant[d]
State maintenance of effort/distribution options	States must pay at least 75% of 1994 benefit levels; 80% if they failed to meet work requirements; state option to transfer up to 30% of cash assistance to other social programs (child care, child protection, social services)	States pay at least 75% of 1994 benefit levels; 80% if states fail to meet work participation requirements ($1 reduction in funding for each $1 states fail to match); 15% cap on administrative spending (technology exempted); up to 30% of grant could be transferred to social programs that benefit children and families	States pay at least 80% of 1994 benefit levels; 15% cap on administrative spending (technology exempted); up to 30% of grant could be transferred to child care programs; funds may be used to set up individual development accounts	Same as House provisions except funds could not be transferred to child-protection programs and must be spent on poor families; funds could be spent on individual development accounts

TABLE 4.2 *(cont.)*
SUMMARY OF WELFARE REFORM PROPOSALS, 1996

Issue	National Governors' Association Proposal (February 1996)[a]	HR 3734 (July 18, 1996)[b]	Senate bill (July 23, 1996)[c]	"Personal Responsibility and Work Opportunity Reconciliation Act of 1996" (HR 3734-H Report 104-725) (August 1, 1996)
Additional funding sources	$2 billion contingency fund with no matching constraints	$800 million for states with high population growth and low benefit levels $2 billion contingency fund over five years (available if states maintain 100% spending); $1.7 billion revolving loan fund; $3 billion grant in 1999 to fund state work programs	$800 million over four years for states with high population growth and low benefit levels; $2 billion contingency fund over four years; $1.7 billion revolving loan fund	$800 million over four years for states with growing populations and low benefits; $2 billion over five years in a matching grant contingency fund; $1.7 billion over five years in revolving loans
Time limits	Five-year lifetime benefit limit; 20% caseload exemption for hardship	Five-year lifetime benefit limit that could be extended with state funds; 20% caseload exemption for hardship; abused individuals could be exempted	Five-year lifetime benefit limit; states could legislate tougher limits; 20% caseload exemption for hardship; some Native Americans exempted[e]	Five-year lifetime benefit limit; limits extended or shortened at state option; 20% caseload exemption for hardship; some Native Americans and abused individuals exempted[f]

TABLE 4.2 (cont.)
SUMMARY OF WELFARE REFORM PROPOSALS, 1996

Issue	National Governors' Association Proposal (February 1996)[a]	HR 3734 (July 18, 1996)[b]	Senate bill (July 23, 1996)[c]	"Personal Responsibility and Work Opportunity Reconciliation Act of 1996" (HR 3734-H Report 104-725) (August 1, 1996)
Work requirements	Mandatory participation in work activities within two years	Mandatory participation in work activities within two years; 25% of single-parent caseload working by 1997, 50% by 2002; 50% of two-parent families working by 1996, 90% by 1999; mandatory responsibility contracts for those without high school diplomas	Same work requirements as House; mandatory personal responsibility contracts for entire caseload	Same work requirements as House and Senate; state option to mandate community service after two months; mandatory personal responsibility contract for those without a high school diploma
Work definition	For parents with child under 6, 20 hours a week; for other parents, 25 hours a week; job search and job training acceptable for 12 weeks	Private- or public-sector employment, work experience, OJT, job search for eight weeks (four consecutive) community service, or vocational educational training (regardless of	Same work definition as the House, except all postsecondary education permitted for up to twenty-four months for those under age 20; job search permitted for four weeks (or	Same work definition as the House; job search for six weeks (twelve in areas of high unemployment); for single parents, 20 hours a week in 1996 and 30 hours a week by 2000;

TABLE 4.2 (*cont.*)
SUMMARY OF WELFARE REFORM PROPOSALS, 1996

Issue	National Governors' Association Proposal (February 1996)[a]	HR 3734 (July 18, 1996)[b]	Senate bill (July 23, 1996)[c]	"Personal Responsibility and Work Opportunity Reconciliation Act of 1996" (HR 3734–H Report 104-725) (August 1, 1996)
Work definition (cont.)		age, twelve-month maximum); For single parents, 20 hours a week in 1996, 30 hours a week in 2000; for two-parent households, 35 hours a week; only 20% of caseload in training at one time	twelve in areas of high unemployment); single parents must work 35 hours a week by 2002; only 30% of caseload in training at one time	for two-parent families, 35 hours a week; only 20% of caseload in training at one time
Work exemptions	Exemptions for parents with children under 1	Single parents with children under 1 at state option; parents with children under 11 could work 20 hours a week	Single parents with children under 1 at state option (exempted for a total of twelve months); parents with children under 11 could work 20 hours a week	Single parents with a child under age 1 exempted for total of twelve months at state option; single parents with children under 6 who could not find child care; parents with a child under 6 could work 20 hours a week at state discretion; second parent exempted if caring for severely disabled child

TABLE 4.2 (*cont.*)
SUMMARY OF WELFARE REFORM PROPOSALS, 1996

Issue	National Governors' Association Proposal (February 1996)[a]	HR 3734 (July 18, 1996)[b]	Senate bill (July 23, 1996)[c]	"Personal Responsibility and Work Opportunity Reconciliation Act of 1996" (HR 3734-H Report 104-725) (August 1, 1996)
Incentives to meeting work requirements	5% annual bonus for states that exceeded employment quotas; work placement mandates reduced in proportion to caseload reductions	$0.5 billion over five years and lowered maintenance of effort requirements for "high-performance" states; job placement requirements lowered for states with reduced caseloads	$1 billion over four years for "high-performance" states; participation requirements reduced for caseload reductions	$1 billion over four years for states with high job placement rates
Incentives to reducing illegitimacy	Bonuses for reducing illegitimate births	In 1998, bonuses for reduced out-of-wedlock births without increased abortions: 5% grant increase for 1% reduction compared with 1995, 10% increase for 2% reduction	Same as House provisions; $20 million annual grants in 1999–2003 for the five states with greatest reductions in "illegitimacy ratios"	Same as Senate provisions, except funds available between 1999 and 2002
Teenage parents		Benefits denied to unwed parents under 18 not living with an adult and not attending school	Same as House provisions	Same as House and Senate provisions

TABLE 4.2 (*cont.*)

SUMMARY OF WELFARE REFORM PROPOSALS, 1996

Issue	National Governors' Association Proposal (February 1996)[a]	HR 3734 (July 18, 1996)[b]	Senate bill (July 23, 1996)[c]	"Personal Responsibility and Work Opportunity Reconciliation Act of 1996" (HR 3734-H Report 104-725) (August 1, 1996)
Funding for additional children	Benefits denied to children born to mothers on welfare at state option	Benefits denied to children born on welfare unless states pass contrary legislation; grant funds could be used for baby-care vouchers	State option to deny benefits to children born on welfare	State option to deny benefits to children born on welfare
Other eligibility restrictions		Out-of-state families could receive previous state benefit levels for up to twelve months; full or partial benefits denied for failing to help establish paternity; fugitive felons or parole violators denied benefits	"Interstate immigration" provisions same as House; 25% reduction in (or elimination of) benefits for failing to help establish paternity; benefits denied for adults without diplomas not attending school; minor children must attend school; all means-tested programs denied to those convicted of drug felonies and misdemeanors	"Interstate immigration," paternity and school attendance requirements some as Senate provisions; cash aid and Food Stamps denied to those convicted of drug felonies (pregnant women, adults intreatment exempted)

TABLE 4.2 (*cont.*)
SUMMARY OF WELFARE REFORM PROPOSALS, 1996

Issue	National Governors' Association Proposal (February 1996)[a]	HR 3734 (July 18, 1996)[b]	Senate bill (July 23, 1996)[c]	"Personal Responsibility and Work Opportunity Reconciliation Act of 1996" (HR 3734-H Report 104-725) (August 1, 1996)
Child support enforcement/paternity establishment	Stronger enforcement recommended	State and federal automated registries created, including "new hire" registries to facilitate wage garnishing; state option to suspend licenses of delinquent parents; passports withheld from parents owing more than $5000; state option to prosecute grandparents	Same as House provisions	Same as House and Senate provisions
Legal and illegal aliens	No position	Illegal/visiting aliens denied all but emergency medical benefits; current legal immigrants denied SSI, Food Stamps, and Medicaid for ten years or until citizens; state option to deny other	State option to deny Medicaid to legal immigrants; other provisions similar to House bill	Same as Senate provisions

TABLE 4.2 *(cont.)*
SUMMARY OF WELFARE REFORM PROPOSALS, 1996

Issue	National Governors' Association Proposal (February 1996)[a]	HR 3734 (July 18, 1996)[b]	Senate bill (July 23, 1996)[c]	"Personal Responsibility and Work Opportunity Reconciliation Act of 1996" (HR 3734-H Report 104-725) (August 1, 1996)
Legal and illegal aliens (cont.)		assistance after January 1, 1997; no child nutrition aid for illegal immigrants; new legal immigrants denied most federal social services for five years; refugees, veterans, and those granted asylum exempted; sponsor income deemed for eligibility for most public services		
Child welfare	State option to make foster care, adoption assistance and independent living capped entitlements and to fold child welfare and child abuse programs into a block grant; states must maintain protections and standards	Foster care and adoption remained entitlement; eleven child protection programs folded into block grant; same-race adoptions not given preference	No changes in child welfare programs	[House child-protection block grant and adoption proposals dropped]

TABLE 4.2 (cont.)
SUMMARY OF WELFARE REFORM PROPOSALS, 1996

Issue	National Governors' Association Proposal (February 1996)[a]	HR 3734 (July 18, 1996)[b]	Senate bill (July 23, 1996)[c]	"Personal Responsibility and Work Opportunity Reconciliation Act of 1996" (HR 3734-H Report 104-725) (August 1, 1996)
Child care	$15 billion over seven years ($4 billion added to original proposals)	Seven programs folded into the Child Care and Development Block Grant; guaranteed federal funding totaling $15 billion by 2002; $1 billion discretionary funding each year; 70% of funding mandated to benefit welfare or at-risk families; states must maintain 1995 spending levels	Same as House provisions	Same as House and Senate provisions
Earned Income Tax Credit	Savings limited to $10 billion; state option to advance the EITC	EITC income must be disregarded; funding cut by $1.75 billion	Cut by $5 billion	No substantial changes; eligibility somewhat narrowed by disregarding less income and not recognizing some losses

TABLE 4.2 (cont.)

SUMMARY OF WELFARE REFORM PROPOSALS, 1996

Issue	National Governors' Association Proposal (February 1996)[a]	HR 3734 (July 18, 1996)[b]	Senate bill (July 23, 1996)[c]	"Personal Responsibility and Work Opportunity Reconciliation Act of 1996" (HR 3734-H Report 104-725) (August 1, 1996)
Supplemental Security Income	Accepts the provisions regarding children in the September 1995 Senate-passed bill; changes effective January 1, 1998; raised eligibility age from 65 to 67	Child "disabilities" must be expected to cause death or to pro'duce marked and severe functional limitation for more than twelve months; incentives for identifying fraudulent SSI collection by prisoners; recipients convicted of fraud denied benefits for ten years	Provisions similar to House	Provisions similar to House and Senate; 12% cut in overall funding
Food Stamp benefits	Uncapped block grant option; cuts $26 billion	Formulas reworked, benefits cut; penalties for fraud doubled; block grants an option for some states	Formulas reworked, benefits cut; penalties for fraud doubled; no block grant	No block grant; 13% spending cuts by 2002 ($24 billion, plus $3 billion in reduced aid to immigrants); entitlement indexed to inflation

TABLE 4.2 (cont.)
SUMMARY OF WELFARE REFORM PROPOSALS, 1996

Issue	National Governors' Association Proposal (February 1996)[a]	HR 3734 (July 18, 1996)[b]	Senate bill (July 23, 1996)[c]	"Personal Responsibility and Work Opportunity Reconciliation Act of 1996" (HR 3734-H Report 104-725) (August 1, 1996)
Food Stamp eligibility	Able-bodied recipients aged 18–50 lose benefits if unemployed for four months	Minors living at home must apply for Food Stamps with their parents; benefits denied for voluntary failure to work 30 hours a week; three-month lifetime benefit limit for unemployed (20 hours a week) able-bodied recipients aged 18–50 (exceptions in areas of high unemployment)	Most provisions same as House; benefits limited to six months each year if unemployed able-bodied recipients aged 18–50 without dependents searched for a job in at least two of those months; 20% adult caseload hardship exemption	Most provisions same as House and Senate; benefits limited to three months in any three-year period for unemployed able-bodied recipients aged 18–50 without dependents (three-month extension if recently laid off)
Nutrition and social services	School lunches remain entitlement; administrative costs in block grant; cuts in subsidized food for child care	[Nutrition, social service programs dropped from reform efforts]		

TABLE 4.2 (*cont.*)

SUMMARY OF WELFARE REFORM PROPOSALS, 1996

Issue	National Governors' Association Proposal (February 1996)[a]	HR 3734 (July 18, 1996)[b]	Senate bill (July 23, 1996)[c]	"Personal Responsibility and Work Opportunity Reconciliation Act of 1996" (HR 3734-H Report 104-725) (August 1, 1996)
Medicaid	Block grant; elgibility guaranteed for poor children under 12; umbrella fund for emergencies no right to sue the government	Full-scale reform not included in bill; mandatory one-year transitional Medicaid for families newly ineligible because of earnings; four-month transitional funding for families ineligible because of marriage or increased child support; coverage for all those previously covered under AFDC	Same as House provisions	Same as Senate provisions; transitional Medicaid extended throughout the life of the block grant; state option to deny Medicaid to those not meeting work requirements
Status	Released to Congress, February 6, 1996[g]	Passed 256–170, July 18, 1996[h]	Passed 72–24, July 23, 1996	Passed House 328–101, July 31, 1996; passed Senate 78–21, August 1, 1996[i]

[a] The governors' proposal includes provisions for raising the administrative cap on child care funds and requiring states to establish criteria for providing fair and equitable treatment and delivery of benefits.

[b] The House bill's goals included promoting responsible fatherhood and motherhood, preventing out-of-wedlock pregnancy, and reducing out-of-wedlock birth.

[c] The Senate agreed with the House on the issues of marriage and illegitimate births, but added that "teenage pregnancy must deal with the issue of male responsibility, including statutory rape culpability and prevention" and that "protection of teenage girls from pregnancy as well as predatory sexual behavior" was very important.

[d] The block grant, Temporary Assistance for Needy Families, replaced AFDC and several related programs. States must convert to block grants by July 1, 1997, although state welfare reform demonstration waivers granted before October 1996 could remain in effect until they expired. States must comply with bill provisions not included in their waivers.

[e] A state's basic block grant would be reduced by 5 percent if it failed to comply with the time limit.

[f] Failure to comply with the time limit would cost states 5 percent of their basic federal grant. States could use funds from the Social Services Block Grant to provide noncash vouchers for children whose parents exceed the five-year benefit limit. The bill reduces this block grant by 15 percent.

[g] The main points of contention with the governors' proposal included the following: Allowing states to define "disabled"; eliminating options to sue under Medicaid coverage; providing inadequate medical coverage for the young and needy; making Food Stamps an entitlement; not addressing illegitimate births; and linking welfare to Medicaid reform. Overall, the governors' proposal provides billions more in federal funds and allows states to withdraw substantial state funding. The proposal cuts more in Food Stamps, Medicaid, child protection, and child nutrition than the fall 1995 Senate bill did.

[h] Clinton's main points of contention with the House bill were the following: denying Medicaid to noncitizens; cutting back Food Stamps and aid to legal immigrants; smaller contingency funds; and eliminating vouchers for children after their parents reach the time limit. Interestingly, although both the Senate and the House were vigorously opposed to using welfare block grant funds for vouchers, most state waivers make explicit provisions for children if their parents are cut from the AFDC rolls because of a time limit.

[i] Clinton remained opposed to deep cuts in Food Stamps and aid to legal immigrants. The administration, however, was pleased that final legislation did not affect Medicaid as an entitlement or attempt radical changes in foster care and adoption, school meals, or nutritional assistance for pregnant women and young children. In addition, Food Stamps remained an entitlement, and efforts to reduce EITC eligibility sharply were abandoned.

Source: "Conference Report on H.R. 3734, Personal Responsibility and Work Opportunity Reconciliation Act of 1996," 141 *Cong. Rec.*, H. 8829 (July 30, 1996).

Welfare reform was part of a flurry of legislation passed during the end of the 104th Congress in July, just before the August recess and party conventions. The Republicans generally got their way on welfare reform, but Democrats got a new minimum-wage bill, and both parties got a modest health care bill.

WHY DID WELFARE REFORM ULTIMATELY PASS?

Political cartoons captured much of the welfare reform debate between 1994 and 1996, as shown by the two examples on the following pages. But the story deserves additional discussion in three parts: state politics, congressional politics, and presidential politics.

STATE POLITICS   One of the most difficult challenges in fashioning a compromise welfare bill was the question of funding the block grant. Some thirty senators from large, high-growth states formed a coalition to lobby Republican leaders for increasing the size of the block grant. Governors had been very influential in shaping the welfare reform bill; they accepted the tradeoff of more state financial responsibility for more discretion, but some began to express worries about inadequate funding and criticized the final House and Senate bills. That provoked a mocking response from House Budget Committee chair John R. Kasich (R.-Ohio):

> It is not unexpected that Governors will say, "Oh, woe is me, look how tough this is going to be." But this bill was put together with the full knowledge and full support of the Republican governors. I think the governors ought to just stop bellyaching because we gave them the great opportunity to participate in this. . . . Get on with it."[58]

The House Republican welfare reform bill introduced in February 1995 abandoned the ambitious work requirement in the "Contract with America." Governors pressured members to reduce the work mandate and give them the flexibility to impose less costly requirements, such as education and job searching activities. The bill required that only 2 percent of recipients be involved in "work activities" by 1996 and that 20 percent be involved by 2003. States could meet those goals by counting the number of recipients already working part time (an average of 6 percent) and the 5 percent currently working under the JOBS program created in the 1988 welfare reform law. States would be free to define what constituted work activities. Unlike the Contract's earmarking of $9.9 billion in new money to pay for welfare reform, the

House bill included no new funding. States were to require work activities after two years, but no penalties were included. House Republicans and governors traded meager block grants and an end to funding teenage mothers for state flexibility and autonomy in work requirements.[59]

Block grants became a central element of the Republican 1995 welfare reform bill. They were touted as the way to tailor welfare policy to local conditions and concerns and to free state officials from meddlesome federal bureaucrats. Block grants would give states the opportunity to pursue innovative solutions to welfare, producing efficient and effective policies. Perhaps most important, they were a symbolic reflection of the recognition that states are sovereign entities rather than administrative arms of the federal government. But not everyone embraces block grants with enthusiasm. States already had considerable discretion under the old law to determine at what income level their residents are eligible for welfare and the size of the monthly AFDC

check, and could get waivers from the Federal government for state experiments. Block grants lock in levels of Federal payments to states; in a recession, states would not receive additional funds to meet increased needs. Block grants may shrink federal bureaucracies, but state agencies may take their place, with fewer opportunities for the efficiency that comes from economies of scale. State agencies may be more susceptible to political pressure. The more freedom states are given in how they can spend their block grants, the greater the chance of a "race to the bottom" among states who want to discourage welfare recipients from coming to or staying in their state by pushing benefits or participation downward and using the funds for more popular purposes.[60]

In converting the federal AFDC entitlement to a block grant, the 1995 House bill would give states more flexibility in providing AFDC and other social services. However, states could face problems if the number of needy families increases, since the lump-sum payment was to be frozen at the 1994 Federal spending level. The amount of funding for child care was also frozen in the bill at a level below current federal payments to states, despite the assumption that child care needs would expand as more welfare recipients were required to work. State governors like George Voinovich (R.-Ohio) were caught in a bind: As loyal Republicans, they were to support the party's national welfare reform initiative, but as welfare reformers, they knew that moving from welfare to work requires more spending.[61]

The Contract's welfare plank would ban AFDC and housing payments to single mothers under 18 and permit states to ban them for those 20 and younger; children of teen mothers would also be banned for life from receiving welfare. The Contract would also have ended AFDC, housing assistance, the Supplemental Security Income (SSI) program, and Food Stamps and other nutrition programs as entitlements by placing a cap on spending. The cuts to SSI seem particularly harsh. Unlike welfare, that program is limited to those who cannot work because of disabilities. There is some debate over what constitutes a disability, but cutting the benefits of truly disabled persons and leaving them to fend for themselves would be widely viewed as unacceptable.

The key question in 1996 became how to get the Republicans to support with money real welfare reform. Part of the problem was that Democrats were split; Senate Democrats favored requiring welfare recipients to take "real jobs," not workfare, whereas the Clinton administration continued to favor community service jobs as a last resort.[62] There appeared to be room for compromise here, but Republicans used the criticisms of one option or the other to justify their budget cuts: Since any proposal to reform welfare would have its critics, why spend any more money on something that might not work? Better to cut our losses and claim welfare reform through requirements that appear to impose obligations but will not be enforced.

The welfare debate in the Senate turned right, in part, as a result of then–presidential candidate and senator Phil Gramm's proposal to ban cash assistance to noncitizens, teenage mothers who have illegitimate children, mothers who refuse to establish their children's paternity, and children born to welfare mothers. He also pushed for converting most federal poverty programs into block grants.[63]

Governors played an important role in the formation of the specific welfare reform bills, because of the Republicans' interest in state government as a way to reduce the size of the national government. Many Republicans are not antigovernment but only opposed to national government; they are quite interested in state governments' having the power to shape community norms and values. Democrats, in contrast, are less committed to that kind of conservative government and prefer the less normative national power. But Bill Clinton's history of involvement in welfare reform as a governor contributed to the deference given to governors.

CONGRESSIONAL POLITICS   By the summer of 1996, the Republicans had largely failed to enact the Contract with America. During 1995, Congress was able to enact laws that subjected its members to the same laws applicable to private-sector employers, made it more difficult to impose unfunded mandates on states, and increased defense spending. The balanced budget constitutional amendment, the line-item veto, term limits, welfare reform, tax cuts for families, the capital gains tax cuts, tax credit for adopting children, tougher death-penalty provisions, and limits on punitive damages in product-liability and medical-malpractice lawsuits all failed.

Why did the Republican juggernaut, which appeared so formidable during the first one hundred days, fail? The Senate declined to pass many of the bills that were pushed through the House. House and Senate Republicans were sometimes unable to broker differences that arose in conference committees when bills did get through the Senate. Senate leaders gave priority to the regulatory reform bill, but then failed to break a filibuster by Democrats. By the fall of 1995, GOP leadership was forced to halt virtually all other efforts to conduct the budget negotiations.

Even within the House, the leadership failed to keep Republicans together after the first one hundred days. The coalition of libertarians, the Christian right, fiscal conservatives, balance-the-budget-at-all-costs freshmen, and moderate Republicans in the House splintered once most of the bills that sprang from the Contract with America were voted on and the agenda turned to more controversial issues. Moderate Republicans bolted and joined Democrats to defeat appropriations bills that were too heavily laden with riders aimed at preventing enforcement of environmental laws and other measures that dealt with sensitive social issues such as abortion.[64]

The House Republicans greatly contributed to public skepticism and cynicism through their unabashed probusiness initiatives. House Majority Whip Tom DeLay kept a book in his office listing how much the four hundred largest PACs gave to Republicans and Democrats during the past two years. House leaders have created their own PACs to funnel money to the reelection campaigns of loyal Republican members.

Rep. John Boeher, chair of the Republican Conference, coordinated efforts among interest groups to raise money in support of the provisions in the "Contract with America."[65] In 1994, Democrats received about two-thirds of the contributions made by the largest PACs; in 1995, Republicans had received nearly 60 percent.[66]

The access given in return to lobbyists was remarkable, even by Washington standards. Lobbyists were invited to write bills and sit with committee members in hearings.[67] A Senate Banking Committee staff member drafted a bill long sought by the securities industry after he had accepted a job with a banking and securities firm. Other people who worked for securities firms were also involved in writing the bill.[68] Journalists described lobbyists ensconced in rooms next to the House Chamber, tapping out on their laptops talking points for Republican members to use in floor debates. Industry lobbyists helped write the House regulatory moratorium bill.[69]

Republican-proposed spending cuts also contributed to the stalling of the revolution. Most cuts were aimed at Democratic constituents—the poor, mothers on welfare, recipients of Medicaid and Medicare. The cuts were not extended to programs of interest to Republicans, such as home-mortgage deductions for second homes, subsidies to corporations, Social Security payments to wealthy citizens that represent several times the amount they contributed to the Social Security system, or the other $200 billion worth of grants and tax breaks that go to Americans who earn more than $50,000 a year.[70] The House Republican Medicare reform proposal was widely criticized for buying off doctors and other groups in exchange for their support. The tax cuts the Republicans proposed primarily benefitted wealthy taxpayers; the taxes to be increased, through a reduction in the Earned Income Tax Credit, fell on the working poor.[71] Special tax breaks were aimed at the funeral industry, convenience store owners, research and experimentation tax credit for businesses, insurance companies, truckers, newspaper publishers, natural-gas and water utilities, and other interests that had close ties to influential members or had made major campaign contributions. Republicans were quick to identify their own list of corporate tax loopholes they were proposing to close, but failed to disclose the many provisions that would benefit wealthy taxpayers.[72]

Considerable closure appeared between the White House and congressional Republican positions on welfare reform. Both sides appeared to agree on requiring work within two years of receiving benefits, capping lifetime participation at five years, and increasing child care funding for working parents. Differences centered on at least three demands by the Clinton administration: more exemptions to be granted to the five-year limit on lifetime benefits, state obligation to continue assistance to recipients beyond the two-year limit if they had made real effort to find a job but were unable to do so, and guaranteed Medicaid benefits to recipients who moved into the work force.[73]

But not everyone else was so close to compromise. The Wisconsin plan was clearly the most dramatic welfare proposal to be considered by states. It ended welfare as an entitlement, required recipients to work, made available jobs to those who tried unsuccessfully to find work, provided child and health care during the transition to work period, and limited lifetime eligibility to five years. Liberals attacked the Wisconsin initiative because it provided the same benefit to families regardless of size and ended the commitment to welfare as an entitlement. Conservatives complained that the program encouraged mothers to work and to send their children to "impersonal" child care providers rather than to encourage the formation of two-parent families.[74] Broader differences also surfaced. Administration officials and congressional Democrats voiced opposition to deep cuts in spending on welfare, Food Stamps, and benefits for legal immigrants. Some Democratic governors complained that the Medicaid proposal reduced the amount, scope, and coverage of health insurance for the poor to an unacceptable level.

Probably more important than these policy differences were the political calculations. Moderates in both parties seemed anxious to enact welfare reform legislation, while partisans on both sides believed the conflict would produce political advantage. The Republican's May 1996 proposal was a partisan affair as leaders excluded Democrats from participation. The Democratic governor of Vermont, Howard Dean, called the Republican proposal "election-year hogwash" and said Democrats were "content to take this to the election." Some Republicans believed that presidential vetos of welfare reform bills would make potent political ammunition in the 1996 election, whereas some Democrats argued that vetos would only highlight the meanness of the Republicans and the importance of a Democratic president to moderate extreme congressional initiatives.[75]

David Ellwood, the key architect of the Clinton welfare reform proposal, has argued that there were two windows of opportunity for welfare reform. The first was in 1993. By the time the Clinton administration had gotten around to releasing its proposal, the House Republicans had unveiled an even more ambitious and expensive program aimed at converting welfare into a work program. But the unwillingness of some in the administration to push for reform as well as resistance by some congressional Democrats to changing welfare doomed reform. Common ground was close at hand, but the White House and congressional leaders failed to provide the leadership necessary to finish the effort. The second near-consensus over welfare reform, which occurred in the summer of 1994, was transformed through the congressional election that fall into a number of competing factions within the Republican party.

David Ellwood has argued that welfare reform is best understood as the clash of four competing Republican groups. One group of reformers emphasized the importance of turning welfare into work, even if it required increased spending to provide the training and jobs. A second group believed that welfare itself was the root of many social ills and the program should be greatly reduced by tightening eligibility rules. A third group, led by Republican governors, wanted policy responsibility to be delegated to states. The fourth faction saw welfare reform as a way to cut spending and were uninterested in any issue save that of how to save money.

Although these four positions are to some extent mutually exclusive, Republicans in Congress embraced all of them. The reform-through-work group had dominated the Republican Congress in 1993 and 1994, but in 1995 they had fallen victim to the budget cutters, the welfare-as-the-root-of-social-ills bloc, and the devolutionists. The House started with a bill that did little more than create a block grant and delegate great discretion to states. When opponents branded that effort as weak on work, Republicans added so many requirements that governors rebelled at the micromanagement. The Senate bill blunted the budget cuts but failed to ensure that the work requirements would be funded.[76]

The debate over Medicare in 1995 and 1996 was not unlike the welfare reform debate. Republicans sought to save $270 billion over seven years by limiting the growth in spending to 7 percent instead of the projected 10 percent. Democrats charged that the reduction in expected spending would force doctors to abandon their Medicare patients. Even though the Republicans were successful in making the case that they were not proposing cuts but reductions in increases, Democrats were successful in raising doubts and fears about Republican intentions. Democratic charges that the Republican savings would put Medicare payments below levels accepted by doctors and hospitals were also disingenuous, since in many areas Medicare has started making higher payments than private insurance plans. Republicans were no less innocent in devising a proposal that would reward doctors and HMOs not practicing cost-effective medicine. If the Republican plan were enacted, giving seniors vouchers with which to buy coverage in HMOs,

costs for providers who could recruit healthy, low-cost Medicare pa-
tients were expected to drop while Medicare payments were be maintained, creating a financial bonanza for the medical profession. The
AMA supported the proposal because its members can form their own
provider networks to catch part of the windfall from Medicare over-
payments. Democrats refused to acknowledge that savings could occur.
Contrary to their usual position, Republicans refused to promote competition but are happy to pay off an important political constituent.[77]
Democrats appeared to win the debate as Republican proposals to prevent Medicare from going bankrupt were overridden by Democratic
fears that benefits would be cut and seniors would be forced to move
into HMOs.

President Clinton's decision to challenge the House Republicans'
agenda, rather than cooperating with their legislative plans, was of profound importance. The president found the most political success in
confronting the Republicans over Medicare, and to a lesser extent, the
environment. The president's favorableness ratings wavered around 45
percent throughout the first half of 1995 (except for a brief spurt after
the Oklahoma City bombing). After the president and the speaker met
together New Hampshire in June and shook hands over a commitment
to balance the budget within ten years, the president's rating fell back
to 46 percent, where it stayed until November, when he turned to
Medicare and other polarizing budget issues. Even his threat to veto
the welfare reform bill, despite promises to sign a very similar version
several months earlier, seemed to boost his political stature, and he
finished 1995 with a 52 percent approval mark.[78]

The budget battle, Medicare, and the perception that the Republican
Congress was too far to the right gave Clinton the opportunity to occupy
the center. A 1996 Gallup Poll reported strong negative job ratings for
Gingrich (55 percent) and Congress as a whole (57 percent). Respondents said that balancing the budget should be the number one priority
of the federal government, but they trusted Clinton as much as they
did the congressional Republicans (42 percent to 42 percent) to deal
with the deficit. Similarly, the public trusted Clinton (44 percent) and
the Republicans (41 percent) about the same to deal with taxes. And
they gave Clinton a thirteen-point edge in dealing with welfare. There
were dramatic reversals in opinion over 1995 as Clinton captured or at
least defused issues long dominated by Republicans. As the political
commentator William Schneider put it, "Speaker Newt Gingrich and
the Republican Congress have moved so far to the right that they've
ceded the center to Clinton."[79]

Clinton saw his popularity take off when he resisted Republican cuts to Medicare and Medicaid.[80] But it was hard to maintain a difference between Democrats and Republicans on that issue in the budget talks, since both sides recognized the need to tame entitlements in order to achieve a balanced budget, or at least to reduce the deficit significantly. But Clinton's threats to veto environmental legislation were easier to make because those bills included extraneous provisions that were not required to meet budget goals. Republicans stubbornly held on to their wish list of deauthorization while Clinton was just as adamant in protecting environmental and social programs. As a result, there emerged a clear difference between the White House and Congressional Republicans.

Personality clashes among Clinton, Dole, and Gingrich prevented progress from occurring on welfare reform as well as other policy initiatives. The competition between Dole and Gingrich over who would control the Republican congressional agenda contributed to the deadlock. At least through the first half of 1995, Dole appeared to be beholden to Gingrich to ensure he could gain the support of conservative Republicans for the party's presidential nomination. But as Gingrich's popularity plummeted, Dole began to separate himself from the Speaker. Journalist Elizabeth Drew wrote that by the end of 1995 Gingrich did not dominate the relationship, but he sought to accommodate Dole's concerns, and had confessed that he was Dole's "junior partner."[81] She described the ties between the Clinton White House and Republican leaders in Congress as the "worst relations in memory," as Gingrich mistook Clinton's agreeableness in negotiations as agreement and Dole also mistrusted the president. Both Republicans were victims of Clinton's charm and wiliness as he focused blame on Congress for the government shutdowns and for proposing extreme budget cuts and other policy proposals. Neither Dole nor Gingrich came up with an effective strategy to deal with their diminished role in setting the agenda. Welfare reform continued to be a key issue, but Republicans were split. Some wanted to pass another bill that the president would likely veto then use it as electoral ammunition. Others feared the president would sign a welfare bill and then capture credit for reforming welfare.[82] Although the final welfare bill kept the Republican structure, its fate was ultimately determined by presidential politics.

PRESIDENTIAL POLITICS   Bill Clinton unleashed welfare reform with his promise to "end welfare as we know it." His credentials and those of Hillary Rodham Clinton as child advocates gave great credibility to such a bold pledge. But "ending welfare" or any other simple slogans aimed at complex problems can backfire. Clinton's intent was to end welfare by replacing it with expanded child care, job training, universal health care, and government-provided jobs as a last resort. But the Republicans pounced on the first two words of the slogan, forcing Clinton to make a choice: "He keeps his promise and he abandons his principles," said Senator Moynihan, "or he keeps his principles and abandons his promise."[83]

One argument is that Bill Clinton was forced into a political box, that he had no choice but to sign whatever bill came to him in order to take away a potent Republican charge. If he did not keep his 1992 promise, then the Republicans would mercilessly attack him. Given the popularity of welfare reform among voters, any politician, member of Congress or president who could claim that he or she reformed welfare would earn some points with voters. Clinton and the Democrats had chances in 1993 and 1994 to pass welfare reform to their liking, and they even had the support of moderate Republicans in Congress in 1993, but they lost control of the process that they had unleashed by making such a sweeping, ill-defined promise.

Another view holds that Bill Clinton successfully branded as extremists congressional Republicans such as Gingrich. He could have vetoed another welfare bill as extremist and renewed his attack on Congress. Polling data indicated that the public trusted Clinton much more than the Republican Congress to reform welfare.[84] However, in signing the welfare bill, he endorsed the Republicans as moderate and reasonable; if he had vetoed the bill, he would have had another opportunity to argue they were mean-spirited, extreme, and ought to be replaced with more reasonable (Democratic) representatives. He would also have solidified his position with the liberal wing of his party instead of alienating so many of them.

Like the Republican assessment of the politics of a welfare bill, the White House position on a welfare veto also evolved. Some aides had expected a harsh bill to come from Congress and were preparing for a third veto. A key turning point occurred when the Senate voted to keep Food Stamps a federal program and softened the spending cuts, apparently convincing White House Chief of Staff and lead negotiator with Congress Leon Panetta that a bill would be passed that the president could sign. Political advisors favored signing the bill. Clinton himself gave mixed signals, praising the bipartisan effort but also criticizing the actual bill: "You can put wings on a pig, but you don't make it an eagle." The challenge for the White House was to nudge the conferees toward its position without making an overt veto threat that might encourage Republicans to put in veto bait.[85]

Republicans could not hide their glee over their political skill. House

Majority Leader Dick Armey exulted, "In the end, the president is going to have to make a determination whether or not he's going to sign this bill and satisfy the American people while he alienates his left-wing political base, or if he's going to veto the bill in order to satisfy the left wing of the Democratic Party and thereby alienate the American people."[86] Other Republicans believe that Bill Clinton had outmaneuvered them, that he was able to go just to the right of Republican presidential candidate Bob Dole without alienating too many within his own party. One Republican House leader, John R. Kasich (Ohio) observed, "It seems like no matter what happens, Clinton wins. No matter what we do—if we get something done, he wins; if we don't get something done, he wins."[87]

Some gave credit to neither side. Senator Bill Bradley called the bill "a politician's dream, a poor person's nightmare, and a continuing source of anger and frustration for the taxpaying public that wants real welfare reform." It permits politicians to claim they will "end poverty and illegitimacy and mind-numbing bureaucracy with one stroke." The bill "creates State chaos, not State experimentation." It "simply pass[es] the buck from Federal politicians to State politicians."[88]

Bill Clinton's role in welfare reform was crucial. He made the idea of welfare reform acceptable in the Democratic party and among liberals. But he assumed that he would always have a Democratic Congress to work with, and he lost control of the effort in 1994. Although many liberals abandoned him, he continued to pursue the idea until he was forced to sign a bill that appeared to be the best that could be gained from a Republican Congress.

Box 4.1 outlines the evolution of the president's welfare reform position. President Clinton's support for welfare reform was indispensable in generating demands and creating expectations for major policy changes. The President's failure in 1993 and 1994 to get Congress to enact welfare reform, however, had a major impact on the eventual outcome, since it meant that Republicans would largely write the new welfare law. The welfare reform bill that President Clinton agreed to sign was much different than the one he proposed in 1994. In some important ways, it was a complete reversal. The federal government would spend much less, rather than more, on welfare. Job training and subsidies to ensure recipients can leave welfare for work are not guaranteed. Benefits are cut for an entire group of recipients, legal immigrants. Budget cuts come from reductions in Food Stamp spending that will unavoidably have an adverse impact on children.

THE NEW POLITICS OF WELFARE POLICY

The passage of the welfare reform bill was the culmination of a year and a half effort by President Clinton to claim the political middle and label congressional Republicans as extremists. He has repeatedly frustrated Republicans by coopting traditional GOP issues and making them his own. Signing a welfare reform bill insulated him from one of the biggest criticisms that Republicans could have launched against him in the 1996 campaign—that he failed to keep his promise to reform welfare and he blocked their effort as well. But Republican members of Congress also claimed victory: their welfare reform bill could not be dismissed as extremism because, after all, it was signed by a Democratic president.[89]

The welfare reform law reflects some common ground between the two parties, but it is clearly a conservative bill. Many liberals sought welfare reform that would maintain a strong federal commitment to helping poor families, especially poor children, while also accepting time limits as an incentive to encourage families to move from welfare to work. President Clinton and others also favored an increase in federal spending on job training and job creation to ensure recipients could find work when eligibility ends. They got none of these. Both liberals and conservatives championed increased spending on child care and increased enforcement of child-support orders, and those reforms were included. Conservatives got much of what they wanted: block grants and increased discretion to states; the family cap, limits on aid to teen mothers, and other efforts to reduce illegitimacy; spending cuts, including making legal immigrants ineligible for most social programs; prohibiting those with drug convictions from receiving welfare benefits. They did not get devolution of Medicaid and Food Stamps.

Both parties faced a schism between moderate and extreme wings. The Republicans started out with a bill pushed by the more conservative wing, and moderated it with amendments and changes pushed by moderate Republicans. Moderate Democrats joined them in an important reflection of bipartisan support. Liberal Democrats got little of what they wanted, but were able to join with moderates to block some provisions that they strongly opposed. But in the end Republicans were rather united. Only two House Republicans voted against the final bill, both because of objections to cutting benefits to legal immigrants; House Democrats split their vote exactly, 98–98. All twenty-one Senate votes in opposition to the final bill were cast by Democrats.[90]

Box 4.1
THE EVOLUTION OF BILL CLINTON'S
WELFARE POLICY PROPOSALS

1988   As Governor of Arkansas and president of the National Gover-
        nors Association, Bill Clinton played a key role in the develop-
        ment and passage of the Family Support Act, which
        emphasized education and training programs to move welfare
        recipients into the work force.[a]

1992   One of the most popular messages of his presidential campaign
        was his promise to "end welfare as we know it," it signaled his
        status as a "New Democrat," independent of the liberal wing of
        the party and seeking middle class and suburban voters.[b]

1993   President Clinton established an interagency Working Group
        on Welfare Reform, chaired by Bruce Reed, Deputy Assistant
        to the President for Domestic Policy, and David Ellwood, Asp-
        sistant Secretary for Planning and Evaluation, Department of
        Health and Human Services (and a leading welfare scholar).
        The working group focused on four principles: making work
        pay so that people who work get out of poverty, dramatically
        improving child support enforcement, providing education,
        training, and other services to help people get and stay off wel-
        fare, and imposing a time limit on welfare followed by work.
        However, presidential attention focused on health care reform
        rather than welfare.[c]

1994   The administration's welfare plan, announced in June, called
        for a two-year lifetime limit on benefits for most able-bodiedre-
        cipients born after 1971; required participation in work and
        training programs for all recipients unless they had children be-
        low age one; increased federal spending on job training and
        child care and federal subsidies for jobs (welfare would con-
        tinue as a federal entitlement); required unmarried minor
        mothers receiving welfare to live at home; permitted states to
        deny benefits to children born to AFDC mothers; increased the
        EITC to help working families get out of poverty; and establish
        a national deadbeat databank to enforce child support orders.
        The plan would increase federal spending by more than $9 bil-
        lion over five years.[d] The proposal was introduced by the chairs
        of the House Ways and Means and Senate Finance commit-
        tees, and hearings were held, but the bill was not aggressively
        pushed and Congress did not act on it.

1995   President Clinton criticized the reform bill passed by the
       House Republicans in March 1995 as "weak on work and tough
       on children." He praised the September 1995 Senate bill as the
       basis for real welfare reform. But he vetoed in December the
       final bill prepared by a conference committee. (The bill was at-
       tached to a deficit reduction or reconciliation bill.[e]) The bill
       would have pushed more than a million children into poverty
       and did too little to help move recipients into the work force.
       Clinton also disagreed with the proposals to reduce the deficit.

1996   Congress repassed its welfare bill apart from the balanced
       budget proposals and Clinton vetoed it in January.
           In his January 23 State of the Union Adress, the president
       challenged Congress to send him a bipartisan welfare plan. He
       announced the creation of a National Campaign to Reduce
       Teenage Pregnancy, an effort to mobilize business, the media,
       entertainment, religious leaders, and others to work to reduce
       teen pregnancy by one-third over the next ten years, and a plan
       to strengthen enforcement of child support orders.[f]
           In February, the administraton's FY 1997 budget document
       outlined the main elements of its welfare reform position: time
       limits (now two years, then work; five-year lifetime cap), vouch-
       ers for children whose parents exceed the time limit, new flexi-
       bility for states in designing their own programs, and new
       child-support enforcement measures. The proposal would also
       tighten eligibility for SSI, limit eligibility for Food Stamps for
       able-bodied persons between 18 and 50 who had no depen-
       dents and were not working, tighten eligibility rules for legal
       immigrants and increase responsibility for their sponsors, and
       save $40 billion over seven years.[g]
           Clinton also hailed as "encouraging" the proposal from the
       National Governors Association to give states more flexibility
       and increase child support payments. Republicans planned to
       link welfare reform with changes in Medicaid, prompting a
       White House veto threat.
           In May, Clinton praised Wisconsin's welfare reform proposal
       because it required people who can work to take a job immedi-
       ately or lose benefits; provided for state-subsidized private-
       sector jobs or community service jobs; ensured health care and
       child care "so that parents can go to work without worrying
       about what will happen to their children"; and required teen-
       age parents to stay in school and live at home in order to re-
       ceive benefits.[h] When the administration failed to approve the
       waivers immediately, House Republicans passed legislation in
       June to authorize the changes,[i] but the bill died in the Senate.

In May, the administration also issued an order that required teenage mothers on welfare to complete high school or lose benefits and to live at home or with responsible adults; those who drop out of school must obtain a GED and sign a personal responsibility plan. Many states already had such provisions in place.[j]

In June, the administration issued another order requiring AFDC mother, to establish paternity or lose their share of the benefits and strengthening governmental power to track deadbeat parents and enforce child support orders.[k]

In July, Clinton ordered the Department of Health and Human Services to issue a regulation that required welfare recipients to go to work within two years of receiving benefits.[l]

In August, Clinton signed the Personal Responsibility and Work Opportunity Reconciliation Act of 1996.

[a] PL 100-485.

[b] Jeffrey L. Katz, "Clinton's Changing Welfare Views," *Congressional Quarterly Weekly Report* (July 27, 1996): 2116.

[c] The White House, letter to members of Congress (June 11, 1993).

[d] H.R. 4605/S. 2224.

[e] H.R. 2491.

[f] The White House, Office of the Press Secretary, "President Clinton Announces Appointment of Dr. Henry Foster as Senior Advisor on Teen Pregnancy" (January 29, 1996).

[g] Executive Office of the President of the United States, Office of Management and Budget, *Budget, Fiscal Year 1997* (Washington, D.C.: U.S. Government Printing Office, 1996: 10-11.

[h] Associated Press, "Clinton Calls for Welfare Plan Like Wisconsin's," *The Deseret News* (May 19, 1996): A1.

[i] H.R. 3562.

[j] Michael K. Frisby, "Clinton's Welfare Move Boosts His Claim of Improving System Without GOP Help," *The Wall Street Journal*, May 6, 1996, p. A14; Barbara Vobejda, "President Limits Teens on Welfare," *The Washington Post*, May 5, 1996, p. A1.

[k] John F. Harris, "Clinton Vows Tougher Rules on Finding Welfare Fathers," *The Washington Post*, June 19, 1996, p. A2; Robert Pear, "Clinton Announces Plan to Find Parents Who Owe Child Support," *The New York Times*, June 19, 1996, p. A13; and Dana Milbank, "Clinton Seeks Tougher Paternity Rules for Mothers Applying to Get Welfare," *The Wall Street Journal*, June 19, 1996, p. A4.

[l] Adam Clymer, "Clinton Will Limit Those on Welfare to 2 Years of Aid; Tells Governors of Plan; Move Is in Accord With GOP Bill—Dole Says President has Moved Too Slowly," *The New York Times*, July 17, 1996, p. A1.

The welfare reform law poses serious challenges to the Democratic party. If the law is successful—that is, if it leads to less welfare dependency and does increase the poverty of families and children—then Democrats will be able to share some of the credit. If it fails, it may split the party. The fissure is already in place. Almost all of the members of the Congressional Black Caucus, as well as leading proponents of Latinos and women, voted against the Republican welfare reform bills. Former presidential candidates Representative Dick Gephardt (Mo.) and Senator Bob Kerrey (Nebr.) voted against the bills, as did retiring Senator Bill Bradley and many other prominent Democrats, including both California Senators Dianne Feinstein and Barbara Boxer, and Senate minority leader Tom Daschle (S.D.). Democratic governors also warned that the reforms are underfunded and will put states in a major financial crunch during economic downturns. Labor unions, civil rights, groups, children's advocates, and feminist groups were virtually united in their opposition. Bill Clinton was virtually alone on the other side, in terms of major elements of the traditional Democratic political base.[91]

What might be the impact of welfare devolution on the political system? Has it been enhanced? Has our problem-solving capacity been improved? Devolution increases the discretion of states: They will have more freedom to act and will be more responsible for their actions. It will decrease the power of the national government and may diminish our collective, national, policy-making power. At another level, reforming welfare has been so difficult that if progress is made here, it can boost our capacity to address other issues.

From the perspective of national politics, welfare has been fundamentally changed. Political leaders made good on their promise to "end welfare as we know it." The sixty-year federal commitment to providing assistance to poor children and their families is ended. From the perspective of families that are on welfare or may be so in the future, however, welfare may continue much like it has been in the past. Some states will have insufficient funding of training and job placement programs, so many recipients will continue to be locked in a system of dependency. Some will face the threat of benefit termination, but others will qualify for exemptions. Welfare may be little different for them than it has been for decades.

One of the clearest consequences of welfare reform is that different states will take different approaches. States such as Wisconsin will commit to increasing spending on welfare so that more recipients can participate in job training and placement activities. Other states such as

Michigan will cut spending by reducing eligibility, and may achieve enough savings to fund training and subsidize job creation. The key will be whether states are willing to cut programs such as General Assistance in order to save money and generate resources for the increased expenses that welfare-to-work reform anticipates.

Although it is true that, at the policy level, Republicans and Democrats seem to agree on much of the welfare reform agenda, there is an underlying important debate over political ideology—between liberal and conservative views of the role of government and the kind of values that society should encourage. But this is a difficult debate, and Congress and the White House both fall short in making it a productive one. The debate over welfare was very mean spirited. In the House, some Republicans compared recipients to animals; there was a remarkable effort to blame welfare recipients for the problems in America; the fights between Democrats and Republicans lacked civility, making compromise all the more difficult.

Bill Clinton was in the middle, between the proposals of the Republican leaders and the moderate alternative. He tried to balance the toughness on adults and the protection of children. He was roundly criticized by Republicans for being unprincipled and politically calculating, and that may be true. But it may be that he was struggling with the balancing act without really knowing how to achieve the elusive goal of most welfare reformers. At least he knew that it is not at all clear how to draw the line; many of his critics were so sure of their position that they could not understand or acknowledge the difficulty of the debate.

The Democratic Leadership Council and its think tank, the Progressive Policy Institute, has proposed a third course rather than split the difference between liberal Democrats and conservative Republicans. Once headed by Bill Clinton, the D.L.C. has had an uneven relationship with the Clinton White House and has struggled to have an impact in the Democratic party. It appeared increasingly influential in Democratic circles after the 1994 election, despite the electoral defeat of members who had strong supporters on the Council. Its core agenda of helping middle-class families through job training and tax cuts, reducing the deficit, reinventing the federal bureaucracy, curbing teenage pregnancy, and welfare reform have found their way in to congressional Democrats' legislative proposals. New Democrats sound much like Republicans on these issues. The Institute's welfare experts developed Work First and other elements of the congressional Democrats' welfare reform proposals. The agenda of the D.L.C. is to reach independent voters as well as establishing a network of local, state, and national legislators, academics, and activists. Nine states have adopted provisions from the P.P.I.'s Work First program. Four have created "second chance" homes—supervised group residences for teen mothers. D.L.C. proponents see a less partisan and more independent electorate, whereas Congress itself seems to be more divided and partisan, and the Council has been unable to bring both parties together to support commonsense reforms.[92]

The Clinton administration was deeply divided over how to respond to the welfare reform bill. Policy advisers favored a veto, but political staff urged him to sign it. The administration's support for welfare reform deprived it of one of the most potent weapons Democrats had in 1996—to be able to describe congressional Republicans as extremists, willing to shut down government to their way.[93] But some Democrats voted for the bill for strictly political reasons. New York Representative Gary L. Ackerman confided, "It was not a happy decision. This is a bad bill but a good strategy. . . . We had to show Americans that Democrats are willing to break with the past, to move from welfare to workfare. Sometimes in order to make progress and move ahead, you have to stand up and do the wrong thing. If we take back the House, we can fix this bill and take out some of the Draconian parts." Ackerman blamed the Democrats for being in a fix: "Shame on us. We must bear the burden of blame. We should have fixed it when we had the opportunity. Then we would not have had the anguish of this particular vote this week.[94]

Others also blame liberals for not acting sooner to remedy the problems plaguing the welfare system. Their unwillingness to support earlier proposals to impose modest work requirements helped fuel the dissatisfaction with welfare that culminated in more harsh reforms.[95]

Welfare reform has also energized antipoverty groups that are now calling for public jobs. Other programs that build on the work ethic are much more popular than AFDC. Mickey Kaus believes that the popularity of the GOP Congress's antigovernment position in 1994 and 1995 was really antiwelfare. Republican leaders tried to attack all government as the welfare state, but the public was primarily frustrated with cash welfare. Now that welfare is a Republican as well as a Democratic problem, Republicans cannot use it to attack Democrats. Democrats are now free to develop new programs that reinforce the idea of work and help poor Americans. The Republicans, having reformed what the voters really wanted changed, are no longer necessary: "Sorry, Newt. Congratulations, and goodbye."[96]

Pessimists such as Robert Kuttner argue that the new welfare bill will harm the poor but it will also harm liberals. Passage of the new law will reenergize conservative Republicans, not as extremists but as commonsense politicians who can get things done. Democrats can no longer argue that the Republican revolution was too radical, when they have embraced one of its central planks. Kuttner argues that the bill Clinton signed was just as guilty as were the ones he vetoed of being "soft on work and tough on children." He could have vetoed the bill and demanded that Congress send him one minus the cuts in Food Stamps, spending on disabled children, and spending on legal immigrants, and insist that any spending cut be rechannelled to job creation programs.[97]

The specific provisions of the welfare reform bill came from different sources and were not part of a comprehensive, integrated package. One of the key provisions, the two-year time limit, for example, originated in a 1991 speech then-Governor Bill Clinton gave at Georgetown University. His speech writer, Bruce Reed, had read a paper by David Ellwood that explored the possible consequences of placing a limit on cash benefits of 18 to 36 months; he split the difference and drafted a speech that proposed welfare benefits end after two years. The two-year limit on benefits became a key welfare reform provision.[98]

The welfare reform debate was remarkable for many reasons. One of the most interesting aspects was the willingness of conservatives to engage in some social engineering, in trying to use government programs to shape sexual behavior, marriage decisions, family formation, and other social/cultural characteristics of Americans, particularly poor ones. After years of castigating liberals for thinking that they could change human behavior through government programs, they now jumped into the fray. But although libertarian conservatives may still be skeptical, a central tenet of conservatism is that the polity should encourage and reward certain behaviors. Creating incentives for welfare recipients to change their behavior is nothing new. The problem is that neither liberals nor conservatives have had much success in consciously redirecting behavior. The unintended consequences of public policies are legendary; the ability of government programs to change counterproductive behavior is underdeveloped at best.[99]

The important questions raised by the new welfare law are whether it will achieve its goals, and how appropriate are those goals, given the persistence of poverty in America and the fundamentally important public values implicated in welfare policy. These and related questions are raised in Chapter 5. It is clear that the new law did not resolve all or even most of the perplexing issues surrounding welfare. President Clinton vowed to reform welfare reform during the 1996 campaign, and pushed Congress in 1997 to increase spending on programs whose budgets were cut in the 1996 law. Representative Clay Shaw promised, as the bill passed the House, to introduce in the next Congress the "mother of all technical corrections bills" to solve some of the problems with the law, and urged Democrats and Republicans to "work together over the next few years to be sure this works."[100]

But the political consequences of welfare reform were significant. Welfare reform was part of a flurry of legislative activity in anticipation of the 1996 election. Members of Congress were anxious to have some achievements to put in front of the voters and justify their reelection. The Clinton White House could deliver on a promise four years before just in time to be reelected and take a potentially powerful issue from the Republicans. In addition to welfare reform, Congress increased the minimum wage by 90 cents to $5.15 an hour. It made health insurance portable from one job to another and curtailed the limits on coverage insurance companies could place on previous conditions.

The politics of welfare reform was played out at the highest level. For the Clinton administration, either an agreement on a welfare reform bill could be a way to keep a 1992 campaign promise, to burnish the president's credentials as a "New Democrat," and to show that divided government could work and he played a key role in moderating the extreme position of the Republicans in Congress, or a veto could be a way to differentiate himself from the Republicans, demonstrate their nastiness and mean-spiritedness, and show the need for a president who would use his veto to protect Americans from extremism. For Republicans, a similar political calculus occurred. Should they pass a welfare reform bill and show that they could accomplish something, that they could deliver on their 1994 campaign promises, or should they use the failure of welfare reform to blame the president for blocking changes the American people demanded and to highlight the need for a Republican presidential victory?

The Republican strategy in the spring of 1996 was to use welfare reform as a way to embarrass the president and improve the prospects of Republican candidate Dole. By linking Medicaid and welfare, they ensured a presidential veto that Dole could then use in the summer months to blast away at the president. However, some Republicans began to fear for their own political safety when opponents criticized the Congress for inaction. Behind-the-scenes meetings between White

House officials and members of Congress made it clear that the president would sign a bill on welfare reform if Medicaid cuts were not part of it. House and Senate Republicans passed welfare reform again, but then tailored the final package around the Senate version that was more acceptable to the president.[101] The Republicans in Congress claimed victory, albeit by weakening Bob Dole's candidacy, because they showed that they could govern responsibly and that reelecting them was essential: After all, if it were not for their election in 1994, welfare reform would never had occurred. The Clinton campaign also got a boost, as the president's triangulation separated him from the more liberal Democratic congressional leadership and showed he was essential in reining in the otherwise extreme Republican congressional leaders. As had happened in many states, welfare reform was good national politics. But was it good policy?

REFERENCES

[1] Laurie Goodstain, "Bishops Critical Of Gingrich on Welfare Cutback; Panel on Sexual Abuse Recommends Compassionate Response to Victims," *The Washington Post*, November 15, 1994, p. A3.

[2] Jeffrey L. Katz, "Parts of Welfare Plan Concern GOP Moderates, Governors," *Congressional Quarterly Weekly Report* (December 10, 1994): 3510–3512, at 3510.

[3] Ibid.

[4] Republicans were divided between two approaches: More conservative members favored Representative Talent's bill, 103rd Congress, H.R. 4473. Moderates favored then–Minority Leader Robert Michel's approach, H.R. 3900.

[5] Katz, "Parts of Welfare Plan Concern GOP Moderates, Governors."

[6] Ibid., at 3510.

[7] Ibid.

[8] Barbara Vobejda, "GOP Outlines Broad Welfare Reform; Proposal Would Replace Federal Programs With Block Grants to States," *The Washington Post*, January 7, 1995, p. A1.

[9] Kevin Merida, "Gingrich Softens Stance Against Aliens' Benefits; Speaker Suggests GOP Will Revisit Welfare Question," *The Washington Post*, January 10, 1995, p. A1.

[10] Barbara Vobejda, "Republicans Open Hearings On Welfare; Grants Likely to Come With Strings Attached" *The Washington Post*, (January 14, 1995): A4.

[11] "Some Antiabortion Activists Question Consequences of GOP Welfare Reform," *The Washington Post*, February 1, 1995, p. A4.

[12] "After Bipartisan Meeting, GOP Vows to Pass Own Welfare Plan; Officials Disagree on How Much Power States Should Get," *The Washington Post*, January 29, 1995, p. A6.

[13] "President Clinton Claimed Credit Yesterday for Creating Nearly 6 Million Jobs in His First Two Years in Office and He Pushed for a 90-cent Increase in the Minimum Wage," *The Washington Post*, February 5, 1995, p. A4.

[14] Judith Havemann, "White House Says GOP Welfare Plan Is Too Lenient in Work Requirement," *The Washington Post*, February 14, 1995, p. A5.

[15] Judith Havemann, "Clash Delays Ways and Means Vote On GOP Welfare Reform Proposal," *The Washington Post*, March 4, 1995, p. A6.

[16] Judith Havemann, "Prominent Conservative Faults GOP Welfare Plan; Foundation Analyst Seeks Tougher Work Criteria," *The Washington Post*, February 19, 1995, p. A14.

[17] Judith Havemann, "GOP Drops Child Support Penalties From Welfare Bill," *The Washington Post*, March 3, 1995, p. A17.

[18] John Harris, "Clinton to Push Child-Support Enforcement Idea; Welfare Talk Scheduled Today; Plan Would Link Driver's License Eligibility, Parents' Obligations," *The Washington Post*, March 7, 1995, p. A4.

[19] Barbara Vobejda, "Welfare Bill Restrictions Are Softened; Legal Immigrants Still Face Major Exclusions," *The Washington Post*, March 15, 1995, p. A4.

[20] "Welfare Sparks Warfare," *Salt Lake Tribune*, March 23, 1995, p. A1.

[21] Kenneth J. Cooper, "Welfare Reform Debate Opens on Partisan Note," *The Washington Post*, March 22, 1995, p. A1.

[22] Nita Lelyveld, "Welfare Reform Turns into Abortion Fight," *The Daily Herald*, 22 March 1995, p. A5.

[23] Nathan Deal (D.-Ga.) was the leading sponsor of the Democratic bill; another Democratic alternative proposed by Patsy Mink (D.-Hawaii) would have built on the 1988 law and set no time limit. See Judith Havemann and Ann Devroy, "Bishops Win Concessions on Welfare Bill; Rules Chairman to Urge Easing of Restrictions Aimed at Teen Mothers," *The Washington Post*, March 21, 1995, p. A6.

[24] "Welfare Reform Clears the House," *Salt Lake Tribune*, March 25, 1995, p. A1.

[25] Kenneth J. Cooper, "House Endorses Overhaul of Welfare System; States Would Gain Under GOP Plan but Senate May Slow Bill," *The Washington Post*, March 25, 1995, p. A1.

[26] Jeffrey L. Katz, "House Passes Welfare Bill; Senate Likely to Alter It," *Congressional Quarterly Weekly Report* (March 25, 1995): 872–75.

[27] Judith Havemann, "Senate Welfare Draft Splits With House; GOP Plan Scraps Some Limits on Teenage Mothers, Aid to Noncitizens," *The Washington Post*, April 13, 1995, p. A4.

[28] Ibid.

[29] Barbara Vobejda, "Clinton Says GOP Governors' Welfare Revisions Fall Short; President Favors Some Changes but Balks at Replacing Food Stamps With Block Grants," *The Washington Post*, April 14, 1995, p. A13.

[30] "Reforming Welfare Tops Clinton's List," *Deseret News*, April 16, 1995, p. A5.

[31] Barbara Vobejda, "Welfare Debate Turns to Work; House Approach Offers Tough Targets, but Less Support for Programs," *The Washington Post*, April 21, 1995, p. A6.

[32] Paul Offner, "So Now You Know," *The New Republic* (July 10, 1995): 11–12.

[33] Paul Offner, "Flippers," *The New Republic* (February 12, 1996): 10–11.

[34] Congressional leaders decided to include the welfare reform proposal in the budget bill that Clinton promised to veto. Conferees apparently agreed to prohibit funds for teenage mothers and for children born to welfare mothers (but states could opt out), and to require states pay in the future at least 75 percent of their current level of welfare spending. See *The Wall Street Journal*, November 11, 1995, p. A1.

[35] Offner, "Flippers."

[36] Actually, the issue was complicated. Under current law, the premium would go down

on January 1, 1996; the Republicans wanted to raise it on that date, and wanted to start reprogramming the computers in order to have it in place by January 1 so that it would be masked by a cost of living increase in Social Security that will take effect on the same date. Democrats wanted the Republicans to have to raise the premium in 1996 so it would appear as a tax increase for senior citizens during the election year.

[37] David E. Rosenbaum, "Real Stakes in Shutdown," *The New York Times*, November 14, 1995, p. A1.

[38] 104th Congress, Con. Res. 67.

[39] 104th Congress, H.R. 2491.

[40] For a discussion of who benefitted from the reconciliation bill, see Michael Lind, "Reaganomics, RIP" *The New Republic* 213 (November 13, 1995): 6; "Trick or Treat?" *The New Republic* 213 (November 13, 1995): 7–8.

[41] Because of Senate rules that nongermane provisions attached to budget bills be subject to a supermajority, or sixty-vote majority for passage, several provisions of the welfare proposal had been removed from the bill.

[42] Keith Bradsher, "Republican Compromise Eases Restrictions on Farmers' Subsidies and Crops," *The New York Times*, November 14, 1995, p. A10.

[43] H.R. 4, H. Rept. 104–430.

[44] William J. Clinton, text of message to Congress vetoing H.R. 4, reprinted in *Congressional Quarterly Weekly Report* (January 13, 1996): 103.

[45] For commentary on these bills, see Jeffrey L. Katz and David Hosansky, "Provisions of House Welfare Bill," *Congressional Quarterly Weekly Report* (March 18, 1995): 815–18; Jeffrey L. Katz, "Highlights of House Welfare Bill," *Congressional Quarterly Weekly Report* (March 25, 1995): 874; "Welfare Reform: The House-Passed Bill (H.R. 4)," *CRS Report for Congress* (Washington, D.C.: Congressional Research Service, April 5, 1995); Jeffrey L. Katz, "GOP Draft Bill relies Heavily . . . On Block Grant Flexibility," *Congressional Quarterly Weekly Report* (August 5, 1995): 2372–73; Jeffrey L. Katz, "Uneasy Compromise Reached on Welfare Overhaul," *Congressional Quarterly Weekly Report* (September 16, 1995): 2804–08; Jeffrey L. Katz, "Senate Overhaul Plan Provides Road Map for Compromise," *Congressional Quarterly Weekly Report* (September 16, 1995): 2908–11; Barbara Vobejda, "Senate Passes Welfare Overhaul; President Indicates His Support," *The Washington Post*, September 20, 1995, p. A1; "Welfare Reform: The Senate-Passed Bill (HR4)," *CRS Report for Congress* (Washington, D.C.: Congressional Research Service, September 29, 1995); Christopher Georges, "GOP Completes Welfare-Overhaul Plan; Veto Looms, Clinton Aides Suggest," *The Wall Street Journal*, November 13, 1995, p. Ann Devroy, "Balanced Budget Talks Still Mired in Politics," *The Washington Post*, January 5, 1996, p. A1; Judith Havemann, "Clinton Vetoes Welfare Measure That Would Have Shifted Power to States," *The Washington Post*, January 10, 1996, p. A4; Daniel Patrick Moynihan, "Close Call," *The Washington Post*, January 11, 1996, p. A23; Robert Pear, "GOP May Revive A Welfare Plan to Snare Clinton: Aim is Democratic Split," *The New York Times*, January 29, 1996, p. C22; Robert J. Samuelson, "Compromise Is No Sin," *The Washington Post*, January 30, 1996, p. A15; Jeffrey L. Katz, "Administration's Objections," *Congressional Quarterly Weekly Report* (February 3, 1996): 35; Clay Shaw Jr., "Welfare: 'This Fight is Not Over,' " *The Washington Post*, February 4, 1996, p. C7; "Governors' Statement on Welfare Reform," (National Governors' Association, February 6, 1996); Judith Havemann, "Governors' Reform Plan Ends Welfare Guarantee," *The Washington Post*, February 7, 1996, p. A4; John F. Harris and Ann Devroy, "Governors Agree on Entitlement Overhaul; Clinton, Hill Leaders

Offer Qualified Praise for Welfare and Medicaid Plans; Overhaul Could Help Budget Talks," *The Washington Post*, February 7, 1996, p. A1; Judith Havemann, "Hill GOP Leaders to Study Governors' Welfare Plan; Gingrich Predicts House Will Act by Early March; Senate Appears More Problematic," *The Washington Post*, February 8, 1996, p. A8; "The Governors' Welfare Proposal," (Center on Budget and Policy Priorities, February 13, 1996); Jeffrey L. Katz, "GOP Prepares to Act on Governors' Plan," *Congressional Quarterly Weekly Report* (February 17, 1996): 394–95; "Welfare-Reform Proposal Is Snubbed by Democrats," *The Wall Street Journal*, February 21, 1996; Dana Milbank, "Clinton to Ask For Changes To Welfare Plan," *The Wall Street Journal*, February 29, 1996; Judith Havemann and Barbara Vobejda, "GOP Tailors Welfare Package to Clinton's Veto Objections," *The Washington Post*, May 23, 1996, p. A6; Jeffrey L. Katz, "Highlights of GOP's Welfare Plan," *Congressional Quarterly Weekly Report* (May 25, 1996): 1466; Judith Havemann, "Governors' Welfare, Medicaid Deal Blows Up Amid Charges of Partisanship," *The Washington Post*, May 30, 1996, p. A7.

[46] "Welfare Reform" (National Governors' Association, adopted February 6, 1996).

[47] "The Governor's Welfare Proposal" (Washington, D.C.: Center on Budget and Policy Priorities, February 13, 1996).

[48] Jeffrey L. Katz and David S. Cloud, "Welfare Overhaul Leaves Dole With Campaign Dilemma," *Congressional Quarterly Weekly Report* (April 20, 1996): 1023–26.

[49] Christopher Georges, "GOP to Tie Minimum-Wage Increase To Overhaul of Welfare and Medicaid," *The Wall Street Journal*, May 6, 1996, p. A14.

[50] Michael K. Frisby, "Clinton's Welfare Move Boosts His Claim Of Improving System Without GOP Help," *The Wall Street Journal*, May 6, 1996, p. A14.

[51] Dana Milbank, "House Passes Welfare Plan, Pressing Clinton," *The Wall Street Journal*, June 7, 1996, p. A16.

[52] Rochelle L. Stanfield, "Lots of Spin, But No Signs of Movement," *National Journal* (June 1, 1996): 1210–11, at 1210.

[53] Jeffrey L. Katz, "Ignoring Veto Threat, GOP Links Welfare, Medicaid," *Congressional Quarterly Weekly Report* (May 25, 1996): 1465–67, at 1467.

[54] Ibid., at 1466.

[55] Stanfield, "Lots of Spin, But No Signs of Movement."

[56] Barbara Vobejda and Helen Dewar, "Conferees Finish Work on Welfare Bill; Clinton Indicates Desire to Sign Measure, But Offers No Endorsement," *The Washington Post*, July 31, 1996, p. A1.

[57] For commentary on these bills, see "Governors' Statement on Welfare Reform," (National Governors' Association, February 6, 1996); Alissa J. Rubin, "Governors Hope Welfare, Medicaid Plan Will Lead to Overall Budget Deal," *Congressional Quarterly Weekly Report* (February 10, 1996): 352–53; "The Governors' Welfare Proposal," (Center on Budget and Policy Priorities, February 13, 1996); John F. Harris, "Clinton Talks Budget with moderates; Meeting Bypasses GOP Leadership," *The Washington Post*, May 3, 1996, p. A6; Lori Nitschke, "Committees Stoke the Fires for Another Veto Battle," *Congressional Quarterly Weekly Report* (June 15, 1996): 1684–86; Robert Pear, "House Approves Shift on Welfare; Bill Would Give States Power—Vote Follows Party Lines," *The New York Times*, July 19, 1996, p. A1, A10; Barbara Vobejda, "House Passes Major Overhaul of Nation's Welfare," *The Washington Post*, July 19, 1996, p. A1; Jeffrey L. Katz, "Conferees May Determine Fate of Overhaul Bill," *Congressional Quarterly Weekly Report* (July 20, 1996): 2048–51; Jeffrey L. Katz, "Welfare Overhaul Highlights," *Congressional Quarterly Weekly Report* (July 20, 1996): 2049; Robert Pear, "Senate

Eases Work Provisions in Welfare Bill," *The New York Times*, July 23, 1996, p. A11; Robert Pear, "Senate Approves Sweeping Change in Welfare Policy; Big Role to States," *The New York Times*, July 24, 1996, p. A1; Christopher Georges, "Senate Votes to Overhaul Welfare System; Broad Support, Big Margin Boost Chances a Version of Bill Becomes Law," *The Wall Street Journal*, July 24, 1996, p. A3; Todd S. Purdum, "President Says He Can Sign Welfare Bill, Within Limits," *The New York Times*, July 28, 1996, p. A14; Barbara Vobejda and Helen Dewar, "Conferees Finish Work on Welfare Bill; Clinton Indicates Desire to Sign Measure, but Offers No Endorsement," *The Washington Post*, July 31, 1996, p. A1; Monica Borkowski, "Points of Agreement, and Disagreement, on the Welfare Bill," *The New York Times*, August 1, 1996, p. A8; Jeffrey L. Katz, "Main Issues Resolved," *Congressional Quarterly Weekly Report* (August 3, 1996): 2191; Jeffrey L. Katz, "Provisions of Welfare Bill," *Congressional Quarterly Weekly Report* (August 3, 1996): 2192–94; Cheryl Wetzstein, " 'Real Welfare Reform' Passes Senate, 74–24," *The Washington Times*, August 4, 1996, p. 3; Robert Pear, "Changes in How Welfare is Operated, While Sweeping, Will be Taking Shape Slowly," *The New York Times*, August 6, 1996, p. A11.

[58] Jerry Gray, "Kasich Criticizes Governors on Welfare Bill," *The New York Times*, August 2, 1996, p. A9.

[59] Mickey Kaus, "Workfare Wimp-out," *The New Republic* (March 13, 1995): 4.

[60] "Blockheads," *The New Republic* (March 20, 1995): 7.

[61] Paul Offner, "GOP Welfare Scam," *The New Republic* (May 29, 1995): 11.

[62] "Work Fear," *The New Republic* (July 17 & 24, 1995): 7.

[63] Eliza Newlin Carney, "Roadblock For Welfare Block Grants?" *National Journal* (July 29, 1996): 1954–55.

[64] Katharine Q. Seelye, "House G.O.P. to Face the Divisive Issues," *The New York Times*, March 27, 1995, p. A8; Robin Toner, "Rifts Emerge Inside G.O.P.," *The New York Times*, March 16, 1995, p. A1.

[65] David Maraniss and Michael Weisskopf, "Cashing In: The GOP Revolutionaries Have a Sure-Fire Way of Telling Friend from Foe," *The Washington Post*, National Weekly Edition, December 4–10, 1995, pp. 6–7.

[66] Nancy Gibbs and Karen Tumulty, "Master of the House," *Time* (December 25, 1995/January 1, 1996): 68.

[67] "A Lobbyists' Perk Will Die," *The New York Times*, May 25, 1995, p. A13.

[68] Jane Fritsch, "Securities-Bill Staff Has Ties to the Industry," *The New York Times*, May 25, 1995, p. A1.

[69] Maraniss and Weisskopf, "Cashing In: The GOP Revolutionaries Have a Sure-Fire Way of Telling Friend from Foe."

[70] Matthew Miller, "It's Christmas: Let's Means-Test," *The New Republic* (January 8–15, 1996): 28–30.

[71] John F. Stacks, "Good Newt, Bad Newt," *Time* (December 25, 1995/January 1, 1996): 93.

[72] Clay Chandler, "Something for Almost Everyone," *The Washington Post*, National Weekly Edition, January 1–7, 1996, p. 19.

[73] Katz, "Ignoring Veto Threat, GOP Links Welfare, Medicaid," 1466.

[74] Stanfield, "Lots of Spin, But No Signs of Movement," at 1210.

[75] Katz, "Ignoring Veto Threat, GOP Links Welfare, Medicaid," at 1466.

[76] David Ellwood, "Welfare Reform As I Knew It," *The American Prospect* (May–June 1996): 22–29.

[77] Matthew Miller, "The Medicare Boom," *The New Republic* (December 11, 1995): 20–21.

[78] Thomas B. Edsall, "It's Confrontation That's Paying Off For Bill Clinton," *The Washington Post*, National Weekly Edition, January 1–7, 1996, p. 12.

[79] William Schneider, "Backlash Boosts Clinton's Prospects," *National Journal* (April 20, 1996): 910.

[80] Paul A. Gigot, "Why 1996 Is Up For Grabs" *The Wall Street Journal*, November 11, 1995, p. A14.

[81] Elizabeth Drew, "Can This Leadership Be Saved?" *The Washington Post*, National Weekly Edition, April 15–21, 1996, p. 27.

[82] Ibid.

[83] Jason DeParle, "Get a Job: The New Contract with America's Poor," *The New York Times*, July 28, 1996, p. IV-1.

[84] See Matthew Cooper, "Where Do I Sign?" *The New Republic* (August 12, 1996): 12–14.

[85] Ibid.

[86] Reprinted in 104 *Cong. Rec.*, S. 9333 (August 1, 1996).

[87] Jerry Gray, "Kasich Criticizes Governors on Welfare Bill," *The New York Times*, August 2, 1996, p. A9.

[88] 104 *Cong. Rec.*, S. 9366 (August 1, 1996).

[89] See Jonathan Alter, "Washington Washes Its Hands," *Newsweek* (August 12, 1996): 42–44.

[90] Jeffrey L. Katz, "After 60 Years, Most Control Is Passing to States," *Congressional Quarterly Weekly Report* (August 3, 1996): 2190–96, at 2196.

[91] David S. Broder, "Clinton's Big Gamble," *The Washington Post*, National Weekly Edition, August 12–18, 1996, p. 4.

[92] Eliza Newlin Carney, "Party Pooper?" *National Journal* (April 6, 1996): 767–71.

[93] Richard E. Cohen, "The GOP Tries Winning With Legislation," *National Journal* (August 10, 1996): 1714.

[94] Robert Pear, "Politics: The Democrats; Many Subtleties Shaped Members' Welfare Votes," *The New York Times*, August 4, 1996, p. I-22.

[95] See Jonathan Alter, "Washington Washes Its Hands."

[96] Mickey Kaus, "The Revival of Liberalism," *The New York Times*, August 9, 1996, p. A27.

[97] Robert Kuttner, "Clinton Joins the GOP," *The Washington Post* (August 11, 1996): C7.

[98] Cooper, "Where Do I Sign?"

[99] See Richard Nelson, *The Moon and the Ghetto* (New York: Norton, 1977); and Charles E. Lindblom, *Inquiry and Change* (New Haven: Yale University Press, 1990). For a more optimistic view, see John E. Schwarz, *America's Hidden Success* (New York: Norton, 1988).

[100] Quoted in Katz, "After 60 Years, Most Control Is Passing to States," at 2196.

[101] See Peter Edelman, "The Worst Thing Clinton Has Done," *The Atlantic Monthly*, vol. 279, no. 3 (March 1997): 43–59, at 45–46.

5

Assessing the Great
Welfare Reform Debate

What will be the consequences of the new welfare reform law? Some of the goals are rather straightforward. The law clearly will reduce federal spending on welfare from projected levels. It will give states more discretion in making welfare policy. It will reduce the length of time people remain on welfare. It will shift the focus of welfare toward preparation for work. But the other goals of welfare reform are much more difficult—empowering women, helping families become more self-sufficient, discouraging illegitimacy, promoting responsible parenting, encouraging policy innovation, and protecting poor children against hunger and suffering. We may not achieve some of these goals because Congress has not provided the resources or authority to achieve them. In many cases, we simply do not know how to create effective incentives for families to move from welfare to work without harming the parents and children who are unable to do so.

Below are three statements, each offering a different analysis of the new law. In a few years, we may be able to see who was the best social forecaster. The first is from Senator Pete Domenici (R.-N. M.), chair of the Senate Budget Committee and a key proponent of the bill. He described on the Senate floor on August 1, 1996, what the bill would do: The new law would "encourage and make people work," reestablish the idea that "parents should take care of their children," and "change the culture of welfare . . . It will be a helping hand—and not a handout," turn "power and flexibility over to the states and communities," and "slow the growth of federal and state spending."[1]

In contrast, Senator Daniel Patrick Moynihan (D.-N.Y.), the undisputed Senate expert on welfare, predicted that the legislation "would substantially increase poverty and destitution," cause "2.6 million persons to fall below the poverty line," fail to meet the work requirements in the bill, and serve as the "first step in dismantling the social contract that has been in place in the United States since at least the 1930s."[2]

President Clinton, in announcing he would sign the welfare bill, offered the following assessment of the new law: "it gives us a chance we haven't had before to break the cycle of dependency," it is "strong on work" and "gives states powerful performance incentives to place people in jobs," it "gives states the capacity to create jobs by taking money now used for welfare checks and [gives] it to employers as income subsidies as an incentive to hire people or [is] used to create community service jobs," it "keeps the national nutritional safety net intact" and it "preserves the national guarantee of health care for poor children, the disabled, pregnant women, the elderly and people on welfare."[3]

Given the nastiness of the debate in Congress, devolution to the states may be a positive development. Given our lack of knowledge about how to solve the problems facing disadvantaged families, experimentation makes sense. The debate will continue. What are the issues we should have in mind as we watch or participate in that debate? The hypothesis of reformers is that if we change the welfare system, we will also change the system of incentives and resources that perpetuates the urban underclass. Although some policy makers and observers are quite confident about what the consequences and impacts of welfare will be, the rest of us will have to be content with making guesses. Despite years of debate, experimentation, and legislation, welfare reform continues to raise questions, a host of them unanswered:

How many welfare recipients are incapable of working and will not be able to meet the obligation to take a job?

How many jobs will be available for welfare recipients, particularly in economically depressed and isolated areas?

Will eliminating benefits to teenage mothers reduce illegitimacy? Will it increase family formation?

How much will it cost to shift from welfare to government employment as a last resort?

How many states will be willing to fund such a solution to welfare?

Will the increased cost of providing a job be balanced by the savings from making welfare less attractive to those who will decide not go on welfare?

States that have in the past offered relatively generous benefits may have the resources to subsidize job creation, but what about the poorer states that traditionally spend much less on welfare?

If workfare programs are successful in the better-off states, will poorer states be able to appeal for increased funding to help them develop similar programs?[4]

How can public jobs of last resort avoid the problems that past public-sector employment initiatives have suffered from, such as the perception that they are make-work or dead end? How can opposition from public employee unions be overcome?

What percentage of the welfare caseload will have to be exempted because of disabilities or inability to find or hold a job?

Will states give up on helping those who are least prepared to take jobs gain the preparation they need for successful integration into the work force?

These and other questions cannot all be addressed here. The discussion in this chapter focuses on three questions that examine some of these issues: (1) Will the new welfare law achieve its goals? (2) Do the goals of welfare reform make sense—how appropriate are they, given the nature of the problems at which they are aimed and the public values to which they appeal? (3) What lessons can we learn from state welfare experiments before the 1996 law was enacted that can illuminate the prospects for the new welfare system? Before turning to these questions, the chapter begins with a review of the main provisions of the new law.

PROVISIONS OF THE NEW WELFARE LAW

The Personal Responsibility and Work Opportunity Reconciliation Act of 1996 makes dramatic changes in welfare policy, as Table 5.1 illustrates.

THE GOALS OF THE NEW WELFARE LAW

Welfare reform encompasses a number of ambitious and challenging goals. Among the most important are the following.

TABLE 5.1
COMPARING THE NEW WELFARE LAW WITH EXISTING LEGISLATION

Issue	Previous Legislation	"Personal Responsibility and Work Opportunity Reconciliation Act of 1996" (H.R. 3734, H. Rept. 104-725) (August 1, 1996)
Projected savings	None[a]	$55 billion over six years
Program structure and funding	Various programs provide federal uncapped matching funds for benefits to all whose income and resources are below set limits	Entitlement ended; $16.4 billion annual block grant[b]
State maintenance of effort/distribution options	Under the 1988 Family Support Act (FSA), states match 50% of administrative AFDC costs; most states match between 50 and 78% of other federal AFDC expenditures[c]	States pay at least 75% of 1994 benefit levels, 80% if states fail to meet work participation requirements ($1 reduction in funding for each $1 states fail to match); 15% cap on administrative spending (technology exempted); up to 30% of grant may be transferred to social programs that benefit poor children and families; funds may be used to establish individual development accounts
Additional funding sources	No adjustment for population growth or other needs; instead, unlimited matching funds automatically increase to meet state needs	$800 million over four years for states with growing populations and low benefits; $2 billion over five years in a matching grant contingency fund; $1.7 billion over five years in revolving loans
Time limits	None	Five-year lifetime benefit limit; limits extended or shortened at state option; 20%

TABLE 5.1
COMPARING THE NEW WELFARE LAW WITH EXISTING LEGISLATION (*Cont.*)

Issue	Previous Legislation	"Personal Responsibility and Work Opportunity Reconciliation Act of 1996" (H.R. 3734, H. Rept. 104-725) (August 1, 1996)
Time Limits (cont'd.)		caseload exemption for hardship; some Native Americans and abused individuals exempted[d]
Participation/ work requirements	7% of single parents participating by 1990, 20% by 1995; 50% of two-parent families participating by 1995, 75% by 1998; states may require JOBS participants to negotiate and enter into a personal responsibility contract	Mandatory participation in work activities within two years; 25% of single-parent caseload working by 1997, 50% by 2002; for two-parent families, 50% working by 1996, 90% by 1999; mandatory responsibility contracts for those without high school diploma
Work definition	JOBS programs must include educational activities, jobs skills training, job readiness activities, and job development and placement; states must offer at least two other options such as job search, OJT, or work experience; postsecondary education must be offered to some; For single parents, at least 20 hours a week in work activities; one parent of a two-parent family must complete 16 hours of work experience per week	Private- or public-sector employment, work experience, OJT, job search for six weeks, (twelve in areas of high unemployment) community service, or vocational educational training (regardless of age, twelve months maximum); For single parents 20 hours a week in 1996, 30 hours a week in 2000; for two-parent households, 35 hours a week; only 20% of caseload in training at one time

TABLE 5.1
COMPARING THE NEW WELFARE LAW WITH EXISTING LEGISLATION (*Cont.*)

Issue	Previous Legislation	"Personal Responsibility and Work Opportunity Reconciliation Act of 1996" (H.R. 3734, H. Rept. 104-725) (August 1, 1996)
Work exemptions	A parent whose youngest child is under 3 (or 1 at State option); those that are ill, incapacitated, or caring for someone ill or incapacitated; parents of children under 6, unless the State guarantees child care and requires no more than 20 hours weekly of JOBS activity	Single parent with a child under age 1 exempted for total of twelve months at state option; single parents with children under 6 who cannot find child care; parents with a child under 6 could work 20 hours a week at state discretion; second parent exempted if caring for severely disabled child
Incentives to meeting work requirements	Federal JOBS reimbursement money to states is halved if they fail to meet participation requirements	$1 billion over four years for states with high job placement rates
Incentives to reducing illegitimacy	None[e]	In 1998, bonuses for reduced out-of-wedlock births without increased abortions: 5% grant increase for 1% reduction compared with 1995; 10% increase for 2% reduction; $20 million annual grants for four years for the five states with greatest reductions in "illegitimacy ratios"
Teenage parents	State option to require teenagers to live in supervised settings; states with sufficient resources must require most teenage mothers to receive education	Benefits prohibited to unwed parents under 18 who do not live with an adult and do not attend school

TABLE 5.1
COMPARING THE NEW WELFARE LAW WITH EXISTING LEGISLATION *(Cont.)*

Issue	Previous Legislation	"Personal Responsibility and Work Opportunity Reconciliation Act of 1996" (H.R. 3734, H. Rept. 104-725) (August 1, 1996)
Funding for additional children	Grants increased for additional children	State option to deny benefits to children born on welfare
Other eligibility restrictions	The Social Security Act forbids states to deny AFDC eligibility to a child on grounds of new residency; recipients must help establish paternity as a condition of eligibility;ᶠ permanent ineligibility for Food Stamps for second drug or first arms trafficking violation	Out-of-state families may receive previous state benefit levels for up to twelve months; 25% reduction in (or elimination of) benefits for failing to help establish paternity; benefits denied to adults without diplomas who do not attend school; minor children must attend school; cash aid and Food Stamps denied those convicted of drug felonies (pregnant women, adults in treatment exempted)
Child support enforcement	Wage withholding must be administered by a public agency that tracks and monitors payments; in general, no "new hire" provisions; child support orders must be reviewed and adjusted at least once every three years; Wisconsin and Hawaii make grandparents financially responsible	State and federal automated registries created, including "new hire" registries to facilitate wage garnishing; state option to suspend drivers' and other licenses of delinquent parents; passports withheld from parents owing more than $5000; state option to prosecute grandparents
Legal and illegal aliens	Benefits for most federal social services are generally allowed for legal immigrants, refugees, asylees, and parolees; illegal and	Current legal immigrants denied SSI, Food Stamps, for ten years or until citizens; state option to deny Medicaid and other

TABLE 5.1
COMPARING THE NEW WELFARE LAW WITH EXISTING LEGISLATION *(Cont.)*

Issue	*Previous Legislation*	*"Personal Responsibility and Work Opportunity Reconciliation Act of 1996" (H.R. 3734, H. Rept. 104-725) (August 1, 1996)*
Legal and illegal aliens (cont'd.)	visiting aliens have limited eligibility for SSI, AFDC, housing assistance, and Food Stamps, but may receive emergency medical, nutritional and educational aid; sponsor income deemed for eligibility for a few programs	assistance after January 1, 1997; new legal immigrants denied most federal social services for five years; refugees, veterans, and those granted asylum exempted; emergency Medical aid only for illegal aliens (no child nutrition or other aid): sponsor income deemed for eligibility for most public services
Child care	Child Care and Development Block Grant funded at $935 million in 1996; entitlement funds available under the AFDC Child Care, Transitional Child Care (TCC), and At-Risk Child Care programs authorized by Title IV-A of the Social Security Act; unlimited matching funds for AFDC/JOBS child care and mandatory one-year TCC (but a capped amount for "at-risk" care); child care guaranteed for JOBS participants with children under 13 (older must be incapable of self-care); income-related fee charged for TCC	Seven programs folded into the Child Care and Development Block Grant; guaranteed federal funding totaling $15 billion by 2002; $1 billion discretionary funding each year; 70% of funding mandated to benefit welfare or at-risk families; states must maintain 1995 spending levels

TABLE 5.1
COMPARING THE NEW WELFARE LAW WITH EXISTING LEGISLATION (*Cont.*)

Issue	Previous Legislation	"Personal Responsibility and Work Opportunity Reconciliation Act of 1996" (H.R. 3734, H. Rept. 104-725) (August 1, 1996)
Earned Income Tax Credit	Advance EITC payments must be disregarded	No substantial changes; eligibility somewhat narrowed by disregarding less income and not recognizing some losses
Supplemental Security Income	Minors are considered "disabled" if impairment is of "comparable severity" to that which would qualify for an adult work disability; it must also be expected to result in death or to last for a continuous period of at least twelve months	Child "disabilities" must be expected to cause death or produce marked and severe functional limitation for more than twelve months; incentives for identifying fraudulent SSI collection by prisoners; recipients convicted of fraud denied benefits for ten years
Food Stamp benefits	Food Stamps is an uncapped entitlement program	No block grant; 13% spending cuts by 2002 ($24 billion, plus $3 billion in reduced aid to immigrants); entitlement indexed to inflation
Food Stamp eligibility	Parents and their children 21 years of age or younger who live together must apply for Food Stamps as a single household unless those children are themselves married or parents; sanctions for two months or ninety days for refusing to work	Minors living at home must apply for Food Stamps with their parents; benefits denied for voluntary failure to work 30 hours a week; benefits limited to three months in any three-year period unless able-bodied recipients aged 18–50 without dependents work 20 hours a week (three-month extension if recently laid off)

TABLE 5.1
COMPARING THE NEW WELFARE LAW WITH EXISTING LEGISLATION (*Cont.*)

Issue	Previous Legislation	*"Personal Responsibility and Work Opportunity Reconciliation Act of 1996" (H.R. 3734, H. Rept. 104-725) (August 1, 1996)*
Medicaid	All AFDC families are covered by Medicaid; states must provide six months of transitional Medicaid to families that leave the rolls because of earnings (four months for families that leave because of new spouse income or increased child support); transitional Medicaid may be extended for an additional six months with certain restrictions	Full-scale reform not included in bill; Mandatory one-year transitional Medicaid for families newly ineligible because of earnings; four-month transitional funding for families ineligible because of marriage or increased child support; coverage for all those previously covered under AFDC; state option to deny Medicaid to those who don't meet work requirements
Status	Provisions of several acts overhauled by 1996 congressional action	Passed House 328–101, July 31, 1996; passed Senate 78–21, August 1, 1996[g]

[a] The Congressional Budget Office estimated that the Family Support Act of 1988 would have a net cost of $3.3 billion over five years (1989–1993).

[b] The block grant, Temporary Assistance for Needy Families, replaces AFDC and several related programs. States must convert to block grants by July 1, 1997, although state welfare reform demonstration waivers granted before October 1996 can remain in effect until they expire. States must comply with bill provisions not included in their waivers.

[c] The Family Support Act of 1988 (P.L. 100–485) was enacted on October 13, 1988.

[d] Failure to comply with the time limit would cost states 5 percent of their basic federal grant. States could use funds from the Social Services Block Grant to provide noncash vouchers for children whose parents exceed the five-year benefit limit. The bill reduces this block grant by 15 percent.

[e] State payments are reduced by 1 percent for failure to offer and provide family-planning services to all eligible AFDC recipients who request them.

[f] This provision is often not strictly enforced.

[g] Clinton remained opposed to deep cuts in Food Stamps and aid to legal immigrants. The administration, however, was pleased that final legislation did not affect Medicaid as an entitlement or attempt to radically change foster care and adoption, school meals, or nutritional assistance for pregnant women and young children. In addition, Food Stamps remained an entitlement, and efforts to reduce EITC eligibility sharply were

abandoned. In July 1997, Congress restored some of the projected cuts in spending made in the 1996 law: it provided $13 billion in new grants to states to provide Supplemental Social Insurance benefits to legal immigrants who were in the United States on August 22, 1996 (when the new law was enacted), gave Medicaid benefits for disabled children who lost SSI benefits under the 1996 law, extended benefits to 15 percent of the able-bodied and childless adults between 18 and 50 who had been denied eligibility for Food Stamps in 1996, and allocated an additional $3 billion to spend on moving welfare recipients who were poorly prepared for work into jobs. The 1997 changes also prohibited states from contracting to private entities decisions concerning eligibility for Food Stamps and Medicaid and expanded Medicaid benefits to reach an additional five million poor children.

Sources: "Conference Report on H.R. 4, Personal Responsibility and Work Opportunity Act of 1995," 141 *Cong. Rec.*, H. 15317 (December 21, 1995); "Conference Report on H.R. 3734, Personal Responsibility and Work Opportunity Reconciliation Act of 1996," 141 *Cong. Rec.*, S. 8829 (July 30, 1996).

SAVING MONEY

One of the most important goals of reformers was to end welfare as a federal entitlement, in which benefits would be guaranteed to everyone who met the eligibility standards. This open-ended budget commitment was replaced with a block grant to states that placed a ceiling on how much money the federal government would spend each year. The law creates a new Temporary Assistance for Needy Families block grant, funded at $16.4 billion a year, from fiscal years 1996 to 2001. The size of a state's grant is based on the amount of federal money it received in fiscal years 1995, 1994, or an average of 1992–1994, whichever is higher. Additional funding is available for states with growing populations and low welfare benefits ($800 million over four years), high unemployment, or rapidly growing Food Stamp payments ($2 billion in matching funds over five years), and for those that were successful in moving recipients into the work force ($1 billion over five years). A $1.7 billion revolving loan fund was also created; states must repay their loans, with interest, within three years. States were given an additional $3 billion in 1997 to help move recipients into work.

The welfare block grant cuts spending by $54.1 billion through fiscal year 2002 from what would have been spent if the old program had remained in effect. Much of the savings comes from denying welfare benefits to legal immigrants and to nonimmigrants such as students and tourists who are in the country legally, except for emergency medical care and disaster relief. Legal immigrants can become eligible for Food Stamps once they become U.S. citizens or have worked in the country for at least ten years. Legal immigrants who come to the U.S. after the new law takes effect are ineligible for cash welfare, Medicaid, Food

Stamps, and other benefits for five years, but, under the 1997 spending law, are eligible for SSI benefits. However, refugees, veterans, and immigrants who have been granted asylum can receive these benefits. The old law's requirement that the resources of immigrants' sponsors be used in calculating eligibility for Medicaid, Food Stamps, and AFDC is maintained and expanded to cover eligibility for other assistance programs. Sponsors are now financially responsible until immigrants have worked ten years or become citizens. Otherwise, the Medicaid program is unaffected by the new welfare law.

About $23 billion in savings will come from reducing Food Stamp benefits. Able-bodied persons between the ages of 18 and 50 without dependents are eligible for only up to three months of Food Stamps every three years unless they are working at least 20 hours a week; those who are laid off from their jobs are eligible for an additional three months of benefits. But under the 1997 spending law, states can protect up to 15 percent of those Food Stamp beneficiaries from loss of benefits. Most legal immigrants are also prohibited from receiving Food Stamps. Individual grants are reduced from 103 to 100 percent of the Agriculture Department's "Thrifty Food Plan." The deductions that recipients are able to count against their income in determining Food Stamp benefits have also changed. The standard deduction of $134 will now be indexed to inflation; the fair-market value of a vehicle owned is raised to a ceiling of $4,650; the housing deduction will be capped at $300 a month by the year 2001. The federal government must deny Food Stamps to recipients of welfare who fail to comply with work requirements. As a result, food stamp spending is expected to decline by 2002. But Food Stamps continue as a federal entitlement.[5]

Spending for Supplemental Security Income (SSI) is expected to fall by tightening eligibility for disabled children. Children who have a disability that is comparable to what is considered to be a work disability in adults would no longer be eligible; children must now be shown to have a medically proven physical or mental disability that represents a severe functional limitation, and is expected to cause death or last more than one year.[6] However, under the 1997 spending law, they can continue to receive medicaid benefits.

Saving money comes at a cost. The Center on Budget and Policy Priorities estimates that Food Stamp benefits for the poorest families —those whose income is less than half of the federally defined poverty level—will be cut by an average of $650 a year. The average reduction in Food Stamp benefits for all recipients will be sizable, as shown in

TABLE 5.2
Cuts in Food Stamp Benefits Under the New Welfare Law

State	Average Food Stamp Cut per Household	Number of Families Receiving Food Stamps
California	$530	1,178,423
New York	624	984,579
Florida	403	591,268
Pennsylvania	351	496,431
Illinois	344	466,856
Michigan	372	414,984
Utah	346	41,233
North Dakota	270	16,322

Source: Center on Budget and Policy Priorities, reprinted in Jonathan Alter, "Washington Washes Its Hands," *Newsweek* (August 12, 1996): 42–44, at 44.

Table 5.2. It is hard to imagine how cuts of this magnitude will not have an adverse impact on millions of poor families, particularly children. A Congressional Budget Office study projects that by the year 2002, three hundred thousand, or 22 percent of children who would have received SSI under the old standards will not be eligible.[7]

Bill Clinton often argued in debating welfare reform that in order to move welfare recipients into the work force, more money needs to be spent on job training and placement efforts. Wisconsin Republican governor Tommy Thompson agrees, arguing that his state has been able to reduce its welfare caseload by 44 percent since 1987 by investing millions of dollars in job training, health benefits, child care, and other assistance. States must be prepared to take an average of eighteen months to help prepare recipients for work; in the long term, savings can be obtained, but "you can't just pass a bill and assume you'll save money the next day." Thompson asked, "How can you ask a welfare mom to get a job if she has to give up the medical insurance she gets on welfare, if she has no training or bus ticket to get there, if she can't find a safe place to leave her children?" Other governors, however, argue that reform and savings can be pursued together. Tighter eligibility or even no benefits at all for able-bodied adults with no children, improved management, and other changes can generate the funds to finance training and placement efforts. But some states have already reduced spending and will have to find new sources of revenue to finance expensive new programs. Some states will be particularly hard hit by eliminating legal immigrants from welfare programs. California projects a shortfall of $20 billion over six years. New York officials describe the reform as an "unfunded mandate," where states will have to finance assistance for which Congress has created an expectation but now no longer helps fund.[8]

Perhaps even more serious is the financial crunch cities and counties will likely find themselves in. Although governors have been the most ardent cheerleaders for devolution, the threat of limited funding for the poor will fall not on their shoulders but on those of city and county officials, many of whom lobbied against block grants. Mayors argued that although they are not primarily responsible for administering welfare services, they will be forced to deal with homelessness, inadequate health care, and the other problems that may come from welfare cuts. Randall Franke, president of the National Association of Counties, warned that local officials will bear the brunt of welfare reform failures: "They're our citizens, and we can't hide from them."[9]

Is it a national concern that some states may choose to give so little assistance to poor children that they go hungry or homeless? The new law reduces projected spending by $42 billion after the 1997 changes are taken into account, but those savings come from cuts in Food Stamps and assistance to legal aliens. Federal spending on cash benefits and child care will actually increase by at least $3 billion a year. The key issue is whether this will be enough to pay for the increased cost of job training and placement. Proponents argue that the more stringent eligibility standards will reduce the rolls and free up resources; pessimists argue that state resources will be overwhelmed by the costs of such efforts.[10]

Clinton failed to make the case that real welfare reform must include a program of public or community-service jobs. He was successful in painting the Republicans as mean spirited, but he only blocked their proposal and did not help lay the groundwork for a real solution. His campaign speeches on welfare reform argued for private-sector jobs, with community service jobs as a last resort. But the cost of one public job, according to one estimate, is $6,000 a year for overhead and child care in addition to the cash benefit or salary. The Clinton plan exempted much of the caseload so that only about 170,000 public-service jobs would be needed by 1999. He continued to argue that the private sector can be encouraged to hire welfare recipients, despite the lack of success with such efforts in the past. As a result, the Republicans were free to retreat from their commitment to turn welfare into work. Instead of increasing spending by $10 billion, as the "Contract with America" proposed, Republicans pursued budget savings through block grants.

Cuts in welfare, from the Republican perspective, would have two benefits. First, government spending is reduced. Second, as welfare benefits become more difficult to come by and more meager when received, some potential recipients will be discouraged from applying and some recipients will be encouraged to leave the program. If the goal is to reduce the attractiveness of welfare, cuts will surely contribute to that end. But the law provides no solution to the possibility that hundreds of thousands of children will suffer as a result. Nor does it give welfare recipients the help they need to become integrated into the work force.[11] Despite their talk about jobs, Republicans abandoned that commitment, preferring instead to save money by spending less and talking tough on welfare.[12]

But Clinton and Congress were not the only ones who made reform difficult. In contrast to other areas of social policy, there are only a few stakeholders in the debate over welfare reform who have much influence with Congress: the governors, who pay part of the bill, and think tank/advocacy groups, who provide the political rhetoric and the research to back it up. Governors seemed to be uneasy about the congressional Republican proposal but seemed unwilling to challenge it. They appeared unwilling to risk offending the Republican lawmakers, who had finally begun addressing the agenda of states—unfunded mandates, burdensome regulations, inflexible federal bureaucrats, and the lack of state power in policy making.[13]

The congressional Republicans' 1995 attempt to balance the budget included spending cuts or slowed the growth in spending for a range of programs affecting veterans, retired federal employees, students, doctors, hospitals, and welfare and Food Stamp recipients. Ironically, the president's veto of the reconciliation bill in December 1995 meant that deficit reduction would be limited to welfare. Two other deficit-reduction bills were scheduled for 1996, but they were not pushed by the leadership.[14]

However, during the first year after the new law was passed, states were more generous with benefits than many expected. Block grants are allocated based on the size of states' caseloads in earlier years, when levels were much higher. The dramatic drop in welfare rolls of nearly 24 percent between March 1994 and May 1997 and increased federal spending on child care gave states much more money to spend on welfare under the new law than they received under the old law. States like Wisconsin and Minnesota spent more on each welfare recipient than they had in the past, and Minnesota actually used new welfare spending to move recipients above the poverty level. Restoring cuts to the SSI and Medicaid programs in 1997 has also softened the impact of the new law. And an economy more robust than projected has made welfare reform appear much easier than expected. The real test will come when state economies weaken and demand for assistance increases.[15] The decline in the caseloads may also reflect the relative ease of weaning the recipients who are best prepared to enter the job market; those who remain on the rolls face greater barriers to work.[16]

BLOCK GRANTS

Proponents of block grants argue vehemently that governors and state legislators are just as concerned about poor children as are federal bureaucrats and members of Congress. But in most other policy areas, we have embraced national standards, national minimums. Devolution will also prohibit the federal government from requiring all states to pursue reforms that work. Part of the problem with welfare has been that the split in responsibility between state and federal agencies has muddied accountability. Senator John D. Rockefeller IV (D.-W.V.) argues that "the block grant is a risk but it has the advantage of shifting power to the states, where it will be much more visible.[17]

The block grant approach is "dead wrong," "an obscene act of social regression," Senator Moynihan and others have argued. A federal entitlement redistributes money to states in need, increases spending during economic downturns, thereby stabilizing the economy as well as providing assistance to areas that are hardest hit, and provides a modest incentives for states to be generous because of the way matching federal funds are provided. Devolution poses much greater challenges to some states than to others. Welfare dependency is not distributed uniformly throughout the nation; there are pockets of dependency such as Detroit, where 67 percent of children are on AFDC, or New York, where 39 percent receive cash assistance. California, Florida, and other states with high numbers of legal immigrants face similar, difficult challenges in helping poor residents.

Block grants are a leap of faith. It is true they may encourage states to experiment, but a great deal of experimentation occurred between 1993 and 1996, encouraged by the Clinton administration's freely granting waivers. But there is little evidence that states are so efficient in administering welfare that great savings will be realized through devolution. Nor is there evidence that the challenges facing states in reforming welfare are dramatically different from those facing the federal government. Republican reformers repeatedly declared that a "one-size-fits-all" welfare policy was a major mistake, but they never offered an explanation of why problems of discrimination, teen pregnancy, urban decay, and suburban flight in Detroit were fundamentally different from those in Chicago, New York, Cleveland, or any other large city.

There are several advantages to the block grant approach, however. It will necessarily encourage state experimentation. It will silence governors who have blamed the federal government for the difficulties in reducing poverty and place responsibility squarely on their shoulders. It will shift debate from a rehash of problems with the current system that dominated congressional thinking and speaking on the issue, and force attention to alternatives. Some governors, such as Tommy Thompson and John Engler, seem to welcome the challenge and are confident they can turn it into political advantage. But some governors may not be so fortunate.

Devolution also poses political challenges. The pressure of the timetable required to have state welfare programs in place will fuel controversy. Republican governors and Democratic-controlled state legislatures have already clashed over welfare reform, and as the stakes become greater, so likely will the conflict. Six states in the South, for example, had in 1996 Republican governors and Democratic legislatures; two states have Democratic governors and Republican legislatures. The Pacific rim states all have divided party control, as do eight states in the Northeast and the mid-Atlantic region.[18]

The old welfare system, a patchwork of federal and state policies, provides clear evidence that states have differing levels of commitments to help poor families. The level of welfare reform activity varies significantly, as will be discussed in chapter 6. The old system's disparity of benefits, ranging from Alaska's AFDC payment of $923 for a family of three, to Mississippi's $120 benefit, itself reflected major inequities across the nation (see Chapter 1). States that have spent more of their own money on welfare in the past, and have consequently received higher federal grants, will get bigger block grants than states that traditionally provided lower benefits. The block grant formula in the new law will not equalize benefits, but will likely maintain the inequality of the old system. Critics argued that governors pushing welfare reform are from states with stable populations and histories of generous benefits, meaning that their states will do well in the block grant formula. Governors of states with high population growth rates and lower welfare benefits opposed the block grant provisions of the welfare reform bills.[19]

Senator Hank Brown (R.-Colo.) argued that although some state programs would be successful, "some states are going to drop the ball. Some states are not going to do much better than what the federal government does right now."[20] That is a key difference between proponents and opponents of the Republican welfare reform bills. For those who are convinced that the current system is a disaster, states could not do worse. Others had no trouble envisioning a worse system of poor families, without any cash benefits, living in the streets, scrounging for food. The new welfare system continues to send money to states, but there is no guarantee that money will be spent on effective reforms. Michael E. Laracy of the Annie E. Casey Foundation, an organization that helps disadvantaged children, argues that welfare reform in the states before the new law was signed has been uneven: "for as many states that claim success, there are at least as many states where the results were minimal or absolutely abysmal."[21] But under the new law, the federal government has lost most of its leverage to force states to provide certain kinds of programs.

Block grants have been popular among Republicans. Defenders of block grants point to the experience of those created in the Nixon and Reagan administrations. The Nixon administration pushed for three block grants, including the Community Development Block Grant, which still provides federal assistance for communities with low-income residents. President Reagan's 1981 budget reconciliation bill created nine block grants by consolidating 57 categorical programs. Congress, however, could not resist imposing new conditions and imposed spending ceilings or earmarked funds for these nine block grants fifty-eight times between 1983 and 1991. By 1995, the number of categorical grants had grown to 618. House Republicans promised to combine 336 of those programs into block grants; the Clinton administration countered with its own list of 271 programs to be combined into twenty-seven Performance Partnerships, a form of block grants.[22]

Block grants have traditionally been aimed, for the most part, at capital expenditures of state and local governments. The proposals in 1995 and 1996 were predominantly for social service block grants. Block grants appeal to states by balancing spending cuts with increased discretion, and appeal to everyone who is critical of big government and federal bureaucracies. But critics argue that Congress has largely been unwilling to use federal funds as a leverage over states and improve the efficiency and effectiveness of public services.[23] Between 1972 and 1986, about $6 billion a year in federal money went to states, with few restrictions. A study by the Finance Project, for example, found that spending by states on social services under block grants "received surprisingly strong support." But "despite greater flexibility, many states did not rush to radically gut or overhaul their programs, management systems or service delivery systems."[24] But the federal government has not carefully assessed the effects of block grants, and the new law does not require rigorous evaluation of state welfare reform experiments.

We can find another indicator of what states might do by looking at the experience under waivers granted in 1995 and 1996. These reforms contributed to a drop in the welfare rolls, but most states did not end up spending more for job training, child care, or subsidized jobs.[25] Defenders of states respond that in weeding out from welfare those who can take care of themselves, enough money is saved to provide the services to those who really need them, as happened in 1996 and 1997.

But some conservatives challenged the idea of states as policy innovators. Devolution, they argued, permits members of Congress to claim they have "reformed" welfare, but have failed to impose the tough changes that are necessary, and instead have simply punted to the states. Heritage Foundation welfare policy expert Robert Rector said that "a lot of Republicans have really deluded themselves that the states are at the vanguard of reform. That has never been true, and it is not true now." Charles Murray, speaking at a Cato Institute conference on welfare reform, said, "I do not trust those welfare bureaucracies at the state level." S. Anna Kondratas of the Hudson Institute also doubted the capacity of states for bold reform: block grants "will be sending an awful lot of federal money out to the states and localities, and decreasing accountability dramatically." Conservatives have noted that although the number of federal bureaucrats has actually declined over the past few decades, state bureaucracies have mushroomed. But Republican governors pushed for block grants, particularly those who had already achieved considerable political success at home as welfare reformers. Part of the compromise was to include goals that states were to achieve in order to receive their entire block grant. One of the ironies of welfare reform is that governors wanted Congress to give them financial assistance with few conditions or demands, in much the same way as the old program welfare distributed benefits without demanding much in return.[26]

One of the key issues in the debate has been whether states should be given primary responsibility for welfare policy. The new law clearly gives states the dominant role. But states have always had a great deal of discretion in setting benefit levels. The funding mechanism under the old system had a very modest redistributive and equalizing effect: The poorest states received four federal dollars for every one of their own dollars they spent on welfare payments. Even then, benefits in the stingiest states have been only one-fifth of those offered in the most generous states. So one likely consequence of the new law is that there will continue to be dramatic differences among the states in terms of the assistance they offer to poor families. Those differences may even become greater as states have more freedom to spend less money on welfare. Without the federal match, states have clear incentives to cut people off welfare. If state spending cuts are combined with reduced federal benefits for Food Stamps, it is hard to see how poor families will not be worse off. Other incentives in the new law will also encourage states to cut welfare rolls. The new law requires that states eventually move 50 percent of their caseload into the work force. But given the cost of work programs, states will have the incentive to set time limits and then cut off assistance. The new law permits states to cut off benefits to recipients even if they are unable to find jobs.

The biggest question facing states is whether they will be able to reform welfare into a work program, or whether it will continue but at a lower level of funding. David Ellwood estimated that the poorest states, such as Mississippi and Arkansas, will receive under the new block grant only about $15 per child per week to pay for cash benefits, child care, and training and work.[27] Paul E. Peterson charged that the "block grant is the secret device for cutting welfare benefits. It is a way of avoiding blame for loading deficit reduction on the backs of the poor."[28]

Mickey Kaus argues that the new welfare reform law will encourage state innovation. Governors "will be competing for the national prominence that will go not to the cruelest state, but to whoever figures out how best to get welfare recipients into the work force." If state welfare-to-work initiatives prove to be too costly, governors will demand more money and Congress will be compelled to give it because of its promise to replace welfare with work.[29] The new law required states to convert their AFDC system to the new block grant on July 1, 1997. While there are numerous restrictions on how federal funds can be used, and several incentives are provided for increased funding, states are still largely free to spend their own money as they wish. States that received waivers under the old system can continue to implement them until the waivers expire. In order to receive the full block grant, states must continue to spend at least 75 percent of the state funds they previously spent on welfare programs. If states fail to place the required percentage of recipients into the work force, they must spend at least 80 percent of their previous funding or lose $1 in federal grants for every dollar they fall short. States are authorized under the new law to establish a single set of eligibility and work requirements for Food Stamps, welfare, and other programs. They can also take food stamps funds and give them to employers for wage subsidies; employees would then receive wages instead of food stamps.

Previous experience of states with block grants is mixed. Some twenty-two states are partially or totally under court supervision because of problems with their foster-care and child-protection programs. Some states will take care of poor children, but other states will not, if past trends continue. Katha Pollit argues that congressional welfare reformers' belief that "impoverishing the poor will bring about a reign of virtue and industry . . . bears no connection to how people actually live."[30] Welfare "as we know it" did not end when Congress passed and President Clinton agreed to sign their welfare reform bill, wrote Theda Skocpol. The new law is better described the "Shirk Responsibility for the Poor Act of 1996." Members of Congress and the president can claim they have ended the failed program of the past, but they have not ensured that the problems facing welfare families will end as they know them. They have simply turned responsibility to states. States have few requirements imposed on them. They can choose to save money in their welfare system. Few states will "turn AFDC into an effective work program."[31]

According to an estimate by the Center for Law and Social Policy, administrative costs only make up 12 percent of AFDC expenditures, so improving administrative efficiency by 20 percent yields only a 2.4 percent budget savings. How much can states save through administrative streamlining or contracting out services to private organizations?

John W. Tapogna, a Congressional Budget Office welfare analyst, estimated that meeting the work requirements in the 1995 Senate bill would cost the states at least $10 billion a year; the entire block grant in the bill was only $16.7 billion. As a result, he argued that many states would opt out of the work requirement rather than commit their own money. (Congress did give states an additional $3 billion in 1997.) During a recession, the $2 billion matching grant contingency fund and the $1.7 billion in revolving emergency loans could quickly be exhausted; during the 1990–1992 recession, AFDC spending increased by nearly $6 billion.[32] And under the new law, states will have to repay loans and match grants. Paul Offner, a former aide to Senator Moynihan, argues that states will face tremendous pressure to cut benefits: "The first thing that will happen is [that] faced with a shortage of funds, [states] will squeeze the money that is spent on education and training and job search and all the activities that help get people off welfare."[33]

Paul Peterson, a Harvard University political scientist, argues that since the new law places the entire burden for additional welfare recipients on states, "every state is going to try very hard to keep poor people [from] moving into their state. And the best way to do that is to reduce the cash benefits to recipients."[34] Scholars have debated whether there is a welfare magnet effect, but even if the effect is small, it can have a significant impact on state officials who are struggling to keep spending in check.[35] As indicated in Chapter 3, there is already some evidence of a race to the bottom. Many state welfare reforms have been aimed at cutting benefit levels; once one state takes such an action, neighboring states have followed.

Discouraging Welfare Dependency, Encouraging Work

Like the goal of saving money, Congress's objective of restricting welfare eligibility will also likely be achieved. The new law prohibits states from using their block grants to provide benefits for adults who do not begin working after two years of receiving welfare or who have received benefits for a lifetime total of five years. Single parents are required to work at least 20 hours a week, beginning in fiscal 1996, and 30 hours by the year 2000; members of two-parent families must work at least 35 hours a week. States are required to provide Medicaid benefits for one year to recipients who leave welfare for work (see Table 5.3).

These work requirements and benefit limitations are relatively clear and straightforward, with strong support for time limits in the states. But the real test will come when families reach their time limits but do not have jobs. The law permits states to use their own funds to extend payments beyond these deadlines. Will they do so rather than cutting families loose from any assistance? States may allow parents with children under six to work 20 hours a week. They may exempt parents of children under the age of one, but that exemption can only be used for a lifetime total of twelve months. States may exempt up to 20 percent of their caseload from the time limits. But there are some incentives for states to be tough on work requirements. They can impose shorter time limits than the two-year/five-year maximums. If states fail to move at least 20 percent of recipients into the work force by 1997 and 50 percent by the year 2002, their block grants will be reduced. If they fail to ensure recipients meet the work requirements, the federal government must reduce their block grant by 5 percent during the first year, and by an additional 2 percent a year to a maximum 21 percent reduction (see Table 5.3).

Another area of widespread agreement is increased spending for child

TABLE 5.3
REQUIREMENTS FOR MOVING RECIPIENTS INTO WORK
AND INCREASING THE NUMBER OF HOURS WORKED

MINIMUM PERCENTAGE RATES

	1997	1998	1999	2000	2001	2002	thereafter
Single-parent families	25	30	35	40	45	50	50
Two-parent families	75	75	90	90	90	90	90

HOURS OF WORK ACTIVITIES PER WEEK REQUIRED

	1997	1998	1999	2000	2001	2002	thereafter
Single-parent families	20	20	25	30	30	30	30
Two-parent families	35	35	35	35	35	35	35

care. Most existing child care programs are folded into a Child Care and Development block grant, to be funded at $1.1 billion in FY 1996, and increased to $2.7 billion in 2002, for a total of $15 billion. An additional $1 billion a year is available for discretionary funding. States are required to spend at least 70 percent of these funds to help welfare recipients and those moving from welfare to work. The existing social services block grant, which provides funds for child care and other programs, was cut by 15 percent.

The new law also tightens eligibility for the Earned Income Tax Credit. It adds new categories of income such as capital gains and eliminates certain losses such as net capital losses in determining the adjusted gross income on which the tax credit is based. It also makes it easier for the IRS to track the identity and income of those claiming the tax credit.

For women on welfare who can go to work, the new law sends a clear signal that they must. In many areas of the country, however, they will likely not find jobs. For the relatively small percentage of recipients who cannot work, there is great risk. Some may be given exemptions or transferred to SSI, but some may simply be left on their own. Nor is it clear what will happen once the next recession hits. States with strong economies and those with relatively generous block grants (because of relatively generous state benefits used in calculating the block grant formula) may be quite successful. But states facing high unemployment and a relatively small block grant may ultimately decide they cannot provide much help.[36]

Even more threatened by the new law are city and county governments who will now have to meet the needs of poorer legal immigrants within their jurisdiction who no longer can receive federal welfare benefits. In some states, devolution to counties is occurring more dramatically than devolution to states. In Michigan, for example, although much attention has been focused on welfare reform, social services that have traditionally been state responsibilities have increasingly been delegated to counties.[37]

As indicated above, the new welfare law requires states to ensure that a minimum percentage of recipients are enrolled in work activities. "Work activities" are defined broadly to include:

Unsubsidized employment
Subsidized private-sector employment
Subsidized public-sector employment
Work experience (if private sector employment is not available
On-the-job training
Job search and job readiness activities
Community service
Vocational educational training (not to exceed twelve months)
Providing child care services to a parent participating in a
    community-service activity

THE ROLE OF TIME LIMITS IN PROMOTING WORK   What will happen when recipients reach the five-year eligibility limit? This may not be a major problem, since the new law prohibits states from spending federal funds on benefits only beyond five years. But state funds can be used for those families, and the federal funds be used for some other program, so state budgets will not suffer and governors will not have to bear responsibility for forcing poor families into the streets. The projections about the impact of the welfare reform bill on poor children assume that states will actually cut off all assistance to poor families. Will they?

Moving people from welfare to workfare has been an essential development in finding common ground between liberals and conservatives. Sheila Zedlewski of the Urban Institute argues that disabled parents and children already make up about 20 percent of the caseload, thus negating any cushion from the provision in the law that permits states to exempt one-fifth of their caseload from the time limits. And no one knows what will happen to states caught in an economic downturn. Some will spend more of their resources on welfare to work transitions, while others may not.[38]

The 1988 Family Support Act failed to provide the necessary funding for training programs, child care, and job search and placement activities, and did not create sufficient incentives for parents to leave the system. Time limits and work requirements are the key provisions to get the attention of adults and compel their compliance with efforts to move from welfare to work. The 1996 law seems to have repeated part of the same mistake, while at least creating the incentive through time limits to leave the system. The new law does permit states to exempt up to 20 percent of the caseload from the deadline, but that may not be enough: an Urban Institute study estimates that 33 percent of adults whose eligibility will run out will be unable to find or keep a job; a Health and Human Services study estimated 40 percent. Another Urban Institute study concluded that half the families who would lose benefits under the new law are working: The reform does not necessarily encourage work, but it is tough on children.[39]

Jobs need to be available for welfare reform to work. But what if jobs are not available? Are there enough jobs to employ former welfare recipients? Can they be created within the next few years? Creating, say, 2.5 million new jobs for about half of current adults on welfare may not be a major challenge in an economy that employs well over 100 million people. What will be the impact on the wages of low-income workers? Frances Fox Piven, a long-time critic of inadequate social policies, argues that the prospects for helping families on welfare is greatly constrained by the current difficulties facing low-income workers: "The conditions of people on welfare are unlikely to improve when the terms of low-wage work are deteriorating."[40] Even if jobs are available, some welfare recipients will be unprepared to take them. According to some estimates, it takes at least two years of counseling and assistance to help a person gain basic job skills, self-confidence, and discipline, and to overcome the crushing effects of a neighborhood racked by crime, drugs, and decay.[41]

Journalist Alex Kotlowitz's description of Benton Harbor, Michigan, demonstrates one of the challenges states face. In Benton Harbor, 45 percent of the households receive public assistance. Industries in the city recruited Southern blacks to come and work in their foundries and auto parts plants. But as the factories closed, no new jobs were created, and families became dependent on welfare.[42] The welfare reform law "will flush a torrent of additional low-skilled or unskilled people into a job market where the demand for them already may have reached the saturation point," wrote another journalist. A legislative aide to the American Federation of State, County and Municipal Employees called job creation the "big black hole of the welfare bill: The jobs are not there." Economists argue that the influx of new workers will depress the wages of low-paying jobs: one estimate, by Lawrence Mishel, is that adding 1 million people to the work force would lower wages by 12 percent for those in the bottom third of wage earners.[43]

WELFARE REFORM AND CHILDREN

The challenge for policy makers was to be tough on parents but not on their children, a view that finds strong support throughout the country. But that is a difficult balance to strike, particularly with a commitment to keeping families together. The Senate rejected an effort to provide funds for vouchers to meet the basic needs of children whose parents are forced off welfare, but was defeated because it clashed with the goal of ensuring that welfare offers only temporary assistance. Congressional welfare reformers argued that the most important thing to do for children on welfare is to ensure that their parents work. But adequate food, health, and care are also important to these children.[44] Perhaps the best that can be said is that some children may suffer in order, eventually, to get the word to their parents that they need to work. The price is high for the children of the parents who must learn that lesson the hard way.

LaDonna Pavetti of the Urban Institute has estimated that if the five-year limit on welfare benefits had been in effect just before the new law was passed, about 2 million adults and 4.5 million children would be forced off the rolls.[45] Few voices were raised to defend the current system. Its successes in reducing want and providing families a way to survive were rarely mentioned; its flaws were widely displayed. But there was an unspoken assumption among advocates that even the stingiest reform would not make it worse. Opponents painted one picture: millions of poor children spilling out into the streets, begging for food and sleeping on grates. That does not seem likely; governors will not be rewarded for such results. Americans are not likely to tolerate such a tragedy. But conditions for poor families could get worse: Their lives could be more chaotic, frustrating, and demeaning as they try to find jobs, overcome health and other problems, and have less insulation against decaying neighborhoods.[46]

One of the biggest challenges will come if welfare-to-work efforts succeed. Frances Fox Piven fears that, "Slashing welfare does not create stable jobs or raise wages. It will have the opposite effect. By crowding the low-wage labor market with hundreds of thousands of desperate mothers, it will drive wages down."[47]

REDUCING POVERTY

The ultimate criterion by which many will judge the new welfare law will be its impact on poverty. Although reducing poverty was not typically cited as an express goal of welfare reformers, it was certainly an implied objective. In some cases, families that leave the welfare rolls and take low-paying jobs may have less money to spend, especially if they live in states that pay relatively high benefits. But the assumption is that over time their work experience will translate into higher earnings.

Some poor families will do better, financially and otherwise, as a result of welfare reform. They will be encouraged to leave or avoid altogether the welfare system and be more self-sufficient. They will rely on work and assistance through Food Stamps, child care, and other programs. Other families will fare worse than they do under the current system; perhaps the biggest question about welfare reform is what will happen to families when their eligibility runs out, they are not eligible for an exemption, and they do not have a job? Is it necessary to permit some families to fall into greater poverty in order to create the incentives to push other families toward self-sufficiency?[48] Or, as Senator Daniel Patrick Moynihan lamented, "the premise of this legislation is that the behavior of certain adults can be changed by making the lives of their children as wretched as possible."[49]

STRENGTHENING FAMILIES, REDUCING ILLEGITIMACY

One of the most difficult goals to achieve will be reducing illegitimacy. The new law creates a financial incentive for states: Beginning in 1998, if they are able to reduce out-of-wedlock births, by 1 percent or more in any year when compared with 1995 rates, they can receive an additional 5 percent of their block grant. States can earn a 10 percent increase by reducing these births by 2 percent. Abortions are excluded from calculations to determine illegitimacy rates. Several restrictions on eligibility are also aimed at reducing illegitimacy. States can reduce by at least 25 percent and can even eliminate benefits to parents who refuse to cooperate with child-support agencies or state efforts to establish paternity. States can deny benefits to children born to mothers on welfare and to unwed parents under 18. They may use federal funds only to provide benefits to unmarried parents under 18 if they are living with an adult and are attending school.

Even more difficult to achieve is the goal of strengthening families and, in particular, encouraging the formation of two-parent families. Some indirect, modest steps are included. One of the most universally supported initiatives aims to increase the payment of child support orders. The law orders each state to create a central registry to track all child support orders issued after October 1, 1998 and to share that information with other states and the federal government in order to track down parents who fail to meet child support orders. By October 1, 1997, states must also create a new-hire registry that requires employers to submit information on newly hired employees that can then be checked against the child-support registry. States must order businesses to withhold wages from workers owing child support and may suspend driver's, professional, occupational, and recreational licenses of deadbeat parents.

The purpose of these provisions may be to save money on welfare as much as any other goal. As more child support orders are paid, the need for welfare will decline. Ending the attractiveness of welfare as a way for a young woman to be able to have a baby and set up her own household will also likely save some money. Requiring unwed parents to attend school and live with an adult appear to be reasonable ways to reduce dependency, but it is not at all clear that such actions will actually strengthen families. Nor is it clear that this is an effective way to help teenage mothers. Some people argue that a significant number of teenage pregnancies are the result of statutory rape, in which a young girl has sex with an older man, often her mother's boyfriend. Requiring teenage mothers to live with their parents or some other adult may simply expose them to continued violence and sexual predators. "Second chance" group homes for these girls may be a much better alternative, but no funds are provided for pilot projects to experiment with that option.[50] Nor does the new law address the actions of typically older men who prey on young girls. Political scientist James Q. Wilson suggests, for example, that if we were really serious about this problem we would identify the men who father the children borne by teenage mothers and give them the choice of marriage or prosecution for statutory rape.[51] But what if the girl does not want to marry the father, or has been a victim of rape or incest?

Although it is debatable that welfare really can be blamed for causing the tremendous increase in illegitimacy among teenagers, especially among blacks, it is clear that welfare at least helps perpetuate the problem. But will ending welfare as a federal entitlement result in reduced out-of-wedlock births? The decline of marriage and the rise of illegitimacy are global trends, functions of widespread social and cultural developments; welfare policy can only have played a modest role at best. Changes in welfare policy will likewise only have a modest impact. That impact will likely be greater among poor women who have children out of wedlock and then go on welfare. For other nonmarried women who have children, the problems of single-parent families will continue.[52]

The goal seems to be, as Glenn Loury put it, "to make unwed child-bearing so miserable an experience that no young woman would choose to endure it." But Loury argues that the "Samaritan's Dilemma" will continue to result in a system that permits women to have children out-of-wedlock. If the federal government no longer provides assistance to these families, other groups will step in: we are a wealthy society and we will not tolerate the suffering of innocent children. But we will rarely intervene to remove children from families, so women will know that somewhere they will be able to get help for their children and stymy reformers.[53]

We do not know how to restore fatherhood and stable two-parent families. We know that education and training programs for those who face major barriers to employment are difficult, expensive, and long term. But how will reducing benefits to poor families make them stronger? Will the increased suffering signal other organizations to step in and provide assistance? Where are these organizations now?

Some conservatives insisted on a family cap so that additional benefits would not be paid to women who have more children while on welfare. The House included the cap in the bill it passed in 1995; the Senate left it up to states, as did the final version of the bill. The cap would prevent welfare mothers from getting another $50 to $60 a month, on average, if they have another child while on welfare, but they would get additional Medicaid and Food Stamp benefits. But even under the House version states could pay additional benefits for additional children out of their own funds. The political potency of the cap greatly exceeded its practical impact. Bill Clinton denounced it as an extreme measure that would punish children. The Christian Coalition launched a grassroots campaign to pressure Congress to include it in the final bill. Senators latched onto the issue as a way to be tough on illegitimacy. However, the symbolic importance of the cap pales in significance to the practical importance of funding the work requirement. A strict, effective work requirement seems to send a much stronger signal to prospective and current welfare recipients than a threat not to increase benefits if they continue to have children once on welfare.[54]

Douglas Besharov argues that "the main route off welfare for good is marriage."[55] But how viable an option is that for many welfare recipients? Can public policies promote those kinds of outcomes?

THE FUTURE OF WELFARE REFORM: LESSONS FROM THE STATES

Proponents of the new welfare reform law, particularly Republican governors and members of Congress, have created tremendous expectations for the new welfare system. The public may be sufficiently wary of grandiose political promises, but the states are nevertheless under some pressure to deliver. As the discussion below emphasizes, there is great uncertainty about the likely effects of the new welfare reform law. We simply do not know how recipients will respond to the new requirements, whether state officials can create new and effective programs quickly enough, whether there will be enough jobs for former welfare recipients, and how voters and politicians will respond to the inevitable problems and shortcomings. But the operation of the old welfare system, the way in which block grants have worked or not worked in the past, and the experience of state welfare reform before the new law took effect provide some fair indicators of how the new system might work and where the problems might be.

The balance of this chapter provides an overview of where the states are in reforming welfare as they take on new responsibilities.

Between January 1993 and January 1996, the Department of Health and Human Services granted waivers for welfare demonstration projects in forty-one states. Under the 1996 welfare reform law, these waivers can continue; most of them will serve as the basis for new state welfare programs. These waivers authorized the following kinds of experiments:[56]

Time limits: In 1996 at least thirty states required recipients to establish personal employability and self-sufficiency plans that involve specific goals and timetables. The states can enforce those plans through sanctions and reductions in or denial of benefits, including time limits on receipt of welfare. In return for compliance, states can offer additional counseling, training, Medicaid, child care, wage subsidy, and other benefits. These states include Arizona, Colorado, Connecticut, Delaware, Florida, Georgia, Illinois, Indiana, Iowa, Louisiana, Maryland, Massachusetts, Michigan, Missouri, Montana, Nebraska, North Carolina, North Dakota, Ohio, Oklahoma, Oregon, South Carolina, South Dakota, Tennessee, Texas, Utah, Vermont, Virginia, Washington, Wisconsin; other states have simply reduced benefit levels or tightened eligibility rules.

Encouraging parental responsibility: In 1996 at least thirty-five states limited benefits in order to encourage education; required teenage parents of welfare to complete high school; discouraged recipients from having additional children while on welfare; required minors on welfare to live at home or with a responsible adult; and required children to attend school, be immunized, and receive regular health check-ups. Specific options included limiting or ending benefit increases for additional children—family cap (eighteen states in 1996) or requiring school attendance—learnfare (thirty-one states in 1996), requiring childhood immunization and preventive health care in twenty-two states in 1996, and requiring unwed minor parents to live with parents or guardians (seventeen states and two territories in 1996).

Requiring work: In 1996 at least thirty-three states had waivers aimed at expanding the JOBS program by narrowing exemptions from participation, extending job search requirements, expanding employment and training services, securing private-sector jobs for welfare recipients through wage subsidies and other partnerships, and establishing special accounts that recipients can use to increase their education and training. States also experimented with education and training programs, job search requirements, community service jobs, subsidized work, and other programs already provided for under the 1988 act.

Supporting work: In 1996 at least thirty-seven states had created incentives for AFDC families to move from welfare to work—the most widely embraced experiment—through increasing the resource limits families on welfare can possess and increasing earnings disregards under AFDC so families can work and save money; some states have extended child care and Medicare benefits to families that leave welfare for work; and several states offer a one-time payment to families to meet temporary needs and help prevent the need for AFDC. These states include Arizona, California, Colorado, Connecticut, Delaware, Florida, Georgia, Illinois, Indiana, Iowa, Maine, Maryland, Massachusetts, Michigan, Minnesota, Mississippi, Missouri, Montana, Nebraska, New York, North Carolina, North Dakota, Ohio, Oklahoma, Oregon, Pennsylvania,

South Carolina, South Dakota, Tennessee, Texas, Utah, Vermont, Virginia, Washington, West Virginia, Wisconsin, Wyoming. Other initiatives included: extending aid to two-parent families with a full-time worker (nineteen states in 1996); increasing resource/asset limits (twenty-nine states in 1996); and allowing restricted savings accounts for retirement, housing, and education (fourteen states in 1996).

Limiting eligibility of teenagers: Proposals focused on mandatory schooling (learnfare), driver's license restrictions for recipients, marriage status, and residency requirements.

Reforming and simplifying administration: States have undertaken a number of measures to reduce fraud, consolidate paperwork, enforce child-support payments, move to electronic provision of benefits, and provide more efficient and effective case management.[57]

Welfare reform has meant different things in different states. Its goals have varied from saving money to empowering women to become productive participants in the labor market and society. States have selected from a variety of options in designing their welfare reform programs. One set of options seeks to reform welfare by imposing new restrictions and conditions on eligibility. Some states are using new requirements to reduce their welfare rolls and to make welfare tougher to get and less attractive. Others are intent on changing the behavior of welfare families by encouraging preventive health care for children, education for parents and children, and responsible childbearing. Some groups, such as immigrants and teenage mothers, are singled out for particular attention in regard to saving money and changing behavior.

The most important restriction placed on welfare eligibility has been the imposition of time limits on receipt of benefits and requirements for work. Virtually every welfare reform initiative centers on education, training, and work requirements. Labor-market-oriented, low-intensity, broad-coverage programs provide modest services such as help with job placement and apply to most recipients who are able to work. These programs emphasize moving recipients into the labor force as quickly as possible. In contrast, other programs provide comprehensive services aimed at giving recipients basic educational opportunities and developing their work-related skills. Usually these intensive programs are extended to only part of the welfare caseload. A mixed-strategy approach emphasizes initial assessment of recipients' needs and resources, regular counseling, and more intensive case management for a larger proportion of the caseload. All three work preparation approaches may be offered either as voluntary programs with positive participation incentives or as mandatory programs in which participation is encouraged through financial benefits or sanctions (see Chapter 6).

Another set of policy options provides support to welfare recipients as they move into the work force. Many options, such as disregarding earnings when determining welfare eligibility, providing assistance for child care, subsidizing travel to work, and extending Medicaid eligibility, make gainful employment more attractive than welfare (see Chapter 7).

A final set of reforms seek to change the way in which welfare programs are administered. States are experimenting with streamlining the application process, consolidating welfare and other programs aimed at low-income residents, shifting the location of welfare offices from human resource to employment agencies, and broadening the interaction of welfare agencies with community programs (see Chapter 8).

There are many similarities across the states in terms of reforms aimed at facilitating the shift from welfare to work, discouraging teenage motherhood, and placing time limits on participation in the welfare system. But there is considerable diversity in detail: States vary on how long the time limits should be, how much earnings should be disregarded, how long health and child-care transitional benefits should be extended, what resources welfare families should be permitted to keep, how to integrate welfare with other social services, and many other issues. While the broad similarities encourage comparison, the differences in the details make that difficult.

Many state reforms sound aggressive, but most are still in the pilot or demonstration stage and do not apply to the entire AFDC caseload. Many exemptions are provided for recipients who need not comply with the reform requirements. Some programs are voluntary, and participants are not representative of the typical welfare family. These pilot programs are sometimes more expensive than the traditional programs, but their limited scope makes experimentation possible. However, it is not clear that most states will be willing to spend more on welfare in order to fully implement these reforms.

From one perspective, it is remarkable that some states have spent as much as they have on welfare reform. Why should states spend more money on problems that seem so intractable? Why not divert welfare spending toward programs that are much more popular and have strong political constituencies? Some welfare reform experiments are pursued for political purposes by policy entrepreneurs. Perhaps motivation is irrelevant; if programs work, let politicians take credit for them. In other states, reforms are pushed quietly by welfare officials who appear to care deeply about helping the clients they serve. In some areas, the primary force seems to be saving money. In order to understand the future of welfare reform, we need to look broadly at states and appreciate the differences among them. The debate in Washington often appears to depict welfare reform as devolution to states. But given these differences, devolution is only the first step in changing the current welfare system.

It is too early to assess many reforms, although some initial conclusions are warranted. Persuasive critiques of the traditional welfare system can serve as a guide in assessing reforms. Prescriptions are fraught with potential for producing unintended consequences and perverse incentives. Most important, the kinds of welfare reforms being discussed will have only a limited impact on the challenges that face welfare families. Successful reforms are critical in making incremental differences and in encouraging efforts to make public policies more effective. But welfare reform agenda in states, just like the federal debate, has focused narrowly on the welfare system itself. But incremental change will not solve the problems plaguing poor families; comprehensive, integrated approaches are required.

SOME CHALLENGES IN ASSESSING
WELFARE REFORM OPTIONS

Evaluating welfare and other social experiments poses daunting challenges. Analysts must decide how to extrapolate from case studies or small sample sizes, how to account for the wide range of factors affecting welfare participation and exit, and how to compare welfare reform across states. Those interested in political implications must determine how experimental results can generate and sustain support for particular policies or program innovations. Finally, administrators must translate innovations into concrete programs and create the incentives necessary to change standard operating procedures.[58]

ANALYZING DEMONSTRATION DATA   While many welfare reform efforts have been analyzed, certain studies are unreliable or inadequate for a number of reasons. Some questionable studies lack appropriate comparison groups; others may not apply to current demonstration projects because key elements of the programs—mandatory or voluntary education, work incentives and supports, child care and medical support, or case management and monitoring procedures—have been changed since the earlier experiments. In addition, studies generally track participants for three years or less, a time frame that may fail to show long-term effects of high-cost programs or detect the fading effects of lower-cost programs.

Often, program evaluations are not helpful because they are incompatible with each other. Programs vary considerably in components and cost: some studies investigate welfare-to-work *systems* (broad coverage programs), while others evaluate *components* within the system (selective-voluntary demonstrations). Within evaluation design, there are differences in targeting, screening, selection, participation mandates, project scale, and other elements of program design, as well as in local conditions.[59]

Evaluation findings may also be misleading. Much of the focus of welfare reform evaluations is on the earnings of recipients who move off welfare. Generally, however, income averages are skewed by substantial income changes for a very small group of people. Analysts might report that a job search program raised the earnings of participants by an average of $300, whereas in actuality only a small percentage of the participants—perhaps 5 to 10 percent—may have received annual earnings gains of several thousand dollars because they were able to secure stable employment, though most participants had no gain. A similar situation exists for welfare spending: "reductions of several thousand dollars can occur for the small number of long-term recipients who are induced to leave the rolls, with only minimal effects for the other program enrollees."[60]

ASSESSING EFFECTIVENESS   Analysts usually look at welfare reform evaluation in order to pinpoint how programs can improve their effectiveness, usually understood as increasing the extent to which programs achieve the goals established for them. The goal of most welfare reform efforts has been to move recipients out of the system and into the work force. Indicators used to measure effectiveness in these welfare-to-work programs typically include changes in the overall caseload, in recipient income or earnings, and in the number of welfare recipients who leave the system. The ultimate goal is usually to help recipients move to self-sufficiency, but that is not a simple criterion. How long should recipients be in the work force before they are considered to be out of the welfare system, for example? How can assessments account for the part of the welfare population that will never become self-sufficient because of physical or mental disabilities or because of caring for other persons who will never be able to take care of themselves? Some observers will judge welfare initiatives to be effective, whereas others who define effectiveness differently may come to the opposite conclusion.

The following criteria might serve in assessing the effectiveness of welfare reforms. First, welfare reforms should move recipients into the work force in ways that keep them from needing welfare assistance within the next two or three years or longer. Some might even argue that success requires lifetime freedom from additional welfare dependence. But that makes assessing welfare reforms almost impossible. The shorter the time period chosen, the more definitive the data, but the less clear the long-term impact will be. Second, effectiveness could be measured in the change in family earnings that result; a threshold could be established that examines whether the postwelfare earnings exceed welfare benefits. Third, reforms can be judged by their impact on the money available to meet the needs of children, but it is always difficult to separate out funds that go to children from overall grants to families that are largely within the control of adults. Fourth, welfare reforms can be assessed in terms of how well they enable recipients to take charge of their lives, but that is difficult to measure. Fifth, reforms must also ensure that benefits provide a decent income for those who are incapable of self-sufficiency.

FACTORS AFFECTING WELFARE REFORMS   Since there is no consensus over these or any other factors to consider when determining a welfare reform's effectiveness, such assessments are difficult to compare and aggregate and must be examined carefully. But other difficulties surround assessments of welfare reforms. One obvious problem with caseload measures is that the need for welfare is, in part, a function of the local economy. If jobs are plentiful and accessible to those with levels of experience and skill typical of welfare recipients, the number of new applicants will decline. Caseloads are affected by other factors as well. For instance, benefits may be so modest and/or application procedures and eligibility requirements so onerous that some would-be applicants may be discouraged from applying. In brief, caseload reduction may result from many different factors: a program that empowers recipients to become self-sufficient, a healthy local economy that can draw welfare recipients into the work force, or administrative changes that limit recipient eligibility. Some of the conditions that appear to have the greatest impact on program effectiveness include (1) cost-determining factors such as the nature and intensity of the program and administrative capacity and expertise; (2) aspects of the local environment; and (3) target group characteristics.

The intensity of programs is a function of factors such as program objectives, type and sequencing of services, voluntary or mandatory participation requirements, enforcement, provision of support services, and extent of case management and monitoring. Program costs are generally directly related to program services: Lower-cost programs emphasize job search and work experience; higher-cost programs offer training and wage subsidies.

Just as program intensity affects program costs, the local environment does as well. The local environment includes such factors as labor market conditions; AFDC grant levels; and the number, capacity, and quality of community training institutions. Successful low-cost programs in states that provide low levels of benefits may disguise the real relationship between cost and impact. In Arkansas, for example, the AFDC grant levels are extremely low; recipients are on welfare primarily because they have few other options in a depressed labor market. But those who do find jobs almost immediately earn enough money to exceed benefit levels and leave welfare rolls. In contrast, in states with higher AFDC benefits such as California or New York, recipients might work and continue to qualify for benefits for some time.[61] Caseload reduction statistics might be impressive in a state with a poor economy and low benefits, but the overall economic status of families may have not significantly improved.

Target group characteristics also influence program effectiveness. Recipient characteristics vary widely. As discussed in Chapter 1, among the most important factors influencing welfare receipt are work history, number of preschool and school-age children, age, education, and marital status. High-cost programs usually focus on volunteers who are generally less disadvantaged than most recipients; in contrast, lower-cost services are usually mandatory and nonselective. Overall program effectiveness statistics change as different populations are targeted; "Screening," or "creaming," significantly affects program impact. For instance, a program in Maine officially targeted single heads of household who had been on welfare for at least six months, but the staff were also told to screen out women with low literacy levels and women who had child care, transportation, health or other problems that would make participation more difficult. The staff also imposed their own informal screening criteria when they enrolled only the most motivated people—those with high school diplomas and those whose job goals were commensurate with their current skills.[62]

The effectiveness of a welfare program requires an assessment of its long-term consequences. In general, both high- and low-cost programs can have lasting effects. However, low-cost programs usually lead to low-wage jobs, and average earnings increases usually result from more people working, not more people earning higher wages.[63] Higher-cost services in selective-voluntary programs may increase wage rates or weekly hours of work, but evidence that they lead to higher-quality jobs (offering good pay, benefits, and promotion opportunities) is spotty. Some average earnings gains in these programs have also been attributed simply to an increase in employment.[64] However, within a fixed budget, providing higher-cost services for some means denying service to many others, resulting in a lower aggregate impact: Low-cost services may produce larger benefits because they can be offered to more individuals at the same overall cost. Broad-coverage programs may become so broad that services are diluted and their impact is negligible. Higher-cost programs take longer to break even and sometimes do not pay for themselves, particularly during a brief evaluation time period. Cost effectiveness and impact on welfare receipt appear to decrease from low- to higher-cost programs because components in addition to basic job search and work experience result in decreasing returns. Lower-cost programs yield quicker and more consistent savings for taxpayers.[65] One way to use scarce resources and increase the help given to selected recipients is to concentrate intensive services on long-term welfare recipients. But others argue that high-cost services should be used in tandem with lower-cost services to reach both at-risk and general welfare populations.[66]

Welfare reform programs often produce gains in earnings for recipients more than they produce reductions in the caseload. Some earnings gains occur among recipients who are on welfare for a short time and would likely have left welfare even without assistance. Earnings can increase without making recipients ineligible for AFDC; increases in welfare savings for some recipients may be canceled out by increases in welfare benefits to others who stay on welfare longer in order to participate in the new programs.

Most states have pursued a mixed strategy of providing limited services to a large proportion of the caseload. The actual mix of services provided may be determined by the assessed needs of the client, may focus on job search or other strategies to move applicants into the labor market, or may funnel recipients into basic education programs. These programs have achieved some gains in job placement and earnings, even among the most disadvantaged recipients.[67] It is difficult to compare the advantages and disadvantages of high-intensity, human capital investments with more modest services aimed at job search and placement and participation in the labor force. Participation in a mix of low-cost services had different results for different segments of the welfare population. These programs can save money but do not usually increase the employability or economic self-sufficiency of recipients. A five-year follow-up study of one such program found that it helped people to take jobs and leave the rolls more quickly than they would have on their own, but did not reduce the number of people still on welfare five years after leaving the program.[68]

Because of differences in caseload demographics, higher-cost, more selective programs cannot be easily compared. Recipients who partici- pate in these selective programs may be more successful because they are more motivated and freer from child care and other barriers to partici- pation. Some research concludes that selective programs produce consis- tent, sustained increases in employment and earnings but result in small welfare savings. The gain in earnings results from improvements in job quality and increased hourly wages, rather than from expanding the num- ber of people working. Selective programs have had little success with the most disadvantaged recipients, with the exception of supported work pro- grams. The National Supported Work Demonstration, for example, found some success through offering "highly structured, full-time, in- creasingly more demanding work experience paying approximately the minimum wage for up to a year or eighteen months," along with "close supervision and peer support" to "improve basic work habits and skills."[69]

Another assessment of welfare reforms concluded that the more expensive and complex programs produced greater benefits than labor- market approaches. Highly successful programs emphasize employ- ment, but they combine job search and placement efforts with education, training, and support services. Few programs, however, have removed participants from poverty, and the multiple objectives of most programs have been difficult to achieve. Innovations that increase em- ployment or earnings may not reduce dependency or reduce gov- ernment costs. Programs that seem promising initially may not have positive long-term results. Educational and training programs that re- quire substantial initial investment may not show favorable results for several years. Programs that target teenagers and promote responsible behavior have had little success, at least according to short-term mea- sures. No programs have been shown to significantly reduce repeat pregnancies, and most young women served by the programs remain on welfare. Finally, the messages conveyed by programs are very im- portant. For example, the Riverside, California GAIN program is more successful than other GAIN programs because it includes the following components: extensive job development (direct links to employers), pos- itive messages about work and client potential, a combination of edu- cation and timely job entry, and strictly enforced mandates.[70]

Although it is often difficult to separate out the effects of changes in welfare programs from broader economic and social forces that affect recipients in assessing reforms aimed at promoting work, it may be even more difficult to assess the impact of other reforms aimed at other goals such as reducing teenage pregnancy or promoting two-parent families. Out-of-wedlock births are a function of a number of social phenomena and norms, only some of which are even addressed by welfare policy, let alone affected by them. Social values concerning sexual activity, the obligation men feel—or do not feel—for the children they father, the lack of marriage prospects in economically depressed areas, and other factors may have a much greater impact on teenage pregnancy than the level of welfare benefits. However, if the very existence of welfare makes it financially feasible and thus attractive for teenage girls to get pregnant, go on welfare, and set up their own "independent households," then reducing eligibility of teen parents may have clear consequences for the welfare system as a whole.

ASSESSING WELFARE REFORMS:
EXAMPLES FROM WISCONSIN

The analytical, political, and administrative challenges in assessing the experience of states in welfare reform are illustrated in a brief case study of Wisconsin's one hundred-hour-rule experiment. Unlike most welfare reform initiatives, which were proposed by the Republican governor Tommy Thompson, the one hundred-hour rule reform was proposed by Wisconsin's state legislature. The legislature's goal was to eliminate a major work disincentive within AFDC-UP: Under the "one hundred-hour rule," a standard AFDC-UP rule, families lose all benefits when the primary wage earner works more than one hundred hours, even if the job pays poorly. Because of this rule, recipients sometimes reject full-time employment offers if the family would be worse off as a result. The Wisconsin proposal eliminated the rule, hoping to increase recipient labor-force attachment and to decrease the likelihood of eligibility assessment errors that would make the state liable for federal sanctions under AFDC rules. Finally, the state's implicit goals were to decrease benefit spending (since payments are inversely related to family income) and to increase family stability (since under the existing one hundred-hour rule, families might break up so that one parent could work full time and family members could still receive benefits).[71]

From an analytic perspective, the experiment was amenable to random assignment of participants, since a small rule change could be tracked easily and inexpensively with automated management information systems. Including up to eight states as test sites increased the possibility of using the experiment to build further support for the reform's replication: The use of good-sized traditional control and experimental groups could create credible evidence for persuading Congress to extend this innovation to all states. Administrative innovation also appeared relatively simple: Programming changes in the management information system used in caseload eligibility determinations could be made centrally without involving local staff.

Nevertheless, several problems in planning, implementation, and analysis emerged. Fifty percent of families were randomly assigned to participate in the rule change; however, Wisconsin families were already involved in another experiment aimed at encouraging work by disregarding earnings. So some recipients were exempt from the one hundred-hour rule and also had earned-income disregards, whereas others experienced only the one hundred-hour rule change. Only 10 percent of all cases constituted the "true" control group—those ineligible for either the elimination of the one hundred-hour rule or participation in the earnings disregard program. As a result, it was impossible to evaluate the independent effect of eliminating the one hundred-hour rule.

Additionally, Wisconsin's research design did not meet the Family Support Act's mandate for producing an evaluation of independent impacts. The program did not propose any way to measure employment earnings of the primary wage earner and the second parent. Work decisions depend on how parents pooled their resources: Increased earnings of the primary wage earner could decrease the earnings of the second parent, or they could be an incentive for the second parent. Neither possibility was evaluated. State and federal officials also argued over how the evaluation should take place and whether to have an in-house or an external reviewer.

Part of the problem was insufficient resources: Decisions regarding the evaluation were driven by fiscal constraints. Resources were also misallocated and aimed at activities with little benefit. Some mistakes were recognized as the initiative progressed, but adjustments were inappropriate; other problems were never even identified. More involvement by outside experts could have prevented some of these problems. Obviously, funding for careful, effective evaluations is essential.[72] However, difficult tradeoffs exist. Should scarce public funds be spent on more research and assessments, or should the funds go directly to help recipients? If assessments fail to measure the characteristics and behaviors we are concerned about, but instead measure indicators that are easier to obtain, how should we use their results? How do we use as-sessments that conclude some values will be enhanced while others will be weakened—what if, for example, reforms impose more responsibility on parents but in so doing reduce benefits to needy children?

THE GREAT WELFARE REFORM DEVOLUTION

Assessing the results of state welfare experiments can help identify the issues and focus attention on the choices we face, as well as identifying where states stand as they take over more responsibility for welfare policy. The experience of states in getting welfare recipients into the work force, changing eligibility rules, and restructuring welfare agencies and programs to make them more supportive of work are three key areas of activity and are the subject of Chapters 6, 7, and 8. The suc-cesses and failures of past state efforts provide one indication of how far we have to go in order to achieve the goals of welfare reform. Is devolution a reasoned political calculation, a result of good policy anal-ysis, or a leap of faith? There is great variety in what states have done and are beginning to do in reforming welfare. One clear implication is that welfare policy will differ considerably across the nation. Some states are well prepared to shift to new ways of helping low-income families, but other states have much to do. And poor families will suffer the brunt of the costs of missteps and the price of learning by trial and error.

The prospects for successful welfare reform will likely depend to a great extent on the following factors. First, the health of the economy is critical. If unemployment is low, welfare rolls will likely continue to decline without great hardships on poor families, and many recipients will be able to find work. Block grants will be large enough to fund programs, since they were based on a formula calculated when the number of recipients was fairly high. But when the next recession comes, the welfare systems in the hardest-hit states will likely be over-whelmed, and new federal support will be needed. Second, the com-mitment to creating jobs is essential. The key to real reform of welfare is transforming it into a work-preparation system. That will require a renewed commitment to ensure that everyone who is able to work can find a job. States will have to invest considerable resources in achieving that goal and in devising a new generation of more effective education and job training programs to reach those who are least prepared to work and most dependent on assistance. Third, implementation is the key to policy success. States will need to develop the institutional capacity to transform their welfare agencies, policies, and processes; improve accountability; make programs more cost effective; effectively integrate assistance with other social services; and accomplish all the goals underlying welfare reform. Fourth, the federal government still has a major role to play in holding states accountable for how they spend block grants and in accumulating evidence from states about what policy initiatives work and don't work. Finally, efforts to make welfare work cannot substitute for a continued discussion of how to ensure that jobs are available for everyone who can work and pay and benefits are sufficient to provide a decent living, how to provide more assistance to poor children so they can grow and develop, how to promote responsible fatherhood and strong families, and how to come closer to the goal of equality of opportunity.

REFERENCES

[1] 140 *Cong. Rec.*, S. 9322-23 (August 1, 1996).

[2] Ibid.

[3] Bill Clinton, statement announcing he would sign the welfare bill, reprinted in *The Washington Post*, August 1, 1996, p. A6.

[4] See "Sign It," *The New Republic* (August 12, 1996): 7–8.

[5] Jeffrey L. Katz, "After 60 Years, Most Control Is Passing to States," *Congressional Quarterly Weekly Report* (August 3, 1996): 2190–96.

[6] Ibid.

[7] Ibid.

[8] Jonathan Alter, "Washington Washes Its Hands," *Newsweek* (August 12, 1996): 42–44, at 44.

[9] Eliza Newlin Carney, "Taking Over," *National Journal* (June 10, 1995): 1382–87, at 1386.

[10] Mickey Kaus, "The Revival of Liberalism," *The New York Times*, August 9, 1996, p. A27.

[11] "Work Fear," *The New Republic* (July 17 and 24, 1995): 7.

[12] Mickey Kaus, "They Blew It," *The New Republic* (December 5, 1994): 14–19.

[13] Paul Offner, "GOP Welfare Scam," *The New Republic* (May 29, 1995): 11.

[14] Robert Pear, "Putting the Burden Largely on the Poor," *The New York Times*, July 25, 1996, p. A10.

[15] Jason DeParle, "U.S. Welfare System Dies As State Programs Emerge," *The New York Times*, June 30, 1997, p. A1.

[16] Dana Milbank, "Under the Underclass," *The New Republic* (August 4, 1997): 20–24.

[17] Quoted in Robert Pear, "Politics: The Democrats; Many Subtleties Shaped Members' Welfare Votes," *The New York Times*, August 4, 1996, p. I-22.

[18] Louis Jacobson, "Devolve, Then Run For Cover," *National Journal* (May 13, 1996): 1177–79.

[19] Eliza Newlin Carney, "Taking Over," *National Journal* (June 10, 1995): 1382–87, at 1386.

[20] Ibid., at 1387.

[21] Ibid., at 1384.

[22] Ibid., at 1384.

[23] Neal R. Peirce, "Are Block Grants Really A Better Idea?" *National Journal* (July 8, 1995): 1787.

[24] Carney, "Taking Over," at 1384.

[25] Frances Fox Piven, "Was Welfare Reform Worthwhile?" *The American Prospect* (July–August 1996): 14–15.

[26] Eliza Newlin Carney, "A Handout for the States?" *National Journal* (April 15, 1995): 951.

[27] David T. Ellwood, "Welfare: Where Do We Go from Here? The End of Work," *The New Republic* (August 12, 1996): 19.

[28] Quoted in Michael Golay, "America's Welfare System: A Hand Up or a Hand Out?" in Michael Golay and Carl Rollyson, *Where America Stands 1996* (New York: Wiley, 1996): 69–87, at 81.

[29] Mickey Kaus, "The Revival of Liberalism," *The New York Times*, August 9, 1996, p. A27.

[30] Katha Pollitt, "Welfare: Where Do We Go from Here? What We Know," *The New Republic* (August 12, 1996): 20.

[31] Theda Skocpol, "Welfare: Where Do We Go from Here? Bury it," *The New Republic* (August 12, 1996): 20–21.

[32] Carney, "Taking Over," at 1384.

[33] Ibid.

[34] Ibid., at 1385.

[35] See Paul E. Peterson and Mark C. Rom, *Welfare Magnets: A New Case for a National Standard* (Washington, D.C.: Brookings Institution, 1990).

[36] Joe Klein, "Monumental Callousness," *Newsweek* (August 12, 1996): 45, Jonathan Alter, "Washington Washes Its Hands," *Newsweek* (August 12, 1996): 42–44.

[37] Jonathan Walters, "Cry, the Beleaguered County," *Governing* (April 1996): 31–37, quotes are from pp. 33–34; see also David S. Broder, "Clinton's Big Gamble," *The Washington Post National Weekly Edition*, August 12–18, 1996, p. 4.

[38] Peter Passell, "The Nation's New Welfare Law is Really Reform on a Shoestring," *The New York Times* (August 8, 1996): C2.

[39] Rochelle L. Stanfield, "This Reform May Not Be The Answer," *National Journal* (August 3, 1996): 1664.

[40] Piven, "Was Welfare Reform Worthwhile?"

[41] Alex Kotlowitz, "Welfare: Where Do We Go from Here? Hit and Myth," *The New Republic* (August 12, 1996): 19.

[42] Ibid.

[43] Patricia Lamieli, "Future May Be Bleak for Welfare Recipients," *Deseret News*, August 17, 1996, p. A5.

[44] Stanfield, "This Reform May Not Be The Answer."

[45] Jason De Parle, "Get a Job: The New Contract with America's Poor," *The New York Times*, July 28, 1996, p. IV-1.

[46] Ibid.

[47] Frances Fox Piven, "From Workhouse to Workfare," *The New York Times*, August 1, 1996, p. A19.

[48] 140 *Cong. Rec.*, S. 9322–23 (August 1, 1996).

[49] Quoted in Jonathan Alter, "Washington Washes Its Hands," *Newsweek* (August 12, 1996): 42–44, at 44.

[50] Joe Klein, "Monumental Callousness," *Newsweek* (August 12, 1996): 45.

[51] James Q. Wilson, "Welfare: Where Do We Go from Here? In an Ideal World," *The New Republic* (August 12, 1996): 21.

[52] Glenn Loury, "Welfare: Where Do We Go from Here? Samaritan's Dilemma," *The New Republic* (August 12, 1996): 20.

[53] Ibid.

[54] "Big Deal," *The New Republic* (October 9, 1995): 7.

[55] Robert Samuelson, "Welfare as We Know It," *The Washington Post*, National Weekly Edition, August 5–11, 1996, p. 5.

[56] U.S. Department of Health and Human Services, Administration for Children and Families, Office of Family Assistance, "State Welfare Demonstrations," *HHS Fact Sheet* (Washington, D.C.: Government Printing Office, July 1996): 1–3.

[57] Jennifer A. Neisner, "State Welfare Initiatives," *CRS Report for Congress* (Washington, D.C.: Congressional Research Service, January 24, 1995); U.S. Department of Health and Human Services, "State Welfare Demonstrations."

[58] Matthew Birnbaum, "Policy, Planning and Social Experimentation: The Sad Case of the Wisconsin One Hundred-hour Rule Experiment" (Madison: Department of Urban and Regional Planning, University of Wisconsin–Madison, November 1995).

[59] Daniel Friedlander and Judith M. Gueron, "Are High-Cost Services More Effective than Low-Cost Services? Evidence from Experimental Evaluations of Welfare-to-Work Programs" (New York: Manpower Demonstration Research Corporation, 1990): 3.

[60] Ibid., 26.

[61] Ibid., 16, 30.

[62] Ibid.

[63] Ibid., 41.

[64] Although higher-cost programs appear to have had a greater impact on income, primarily by positively affecting job quality and stability, welfare-to-work programs for AFDC recipients are not enough to end poverty. For maximum effectiveness, these approaches need to be combined with other policies such as raising the minimum wage, increasing the EITC, and increasing child support collections. See Friedlander and Gueron, "Are High-Cost Services More Effective than Low-Cost Services?": 42–44.

[65] Friedlander and Gueron, "Are High-Cost Services More Effective than Low-Cost Services?": 36, 37, 47.

[66] Ibid., 40.

[67] Evelyn Ganzglass, "Research Findings on the Effectiveness of State Welfare-to-Work Programs" (Washington, D.C.: Employment and Social Services Policy Studies, Center for Policy Research, National Governors' Association, 1994): 7.

[68] Ibid.

[69] Ibid., 6.

[70] Ibid.

[71] Birnbaum, "Policy, Planning and Social Experimentation: the Sad Case of the Wisconsin 100-hour Rule Experiment," 15.

[72] Ibid., 25.

6

Getting Welfare Recipients into the Work Force

The 1996 welfare reform law required states to begin shifting welfare recipients into the work place. By 1997, 25 percent of single recipients had to be participating in work activities, and 50 percent by 2002; of married recipients, 50 percent by 1997 and 90 percent by 1999 must be working in order for states to receive their full block grants. Work is defined as private or public-sector employment, on-the-job training, job search activities for six week (twelve weeks in high-unemployment areas), community service, or vocational education. States can grant exemptions to single parents with children under 1, or under 6 if child care cannot be found. Except for those guidelines, states are quite free to develop their own policies to move recipients from welfare to work. The law include financial incentives for states to meet these goals: If states fail to meet them, they must pay more of the cost of the program; if they exceed the goal, bonuses are provided.

The debate over how to restrict welfare benefits has been contentious, but few have dissented from the view that welfare should be aimed at integrating recipients into the work force. In the past, the welfare system was defended by those who sought to make it possible for women to stay at home and raise their children and by those who believed that imposing any kind of requirements on recipients was repressive and illiberal. But those views seem to garner little support today. Although there are advantages to having mothers on welfare stay at home with their young children, many people believe it is more important that those children see their mothers going off to work each day to help their families become independent.

The consensus begins to breaks down a little, however, when the discussion turns to the exact role the welfare system should play in encouraging work. Two main models vie for attention. The *labor force attachment model* views the welfare system as primarily a job search and placement office through which recipients move as quickly as possible before they enter the work force. The *human capital development model* seeks to help recipients prepare themselves for work through basic education, vocational and on-the-job training, and other work-related programs.

Costs are a key factor in the debate over these two models. The labor force attachment approach is much less expensive to operate and is more attractive to budget-cutting reformers. It is also attractive to those who believe that welfare itself breeds dependency and that recipients need to be pushed into the work force where they can quickly learn to be independent. Focusing on a labor force attachment approach, however, fails to acknowledge that some recipients are ill equipped to enter the labor market immediately and need some preparation. Conversely, the human capital development approach aims to help recipients prepare to work and become self-sufficient. This latter approach requires much greater government outlays and keeps recipients in the system for a much longer period of time. It may permit recipients to delay their independence.

A second and perhaps even more difficult issue is what to do when recipients are sent into the labor market but can't find jobs because they aren't available. Comparisons between the labor force attachment or human capital development approaches are irrelevant if recipients fail to find jobs after completing the programs. If recipients cannot find jobs, one option is to keep them in the caseload as long as they continue to seek work or participate in additional training. Another approach is for the state to entice private employers to hire recipients by offering to subsidize wages. States may hire the recipients themselves and pay wages directly to them to replace welfare benefits, or continue to offer benefits on condition that recipients work in community and governmental agencies.

States can also simply terminate benefits once time limits are exceeded and leave families on their own. This final option raises a new set of questions about what states will do if families are unable to find or keep jobs but are also ineligible for further benefits because of time limits.

Table 6.1 summarizes how states have experimented with welfare-to-work reforms. Many of these reforms were introduced in Chapter 5's

TABLE 6.1
WELFARE-TO-WORK EXPERIMENTS

Programs that emphasize labor force attachment	*States*
Programs that emphasize job search/ immediate placement	Arkansas, California, Connecticut, Florida, Hawaii, Illinois, Kentucky, Maryland, Massachusetts, Michigan, Missouri, Nebraska, New Hampshire, North Carolina, Ohio, South Carolina, Texas, Virginia, Wisconsin
Programs that emphasize private sector job placement	Arizona, Georgia, Indiana, Maine, Massachusetts, Mississippi, Missouri, North Carolina, Ohio, Oregon, Vermont, Virginia, West Virginia
Programs that emphasize work experience programs (jobs specifically created by state and local governments; paid or community service)	Arizona, Arkansas, California, Florida, Hawaii, Illinois, Maine, Maryland, Missouri, New Hampshire, New Jersey, New York, Oklahoma, South Carolina, South Dakota, Texas, Vermont, Virginia, West Virginia, Wisconsin, Wyoming
Programs that mandate work at a time limit	Colorado, Connecticut, Georgia, Illinois, Massachusetts, Missouri, Montana, Nebraska, North Carolina, North Dakota, Oklahoma, Oregon, South Carolina, South Dakota, Tennessee, Utah, Vermont, Virginia, Wisconsin, Wyoming
Programs that emphasize human capital development	*States*
Programs that emphasize education/ vocational training	California, Iowa, Louisiana, Maine, Maryland, Massachusetts, Minnesota, New Jersey, North Carolina, Oregon, South Dakota, Texas, Virginia, Wyoming
Programs that emphasize small-business development/entrepreneurial training	Iowa, Maryland, Michigan, Minnesota, Mississippi, New York

overview of welfare reform approaches; the focus here is on efforts to promote job placement, education and training, and related activities. This chapter then discusses some of the major state initiatives and how well they seem to have achieved their goals as of 1996. As is true in other chapters, the discussion of state programs is not exhaustive and states have created new programs and will likely eliminate many of the ones described below. The purpose here is to illustrate the options that states have tried, to assess their strengths and weaknesses, and to explore lessons for states' takeover of policy under the new welfare law. As of July 1996, some thirty-seven states encouraged the transition from welfare to work by allowing recipients to earn paychecks and by increasing education/training opportunities and public/private partnerships. Unless otherwise noted, the reforms reviewed here were all the subject of waivers approved in 1994 or 1995 by the Federal government. Some of these experiments will continue as states revise their welfare programs under the new law.

LABOR FORCE ATTACHMENT EXPERIMENTS

JOB SEARCH AND IMMEDIATE PLACEMENT

Many welfare reforms dispense with detailed assessment programs or education and training programs, seeking to move recipients immediately into job search activities and to place them into jobs as soon as possible. Florida's Project Independence, which requires all participants with at least a tenth grade education or work experience to seek jobs before participating in classes, and Riverside, California's GAIN program, which urges participants to find work "without being too fussy about the kind of job they took or its wages," have prompted other states to change their emphasis away from education training to job search.[1]

Connecticut's "Reach for Jobs First" reform requires recipients to spend twelve weeks in job-search activities.[2] The state also proposed a Job Connection program that targets all able-bodied welfare recipients except teenage parents progressing toward high school graduation. Job Connection would replace a long-range education and training program with brief job placement service because state officials became convinced that training programs were too costly and reached too few people. Under the proposal, all employable welfare recipients would have twenty-one months to find work before losing benefits; benefits would be cut to 1988 levels to make minimum wage-paying jobs look more attractive. Employers would receive a $1,500 tax credit for each welfare employee hired. Transitional Medicaid and child care would be provided for twenty-four months. In addition to benefits, recipients could keep wages up to the Federal poverty level for twenty-one months. Connecticut also experiments with phasing in job requirements. The state's "A Fair Chance" Job Pathways program requires recipients who have been on welfare for two years to work at least fifteen hours a week; after three years, twenty-five hours a week; and after four years, thirty-five hours weekly.[3]

In Hawaii's "Creating Work Opportunities for JOBS Families," recipients who would normally wait at least three months before being placed in a education or training program are required to pursue job leads developed by program officials. Positions are typically part-time (up to eighteen hours a week), minimum wage, private-sector jobs.[4] Illinois' "Work and Responsibility" mandates that new applicants with children aged 5 to 12 participate in job search efforts. They are assigned to community service work if not employed within six months.[5] Maryland's "Family Investment Program" requires able-bodied applicants to make job search efforts; if they fail to comply for six months, the family becomes ineligible for benefits.[6] Massachusetts provides cash assistance to nonexempt families for up to sixty days; during this time the applicant head-of-household must participate in job search. Participants without a job after sixty days or those reapplying must perform twenty-five hours of community service per week and engage in job search activities for at least fifteen hour per week to receive a "subsidy" in lieu of a cash grant, plus child care and health benefits. These subsidies are also available to make up income deficits for those working full time (forty or more hours) at a low-wage job or those doing a combination of private-sector work and community service. If the recipient is working full time, all child-support payments are given directly to the family; Food Stamps are cashed out for those in unsubsidized employment.[7]

Job search programs seem to produce the quickest results in decreasing welfare rolls and increasing work effort. Proponents of job placement programs argue that "the acquisition of basic skills is not a necessary precondition for achieving stable employment at an adequate wage." For many welfare applicants and recipients, quick labor force entry, even in low-paying jobs, is the most direct way to achieve long-term self-sufficiency. Other proponents argue that mandatory job search participation ensures equality of treatment and results in a cost-effective program, since jobs are found during up-front job search activities and labor-market disadvantages are identified. As one study concluded, "no assessment tool is a better judge of who will get a job than who does not get a job."[8] Extensive assessment is costly, unnecessary, and of dubious effectiveness, they argue; assessment for all clients diverts resources from training programs for less-prepared clients. An assessment of California's GAIN program found that intensive assessments "offer very little about who will actually be successful in the job market, and their results are of limited value in setting goals. For example, while documenting educational deficits may be of significant value in setting educational goals, it is not particularly helpful in setting employment goals."[9]

Proponents further argue that job search programs send the right signals to recipients. A study of three states—Georgia, Michigan, California—found that emphasizing work "dramatically increased participation in job search activities, slightly increased the rate of participation in work-directed services, and resulted in a high rate of sanctioning."[10] Most of the increase in activity was centered in job search. The programs substantially increased the number of people who found work and left welfare within two years, an 11 percent reduction in the percentage of recipients on AFDC. There were relatively large impacts (in all three sites) on AFDC receipt, AFDC payments, employment rates, and earnings: AFDC payments were reduced by 22 percent. In the final month of the study, 42.5 percent of the control group was employed and average monthly earnings increased 26 percent. Reductions in AFDC payments "exceeded savings found in prior studies of large-scale welfare-to-work programs." About 20 percent of the control group was sanctioned during the two years of the study. Food Stamp payments during the final month were reduced by 14 percent. The combined annualized savings for AFDC and Food Stamps was $984 per recipient. Earnings gains were particularly large for high school graduates, those with a GED prior to the program, and women with preschool-age children. However, since earnings gains were about the same size as AFDC reductions, the reform approach produced no significant change in measured income.[11]

Anecdotes paint a similar picture. In one rural Alabama county, the main source of jobs is a catfish processing plant. Residents of the county, when informed that they would start working for the plant or lose benefits, found more pleasant jobs on their own. The director of the state's job-training program observed: "Of the first group we referred, we had 14 lined up for work [in the processing plant] on Monday. The week before they were to start, seven had found other jobs. . . . In that county, the word is out: You either find a job, or you're going to work for the catfish plant."[12]

In some areas, however, there are simply not enough jobs available for welfare recipients. Connecticut's Job Connection proposal was immediately criticized, for example, because there were already 92,600 unemployed people in Connecticut in March 1995 and only 51,431 job openings projected between 1992 and 2000. Welfare reform would only

swell the unemployment population. Connecticut state officials promised to place nine thousand welfare recipients in jobs in 1996 and to
move forty thousand of the state's fifty-nine thousand recipients into
jobs by 1999. But one state representative warned that the "jobs [for
forty thousand people] just aren't there."[13]

Florida received permission to experiment with time-limited benefits
and subsidies to employers who hire welfare recipients. Benefits are to
be cut off after two years but recipients will get education and job
training help, as well as subsidized child care and health care after they
start working.[14] But critics argued that welfare workers were being pressured to increase job placements and were doing little more than "giving people bus passes and a copy of the want ads."[15] One recipient
complained that state officials pressured her to accept a job at a fast-
food restaurant instead of waiting for a position as an accounts clerk for
the Dade County Public Schools that she ultimately took. Another
claimed she was forced to quit college after the state refused to continue
benefits when she had taken sixty hours of courses.[16] Other problems
that have been identified include a lack of state officials' contacts with
employers to find jobs for participants,[17] insufficient staffing and other
resources, and the discouragement recipients face from having only low-
wage jobs available.[18]

As mentioned above, subsidies to private employers are an essential
element of many state programs; these subsidies are often funded by
combining welfare and Food Stamp benefits. Massachusetts' "Welfare
Reform '95" program, for example, combines welfare and Food Stamp
benefits to subsidize private sector employment for up to 12 months.[19]
Indiana's "IMPACT" initiative extends the subsidy for up to 24
months.[20] Mississippi's "Work First" reform combines welfare and Food
Stamp benefits to subsidize private sector employment and provides
supplemental payments to recipients when their total income is less
than the combined welfare and Food Stamp benefits they would otherwise receive.[21] The state also permits recipients in six counties to cash
out welfare and Food Stamps to supplement wages in private sector
jobs.[22] Missouri's 1993 "21st Century Communities Demonstration Project" offers welfare recipients the option of having wages subsidized
with welfare funds for up to forty-eight months; direct child support
payments are disregarded if payments affect welfare eligibility status; a
resource allowance of up to $10,000 is provided for participants; and
the hundred-hour rule is eliminated.[23]

Vermont's "Family Independence Project" was given a Federal
waiver in 1993. The state uses welfare money to subsidize wages of

recipients who reach the thirty-month time limit on receiving welfare benefits (in two-parent families, the time limit was reduced to fifteen months). Recipients are placed in public service or community jobs if private employment is not available.[24] The legislation that created the program established three groups to demonstrate the effectiveness of time-limited welfare. Twenty percent of the welfare demonstration group remained in the current welfare system; another 20 percent were given benefits and support services such as training programs, child care and transportation, but were not required to work; and the remaining 60 percent received the support services but were also obligated to go off welfare and take a job after a maximum of thirty months. The program extended Medicaid for an extra twenty-four months in addition to the twelve months welfare recipients get when they make the transition to a job. Those who worked in unsubsidized jobs, but were still below poverty level, were permitted to keep more of what they earned; in addition, they received additional Food Stamp benefits because the state counted less of their earnings against their benefits. Parents with children under thirteen were expected to work twenty hours weekly. Adults in two-parent families and those with no children under thirteen were expected to work 40 hours.[25] Virginia's "Full Employment Program," part of the "Virginia Independence Program," authorizes the state to combine welfare and Food Stamp benefits to subsidize private sector employment.[26] Under West Virginia's "Joint Opportunities for Independence" program (JOIN), employers who provide work experience for participants pay employees an additional $1 per hour for work and travel expenses.[27]

Oregon's JOBS Waiver Project, approved in 1992, permitted the state to require welfare custodial parents under age 16, regardless of the age of their child, and medically able pregnant recipients under age 20 to participate in full-time educational programs. Recipients can also be required to participate in extended job search and mental health and substance abuse programs. State officials can impose an immediate minimum one-month sanction for failure to comply.[28] The state's JOBS Plus program, operating in six counties, encourages private employers to hire welfare recipients and give them work experience. Recipients are paid the minimum wage with funds that previously paid AFDC and Food Stamps benefits. Employers donate $1 an hour after thirty days toward a participant education fund. The state pays wages, payroll expenses, workers compensation, and Social Security taxes for nine months.[29] If employers choose not to offer recipients a permanent position after six months, the firms are obligated to keep them on for another three months and allow them one day a week of pay to search for another job.[30]

The genesis of Oregon's experiment was unusual. Dick Wendt, the founder and head of Jeld-Wen, a company that employs nine thousand people worldwide in the wood products, real estate, and resort industries, bankrolled a controversial workfare measure on the 1990 Oregon state ballot. After that measure failed, he worked to establish Jobs Plus as a way to get people off welfare and into productive jobs. The federal government rejected the reform proposal, but supporters sued then-Governor Barbara Roberts, contending that she did not try hard enough to persuade federal officials. To settle the matter, state officials agreed to negotiate with Jeld-Wen officials, and the result was Jobs Plus. The Federal government subsequently approved the pilot project.[31]

Some Oregonians have criticized JOBS Plus as a free labor program for business and fear that participants are labeled as "damaged goods" because the state is paying employers to hire them. Defenders respond that participating companies pay employees more than the state minimum wage, even though the state will subsidize salaries only to that level. Further, they say that JOBS Plus provides valuable on-the-job training for participants and makes the extra training time required economically feasible for employers.[32] Other critics of subsidized work argue that employers provide little training and supervision for these participants, since they don't have much invested in them and because work assignments are generally in low-skilled, low-paid jobs. However, it is difficult to see how better jobs can be made available to some recipients who lack the educational or experience prerequisites of more attractive jobs.[33] Some fear that subsidized work programs take jobs from non-welfare workers.[34]

WORK EXPERIENCE PROGRAMS

Work experience programs provide an opportunity for welfare recipients to be paid wages or to work in exchange for their benefits. One of the earliest programs was California's Seasonal Employment Opportunities in State Government, begun in 1984, which provided that "AFDC recipients who have necessary qualifications shall be hired before any other applicant, with certain exceptions, for designated State Civil Service positions."[35] Nevada's General Assistance/Temporary Employment program (GATE) proposed to provide job experience for welfare recipients by using grant money to fund salaries and place recipients in public departments, agencies, districts, and nonprofit corporations.

Participants would be obligated to work two days a week and look for jobs three days a week; physically and mentally disabled recipients, those who must care for ill or elderly relatives, or those who live too far away would be exempted.[36]

New York's Working Toward Independence program, approved in 1993, targeted childless adults in the Home Relief Program. The state provided jobs in state institutions and offices; recipients' refusal to participate could result in loss of their Home Relief grant.[37] As a result, one county trimmed its Home Relief caseload by 23 percent and placed 120 Home relief recipients in part-time government jobs that averaged eighteen hours a week.[38] South Carolina created in 1993 a program to train high school dropouts and welfare parents at least 20 years old and who are eligible to participate in the Department of Social Services Work Support Program for work as correctional officers. Participants were to complete high school and receive benefits during their training.[39]

UNPAID WORK/COMMUNITY WORK EXPERIENCE PROGRAMS

Community Work Experience Programs (CWEP) create unpaid public sector jobs for welfare recipients in order to help them gain work experience, promote a sense of obligation among recipients to perform some kind of work in exchange for the benefits they gain, reduce welfare rolls and costs by imposing some conditions on benefits, and help ensure that community needs are addressed.[40] California's 1988 GAIN program was one of the earliest CWEP programs; most were approved between 1982 and 1985. Their most important purpose is increasingly to serve as a default plan if clients are unable to find a job once time limits have expired.

South Carolina's "Self-Sufficiency and Personal Responsibility Program" requires welfare clients to complete Individual Self-Sufficiency Plans, find a job in their field of interest and training within thirty days, or find any job within sixty days. At the end of that period, unemployed recipients must participate in CWEP or lose their benefits.[41] South Dakota's "Strengthening of South Dakota Families Initiative" automatically enrolls unemployed recipients in CWEP after they complete education and training or employment tracks.[42] Supporters of CWEP argue that programs inject the work ethic into the welfare system, prepare welfare recipients for the labor market by teaching them good work habits and skills, enable community work to be performed, and lower welfare costs through job placement or deterrence. Critics counter that they are not effective in getting people off welfare, that enough meaningful jobs cannot be created at a reasonable cost without displacing existing workers, and that recipients are not accorded the same rights, remuneration, or status of regular employees. Organized labor has opposed these and other work requirement programs as a threat to their members in tight labor markets.

The outcomes of these experiments are difficult to assess. Studies show they have high overhead costs and not much impact in moving individuals into private sector jobs.[43] One study of CWEP found "little evidence that unpaid work experience leads to consistent employment or earnings effects." Unpaid work experience "nearly always operated on a limited scale, for a small percentage of the eligible welfare population, and for three-month periods." Programs were sometimes constrained by "staff opposition, administrative difficulties, or insufficient resources." Nor is there clear evidence that "unpaid work experience leads to reductions in welfare receipt or welfare payments." Although some programs combined with job search did reduce welfare payments, "these reductions were not significantly greater than those achieved by running job search alone." In another program, there was a small welfare payment decrease after twenty-one months, but the effect was only temporary.[44]

Unpaid work experience provides free labor for work site sponsors, but it also incurred administrative expenses for work site development; client intake, assignment, and monitoring; support services such as child care and transportation assistance; and participant work allowances. Successful unpaid work programs require sufficient funding; strong staff commitment; adequate worksite capacity; clearly defined procedures for client assignment; client monitoring; client exemptions; effective sanctioning; and no opposition from labor unions, welfare advocacy groups, and community members.[45] The cost of unpaid work experience per participant, in 1993 dollars, ranged from $700 to $2,100. But because of the community and governmental work accomplished through unpaid work experience programs, taxpayers seem to receive a net gain in benefits. In San Diego and West Virginia, for example, the benefit to taxpayers ranged from $260 to $1000 per program group member. Participants and supervisors indicated that the work was meaningful and the work requirement was fair. Most, however, would have preferred a real job.

A 1994 study of unpaid work programs found several constraints. Programs generally excluded mothers with young children; participation was typically voluntary, or had to follow participation in another program component such as job search. Program resources were often limited and designers anticipated opposition by welfare staff, welfare advocates, and labor unions. Some clients were unwilling to work or were exempted. Clients worked as office aides/assistants for nonprofit agencies, mail clerks, day care assistants, workers in street cleaning and repair, and gardeners, but did not teach new skills. Positive earnings effects were found for predominantly female, single-parent welfare applicants in San Diego, but no studies showed welfare savings attributable to unpaid work experience. The annual cost, in 1993 dollars, of keeping a position available was $1,100 to $7,000. The study recommended that states emphasize *"front-end* services that will be offered to welfare recipients *before* reaching the time limit so that the number of people who have to be placed in a work position is minimized," provide reasonable deferral policies for people unable to work, present periodic job search workshops for participants, and require that work site sponsors offer meaningful assignments and hire some participants when jobs become available.[46]

Another evaluation of unpaid work programs found they were constrained by program design decisions, administrative difficulties, inadequate resources, and staff opposition. Unpaid work experience programs were generally meaningful and produced work that offset program costs. However, there was little evidence that unpaid work experience led to consistent employment/earning effects. Benefits to taxpayers generally outweighed the costs, but there were no consistent benefits for individuals.[47]

Overall, studies show that low-intensity, broad-coverage programs that emphasize quick labor force attachment produce "consistent and sustained, but modest, increases in employment and earnings and reductions in welfare receipt of participants, resulting in relatively large welfare savings per dollar spent and a rapid payoff on the resources spent."[48] However, these earnings gains resulted from more people working, not from increases in earnings for those employed. Many remained in poverty and on welfare because of relatively low-paying jobs. Participation in a mix of low-cost services has resulted in different impacts on different segments of the welfare population. Low-intensity, broad coverage programs do not help the most job-ready recipients. The most disadvantaged and long-term recipients experienced the most welfare savings, but the programs did not increase their employment experience or economic self-sufficiency. Clients in the middle group achieved the most consistent earnings gains. A five-year follow-up study shows that participants did significantly better for three to four years after completing the program. The programs helped people to take jobs and leave the rolls more quickly than they would have on their own, but did not reduce the number of people still on welfare five years after leaving the programs.[49]

HUMAN CAPITAL DEVELOPMENT EXPERIMENTS

The human capital development model of welfare reform seeks to help prepare clients for work before expecting them to enter the labor market. Typical services provided to clients range from basic education programs aimed at producing high school diplomas or GEDs to more focused job training and preparation activities. Education and training programs have been a mainstay of the welfare system, but have increasingly come under attack because of their expense, their limited success in moving clients off of welfare, and their inability to compel efforts on the part of recipients to make a contribution to their community in exchange for assistance. Nevertheless, many states still offer education and training programs and have increasingly linked participation to the continued receipt of benefits and to the imposition of time limits.

Proponents of education and training programs for welfare recipients argue that helping individuals gain basic academic skills will ultimately enable them to enter more advanced training programs and/or find jobs with higher wages. This will also improve their chances for good jobs, opportunities for advancement, and the potential for real, long-term self-sufficiency.[50] Some proponents would even extend benefits to two and four years of college education, although others believe that financing college education is not an efficient allocation of scarce resources and shifts resources from recipients who are most at risk of continued dependency to those who are better educated and less at risk. Under this model, states invest in longer-term human capital development by performing up-front, in-depth assessments of clients' education, employment history/experience, interests, health, talents, labor market potential, and need for social services.[51]

Table 6.2 summarizes the experience of states with training programs that target disadvantaged individuals. It is difficult to compare these programs: The net cost per participant, for example, ranged from $136 to $10,147. But the table demonstrates that human capital development has been one of the most active areas of state welfare reform. States have been experimenting with a combination of job search, education, job skills training, on-the-job training, unpaid work experience, and paid work.

Iowa's JOBS welfare reform program illustrates many of the chal-

TABLE 6.2
TRAINING PROGRAMS TARGETING DISADVANTAGED INDIVIDUALS AND
EVALUATED USING RANDOMIZATION TECHNIQUES OUTCOME
(PARTICIPANT-COMPARISON DIFFERENCE)

Program (start date)[a]	Target Group	Mandatory/ Voluntary	Services	Net Cost per Participant ($)	Annual Earnings ($)	Annual AFDC Payments
1. Arkansas WORK Program (1983)	AFDC applicants and recipients with children 3 years of age or older	Mandatory	Job search assistance; unpaid work experience	118	Year: 1. 167[b] 2. 223 3. 337[c]	-145[b] -190[b] -168[b]
2. Baltimore Options Program (1982)	AFDC applicants and recipients with children 6 years of age or older	Mandatory	Job search assistance; education; job skills training; on-the-job training	953	Year: 1. 149 2. 401[b] 3. 511[b]	2 -34 -31
3. Cook County WIN Demonstration (1985)	AFDC applicants and recipients with chil$Xdren 6 years of age or older	Mandatory	Job search assistance; unpaid work experience	157	Year: 1. 10	-40
4. Louisville WIN Laboratory Experiment (1978)	AFDC applicants and recipients with children of any age	Mandatory and voluntary	Individual job search assistance	136	Year: 1. 289[b] 2. 456[b] 3. 435[b]	-75 -164[b] -184[b]
5. Maine On-the-Job Training Program (1983)	Unemployed AFDC recipients on rolls for six or more months with children of any age	Voluntary	Employability training; unpaid work experience; subsidized on-the-job training	2,019	Year: 1. 104 2. 871[b] 3. 941	64 29 80

TABLE 6.2

TRAINING PROGRAMS TARGETING DISADVANTAGED INDIVIDUALS AND
EVALUATED USING RANDOMIZATION TECHNIQUES OUTCOME
(PARTICIPANT-COMPARISON DIFFERENCE) (*Continued*)

Program (start date)[a]	Target Group	Mandatory/ Voluntary	Services	Net Cost per Participant ($)	Annual Earnings ($)	Annual AFDC Payments
6. New Jersey On-the-Job Training Program (1984)	AFDC recipients over 18 years of age with children of any age	Voluntary	Subsidized on-the-job training	787	Year: 1. [d] 2. 591	−190[b] −238
7. San Diego SWIM (1985)	AFDC applicants and recipients with children 6 years of age or older	Mandatory	Job search assistance; unpaid work experience; education; job skills training	919	Year: 1. 352[b] 2. 658[b]	−407[b] −553[b]
8. Virginia Employment Services Program (1983)	AFDC applicants and recipients with children 6 years of age or older	Mandatory	Job search assistance; unpaid work experience; education; job skills training	430	Year: 1. 69 2. 280[b] 3. 268	−69 −36 −111[b]
9A. NSW Demonstration (1976)	AFDC recipients	Voluntary	Structured paid work experience	10,147[c]	Year: 1. 409 2. 386 3. 66 4. 721 5. 735[b] 6. 866[b] 7. 682[b] 8. 619	[d]
9B. NSW Demonstration (1976)	Youths	Voluntary	Structured paid work experience	7,582[c]	Year: 1. 15 2. 259 3. 101 4. 119 5. 28 6. −12 7. 28 8. −56	[d]

TABLE 6.2

TRAINING PROGRAMS TARGETING DISADVANTAGED INDIVIDUALS AND
EVALUATED USING RANDOMIZATION TECHNIQUES OUTCOME
(PARTICIPANT-COMPARISON DIFFERENCE) (*Continued*)

Program (start date)[a]	Target Group	Mandatory/ Voluntary	Services	Net Cost per Participant ($)	Annual Earnings ($)	Annual AFDC Payments
10A. National JTPA Study (1987)	Economically disadvantage women	Voluntary	Job search assistance; job skills training; on-the-job training	[d]	First 18 months: 444[b]	[d]
10B. National JTPA Study (1987)	Economically disadvantaged men	Voluntary	Job search assistance; job skills training; on-the-job training	[d]	First 18 months: 453	[d]
10C. National JTPA Study (1987)	Out-of-school youth	Voluntary	Job search assistance; job skills training; on-the-job training	[d]	First 18 months: Female, −150 Male, −703[b]	[d]
11A. California GAIN (1988)	AFDC applicants and recipients who are single parents with children 6 years of age or older	Mandatory	Basic education; skills training; on-the-job training; job search assistance; unpaid work experience	[d]	Year: 1.223[b]	−231
11B. California GAIN (1988)	AFDC applicants and recipients who are household heads of two-parent families with children of any age	Mandatory	Basic education; skills training; on-the-job training; job search assistance; unpaid work experience	[d]	Year: 1. 309[b]	−346

Note: Dollar amounts are in evaluation year dollars except for rows 4, 9, 10, and 11, which are in 1985 dollars.

ª The start date refers to the start of intake for the research sample and not to the start of the actual program.

ᵇ Significant at the 95 percent confidence level.

ᶜ These figures include the trainees' subsidized wages and fringe benefits. If these are excluded (for example, treated as transfers rather than costs), then the net costs are $3,457 for AFDC trainees and $3,011 for youth.

ᵈ Not available.

Source: U.S. General Accounting Office, "Welfare to Work: Most AFDC Training Programs Not Emphasizing Job Placement" (Washington, D.C.: G.A.O., May 1995).

lenges states face in developing and implementing a human capital development approach. Under the Iowa plan, recipients are given incentives to find and retain employment, including earnings disregards for the first four months of employment (for those with less than $1,200 in earnings the previous year), and transitional child care for two years. Resource limits for assistance and Food Stamps are increased, and interest and dividend income is disregarded to encourage savings. Recipients sign a social contract that outlines mutual obligations and consequences for noncompliance, including a time frame for achieving specific goals. Contracts can be revised if recipients maintain contact with caseworkers; those who do not sign a contract or follow their plan are placed on a Limited Benefit Plan that provides benefits for three months, then reduces them for three months, and then eliminates them six months later. Postsecondary education assistance—including child care, transportation costs, and tuition and fees—is available, but waiting lists are long, and clients must work or volunteer until they reach the top of the list. Recipients can pursue educational opportunities independently through Pell Grants. The entire program is aimed at encouraging self-sufficiency.

The prospects for a comprehensive education and training program are quite good in Iowa, a state that enjoys a low poverty rate, low unemployment, and a strong economy and whose population is largely rural, homogenous, and highly educated.[52] Caseloads increased during the first six months of the reform, from 36,000 to nearly 41,000, primarily because of generous earnings disregards and an increase in unemployed parents. They then declined steadily to below 36,000 by June 1995. The average monthly benefit also declined from $374 to $337 during the same period.

Although the Iowa plan had some success in moving people into the work force, however, most have not become self-sufficient because of barriers such as inadequate education, jobs without benefits, temporary jobs, lack of reliable transportation, and personal or family disabilities.[53] One study of Iowa's reforms randomly assigned cases to treatment or control status in the nine counties, including all ongoing cases as of September 1993 and all new applicants beginning in October 1993. It surveyed recipients, only one-third of whom reported that their "contracts" helped them in reaching their goals. According to some participants, goals were "often vague or generic" and activities were not often linked to reaching the final goal. Those who reported negative experiences felt pressured by staff to pursue the caseworker's goals.[54] Other negative experiences were a result of interaction with caseworkers, long waiting lists for education programs, lack of follow-up by staff, and living with the threat of the Limited Benefit Plan. Some complaints focused on the lack of available jobs and good pay; education plans that could not be implemented because of inadequate funding; limited supply of dependable licensed providers in rural areas, and a shortage of infant care in urban areas; and lack of employer understanding about the need to miss work because of sick children or lack of child care. Those who reported positive experiences with the Iowa JOBS program developed their own ideas and received support from the staff to try new activities. Success was also attributed to positive relationships with caseworkers, the education and training services themselves, self-sufficiency encouragement, and goal-setting assistance.[55]

The cost of welfare reform included benefits and administrative costs, Food Stamp benefits and administrative costs, Medicaid claims paid and administrative costs, and child care costs for JOBS participants. Preliminary calculations found an increase in Medicaid expenditures and an initial increase in welfare spending due to a higher number of claims during the second year. Iowa's program had some success in increasing work effort and creating responsible attitudes among recipients. Some people stayed on welfare longer, but received lower average benefits. Cuts in child care resulted from the increased cost of Medicaid and the federal cost-neutrality requirements; reductions in spending seemed to hurt the goals of making work pay and promoting self-sufficiency.[56]

The Iowa experience makes it clear that the health of the local economy is tremendously important in determining the prospects for welfare reform. In a low-unemployment labor market, a low-cost, employment-oriented approach, coupled with strict sanctions for nonparticipation in job search requirements, will likely reduce the welfare rolls. But it is much less clear how to achieve the goal of helping families become more self-sufficient. The Iowa demonstration, as well as most other experiments, has started so recently that it is not clear for now what its long-term consequences might be.

The Massachusetts Employment and Training Choices (ET) sought to place participants in "meaning full jobs" that paid $5 or more an hour, lasted at least thirty days, and were full-time; reduce welfare dependency; save tax dollars; and increase participant self-sufficiency. It initially targeted women with children aged 14 to 18, teenage parents and their dependents, and two-parent families but also focused on people who had been on welfare at least two years or lived in public housing. The program required officials to prepare an employment plan for each recipient based on a skills assessment. Activities included education (basic, GED, ESL), training, job search, supported work, and direct placement. Child care was provided through vouchers for a twelve-month transition period, but families were not eligible for day care unless both parents were enrolled in ET. One evaluation found that in 1986, 38 percent of recipients earned at least $5 or more an hour and 38 percent found jobs in 1986, 68 percent of which were full-time jobs. Massachusetts spent over $3,300 for each placement.[57]

As part of Oregon's JOBS Plus (grant-subsidized private-sector work program), employers contribute $1/hour of work to an Individual Education Account (IEA). Once the employee's wages are no longer subsidized, the IEA is transferred to the State Scholarship Commission, which reserves the funds until needed for education and training at state colleges.[58]

Tennessee's JOBSWork includes mandatory education, job skills training, job readiness activities, and job development and placement activities; job search and on-the-job training are optional. Tennessee's program is administered through a partnership with the state Department of Human Services, Department of Labor, Department of Education, the Board of Regents, and local and private agencies. Private Industry Councils contributed $3.5 million in JTPA training dollars to JOBSWork.

In one county, Arizona initiated a full employment demonstration project in which selected JOBS participants receive nine to twelve months of on-the-job training (private or public) paying at least minimum wage; wages are subsidized with welfare and Food Stamp funds. Monthly supplemental payments are offered to offset any loss in income. Employers must provide mentoring; after nine months of work they must provide participants with up to eight hours of paid time a week to engage in job search. The state can impose sanctions of up to 50 percent of the client's welfare grant for unjustified failure to comply with requirements.[59]

Some welfare reforms go beyond education and training to help recipients create their own jobs. Iowa initiated in 1989 and Self-

Employment Investment Demonstration (SEID) project, a voluntary entrepreneurship program that "offers small business loans up to $5000 to start microbusinesses and business skills training in finance, marketing and management."[60] Minnesota's SEID program, begun in 1987, provided business loans (up to $3,000) from private and state sources to enable participants to start microbusinesses. Clients receive business skills training, technical consultation, and evaluations from an economic service provider. Between March 1988 and June 1991, 604 AFDC clients received orientation in this program; 335 enrolled and 244 completed training. As a result 103 businesses were launched, 48 recipients became employed and left AFDC, and 31 recipients enrolled in further education. These outcomes involved 75 percent of those who completed SEID training.[61]

Maryland's Self-Employment Initiative Waiver allowed participants to maintain a business bank account to be used exclusively for business, not to exceed $5,000 on the first day of each month, to allow for purchase of capital assets or durable goods as a business expense deduction up to a limit of $5,000. Participants could also to use the money to repay business loans from subsequent receipts. The 185 percent gross income test was waived up to an annual profit of $15,000 to allow entrepreneurs to build businesses up to an adequate level before losing welfare benefits. The program also allowed an unencumbered cash reserve fund, not to exceed $3,000 as a business expense, in which payments are averaged over a quarter. Profits for personal use are prorated over the following quarter as countable income.

ASSESSING THE LABOR MARKET AND HUMAN CAPITAL APPROACHES

The labor force attachment approach relies on rapid job entry, job search, work experience, and short-term educational training for those who did not find jobs. The human capital development approach seeks to increase recipients' earning ability, long-term self-sufficiency, and skill-building. What are the impacts of programs emphasizing human capital development versus those emphasizing immediate job placement? Do investments in human capital development lead to higher-wage jobs, substantially more income, and greater long-term self-sufficiency? Does immediate job placement in a low-wage job lead to continuation in a low-wage job, to eventual employment in a better job, or to job loss and a return to the welfare rolls? How are different subgroups affected by these two approaches?

Some studies offer partial answers. A review of the Washington Family Incentives Program concluded that investment and intensity of services during the two-year period of receipt must be substantial if they are to be more successful than current programs. Two suggestions were made: (1) make an inventory of existing federal and state resources and programs that can be tapped for employment-related services, and (2) identify and track specific target groups (time limited, characteristics, and so on) within the welfare caseload. One study found that populations participating in higher-cost, selective programs "may be more motivated, more likely to use services, and less burdened by child care needs and other barriers to participation." Therefore, effects cannot be directly compared to those of mandatory, broad-coverage programs. Because of heavy preemployment investments, selective programs produce consistent and sustained increases in employment and earnings but result in small welfare savings. Welfare savings are also minimal because more people stay on the rolls: Earnings gains result from improvements in job quality and increased hourly wages, rather than from increased numbers of people employed. And with the exception of supported work programs, selective programs had little success with the most disadvantaged recipients.[62] The National Supported Work Demonstration "provided very disadvantaged recipients with highly structured, full-time, increasingly more demanding work experience paying approximately them minimum wage for up to a year or eighteen months. Close supervision and peer support were provided to improve basic work habits and skills."[63]

Another study evaluated the effects of voluntary subsidized employment programs, mandatory work/training programs, and financial incentives to work in terms of their impact on the AFDC caseload as a whole. The study calculated program effects on the proportion of AFDC recipients receiving grants twenty-four months after program entry, total AFDC benefits over the first twenty-four months of program involvement, and total earnings over the first twenty-four months of program involvement.[64] It found that "while all three of the policy strategies examined have shown the potential to affect participating families in a meaningful way, their penetration is too limited to have a major impact on the AFDC caseload."[65] The results in reducing welfare dependency among participants were mixed. "When dependency is measured in terms of how many participating families are on the rolls at the end of two years, rather than how much assistance they received, the subsidized employment programs show the strongest results."[66] Findings were still inconsistent, however. No program reduced caseloads by even as much as one percentage point or reduced average expenditure for welfare benefits by more than $10 per case per month.[67]

Should programs be voluntary or mandatory? Mandatory work requirements and cutoffs dominate political reform discussion because they are seen as ways to "send messages" to nonworkers about the importance of working for benefits received. On the other hand, some argue that a voluntary program "will be more effective because it focuses on more highly motivated clients and encourages localities to design attractive programs."[68] One study described the tradeoff this way:

> A mandatory program would serve large numbers of participants but would relegate many to low-cost options such as job search or CWEP. A program that relies on volunteers and selective compulsion of targeted groups might serve fewer people but could provide higher-cost services.[69]

Mandatory programs also cost more because of the extent of monitoring required and the resources involved in tracking participants. Ineffective monitoring will send signals that obligations can be ignored. Lengthy notification procedures and cumbersome appeals and adjudications processes may discourage staff members from initiating sanctions.[70]

Welfare-to-work reforms raise other questions. What does the state do with children of parents who refuse to cooperate and so lose benefits? What if jobs don't exist for program graduates? Who will create them? One official in the Oklahoma Department of Human Service's family support service division emphasized that the private sector must help create jobs: "It doesn't matter how well-trained and job-ready our recipients are if the jobs aren't out there. . . . DHS is not the agency that creates jobs."[71] The director of Michigan's Social Services department argued that time limits may not work because of the job market: "You have to recognize the reality of the economy we live in. If you go over to Wal-Mart now, you know what you're going to get offered. You're going to get offered 19½ hours a week. And you know why? Because they don't want to have to pay benefits. That's the real world."[72]

Should the various work-welfare strategies be viewed as competing or as complementary approaches? Do strategies reach identical or overlapping client groups, or do different approaches reach different groups? Does combining multiple strategies result in more success than focusing on one strategy? Evelyn Ganzglass argues that highly successful programs heavily emphasize employment but also integrate education, training and support services. No programs have removed participants from poverty; the multiple objectives of most programs have been difficult to achieve. Strategies that increase employment or earnings may not reduce dependency or cut government costs, and vice versa. Programs that seem initially promising may not have positive long-term effects. Education and training programs that require substantial initial investment may not show positive results for several years. In the short run, programs that target teenagers and promote responsible behavior have had little success: No programs studied reduced repeat pregnancies, and most young women served by the programs remain on welfare.

Many state welfare reforms seek simultaneously to reduce long-term welfare receipt, protect children from extreme poverty, and reduce costs. Mutual responsibility on the part of states and recipients "can simultaneously raise recipients' earnings and employment rates, reduce their reliance on AFDC, and save money for taxpayers."[73] These programs, however, require extensive up-front resource investment and do not end poverty or long-term benefit receipt. Neil Gilbert concludes that "current welfare reforms organized around incentives to work are plagued by three problems: they ignore successes, they create perverse effects, and they require a level of callousness that social workers are unlikely to countenance."[74] Irene Lurie and Mary Bryna Sanger argue, "Job search and CWEP are low-cost options that require clients to make efforts to work but do little to improve their earning capacity. On-the-job training and work supplementation have more promise as investments in human capital but require a supply of both job-ready candidates and prearranged jobs with private or non-profit organizations."[75]

Stephen Freedman and Daniel Friedlander found the following results in three states—Georgia, Michigan, and California—that had pursued reform efforts aimed at improving human capital: a modest increase in GED or high school diploma receipt (7 percent for HDCs versus about three percent for control group members; AFDC reductions of 4 percent and average payments reduced by $38 per month or 14 percent, but smaller than those in the LFA approach; greater participation in employment-oriented activity after attending orientation (64 percent of HCDs versus 33 percent of control group members) and more participation in education and job search. Sanctions had been applied to 25 percent of recipients during the two-year study period, reflecting strict enforcement of rules. Better follow-up and significant impacts were found for full-time employment in the first year. However, only two years of results were available, making long-term assessments impossible.[76]

Other studies emphasized child care, transportation, and the state of the job market as key determinants in job placement for recipients. One official from the Georgia Department of Technical and Adult Education observed that the "biggest barriers for women who want training are child care and transportation."[77] Employment in many areas is difficult to find at all, and the situation may be worse for women, who are commonly hired only for low-wage service jobs. In this sense, the program may work slightly better for men, who are more often eligible for factory- and construction-type jobs, which tend to pay better. According to a welfare rights activist, "The workfare program in [Arkansas], JOBS, is not going to work. The poor already work every day, and they cannot put food on the table for their children. What kind of job you goin' to give me? You work, but it doesn't elevate you above poverty. And even if you give people a year of training, where's the job market? Do you know that the job program in our state created 206 jobs? You had to have a college degree to get a slot."[78]

Douglas North cites many examples of former welfare recipients helped to independence by going to college through a training program before JOBS was in place. In Vermont, Goddard College filled its half-empty dorms with single mothers who wanted an education in order to become independent through a degree and professional career. Goddard College worked with the state Department of Social Welfare to discover that single parents could go to college without the college having to provide more assistance than it already provided to needy students. Additionally, students did not have to incur large student debts, and welfare costs did not increase. The program also increased tuition money paid to the college.[79]

Robert Sheak and David Dabelko's study of welfare reforms conclude that without a major job-creation component, workfare programs "intensify rather than ameliorate the subsistence living conditions of the poor."[80] Even those placed in jobs may find those job placements to be very temporary, as many are forced to return to welfare by low wages and lack of health benefits. A major problem with the JOBS program is that states cannot or will not fully fund the programs. Although the blame is often placed on the participants themselves, much of the problem with these programs is a lack of funding. Other problems center on administrative structure. Many states are moving towards consolidation of welfare, Food Stamp, and other offices to try to promote efficiency. But social service agencies that are smaller, more accessible to clients, and located in their communities may be better able to help clients find jobs.[81]

A final issue that deserves discussion is whether, in the absence of private-sector jobs, states should require some kind of work in exchange for benefit checks, or whether recipients should be paid directly in a joblike salary. In the 1980s, for example, Ronald Reagan promoted "workfare" throughout his presidency, encouraging states to experiment with programs that required welfare recipients to work in order to receive benefits. The welfare grant, divided by the minimum wage, would determine how many hours of work would be required each month. Public employee unions opposed workfare, fearing it would result in job losses for their members; advocates for welfare recipients also opposed this mandatory requirement. President Reagan's efforts culminated in the workfare provisions of the 1988 Family Support Act. Educational and training programs were also part of the FSA, and they were pushed by welfare agency administrators much more than jobs: By 1994, less than 1 percent of AFDC recipients worked in community jobs in exchange for their benefits.[82]

In 1994, the Clinton administration's welfare task force argued against workfare, criticizing it as ineffective in reducing welfare, charging that the "make-work" jobs possessed less dignity than jobs that paid traditional wages. The Clinton plan suggested that, instead of workfare, recipients be offered a job that would require a certain number of hours at an hourly wage. As a "real" job, it would serve as more of a deterrent for those who might seek welfare without work obligations. If recipients failed to show up for work, for instance, they would not get paid and may lose their job. The estimated 10 percent of recipients with physical disabilities or other problems who could show they are unable to work would be excused from the requirement. According to one estimate, however, between 20 and 25 percent of welfare recipients are unable to hold a regular job because of mild illness, drug dependency, lack of personal discipline, and other problems. A strict work-for-wages system might force many of them, and their children, into the streets.[83]

In contrast, workfare is more flexible and can accommodate workers who need more of a transition to work or who at least need time off to stay home with a sick child. Those who miss work without an acceptable excuse would have their benefits reduced rather than losing their jobs. Some of the successful pilot programs, in California and Wisconsin, for example, involve welfare administrators who are not afraid to impose sanctions such as benefit reductions in order to compel participation in required activities. Work-for-wage jobs also cost about $2,000 a year more than workfare because of the number of hours of guaranteed work and benefits. Costs could also increase if recipients lose their jobs and the state needs to intervene with foster care or other services.

However, workfare requires monitoring of recipients' work activities and their absences from work, but state offices lack the resources to do that. Workfare sanctions are typically small—$40 to $70—but the paperwork required to impose them can take months. Perfect welfare reform programs may be impossible to find, and we ought to look for those that have the best chance of working. Work-for-wages is tough on welfare recipients; however, reforms that talk tough but are expensive or appear to threaten children will likely be abandoned.[84] Workfare has the added appeal of possible bipartisan support: It is a modest program that has worked and is less expensive than some alternatives.

States are close to a consensus on equating welfare reform with tough work requirements. But the annual cost of providing training to welfare recipients, including day care and other services, is about $5,000 in addition to the actual cash payments. The overhead cost of providing jobs for welfare recipients is about $4,000, including day care, transportation, and supervision.[85] The challenge in raising expectations for welfare reform is that adequate funding will not be provided to make the reforms work. If money is not available to pay for training and jobs positions then nothing will change for recipients. That has been the experience under the 1988 Family Support Act, which required able-bodied adult welfare recipients to work or participate in job training. But only about one-sixth of the slots were funded and priority was given to volunteers who largely filled the positions that were available.[86] Senator Moynihan has argued that "we must get rid of [the] stigma [of welfare receipt] by emphasizing child support, support to families, and the education and training adults need to get off welfare."[87] Unfortunately, there seem to be some serious questions about whether the JOBS program is indeed productive in either eliminating welfare's stigma or helping participants become independent. According to Moynihan, "our difficulty is that the federal executive branch currently lacks the institutional capacity fully to implement [welfare and related laws]."[88]

JOBS programs have always suffered from a lack of adequate funding. The 1988 funding for JTPA was 70 percent less than CETA's 1980 funding; funding for WIN in 1988 was less than one-third of its 1980 level. Too little funding for programs that try to help too many people moves a large number of people into poor jobs instead of a smaller number into good jobs. Programs also sabotage themselves by trying to cut corners. JTPA abolished training stipends, making it impossible for most people to spare the time for training. WIN used inexpensive "job clubs" to teach interview skills, but they were effective only when participants already had marketable skills.[89]

There are general problems with employment programs. "Creaming," which targets the most employable (those with job experience) instead of helping the least employable, such as single mothers and teenagers with few skills and no work history, is common. Training programs are too short to be of real benefit. Basic education programs have lost favor because they delay working, but many of the poor lack essential literacy and quantitative skills in an age when "a high school diploma no longer guarantees a living wage, and the absence of a diploma almost guarantees failure."[90]

Few programs deal with other barriers to entering the labor force, such as low self-confidence, chaotic lives at home, and unfamiliarity with workplace rules and expected standards of behavior.[91] The city of Milwaukee is one of the few areas that are taking the public jobs route. The city has about 43,000 welfare and general assistance recipients. A committee of city officials, union leaders, and others identified some fifty thousand public service jobs, including five thousand in housing rehabilitation—small scale projects too small to be of interest to unions who prefer large, commercial contracts; ten thousand in neighborhood patrols that, armed with radios, would notify police of problems; ten thousand sanitation workers; and six thousand education aides. But other cities face greater challenges in finding enough public jobs. New York City, for example, has 125,000 employable people on welfare. If it were to hire them all it would have to increase its work force by one third.[92]

The federal government could create incentives for states to develop public-sector jobs programs rather than simply delegating welfare reform to states through a block grant. It could offer to pay, for example, 40 percent of welfare benefits for recipients who don't work but 70 percent of the cost for those working in public jobs. At the minimum, it could at least offer to pay the costs incurred when youngest welfare mothers not in school participate.[93]

Only a few areas of the country have experimented with universal participation in education or work requirements. Ohio's Learning, Earning, and Parenting (LEAP) program required the state's twenty thousand AFDC mothers to stay in school and provided the necessary support services for them. The program was clear about requirements and consequences: If you were a teenage mother, you were in LEAP; if you missed school, your benefits were cut; if you attended regularly, you received a bonus.[94] Requiring all able-bodied recipients to participate in work and training programs is an essential part of reforming welfare, but states must be willing and able to fund these programs and find sufficient jobs. But only a few states such as Wisconsin have done so thus far.

Since part of the welfare reform agenda is to cut spending, a comprehensive, more expensive program seems unlikely. One alternative is to target teenage parents and require that they live with their families rather than moving out on their own and stay in school until they graduate or turn twenty, when they would be offered a job. If they failed to meet any of those requirements, they would lose part of their grant. Targeting teenagers in this manner has several advantages. It would focus resources on the beginning of the welfare dependency cycle and would have the greatest impact on reducing long-term welfare dependency. It would also be affordable, since there are approximately four hundred thousand teenage welfare mothers and the cost would be about $500 million a year. It would send a clear signal that welfare benefits are not a way for teenagers to get out of going to school and live on their own. Teen mothers could also be given priority in efforts to determine paternity and obtain child support payments. And with the schooling and age requirements, even if women waited until twenty to get pregnant and go on welfare, they would be more likely to finish high school.[95]

From a political perspective, it is critical, at least in many states that do not have a strong commitment to improving welfare, to generate modest proposals that would likely work, rather than proposing comprehensive reforms that will not be implemented and will contribute to further cynicism about our ability to solve the problems of poverty and welfare dependency or pursue other public purposes.

REFERENCES

[1] Elaine Stuart, "The Reform Race: Will New State Welfare Reforms Punish the Poor or Push Them to Self-Sufficiency?" *State Government News*, The Council of State Governments (June 1994): 17–20, at 20.

[2] U.S. Department of Health and Human Services, Administration for Children and Families, Office of Family Assistance, "State Welfare Demonstrations," *H.H.S. Fact Sheet* (Washington, D.C.: Government Printing Office, January 1996).

[3] Ibid.

[4] Ibid., 9.

[5] Ibid.

[6] Ibid., 11.

[7] Jennifer A. Neisner, "State Welfare Initiatives," *CRS Report for Congress* (Washington D.C.: Congressional Research Service, January 24, 1995).

[8] Irene Lurie and Mary Bryna Sanger, "The Family Support Act: Defining the Social Contract in New York," *Social Service Review* (March 1991): 43–67, at 55.

[9] Ibid., at 57.

[10] Stephen Freedman and Daniel Friedlander (Manpower Demonstration Research Corporation), "The JOBS Evaluation: Early Findings on Program Impacts in Three Sites" (Washington, D.C.: U.S. Department of Health and Human Services/U.S. Department of Education, September 1995): ES-2.

[11] Ibid., ES-6.

[12] Maureen Balleza, "One Motivator: the Catfish Plant," *The New York Times*, September 21, 1995, p. A10.

[13] State Representative Peter F. Villano (D.-Hamden), quoted in Jonathan Rabinovitz, "Single Mothers Trapped in Welfare Fallout," *The New York Times*, May 19, 1995, p. A12.

[14] "Welfare Reform Will Get Test in Florida," *Chicago Tribune*, January 28, 1994, p. N3.

[15] Laurie Udesky, "Punishing the Poor," *Southern Exposure* (Summer 1991): 12–13.

[16] Brett Campbell, "Red Tape Blues: Poor Texans Ordered to Work Find Themselves Trapped in a Bureaucratic Maze that Ignores the Realities of Poverty," *Southern Exposure* (Summer 1991): 23–26, at 23.

[17] U.S. General Accounting Office, *Welfare to Work: Most AFDC Training Programs Not Emphasizing Job Placement* (Washington, D.C.: G.A.O., May 1995): 5.

[18] Ibid., 4.

[19] U.S. Department of Health and Human Services, "State Welfare Demonstrations."

[20] Ibid.

[21] Ibid.

[22] Ibid.

[23] Neisner, "State Welfare Initiatives."

[24] Ellen Perlman, "Vermont Legislature Explores Welfare Reform," *City & State* (June 7–20, 1993): 18.

[25] Ibid.

[26] U.S. Department of Health and Human Services, "State Welfare Demonstrations."

[27] Ibid.

[28] Neisner, "State Welfare Initiatives."

[29] Neisner, "State Welfare Initiatives"; Hilary Stout, "Oregon Tries Its Own Welfare Reform, Offering Employers Incentives to Put People to Work," *The Wall Street Journal*, May 24, 1995, p. A16.

[30] Susan Kellam, "Welfare Experiments: Are States Leading the Way Toward National Reform?" *CQ Researcher* 4:34 (September 16, 1994): 795–815.

[31] Ashbel S. Green, "Shy Tycoon Spearheads Oregon's Welfare Reform," *Oregonian*, September 26, 1994, p. A1.

[32] Stout, "Oregon Tries Its Own Welfare Reform."

[33] Sarah K. Gideonse and William R. Meyers, "Why the Family Support Act Will Fail," *Challenge* (September–October 1989): 33–39.

[34] Christina Klein, "Aid to Families with Dependent Children (AFDC) Self-Sufficiency Project" (Department of Health and Social Services, Division of Public Assistance, Alaska, February 1993).

[35] Jason Turner, "AFDC Research and Demonstration Projects in Fiscal Year 1991: Section 1115 Grant Projects" (report prepared for Administration for Children and Families, Office of Family Assistance April 10, 1992).

[36] "Nevada Workfare Program Tabled for Consideration," *The Outlook from the STATE CAPITALS* 47:1 (January 1993).

[37] "New York Public Employee Unions Upset over 'Workfare'," *The Outlook from the STATE CAPITALS* 47:1 (January 1993).

[38] Kevin Sack, "New York Shifting Focus of Welfare to Job Placement," *The New York Times*, May 21, 1994.

[39] "South Carolina Will Provide Correctional Work for Welfare Recipients," *The Outlook from the STATE CAPITALS* 47:1 (January 1993).

[40] Klein, "Aid to Families with Dependent Children (AFDC) Self-Sufficiency Project," 20.

[41] U.S. Department of Health and Human Services, "State Welfare Demonstrations."

[42] Ibid.

[43] Tom Morganthau, Bob Cohn, and Eleanor Clift, "The Entitlement Trap," *Newsweek* (December 13, 1993): 33–34.

[44] Thomas Brock, David Butler, and David Long, "Unpaid Work Experience for Welfare Recipients: Findings and Lessons From MDRC Research" (New York: Manpower Demonstration Research Corporation, September 1993), 3–4.

[45] Ibid., 4.

[46] Manpower Demonstration Research Corporation, "Unpaid Work Experience: Findings and Lessons from MDRC Research" (October 1994): 9.

[47] Evelyn Ganzglass, "Research Findings on the Effectiveness of State Welfare-to-Work Programs" (Washington, D.C.: Employment and Social Services Policy Studies, Center for Policy Research, National Governors' Association, 1994).

[48] Ibid., 5.

[49] Ibid.

[50] Manpower Research Demonstration Corporation, "Overview of the JOBS Evaluation" (New York: MDRC, November 1991): 13.

[51] Lurie and Sanger, "The Family Support Act" at 57.

[52] Anne R. Gordon, Carol Prindle, and Thomas M. Fraker, "Initial Findings from the Evaluation of the Iowa Family Investment Program," (Iowa Department of Human Services, paper presented the annual meeting of the Association for Public Policy Analysis and Management, Washington, D.C., 1995).

[53] Ibid., 12–13.

[54] Ibid., 11.

[55] Ibid.

[56] Ibid.

[57] U.S. General Accounting Office, "Work and Welfare: Analysis of AFDC Employment Programs in Four States," *Fact Sheet for the Committee on Finance, U.S. Senate* (Washington D.C.: G.A.O., January 1988).

[58] U.S. Department of Health and Human Services, "State Welfare Demonstrations."

[59] Neisner, "State Welfare Initiatives."

[60] Turner, "AFDC Research and Demonstration Projects in Fiscal Year 1991."

[61] Ibid.

[62] Ganzglass, "Research Findings on the Effectiveness of State Welfare-to-Work Programs," 6.

[63] Ibid.

[64] William L. Hamilton, Larry L. Orr, Stephen H. Bell, Nancy R. Burstein, and David J. Fein, "The Effects of Alternative Welfare-to-Work Strategies on AFDC Caseloads"

(paper presented at the 16th Annual Research Conference of the Association for Public Policy Analysis and Management, Chicago, October 1994).

[65] Ibid., 14.

[66] Ibid., 17.

[67] Ibid.

[68] Lurie and Sanger, "The Family Support Act," 60.

[69] Ibid.

[70] Ibid., 61.

[71] "Task Force Says Private Sector Must Help in Oklahoma Welfare Reform," *The Outlook from the STATE CAPITALS* 47:41 (October 11, 1993).

[72] Eliza Newlin Carney, "Test Drive," *National Journal* (December 10, 1994): 2893–97, at 2897.

[73] Dan Bloom and David Butler, "Executive Summary, Implementing Time-Limited Welfare: Early Experiences in Three States" (New York: Manpower Demonstration Research Corporation, advance prepublication copy, November 1995): 2.

[74] Neil Gibert, *Welfare Justice: Restoring Social Equity* (New Haven, Conn.: Yale University Press, 1995), 168.

[75] Lurie and Sanger, "The Family Support Act," 57.

[76] Freedman and Friedlander (MDRC), "The JOBS Evaluation."

[77] Georgia Department of Human Resources, "The Peach Express" (Winter 1992): 1.

[78] Laurie Udesky, "Looks Like I Got Mad: Welfare Rights Activist Annie Smart Talks About Going on Welfare under Truman—and Fighting for Reform under Bush," *Southern Exposure* (Summer 1991): 27–30, at 30.

[79] Douglas M. North, "Some Single Parents in Vermont are Trading Their Welfare Checks for a Degree," *Public Welfare* (1987): 5–12, at 12.

[80] Robert Sheak and David D. Dabelko, "Conservative Welfare Reform Proposals and the Reality of Subemployment," *Journal of Sociology and Social Welfare* (1990): 41–70, at 49.

[81] Brett Campbell, "Red Tape Blues: Poor Texans Ordered to Work Find Themselves Trapped in a Bureaucratic Maze that Ignores the Realities of Poverty," *Southern Exposure* (Summer 1991): 23–26, at 25.

[82] Paul Offner, "Reagan's Rule," *The New Republic* (May 23, 1994): 14–15.

[83] Ibid.

[84] Ibid.

[85] Paul Offner, "Target the Kids," *The New Republic* (January 24, 1994): 9–11.

[86] Ibid.

[87] Daniel Patrick Moynihan, "Welfare Reform: Serving America's Children," *Teachers College Record* 90:3 (1989): 337–41, at 340.

[88] Ibid.

[89] Gideonse and Meyers, "Why the Family Support Act Will Fail."

[90] Ibid., at 35.

[91] Ibid.

[92] Paul Offner, "The Dole Hole," *The New Republic* (March 14, 1994): 16–17.

[93] Ibid.

[94] Offner, "Target the Kids."

[95] Ibid.

7

Changing the Rules About
Who Should Receive Welfare

A great deal of the effort involved in welfare reform goes into changing the rules about who should be eligible for welfare benefits. The new welfare law places a two-year limit on receiving federally funded welfare during any one eligibility period and a five-year lifetime limit on benefits (states can continue to provide benefits with their own funds). Federal funds cannot be used to provide benefits for unwed parents under eighteen who do not live with an adult and do not attend school; states may deny benefits to children born to welfare recipients; and states can receive bonuses for decreasing out-of-wedlock births without increasing abortions. States can also cut benefits to recipients who refuse to cooperate in establishing the paternity of children on welfare, prohibit benefits to adults without high school diplomas who do not attend school, and deny benefits to those convicted of drug felonies (unless pregnant or in treatment).

These provisions are only minimum requirements; states can be more generous with their own funds, or can they be more restrictive with time limits and other provisions. If they tighten eligibility, states can save money by cutting the caseload as well as by discouraging potential recipients from applying. Changing the rules also appeals to those who believe the current welfare system is harmful to both society and to recipients. If, for example, to those who are convinced that illegitimacy is the most pressing public problem in America and that welfare encourages out-of-wedlock births among teenagers, prohibiting welfare to unmarried teenagers mothers is an enormously important reform.

States have only limited ability to change the rules governing welfare eligibility, however, so they have sought waivers from the federal government to pursue their experiments. Placing time limits on welfare recipients has become the most prominent restrictive reform in eligibility, but other strategies include cutting benefits, limiting benefits available to immigrants, reducing benefits for children born to families already on welfare, and creating positive or negative incentives to encourage welfare families to promote the education or health of their children.

Table 7.1 summarizes the ways states have sought to reform eligibility. Goals and reform efforts generally fall into several broad categories; state programs are grouped in terms of similar goals, but details of individual programs vary from state to state and are discussed later in the chapter. These reforms were in place, unless otherwise noted, when the new welfare law was passed. The new law allows states to continue to choose which strategies to pursue. While some of the programs may have ended, the discussion below illustrates what states have been doing.

CHANGING THE RULES CONCERNING ELIGIBILITY

OUTRIGHT BENEFIT CUTS

Although reducing spending is one of the primary motivations behind many state welfare reform initiatives, few states have simply cut benefits outright, primarily because of Federal regulations. Welfare administrators, however, have been able to save money through reforms that have been justified for other reasons, such as deterring undesirable behavior or creating an incentive to comply with program requirements. In contrast, General Assistance (GA) programs, because they are not federally funded, can and have been cut unilaterally by states. Michigan abolished its General Assistance program, Massachusetts effectively cut off benefits to more than 25 percent of its GA caseload, Illinois cut the duration of GA payments from twelve to nine months, and Ohio reduced grants from $128 to $100 a month and limited eligibility to six months during any year.[1]

Cuts in welfare spending have been particularly noticeable in California. Republican governor Pete Wilson has led the charge for reductions in benefits and restrictions on aid to teenage mothers and pregnant women on welfare. Payments were cut 15 percent between 1991 and 1994, and an additional 5 percent in 1995, saving California taxpayers

TABLE 7.1
POLICY OPTIONS FOR LIMITING ELIGIBILITY

Programs to encourage specific behaviors	States
Programs that provide family planning/effective parenting services (voluntary or mandatory)	Arkansas, Delaware, Georgia, Iowa, Louisiana, Maine, Maryland, Texas, Wisconsin, Wyoming
Programs that limit or end benefit increases for additional children ("family cap")	Arizona, Arkansas, Connecticut, Delaware, Florida, Georgia, Illinois, Indiana, Maryland, Massachusetts, Mississippi, Nebraska, New Jersey, North Carolina, South Carolina, Tennessee, Virginia, Wisconsin
Programs that require school attendance (for either dependent children or teenage parents)	Arkansas, California, Colorado, Connecticut, Delaware, Florida, Illinois, Indiana, Iowa, Louisiana, Maryland, Massachusetts, Michigan, Mississippi, Missouri, Nebraska, New York, North Carolina, Ohio, Oklahoma, Oregon, Pennsylvania, South Carolina, South Dakota, Tennessee, Texas, Utah, Vermont, Virginia, Wisconsin, Wyoming
Programs that encourage preventive health care (mandatory or voluntary childhood immunizations, checkups, prenatal care)	Colorado, Delaware, Florida, Georgia, Indiana, Louisiana, Maine, Maryland, Massachusetts, Michigan, Mississippi, Montana, New York, North Carolina, North Dakota, Ohio, Oregon, South Carolina, Tennessee, Texas, Utah, Virginia
Programs that encourage marriage by disregarding new spouse income	Florida, Mississippi, New York, North Dakota, Pennsylvania, South Carolina, Virginia, Wisconsin

Programs that limit eligibility through rule changes	States
Programs that require unwed minor parents to live with parents or guardians (some require benefits to be issued to adults)	Delaware, Connecticut, Indiana, Iowa, Maine, Maryland, Massachusetts, Michigan, Missouri, Nebraska, New York, North Carolina, Oregon, Puerto Rico, Vermont, Virginia, Virgin Islands, Wisconsin, Wyoming
Programs with outright benefit cuts (eligibility denied to large segment of population)	California, Illinois, Massachusetts, Michigan, Ohio

TABLE 7.1
POLICY OPTIONS FOR LIMITING ELIGIBILITY (*Continued*)

Programs that limit eligibility through rule changes	States
Programs that seek to reduce interstate migration	California, Maryland, New Jersey, Wisconsin[a]
Programs that put a time limit on benefits (benefits may be cut off for entire families, adults only, or the unemployed only)	Arizona, Colorado, Connecticut, Delaware, Florida, Georgia, Illinois, Indiana, Iowa, Louisiana, Maryland, Massachusetts, Missouri, Montana, Nebraska, North Carolina, North Dakota, Ohio, Oklahoma, Oregon, South Carolina, South Dakota, Tennessee, Texas, Utah, Vermont, Virginia, Washington, Wisconsin

[a] These waivers were granted by the Bush administration; the Clinton administration denied similar waivers to Illinois and Wyoming and, in 1996, rescinded California's authority to provide two-tier benefits. At one point, Arkansas and Idaho had also included antimigration measures in reform proposals.

almost $9 billion. A spokesperson for the governor said the budget cuts he proposed had two purposes: "One is budget-driven; welfare rolls are growing at double the pace of population growth, even before the recession." The other was a need for personal responsibility and economic empowerment: "We're not asking [welfare mothers] to get off aid and seek a forty-hour-a-week job; we're asking them to start taking responsibility for [their lives], to do something positive and constructive to increase self-esteem, to go out and start earning on [their] own."[2] Wilson claimed the restrictions doubled the number of welfare recipients in the work force.[3]

MIGRATION MEASURES

The debate in Congress over welfare reform in the mid-1990s largely accepted the idea of prohibiting benefits to legal and illegal immigrants as a way to save money, and the 1996 law reflected that consensus. State welfare reform efforts, in contrast, have sought to stop recipients from migrating to states offering higher benefits. Until approval for such a program was withdrawn in a February 1996 waiver, California imposed a one-year waiting limit before immigrants could receive benefits higher than those provided in the state from which they came.[4] In a six-county experiment, Wisconsin requires six months' residency before recipients who have moved from states paying lower benefits can receive Wisconsin's full benefits.[5] New Jersey and Maryland have similar two-tier programs.

TIME LIMITS

Much of the debate over welfare reform has focused on whether to impose limits on how long recipients can receive welfare.[6] Time limits are often part of a plan that requires recipients to devise personal self-sufficiency plans with specific goals and deadlines that are backed up by sanctions such as reduced benefits. In return, states offer services such as counseling, training, employer subsidies, and extended Medicaid and child-care coverage.[7] In some states, the time limit triggers a work requirement; states may public or subsidized employment to parents who cannot find employment on their own.[8] Alternatively, benefits can simply terminate when recipients reach the time limit, and the state may not provide jobs for those who can't find them.[9] Exemptions are often provided for those who are sixty or older, suffer from poor health, are in their third trimester of pregnancy, or have disabled or preschool children.[10]

Since the early 1980s, exemptions based on the age of the youngest child have become more restrictive: mothers with younger and younger children are required to work. Exemption changes reflect several different objectives. Exemptions send a message about society's expectations: For example, if many mothers with young children can work, so can and should welfare mothers. But exemptions also decrease the number of recipients for whom states must provide education and training programs, thereby reducing program costs.[11]

Many states have also proposed time limits but almost all of the waivers permitting these provisions were granted in 1994 and 1995, so we have little information concerning their impact on welfare recipients. Although interest in time limits is found nationwide, the specific provisions differ considerably. Most state reforms provide for an absolute cutoff, but a few permit extensions if recipients have made "good faith" efforts. Some states insulate benefits aimed at children from the cutoff. Some states treat single- and two-parent families differently. Some states provide lifetime caps on receiving benefits, whereas others focus on the immediate limit on benefits.

Arizona's EMPOWER program, for example, limits welfare participation to twenty-four months in any sixty-month period.[12] Colorado's "Personal Responsibility and Employment Program" requires parents who can work or participate in training to do so after receiving two years of welfare benefits.[13] Delaware's "A Better Chance" program places a time limit of twenty-four months on cash benefits given to able-bodied adults over nineteen years old.[14] Georgia's ten-county "Work for Welfare" demonstration project requires recipients of welfare payments for twenty-four of the previous thirty-six months to work up to twenty hours a month at an assigned job in local, state or federal government, or at a nonprofit agency. If work is not available, the time may be spent in job-search activities.[15] Illinois' "Work and Responsibility" program sets a two-year time limit on benefits when the youngest child is thirteen or older; if recipients are unable to find work within one year after reaching the limit, they must accept up to sixty hours of work per month (subsidized by the welfare grant). If they are not eligible for extensions, these families cannot reapply for welfare for two years.[16] Nebraska's demonstration project limits benefits to twenty-four months during a forty-eight-month period.[17] The Virginia "Independence Program" limits cash benefits to twenty-four months for families headed by employable parents; during those twenty-four months, recipients must be involved in education and training or employment activities.[18]

Connecticut has one of the strictest state time limits (twenty-one months) and has pledged to move more than 50 percent of welfare recipients into jobs within the next four years. Connecticut also provides a "good-faith" extension of the twenty-one-month limit for those who try to find work, and those subject to time limits are given priority for the JOBS program.[19] Florida's "Family Transition Program" limits benefits to a maximum of twenty-four months in any five-year period; those unable to find employment are guaranteed the opportunity to work at a job paying more than their welfare grant."[20] Longer eligibility (thirty-six months) is provided for families at high risk of becoming dependent on welfare.

The Indiana Manpower Placement and Comprehensive Training Program (IMPACT) limits benefits to twenty-four consecutive months once recipients are on the job search/placement track, but children's benefits not affected by the time limit.[21] The "Missouri Families—Mutual Responsibility Plan" includes a two-year time limit; on reaching the time limit, recipients must participate in job search or work experience. Those who have received welfare benefits for thirty-six months and who have completed self-sufficiency plans will not be cut off from welfare, and children's benefits are not affected by the time limits.[22]

Montana's "Families Achieving Independence" sets a twenty-four-month limit for single parent families and an eighteen-month limit for two-parent families. Adults who do not leave welfare when the time limit is reached must enroll in a community services program and serve at least twenty hours a week.[23] Under Oklahoma's "Mutual Agreement—A Plan for Success" (MAAPS), adults that receive welfare benefits for three years in any five-year period and are still unable to find a job are required to work at least twenty-four hours a week in a subsidized job.[24]

The "Strengthening of South Dakota Families Initiative" limits benefits to twenty-four months for those on an employment track and sixty months for those on an education track. Those who cannot find employment on completion of one of these tracks must accept community-service assignments or lose their benefits.[25] Vermont's "Family Independence Project" (approved in 1993) places a thirty-month limit on welfare for single parents and a fifteen-month limit for two-parent families. Recipients must then participate in community or public-service jobs.[26] Washington's "Success through Employment Program" progressively reduces benefits after a family has received assistance for four years in a five-year period: After four years, the grant is reduced by 10 percent, and by another 10 percent for each year thereafter.[27] Wisconsin's 1996 reform requires recipients to enroll immediately in work or training programs and limits assistance from the state to two years at any one time, with a lifetime maximum of five years.[28]

Time limits seem to be aimed primarily at pushing welfare recipients into the work force. But for some states, they also serve to make part-time work acceptable indefinitely and maintain a safety net for those with barriers to work[29] or who "play by the rules" but can't find work.[30] Time limits are often accompanied by expanded services such as education, training, job search and work activities; enhanced case management; child care and transportation assistance; extended transitional child care and medical services for working former recipients; and a variety of other social services.[31]

Although it is too early to assess the impact of time limits, there are some indicators of how they might work. Time limits are more likely to be successful in changing behavior if welfare officials clearly explain new rules, convince recipients that the time limit is real, and accurately monitor recipients' progress toward reaching the time limit.[32] For instance, one study emphasized that whereas it is important for programs to "hit the ground running . . . implementing time limits and related reforms too quickly, without adequate time for planning, can pose sig-

nificant risks for both recipients and for the credibility of the programs."[33] In addition, continually reiterating and reinforcing new
policies, especially those that have been implemented simultaneously,
is crucial. Recipients often get incorrect information through the media
or the neighborhood, and many understand the broad message but not
the details (such as consequences of reaching the time limit). Caseworker confusion or skepticism will also affect recipients' compliance.[34]
Finally, time-limited welfare places heavy demands on management information systems.[35] Poor systems can make it impossible to monitor
and enforce limits, make it difficult to respond quickly to recipient challenges, or distract caseworkers by forcing them to handle too much
paperwork.[36]

Other research conclude that the "imposition of time limits has
spurred new investments and renewed efforts to strengthen many of
the work-focused policies that have been the mainstay of welfare reform
efforts for a decade or more."[37] Many states have added or strengthened
job search, job placement, and work experience programs and restructured some education and training programs in order to fit the new
schedule established by time limits.[38]

Time limits have been shaped in policy and implementation at the
state and local levels by a complex set of factors—characteristics of
welfare recipients, state politics, economic conditions, the difficulties of
changing large organizations, and the demand for programs that reduce
dependency, give support to children, and control costs.[39]

Although most welfare recipients currently spend longer than twenty-
four months on welfare rolls, a much smaller number would be affected
by current time-limit proposals.[40] Regardless of behavioral changes, exemption policies (those that exempt recipients who have a child under
age 18 months, who are disabled, or who combine work and welfare)
reduce the amount of recipients that would be affected by almost 30
percent: "In a time-limited system followed by a work requirement, the
number of publicly subsidized jobs that would be needed for the caseload at a point in time is one-third lower than with no exemptions in
place."[41]

The effects of alternative approaches to time limits are difficult to
assess, but some initial information is available. One option is to allow
no exemptions: Benefits for all are limited to 24 months. Even when
movement on and off the rolls is accounted for, almost two thirds of
those recipients who will eventually spend more than twenty-four
months on the rolls will do so without ever leaving welfare.[42] Ninety
percent of those who eventually spend twenty-four months on the rolls

will do so within five years of their initial receipt.[43] Since most recipients who will be affected by time limits are continuous users, and since 50 percent leave the rolls within the first year, targeting recipients who are on the rolls for twelve continuous months can identify (early) those who will reach the time limit quickly.[44] One study concluded, "Virtually all recipients who will eventually spend 24 months on the welfare rolls will have accumulated 24 months on the welfare rolls within eight years after their initial welfare receipt."[45]

Exempting families with young children is the second option. Child advocates stress policies that are designed in the best interests of the child: Some argue that exemptions should be comparable with the four-month leave policy allowed under the Family and Medical Leave Act. Others are concerned that exemption policies could encourage welfare mothers to have additional children. However, because infant care is so costly, most exemption policies are generally constrained by financial considerations.[46] Exemptions for young children extend the time it takes for recipients to hit a two-year limit and decreases slightly the percentage of recipients who ever hit a two-year time limit. Exemptions for young children would also reduce (by 15 percent) the percentage ever affected by a time limit (from 58 to 49 percent of all new recipients).[47]

Option three would exempt those with disabilities or other barriers to work. When work limitation exemptions are added to young child exemptions, the time it takes to reach a two-year limit is increased and the percentage of recipients who will eventually reach the limit is marginally reduced. This effect may be marginal because work disabilities do not necessarily inhibit welfare exit and because those with severe disabilities are often older recipients who account for a relatively small share of all new recipients.[48]

One study hypothesized that under a comprehensive exemption policy, fewer than 5 percent of all recipients would hit a two-year time limit within two years after their initial welfare receipt (compared with 37 percent with no exemptions).[49] Recipients eventually affected by a two-year time limit would be reduced by almost 30 percent.[50] In a program with a two-year limit followed by mandatory work, "these changes in the timing and percentage of recipients who eventually hit a two-year time limit" would reduce the overall percentage of recipients mandated to work at a specific point in time. Exempting all families with young children, for example, would reduce the mandated population from 72 to 55 percent. Adding exemptions for disabled children, household heads with work limitations, or household heads who participate in the work force would further reduce the mandated population to 47 percent of the welfare caseload.[51]

Time limits will not affect all recipients equally. Younger recipients, those with low education levels and/or no recent work experience, those who have never married, those who enter welfare with young children, and those with more than three children all have a higher than average possibility of spending longer than 24 months on the welfare rolls.[52] Two-thirds of African-American and Hispanic women would be affected by a two-year time limit, compared with 50 percent of white women.[53] Three-quarters of those who have never completed any high school will spend more than twenty-four months on welfare. Although recipients with less than nine years of education represent a small percentage of welfare recipients, recipients in this group will spend an average of ten years on welfare; more than half will spend 8.5 years on the rolls. This group would account for a large share of recipients affected by a two-year time limit.[54] However, two-thirds of recipients with some high school education will spend twenty-four months on the welfare rolls. On average, this group will spend seventy-eight months receiving welfare.[55] Fewer than 50 percent of high school graduates will spend more than two years on welfare. On average, these women will spend fewer than four years on welfare, with half receiving benefits for twenty-three months or less.[56] Just over half of those with recent work experience will spend more than two years on welfare, and two-thirds of those with no recent work experience would be affected by a two-year time limit.[57]

Just as specific exemptions reduce the caseload, and so do behavioral changes. If behavioral changes are considered, the welfare caseload could decrease by as much as one-fourth, further reducing those mandated for public-sector employment programs.[58] A universal health care plan (such as the 1993 Clinton proposal) would have "the largest single effect on reducing" caseloads.[59] A two-year time limit followed by a stringent work requirement results in some recipients exiting welfare sooner than they otherwise would have.[60]

Time limits are enormously popular as a way to save money and to reward and punish particular behavior.[61] But critics warn that states will have to get better at job creation and training if time limits are going to work.[62] Time limits will be ineffective if they are not enforced or if they simply transfer costs to shelter and foster-child services, programs that are often more expensive than welfare payments. One California official said that "flexibility in meeting individual needs and not imposing one-size-fits-all solutions is what we're about, and this is where we part company with [President Clinton's] welfare reform plan. . . . We encounter an appalling range and depth of problems here, and that's precisely why you can't just push people through the same kind of government-formula vocational training program in two years and expect them to succeed in their jobs."[63]

Others agree that a two-year time limit on welfare benefits may not lead to families' self-sufficiency. One study found that single mothers who supported themselves entirely by working need an annual income of at least $15,000. In order to make this much money, they must earn more than $7.50 per hour (the average starting salaries in the JOBS program are much lower in all states), a wage that even after two years of training seems quite unrealistic in the face of youth and lack of previous education.[64]

Imposing a two-year limit on welfare requires some additional policy actions to ensure that families can live on a minimum-wage income. These families will need free medical care and at least $5,000 worth of other resources yearly if they are to survive. One way to close the gap is to increase child support from absent parents, but many fathers do not make enough money for a typical child support order. Moving in with other members of an extended may be an option for some. A mother may have a live-in boyfriend who shares the bills, but this can lead to unplanned pregnancies, abortions, and child abuse.[65] One way for the government to make up the difference is to increase the EITC; alternatively, a guaranteed income for children could be provided. If a parent cannot find employment after the two years she could be treated like others who have been on unemployment insurance (UI). If she is disabled, she could receive disability insurance. If the economy is in a recession, her benefits could be extended, as UI often is.[66]

States face a number of difficult challenges in implementing a time limit for welfare benefits. Costs for supplemental services would be large. One study projected that the two-year time limit on welfare would save $18 billion per year, but that the cost of raising the income level of families below $15,000 would be $33 billion, even if benefits were given to no one else.[67] Perhaps $5 billion could be collected from absent fathers, but that still leaves new costs of $10 billion. States must also devise the supplemental policies that seek to find employment for recipients before they reach the limit.[68] Cutting benefits is one way to end long-term dependency, but that could increase child poverty and raise costs in the child-welfare system.[69] Finally, mental or physical disabilities could keep many welfare recipients from steady employment.[70] The optimal solution is to minimize the number of recipients who reach the time limit. But that is a function of their behavior as well as of the level of job opportunities, two factors that are difficult for welfare agencies to affect.[71]

Time limits raise a number of difficult questions. What happens to the parent who follows all the rules and still can't get a job? What role should government play in providing employment, training activities, and a safety net for poor, mostly single-parent families? How will differing definitions of time limits affect the nature of welfare and the lives of families dependent on the system? Will there be enough jobs in the private sector to accommodate people pushed off welfare? Will the states create subsidized jobs? Will the states subsidize incomes to help families reach the poverty line? Can states design and enforce time limits that end or at least reduce long-term dependency without harming children or raising costs substantially? Will welfare reform be more expensive than "welfare as we know it"?[72] Beebout and Jacobson conclude, "Ultimately, the fate of time-limited welfare is likely to be determined in the 'trenches,' in the interactions between staff and welfare recipients."[73]

REVISED PARTICIPATION MANDATES AND SANCTIONS

As discussed in Chapter 6, one of the most important state innovations has been the linking of participation in services and programs with sanctions—bonuses or benefit cuts to encourage certain behaviors. Many states have moved to a contract-based welfare systems, in which recipients agree to some kind of self-sufficiency plan with sanctions or incentives to foster compliance. States usually exempt parents with young children from participating in JOBS programs, but they differ over whether parents should be required to participate once their children reach one, two, or three years of age. In Alabama, JOBS participation is mandatory unless there are children in the household under the age of three or if the head of the household is under sixteen or over sixty, is physically unable to participate, pregnant and due in at least six months, or already works thirty hours a week. Teenage parents are not exempt on basis of their child's age. In Georgia's "Personal Accountability and Responsibility Project," able-bodied recipients aged 18 to 60 who have no children under age 14 and who refuse to work or who quit their jobs without "good cause" are ineligible for welfare benefits; the rest of the family, however, is not excluded. Exemptions are provided for those without transportation.[74] Iowa's "Family Investment Program" provides exemptions for those with children less than six months old, those working at least 30 hours a week, and those who are disabled; recipients who do not create a Family Investment Agreement will have benefits phased out over six months and cannot reapply for six months.[75] In North Dakota, welfare recipients must pursue education and training both during the first six months of pregnancy and after the child is 3 months old.[76] South Dakota denies benefits to recipients who quit jobs without good cause for three months or until the parents finds a comparable job.[77] In Utah, cash benefits can be terminated if parents do not comply with education, training, and work preparation requirements after repeated efforts by the state to encourage compliance.[78] Virginia's "Independence Program" requires that if a recipient or his or her relative does not assist in establishing paternity for a child born out of wedlock, the family's entire welfare benefit can be terminated until the person cooperates with the state.[79] Wyoming denies benefits to recipients who have confessed to or been convicted of program fraud until full restitution is made to the state.[80]

CHANGING BEHAVIOR OF WELFARE RECIPIENTS

DISCOURAGING PREGNANCY AMONG WELFARE RECIPIENTS

Some states encourage recipients to gain access to birth control information and contraceptives and family counseling. One of the few areas in which the federal government has rejected waivers from states is when they have proposed giving bonuses to welfare mothers for voluntary sterilization or use of the Norplant insert (a contraceptive).[81] Delaware requires teenagers on welfare to attend family-planning classes; Wisconsin holds mandatory sex- and parent-education classes for teenage recipients and parenting classes for welfare parents, including noncustodial parents and spouses. Many other states have similar programs.

The family cap has become the most popular reform. It reduces or eliminates increases in welfare grants for children conceived while a parent is on welfare. These additional children usually remain eligible for Medicaid and Food Stamps. The actual form of the family cap varies considerably. Arizona's EMPOWER reform provides no additional benefits for children conceived on welfare or within twelve months after leaving welfare if the family reapplies.[82] Arkansas' Reduction in Welfare Birthrates Project eliminates benefit increases for additional children born to families on welfare; provides family planning counseling to adolescents aged 13 to 17; and requires minor parents under age 16 to participate in the New Hope component of the state JOBS program.[83] Delaware provides no additional benefits for additional children born on welfare and requires teenage parents to attend parenting and family-planning classes.[84] Georgia's Personal Accountability and Responsibility Project, approved in 1993, includes family-planning and parenting-skills programs and a family cap for families on welfare for more than two years.[85] In Mississippi's "New Direction Demonstration Projects," the family cap is not applicable to first-born children or those conceived through rape or incest.[86] Wisconsin's AFDC Benefit Cap (ABC) Demonstration Project eliminates benefit increases for additional children born more than ten months after family has initially applied for benefits; exceptions are provided for verified cases of rape or incest, or if the child has been placed in the care of a non–legally responsible relative.[87] Connecticut cuts in half the amount of additional benefits for children born to welfare recipients.[88]

New Jersey's Family Development Program has been the most widely discussed family cap experiment. The family cap was first proposed in 1991 by reformers who sought to deny additional benefits to women who gave birth to additional children ten or more months after they began receiving welfare. In January 1992, the prochoice governor, Jim Florio (D.), signed a legislative package that made New Jersey the first state in the nation to deny additional payments to welfare mothers who have more children. Under the previous program, a welfare mother in New Jersey received an additional $64 a month for another child. Florio's package eliminated this grant increase, but women on welfare could marry without losing welfare grants for their children if the husband was not the natural father of the children and if his income was less than $21,180 for a family of four. The measure would increase the amount of income a woman was allowed to earn from working without a reduction in her grant, allow her to earn up to 50 percent of her current grant (working fifteen hours a month or a half-hour a day would replace the $64 grant reduction), and require all parents with children over age 2 to participate in education, training, or job-related activities as a condition of receiving benefits. Recipients would have to get a high school diploma or GED. Those who failed to participate in the Family Development Act would face a grant reduction and an eventual loss of funds.

The New Jersey reform was eventually approved in 1992 for five years. This statewide program seeks "to encourage single mothers receiving welfare to marry (and for men to marry them), to take employment, and to avoid additional childbearing."[89] Parents of children whose youngest child is at least two years old are required to participate. The program increases the family's earned income disregard to 25 percent of the monthly welfare grant, suspends the one hundred-hour rule for two-parent families, extends transitional Medicaid extended to twenty-four months, provides subsidies for child care, and eliminates the $64 monthly increase in welfare payments for the birth of additional children.[90]

A group of religious, legal, and social services activists challenged the family cap because it punished poor children solely on the basis of when they were born. The activists argued that it would "cause tremendous suffering among poor families under the guise of preventing women from having children only for the money."[91] In 1994, eight welfare recipients, New Jersey's NOW Legal Defense Fund, the Legal Services Corporation, and the ACLU filed a suit in federal court challenging the cap and contending that the restriction violates a woman's constitutional right to decide about childbirth without government involvement and that the family cap violates federal laws governing experiments on humans. Plaintiffs argued that the new law "will unfairly penalize poor children, deny women the opportunity to have more children, and deny poor families their rights to privacy, equal protection under the law and freedom of association."[92] Opponents argued that withholding the extra $64 per child threatened women's reproductive freedom; proponents said the lawsuit would enshrine welfare as a constitutional right.[93]

In other states, proposals for a family cap have become embroiled in the politics of abortion policy. In Minnesota, the state's welfare reform proposal became a hostage to abortion politics when a "right-to-know" abortion amendment was added to the state House welfare reform bill in 1995. Shortly after prochoice Republican Governor Arne Carlson told lawmakers that he did not want any controversial amendments "cluttering up" a welfare reform bill, a House committee adopted a proposal calling for a twenty-four-hour waiting period after a woman was informed of the risks of an abortion. The bill would allow women to sue abortion providers who did not provide the required information.[94]

In Illinois, the state welfare reform package brought together abortion-rights and antiabortion groups in opposition to the bill and its family cap provision. The state estimates that about 2,700 babies are born to welfare mothers each month in Illinois. Under the plan, those children would still receive food stamps and medical assistance, but they would not get monthly stipends. (The stipends average about $65 a month.) The antiabortion and abortion-rights movements fear that without those extra funds, pregnant welfare mothers will choose abortion.[95] Similar criticisms of the family cap have arisen in other states.[96]

The potential savings in welfare expenditures from a family cap provision is small but not insignificant. The U.S. Congressional Budget Office estimated that "almost one-third of all families receiving AFDC nationwide include children born to adults already receiving AFDC, and that the benefits paid for these children amount to about 8 percent of all AFDC outlays."[97] Birth rates among New Jersey women on welfare dropped 11.4 percent in the thirteen months after the family cap took effect.[98] Another study also found that New Jersey women on welfare also began having more abortions after the family cap was instituted, but the methodology of both studies have been criticized.[99]

Much more significant than budgetary savings is the symbolic importance of the family cap. The cap has generally been viewed as hostile to welfare and social services, but it has gained increasing support among legislators representing areas with large numbers of welfare recipients. The legislators argue that "ordinary working mothers don't get extra pay because they have more children and there is no reason to treat welfare recipients any better or worse."[100] A similar rationale accounts for the increasingly popular prohibition against "allowing teenagers to use childbearing and welfare for establishing their own homes."[101] On the other hand, mothers might think that they lose part of their existing grant if they report an existing birth, and in not reporting it they might also fail to seek nutritional and health services.[102]

Judith Gueron argues that no study has shown that higher welfare benefits lead to increased childbearing.[103] Others criticize the family cap as punitive. One AFDC recipient pleaded: "Every woman's situation is different. We don't need reform that is punitive. We need resources to help us leave welfare."[104] New Jersey Democratic Assemblyman Wayne Bryant represents Camden, where 70 percent of the residents receive some form of public assistance. He supported the family cap, stating, "You don't go to a job and tell the person you're going to have a child, and all of a sudden they way, 'Well, thank God. I'm going to give you a raise.' . . . We're saying that the same kind of norms, the same kind of values, ought to be in our poverty system."[105]

ENCOURAGING SCHOOL ATTENDANCE

In order to break the welfare cycle, many states have created incentives to help keep children of welfare families and recipients themselves in school. Grants are typically reduced after frequent absences or increased as a bonus to encourage regular attendance; some states require school attendance for teenage recipients and for dependent children. In Arkansas, welfare parents aged 16 or under must attend school or an alternative educational program or face sanctions.[106] California's CAL LEARN program is part of the "Work Pays Demonstration Project" that offers teenage parents a $100 bonus for maintaining a C average and $500 for high school graduation. Benefits are reduced up to $50 a month for two months for those who don't maintain a D average.[107] California's "School Attendance Demonstration Project" requires dependent teenage children in San Diego County to attend high school or participate in job search and training.[108] Colorado's "Personal Responsibility and Employment Program" awards bonuses for school attendance and for graduation from high school or a GED program.[109] Connecticut targets welfare parents under twenty-one without high school diplomas for educational programs.[110] Delaware's "A Better Chance" program requires teenage parents to attend school and gives them a $50 bonus for graduation.[111] Maryland's Primary Prevention Initiative, started in 1992, cuts benefits for families by $25 per child per month if their children are not immunized or if they attend classes for less than 80 percent of school days, or if the rent isn't paid on time. Adults and school-age children receive $20 per year if they have preventive health care.[112] Nebraska reduces benefits by $50 for each minor child who skips school.[113] In Oklahoma, the Learnfare program targets teenage recipients who have not graduated from high school; benefits are cut to recipients whose school attendance drops below 80 percent. Virginia's Incentives to Advance Learning (VITAL) requires school-age recipients to participate in education activities, provides drop-out prevention counseling, and rewards children who stay in school with tickets to movies and rock concerts.[114] Wisconsin's Learnfare project, begun in 1988, targets teenage mothers and welfare children aged 13 to 19 without high school diplomas. It ties welfare benefits to school attendance: Grants are cut by 15 percent for families with habitually truant students and by 45 percent for all teenage mothers who do not attend school regularly.[115] The state provides support services such as child care, transportation subsidies, and case managers to work with at-risk students to identify causes of truancy and help them find support services.[116] Wyoming cuts benefits by as much as $40/month for families whose minor children don't attend school or have suitable employment.[117]

Ohio's Transitions to Independence program targets teenage parents who have not graduated from high school. The program involves enhanced work and training programs and mandatory school attendance. The state's Learning, Earning, and Parenting project (LEAP), begun in 1989, promotes school attendance among teenage parents and expectant parents on welfare who do not have a diploma or a GED. It provides a monthly bonus of $62 for good attendance (four or fewer absences a month) and reduces it by the same amount for poor attendance (the average base benefit level for a mother and one child was $274 a month).[118] Welfare recipients who are pregnant or under age 20 must try to get a diploma or GED, but if educational activities are not appropriate, recipients may participate in approved training and work. A bonus of $62 is given for completion of each grade; a $200 bonus is awarded to high school graduates.[119] A work component was added to LEAP in 1995.[120]

LEAP was the first program to offer rewards, and not just sanctions, for school attendance. It appears to have had a positive effect on high school completion and educational attainment for teens enrolled in school at baseline, but has had no effects on dropouts. Sanctioning has occurred: At least one sanction was requested for 68 percent of the group; 4 percent of enrolled teens and 22 percent of dropouts were sanctioned frequently.[121] One study found that LEAP "appears to provide powerful evidence for an incentive-based strategy"—but only when accompanied by counseling and support.[122] Of the participants already in school, 61 percent kept up attendance or graduated, compared with 51 percent of the control group. Of participants who had dropped out, 49 percent reenrolled at some time during the one-year study period, compared with 33 percent of the control group.[123] LEAP "achieved a 10 percent increase in continuous school enrollment and a 13 percent increase in that rate at which teen dropouts returned to school during the year after they became eligible for LEAP." But no one knows if these figures will translate into increased high school completion, welfare roll reduction, or better employment and earnings.[124]

Learnfare programs—programs aimed at children of welfare families—face some difficult challenges such as lack of understanding of the requirements, few incentives for the most at-risk students to return to school, prior negative experience with counseling, inadequate coordination of Learnfare services with schools, and inadequate case-management services. In relatively successful programs, case managers did more outreach at the outset and had access to a well-developed service agency network.[125] One study found that "children in the counties studied actually missed more often than those not targeted for a benefit reduction."[126]

ENCOURAGING PREVENTATIVE HEALTH CARE

Maryland reduces benefits to families that fail to meet state preventive health-care standards such as annual preventive health visits for preschool, school-age, and adult welfare recipients and regular prenatal care visits by pregnant welfare recipients. The state offers bonuses of $20 a year for each family member who has an annual checkup and provides $14 a month for regular prenatal care for pregnant welfare mothers. (These benefits are to some extent inconsistent with the idea of the family cap).[127] North Dakota's Early Intervention Program (EIP) expands welfare eligibility to include women in their first and second trimesters of pregnancy if they are single and have no other children; recipients must participate in the JOBS program.[128] However, such funding is not usually available until the last trimester of a pregnancy.[129] Montana's "Families Achieving Independence" requires welfare families to choose between a reduced Medicaid benefit package and a partial premium payment toward a private health insurance policy; full Medicaid coverage is provided on an emergency basis if certain services are needed for employment purposes.[130] Idaho Health Check is a free medical service for children on welfare that provides corrective services, transportation, and screening to help find any physical or developmental conditions that may endanger a child's life or well-being in the future.

ENCOURAGING TWO-PARENT FAMILIES

Wedfare or bridefare programs encourage marriage as a way to help single mothers leave the welfare system. California's "Incentives to Self-Sufficiency Project" provides transitional child-care benefits to families who leave the rolls because of marriage.[131] Wisconsin's Parental and Family Responsibility Initiative, approved in 1992 for six counties, seeks to "promote and preserve families by removing disincentives in the welfare system that serve as barriers to young couples from marrying and working."[132] It targets welfare mothers under twenty who are first-time parents as well as the fathers of their children, and allows certain couples—married or unmarried—to receive benefits. Benefits for a second child are cut in half (from $77 to $39), with no money available for additional children. The state also provides expanded eligibility for stepparent families, permits noncustodial parents to be involved in JOBS programs, and increases funding for establishing paternity.[133] As a result, parents receive higher benefits together than they would if separated.[134]

Critics have argued that such programs might create a sort of lottery effect, because teenagers might wait to get married until they see if they can qualify for welfare. Wisconsin will not give benefits before the third trimester of pregnancy, so if benefits are denied, then abortion is no longer an alternative either, but marriage might still not occur. Additionally, the program's scope may be too small to make a significant difference in pregnancy rates; on the other hand, large-scale implementation might have unintended consequences. Such a program might produce higher marriage rates because it might become fashionable to marry. However, general implementation might also encourage young couples with low skills to marry as teenagers and have a child right away to become eligible for benefits. The cost of large-scale implementation would be significant and politically difficult, especially when combined with a general expansion of eligibility for welfare.[135]

Some states have made changes in the way stepparent income disregards are calculated in determining welfare eligibility. Under New York's "Jobs First Strategy," welfare children can receive benefits for up to two years after the caretaker parent marries—if the new spouse's income is not greater than 150 percent of the poverty line.[136] In determining welfare eligibility, North Dakota and New Jersey do not count the income of stepparents during the first six months of marriage.[137]

Other programs also encourage the perpetuation of two-parent families. Arizona's "Two-Parent Employment Program" assists low-income, two-parent families in meeting their needs until the parents' transition back into the labor force. Cash benefits, limited to six months in any twelve-month period, are issued on a semimonthly basis after work assignments are completed. A parent can miss one day per semimonthly work cycle; when more than one day is missed, the work cycle is considered incomplete; when two consecutive incomplete work cycles occur, benefits are terminated. To be eligible, both parents must be in the home, be able-bodied, and have a child in common; the primary wage-earning parent must be unemployed or underemployed and must establish a connection with the work force; and parents must continuously participate in the JOBS program. Child care is guaranteed when necessary for the person to accept or keep employment or to participate in JOBS. The standard transitional one-year benefits of Medicaid and child care are also available.[138]

Finally, several states have waived the one hundred-hour rule to permit some families to continue eligibility who otherwise would have lost it because of work income. Extending welfare benefits to two-parent families seeks to strengthen the parents' participation in the labor force and the stability of the family unit, but the evidence on whether waivers achieve these goals is uncertain.[139]

TARGETING TEENAGE MOTHERS

Except for time limits, no welfare reform issue has garnered more attention than efforts to reduce out-of-wedlock births among teenagers.

Many states have targeted teenage mothers for intensive job-search, training, education, parenting, and other programs, with sanctions such as reduced benefits for failure to participate as a way to discourage girls from getting pregnant and applying for welfare.[140] Delaware's Teen Family Literacy Pilot Program targets out-of-school welfare teenage parents and provides child care payments, transportation assistance, remedial medical and dental care, work and/or training-related equipment and supplies, and incidental expenses involved with community work. Illinois' Young Parents Program in Chicago was established in 1983 and became part of Project Chance in 1990. The program provides a wide range of programs in education, training, development of basic skills, parenting, child development, family planning, health nutrition, child-support enforcement, personal advocacy, computer-assisted literacy, and other programs.[141] Project Advance is another Illinois program that targets teenage parents for mandatory education, training, and employment programs.[142]

Kentucky's MOM (Mothers on the Move) program for unwed teenage mothers provides transportation so girls can attend sessions on goal setting, prenatal care, family planning, hygiene, assertiveness, and other topics. Oklahoma operates a Job Corps II program for women 18 to 21 receiving welfare. These women have proven to be better students, on average, than regular Job Corps members, and this program has received national attention from the Job Corps. The state refers participants, then Job Corps II provides basic and vocational education; recipients continue to get day care, assistance payments, medical care, and Food Stamps. The state's Employment Services provides assessment and applications for eligible clients. Texas' Teen Parent Initiative provides special case management for teenage mothers and fathers. In Washington State, teenage parents in school are guaranteed help with child care costs in the form of vouchers, reimbursed at the 55th percentile of the local market rate.

Ohio's efforts in encouraging education for teenage mothers have been studied more than those of other states. Ohio's GRADS (Graduation, Reality, and Dual-Role Skills) program funds and trains home economics teachers to instruct and facilitate services for pregnant and parenting teenagers in five hundred Ohio schools. In many cases, GRADS teachers have taken the informal role of liaison with the LEAP program. For instance, in one county, LEAP contracts with the GRADS program for case-management services; in another, LEAP case managers are stationed in public schools, or LEAP pays the salary of a school district official who serves as liaison between the school and the LEAP program.[143] Rules require that bonuses be paid to students for whom attendance information cannot be obtained, so some teens receive bonuses without fulfilling the education requirement. However, counties vary in the extent to which they pursue missing information, and in whether they pay presumptive bonuses. The total number of sanction requests was similar to the number of bonus requests—the number of sanctions is large compared with those for mandatory programs of welfare recipients. Bonuses were requested for one-sixth to one-third of teenagers eligible for LEAP. Most sanctions were for failure to start the program (initial assessment) or enroll in school. Exemptions were usually due to the program's inability to provide needed support services. The number of exemptions has been "relatively small," which suggests that the "application of a school attendance mandate appears feasible for the majority of teen parents."[144] Demand for child care was low—most teens preferred informal care by relatives, and Ohio rules prohibit payment to unlicensed child-care providers. However, child care problems are often cited by staff and students as a major barrier to school attendance.[145]

A few states have attacked pregnancy more directly. In 1985, Denver, Colorado began its Dollar-a-Day program, funded by Planned Parenthood, in which teenage girls are paid seven dollars a week for attending a meeting and not becoming pregnant. Most of the participants have already had one child. The rate of repeat pregnancy in that area of Colorado is 50 percent, but by 1991 only 26 percent of the girls in the program had become pregnant. Peer counselors are hired to help discourage pregnancy. A Baltimore, Maryland school-linked counseling program distributes birth control devices. The program was credited with reducing pregnancy by 30 percent while pregnancy rates in other schools increased by 58 percent. To avoid controversy, the program was located near, but not in, the school. Students were required to obtain parental permission to participate.[146]

Assessments of initiatives aimed at teens demonstrate how difficult this problem is to remedy. The Teenage Parent Demonstration project was a federal pilot program in Camden and Newark, New Jersey, and Chicago involving nearly six thousand first-time teenage parents on welfare. Participants were divided into two equal groups. The control group received normal welfare benefits; members of the experimental group received enhanced services aimed at producing self-sufficiency including job training, completion of education, and extensive personal counseling and monitoring by case workers. They were required to be in high school or pursue postsecondary education, job training, or employment options if they had already graduated. The experiment had a positive but minimal impact on promoting school enrollment, job training, and employment. It resulted in lower Food Stamp participation and reduced AFDC benefit levels, but did not lower AFDC participation rates and had little impact on living arrangements, child support, pregnancies, or births.[147] It produced inconsistent results in terms of school completion: Only those who had started the program as high school graduates had any significant earnings gain. The project did not significantly decrease the percentage of participants on welfare, but the average AFDC grant went down, perhaps as a result of sanctioning. Repeat pregnancy rates remained high. Thirty-five percent of participants were sanctioned at least once; 4 percent of enrolled teenagers and 22 percent of dropouts were sanctioned frequently.[148]

Project Redirection, another teen-targeted program, aims to "enhance the education, job-related, parenting, and life management skills of participants and delay further childbearing by linking participants to community services and providing mentoring and counseling services."[149] Five years after the program began, Project Redirection participants had higher earnings and were less likely to be on welfare, but most remained on welfare and in poverty. Participants scored better on parenting skills tests; their children showed higher cognitive skills and exhibited fewer behavioral problems. But the program had no discernible impact on repeat pregnancies.[150] The Summer Training and Employment Program (STEP) targeted fourteen- and fifteen-year-old low-income, low-performing potential dropouts "with two consecutive summers of paid remediation, life skills instruction," and JTPA work experience in order to reduce teenage pregnancy. The program had no apparent impact on sexual behavior or educational and economic experience.[151]

The New Chance program, a "National Demonstration for Adolescent Mothers and Their Children," took place between 1989 and 1992 in sixteen locations in ten states. Recipients were separated into an experimental and a control group. The program sought to promote self-sufficiency in young welfare mothers—AFDC mothers aged 16 to 22 who were high school dropouts and gave birth during their teenage years. Another goal was to improve the well-being of their children by helping mothers expand their intellect and develop decision-making and communication skills. Services included basic education programs; health, personal-development, and parenting instruction; training; employment services; and child care. New Chance participants were expected to attend daily for eighteen months, with services extended for up to one year, but high absenteeism and premature terminations resulted in a briefer, less intensive, and less employment-focused program overall. After eighteen months, New Chance women in the random experimental group were more likely to have a GED, to have earned college credits, or be enrolled in college. The program had no impact on reading skills; levels of depression, stress, and drug use; health; repeat pregnancies; use of contraceptives; employment; or child-rearing behavior. Women in the control group received similar but more limited services. At eighteen months, 615 of the total sample did not have a GED or a diploma; 65 percent were not employed or in an education or training program; and 82 percent were still on welfare.[152] The program continued beyond the initial demonstration period.

Rebecca Maynard's review of programs aimed at teenage pregnancy concluded that "none of the employment or welfare-focused programs succeeded in helping young mothers take control of their fertility." However, there is some promise in programs that "provide clear messages on values."[153] Other reviews have concluded that nearly all programs have trouble achieving high attendance rates and none have successfully reduced repeat pregnancies.[154] Most young women remained on welfare and were economically dependent. Sanctioning is a useful tool, but frequent use means that teenagers are not changing their behavior. Programs have mixed success in achieving employment and education gains and in improving parenting practices.[155] Studies conclude that programs for teenagers are most effective if they are started while the teenagers are still actively participating in high school. However, New Chance, TPD, and other programs have had no effect on literacy levels.[156] Successful pregnancy-prevention programs appear to combine (1) reproductive education; (2) access to contraceptives; and (3) information about life options before teenagers become sexually active or have given birth. Early identification and treatment, long-term program commitment, and greater community and school involvement also appear to be important ingredients.[157]

THE VALUE OF CHANGING WELFARE ELIGIBILITY RULES

Changing eligibility rules will likely change welfare caseload demographics. Those most ready to work will respond to work incentives by leaving the rolls entirely or by combining work and welfare. Time limits will force most longer-term recipients off the rolls, or else recipients will become exempt through work or community service. Time-limit reform programs would lower the average age of welfare populations as families on welfare for long periods are forced off the rolls, and pregnant women or women with young children are exempt from time restrictions.[158] Depending on how time limits are defined, they can lead to lower poverty rates and higher extreme poverty: Time limit policies are estimated to reduce poverty rates slightly among single parent families, but some families will be worse off if lost benefits are not offset by increased earnings.[159]

The majority of the welfare caseload receives benefits for more than twenty-four months. Exemptions are important ways of tailoring restrictions to state concerns and priorities, because they usually reduce the overall size and cost of work and other programs and permit states to target limited resources.[160] The recipients most likely to be affected by time limits are those with the biggest barriers to employment. As will be discussed in Chapter 8, work incentive policies are more effective in moving recipients into private-sector employment than are policies that seek to change welfare rules.[161] But work incentives alone will not result in large reductions in the caseload. Health reform that breaks the links between welfare and health insurance coverage is one of the most important components of improving work incentives.[162]

Welfare reforms that seek to change the behavior of recipients runs the risk of being particularly punitive. Behavior modification programs, Lawrence Mead argues, are a "blend of the 'old conservatism,' which consists of 'cutting welfare to throw off the less deserving,' and the new or 'big-government conservatism,' in which 'the aim is not to save money but to . . . serve public expectations of good behavior.' "[163] Programs range from cutting off aid to able-bodied adults on general assistance to influencing family size and living arrangements.[164] The Family Support Act of 1988 also tried to change welfare recipients' behavior, but it included many support programs for families. Because most recent reform proposals do away with many of these expensive support programs, critics charge that current reformers are more concerned with saving money than encouraging responsibility.[165] Liberal analysts say that most current reforms are punitive. Regarding the family cap, for example, they argue that "The notion of tough love makes sense, but . . . we can't accept the notion that it's OK to hurt kids if whatever we designed for their parents is not working."[166]

Both liberals and conservatives may be uneasy with behavior modification efforts. Little is known about how sanctions or financial incentives influence childbearing and other behaviors. No one knows if the budget savings will be as extensive as promised.[167] Needy persons may exhaust the capabilities of other (nonprofit) assistance organizations. Reduced benefits may translate into neglect of children.[168] Charles Murray warns that trying to manipulate recipients' behavior—social engineering, he calls it—"is a bad idea whether it's done by liberals or conservatives . . . We're very bad at creating rules that punch the right buttons with people. People are complicated and these things tend to backfire."[169]

But the current welfare system includes incentives that encourage certain behaviors, and changing those incentives is central to any effort to improve welfare. Efforts to bring about behavioral changes can be carefully constructed so that they are fair, within the reach of the recipient, and well grounded in public support. But they are quite likely to have unintended consequences. Children will be penalized for the actions of their parents, and vice versa.[170] Determining compliance should be objective, easy, and fair. Sanctions clearly reduce welfare spending; it is less clear whether they are sufficiently large to actually affect behavior. Rewarding positive behavior may be more useful than imposing penalties since it can send the same signal but without reinforcing the discouragement and lack of self-esteem that accompany welfare dependency. Positive incentives place the burden of proof on the recipient. Benefits (or penalties) should encourage the internalization of long-term changes in behavior. Humility and caution should infuse state efforts. Those efforts should proceed step by step, avoid big promises or unrealistic goals, and build in opportunities for learning by trial, error, and experience.[171]

REFERENCES

[1] Julie Kosterlitz, "Behavior Modification," *National Journal*, (February 1, 1992): 272.

[2] Ibid., 273.

[3] B. Drummond Ayres, Jr., "A Forerunner of the House Bill," *The New York Times*, September 21, 1995, p. A10.

[4] U.S. Department of Health and Human Services, Administration for Children and Families, Office of Family Assistance, "State Welfare Demonstrations," *H.H.S. Fact Sheet* (Washington, D.C.: Government Printing Office, July 1996).

[5] Jennifer A. Neisner, "State Welfare Initiatives," *CRS Report for Congress* (Washington, D.C.: Congressional Research Service, January 24, 1995).

[6] Dan Bloom and David Butler, "Executive Summary, Implementing Time-Limited Welfare: Early Experiences in Three States" (New York: Manpower Demonstration Research Corporation, advance prepublication copy, November 1995), 3.

[7] U.S. Department of Health and Human Services, "State Welfare Demonstrations."

[8] Bloom and Butler, "Executive Summary, Implementing Time-Limited Welfare."

[9] Ibid.

[10] Harold Beebout and Jon Jacobson, "The Number and Characteristics of AFDC Recipients Who Will be Affected by Policies to Time-limit AFDC Benefits," (Mathematica Policy Research, Inc., paper presented at the APPAM Annual Conference, Chicago, October 1994): 34.

[11] Ibid., 17.

[12] U.S. Department of Health and Human Services, "State Welfare Demonstrations."

[13] Ibid.

[14] Ibid.

[15] Ibid., 9.

[16] Ibid.

[17] Neisner, "State Welfare Initiatives."

[18] U.S. Department of Health and Human Services, "State Welfare Demonstrations."

[19] Ibid.

[20] Ibid.

[21] Ibid.

[22] Ibid.

[23] Ibid.

[24] Ibid.

[25] Ibid.

[26] Ibid.

[27] Ibid.

[28] Jeffrey L. Katz, "House Passes Wisconsin Waivers," *Congressional Quarterly Weekly Report* (June 8, 1996): 1598.

[29] Bloom and Butler, "Executive Summary, Implementing Time-limited Welfare" 7.

[30] Ibid., 7.

[31] Ibid., 11.

[32] Ibid.

[33] Ibid., 11.

[34] Ibid., 12.

[35] Ibid., 14.

[36] Ibid., 14.

[37] David Gueron, preface to "Executive Summary, Implementing Time-Limited Welfare: Early Experiences in Three States," by Dan Bloom and David Butler (New York: Manpower Demonstration Research Corporation, advance pre-publication copy, November 1995): iv.

[38] Bloom and Butler, "Executive Summary, Implementing Time-limited Welfare" 13.

[39] Ibid., 14.

[40] Beebout and Jacobson, "The Number and Characteristics of AFDC Recipients."

[41] Ibid., 3.

[42] Ibid., 21.

[43] Ibid., 21.

[44] Ibid., 21.

[45] Ibid., 21.

[46] Ibid., 16–17.

[47] Ibid., 22.

[48] Ibid., 22.

[49] Ibid., 23.

[50] Ibid., 23.

[51] Ibid., 23.

[52] Ibid., 23, 26.

[53] Ibid., 26.

[54] Ibid., 26.

[55] Ibid., 26.

[56] Ibid., 26.

[57] Ibid., 27.

[58] Ibid.

[59] Ibid.

[60] Ibid., 4.

[61] Penelope Lemov, "Putting Welfare on the Clock," *Governing*, (November 1993): 29–30.

[62] Ibid., 30.

[63] William Claiborne, "On the Receiving End of Welfare Reform," *The Washington Post*, National Weekly Edition, April 18–24, 1994, p. 31.

[64] According to census data, the average earnings of women who choose to work are as follows:

	No education	Some high school	High school graduate	Some college
18–24	—	$11,033	$13,385	$14,487
25–34	$11,832	$13,825	$17,026	$20,872

Christopher Jencks, "Can We Put a Time Limit on Welfare?" *The American Prospect* (Fall 1992): 32–40, at 35.

[65] Ibid., 36.

[66] Ibid.

[67] Ibid., 39.

[68] Bloom and Butler, "Executive Summary, Implementing Time-limited Welfare."

[69] Ibid.

[70] Ibid.

[71] Ibid., 3.

[72] Lemov, "Putting Welfare on the Clock," 30.

[73] Gueron, preface to Bloom and Butler, "Executive Summary, Implementing Time-limited Welfare," iv.

[74] U.S. Department of Health and Human Services, "State Welfare Demonstrations."

[75] Ibid.

[76] Ibid.

[77] Ibid.

[78] Ibid.

[79] Ibid., 22.

[80] Ibid., 24.

[81] Christina Klein, "Aid to Families with Dependent Children Self-Sufficiency Project" (Alaska: Department of Health and Social Services, Division of Public Assistance, February 1993).

[82] U.S. Department of Health and Human Services, "State Welfare Demonstrations."

[83] Neisner, "State Welfare Initiatives."

[84] U.S. Department of Health and Human Services, "State Welfare Demonstrations."

[85] Ibid.

[86] Ibid.

[87] Neisner, "State Welfare Initiatives."

[88] U.S. Department of Health and Human Services, "State Welfare Demonstrations."

[89] Michael Wiseman, "New State Welfare Initiatives," (Madison: La Follette Institute of Public Affairs, University of Wisconsin–Madison, August 1992): 27.

[90] Elaine Stuart, "The Reform Race: Will New State Welfare Reforms Punish the Poor or Push Them to Self-Sufficiency?" *State Government News* (The Council of State Governments, June 1994): 17–20.

[91] "New Jersey: Florio Signs Welfare Reform into Law," *Abortion Report* (January 22, 1992).

[92] "New Jersey Effort to Cut Welfare Gets Support in Federal Lawsuit," *The Washington Post*, March 4, 1994.

[93] Juliet Eilperin, "Group Moves to Support New Jersey Welfare Reform in Court," *States News Service* (March 2, 1994).

[94] "Minnesota: Welfare Reform Deja Vu as Abortion Rider is Added," *Abortion Report* (January 20, 1995).

[95] Rob Thomas, "GOP's Welfare Reform Sparks Unexpected Illinois Alliance," *St. Louis Post-Dispatch*, February 20, 1995.

[96] "Maryland: Welfare Reform May Demand State-Funded Abortions," *Abortion Report* (March 8, 1994).

[97] Wiseman, "New State Welfare Initiatives," 22.

[98] Iver Peterson, "Results Mixed After Caps Placed on Money for Children," *The New York Times*, September 21, 1995, p. A10.

[99] Ibid.

[100] "Widespread Support for Welfare Reform," *State Policy Reports* 12:10 (May 1994): 4.

[101] Ibid.

[102] Stuart, "The Reform Race."

[103] Kosterlitz, "Behavior Modification."

[104] David Holstrom, "Bay State Plan Sparks Protests from Recipients," *The Christian Science Monitor*, December 8, 1993, p. 3.

[105] Quoted on *60 Minutes*, May 15, 1994.

[106] U.S. Department of Health and Human Services, "State Welfare Demonstrations."

[107] Ibid.

[108] Ibid.

[109] Ibid.

[110] Jonathan Rabinovitz, "State that Was a Step Ahead on Benefit Limits," *The New York Times*, September 21, 1995, p. A10.

[111] U.S. Department of Health and Human Services, "State Welfare Demonstrations."

[112] Susan Kellam, "Welfare Experiments: Are States Leading the Way Toward National Reform?" *CQ Researcher*, 4:34 (September 16, 1994): 795–815.

[113] U.S. Department of Health and Human Services, "State Welfare Demonstrations."

[114] Douglas J. Besharov, "The New Paternalism: Programs and Proposals."

[115] Laura Kliewer Foster, "Welfare Reforms Try to Short-Circuit the Cycle," *Midwesterner* (Council of State Governments, Midwestern Office, June 1992).

[116] Deborah L. Cohen, "Learnfare's Services for Truants Not Often Tapped," *Education Week* (March 2, 1994).

[117] U.S. Department of Health and Human Services, "State Welfare Demonstrations."

[118] Robert C. Granger, "The Policy Implications of Recent Findings from the New Chance Demonstration, Ohio's Learning, Earning and Parenting (LEAP) Program in Cleveland, and the Teenage Parent Demonstration (TPD)" (paper presented at the annual meeting of the Association for Public Policy and Management, Chicago, October 1994).

[119] U.S. Department of Health and Human Services, "State Welfare Demonstrations."

[120] Jason Turner, "AFDC Research and Demonstration Projects in Fiscal Year 1991: Section 1115 Grant Projects" (report prepared for Administration for Children and Families, Office of Family Assistance, April 10, 1992).

[121] Granger, "The Policy Implications of Recent Findings."

[122] Kellam, "Welfare Experiments": 798.

[123] Kathleen Sylvester, "Two State Routes Out of Welfare," *Governing* (June 1993): 14.

[124] Evelyn Ganzglass, "Research Findings on the Effectiveness of State Welfare-to-Work Programs" (Washington, D.C.: Employment and Social Services Policy Studies, Center for Policy Research, National Governors' Association, 1994): 15.

[125] Cohen, "Learnfare's Services for Truants Not Often Tapped."

[126] Klein, "Aid to Families with Dependent Children Self-sufficiency Project," 19.

[127] Besharov, "The New Paternalism."

[128] Neisner, "State Welfare Initiatives."

[129] U.S. Department of Health and Human Services, "State Welfare Demonstrations."

[130] Ibid., 15.

[131] Ibid.

[132] Wiseman, "New State Welfare Initiatives," 19.

[133] Klein, "Aid to Families with Dependent Children Self-sufficiency Project."

[134] Sondra J. Nixon, "States Experimenting with Ways to Help People Stay Off Welfare," *Congressional Quarterly Weekly Report* 53:27 (July 1995): 2002–3.

[135] Wiseman, "New State Welfare Initiatives," 27.

[136] U.S. Department of Health and Human Services, "State Welfare Demonstrations."

[137] Ibid.

[138] Arizona Department of Economic Security, Division of Family Support, Family Assistance Administration, "Assistance Programs in Arizona" (1991).

[139] Matthew Birnbaum, "Policy, Planning and Social Experimentation: The Sad Case of the Wisconsin 100-hour Rule Experiment," (Madison: Department of Urban and Regional Planning, University of Wisconsin–Madison. Paper presented at the 17th Annual Research Conference of the Association for Public Policy and Management, Washington, D.C., November 1995), 10.

[140] Granger, "The Policy Implications of Recent Findings."

[141] Illinois, Department of Public Aid, "Project Chance Annual Report 1992" (1992): 6.

[142] Turner, "AFDC Research and Demonstration Projects in Fiscal Year 1991."

[143] Ibid., 14–15.

[144] Ibid., 12.

[145] Ibid., 13.

[146] Besharov, "The New Paternalism."

[147] Ganzglass, "Research Findings on the Effectiveness of State Welfare-to-Work Programs."

[148] Granger, "The Policy Implications of Recent Findings."

[149] Ganzglass, "Research Findings on the Effectiveness of State Welfare-to-Work Programs," 11.

[150] Ibid.

[151] Ibid., 12.

[152] Ibid., 12.

[153] Rebecca Maynard, "Teenage Childbearing and Welfare Reform: Lessons from a Decade of Demonstration and Evaluation," *Children and Youth Services Review*, vol. 17 (1995): 309–32, at 323, 325.

[154] Ganzglass, "Research Findings on the Effectiveness of State Welfare-to-Work Programs."

[155] Ibid.

[156] Granger, "The Policy Implications of Recent Findings."

[157] U.S. General Accounting Office, *Welfare Dependency: Coordinated Community Efforts Can Better Serve Young At-Risk Teen Girls*, (Washington, D.C.: U.S. G.A.O., May 1995).

[158] Beebout and Jacobson, "The Number and Characteristics of AFDC Recipients," 50.

[159] Ibid., 60.

[160] Ibid., 59.

[161] Ibid., 60.

[162] Ibid., 60.

[163] Kosterlitz, "Behavior Modification," 274.

[164] Ibid., 271–275.

[165] Ibid., 271–275.

[166] Nancy Amidei, antipoverty activist and columnist, quoted in Kosterlitz, "Behavior Modification."

[167] Kosterlitz, "Behavior Modification."

[168] Ibid.

[169] Charles Murray, quoted in Kosterlitz, "Behavior Modification," 274.

[170] Douglas J. Besharov, "Go Slow on the New Paternalism," *The Children's Roundtable* (Washington, D.C.: The Urban Institute, 1992).

[171] Ibid.

8

Reorienting Welfare Administration to Work and Other Reforms

Much of the attention surrounding the new welfare law has focused on its provisions aimed at moving recipients from welfare to work and discouraging dependence on welfare by placing limits on eligibility. As described in Chapters 6 and 7, Congress created financial incentives in the new welfare law to encourage states to enforce these provisions. Among the most popular provisions of the new law are titles that improve the child-support system and provide increased funding for child care. Among the most criticized provisions are those not really part of welfare reform but which are aimed at producing federal budget cuts, such as tightening eligibility requirements for disabled children, banning noncitizens from receiving welfare and many other social services, and cutting Food Stamp benefits for unemployed adults. The law delegates to states the task of creating programs that will encourage work by changing the incentives the old welfare system gave to recipients. States have had some experience in creating incentives to facilitate the transition to work, and those are reviewed in the first half of the chapter.

One of the most important implications of welfare policy devolution is the responsibility of state agencies for implementing the new law. No reform is more important that changing the way in which welfare is administered and increasing the ability of state governments to reorient their welfare bureaucracies toward encouraging self-sufficiency and work. Changing the way welfare offices operate and the signals and messages they send to welfare recipients is critical. All the reforms included in the new law must be implemented by state agencies. They must create the incentives and impose the sanctions that are expected to change behavior and end dependency. They may also choose to integrate welfare with other social programs, such as housing assistance, Food Stamps, and Medicaid, in order to streamline administration and better serve clients. The prospects for increasing the states' capacity to reform welfare are examined in the second part of the chapter.

CREATING FINANCIAL INCENTIVES TO ENCOURAGE WORK

Many states have experimented for years with programs aimed at encouraging work among welfare recipients and providing other ways to encourage the transition from welfare to self-sufficiency. These programs are summarized in Table 8.1.

INCREASING EARNINGS FROM WORK

MINIMUM WAGE   Chapter 2 reviewed efforts to raise the national minimum wage. Some state legislatures have also addressed the issue as part of their welfare reform initiatives. In Vermont, Democrats wanted to raise minimum wage by $1 to $5.25 an hour, but Senate Republicans refused to go along. The state's Human Services agency argued that the cost of raising the wage would be offset by dollars pumped into the economy by people with more spending money.[1] Additionally, a higher minimum wage would serve as a direct incentive to work. One estimate projected that a $1 increase in the minimum wage would raise 100,000 families above the poverty line.[2] However, critics questioned whether the increased minimum wage would reduce job opportunities for young people and minorities.[3] A higher minimum wage may be too blunt an instrument to really help the poor: Five of six people earning minimum wage are not poor, and critics predicted a loss in jobs and a 0.5 percent increase in inflation.[4]

EARNED INCOME DISREGARDS   One of the most frequently requested waivers by states has been to increase the earned income (EI) disregard formula. The existing federal policy rests on an uneasy compromise: Welfare recipients are encouraged to move into the work force, but in order to ensure that welfare benefits are reserved for needy families, earned income a welfare family receives is subtracted from their benefits. In order to encourage work and nudge families into the transition from welfare to work, states have raised the amount of income families

TABLE 8.1
FINANCIAL INCENTIVES TO ENCOURAGE WORK

Programs to increase cash income	States
Programs that disregard more income when determining welfare eligibility (some states disregard children's income as well)	Arizona, California, Colorado, Connecticut, Florida, Georgia, Illinois, Indiana Iowa, Massachusetts, Michigan, Minnesota, Mississippi, Missouri, Montana, North Dakota, New York, Ohio, Oklahoma, Pennsylvania, South Carolina, South Dakota, Texas, Utah, Vermont, Virginia, Washington, West Virginia, Wisconsin

Programs to increase resources	States
Programs that increase asset limits	California, Colordo, Connecticut, Florida, Indiana, Georgia, Iowa, Maine, Maryland, Massachusetts, Michigan, Minnesota, Missouri, Montana, Nebraska, New Hampshire, New York, North Dakota, Ohio, Oklahoma, Oregon, Pennsylvania, South Carolina, Tennessee, Texas, Vermont, Virginia, Wisconsin, Wyoming
Programs that allow specialized savings accounts	Arizona, California, Iowa, Massachusetts, Mississippi, Oregon, Pennsylvania, South Carolina, South Dakota, Tennessee, Texas, Utah, Virginia, Wisconsin
Programs that emphasize taking advantage of the EITC	Delaware
Programs that pass child support payments to families (part or full payment disregarded when determining eligibility; some states ensure collection of minimum levels of child support)	Arizona, Colorado, Connecticut, Iowa, Maine, Massachusetts, Minnesota, Mississippi, Montana, New York, Ohio, Oregon, South Carolina, Vermont, Virginia, Wisconsin

can earn and still receive welfare. States have differed in terms of whose income is disregarded, how long the disregard applies, and how much income is excluded. In Colorado, Florida, and Georgia, for example, the income of children (up to age 18) attending school full time is disregarded. In Montana, North Dakota, Ohio, Oklahoma, Pennsylvania, South Dakota, if children are attending school at least part time, their earnings will be disregarded.

In Illinois, two of each three dollars earned monthly are disregarded for as long as the recipient is working. Indiana uses an EI disregard for Food Stamps for the first six months of employment. Iowa disregards 50 percent of earnings; for those without significant work histories, all income is disregarded for the first four months on welfare. In Missouri, minor parents attending school and working can keep all their income. In Vermont and Virginia, earnings are disregarded if, with the addition of the welfare grant, they do not exceed poverty guidelines.[5] California's Assistance Payments Demonstration Project (APDP), approved in 1992, removes the time limits on EI disregard, lowers welfare grant levels by 5.8 percent, and eliminates the 100-hour rule.[6] Connecticut's "Reach for JOBS first" permits recipients to keep all earned income up to the federal poverty line.[7] The Illinois Work Pays Demonstration Project, approved in 1993, disregards up to $90 per month in employment expenses for each employed person in the family in determining eligibility and allows families to keep more of their earned income.[8] Vermont's Welfare Restructuring Project (WRP) increased the basic monthly disregard from $120 to $150 for a family of three.[9]

Minnesota's Family Investment Program raises EI disregard to 38 percent of EI, up to 158 percent of poverty, and more than doubles basic earnings disregards for a family of three—from $120 to $245.[10] An evaluation of the MFIP projected that annual hours of work would increase by 17 percent, earnings would increase $43 per year, average participants would collect an additional $541 in assistance, net transfers would increase by $125 per year per family because of EITC payments, and disposable income would increase by $660. The program has some flaws, however. Ironically, tax rates encourage unemployed and part-time workers to begin working, but may discourage them from working full time. The percentage of recipients working 1,500 or more hours a year was predicted to decline from 7.7 to 5.5 percent, and the percentage working 500–1,499 hours per year was expected to increase by 8.3 percent, from 17.4 to 25.7 percent of the caseload. The extra benefits of MFIP allow full-time workers to reduce their hours of work with little effect on (or actual gain in) their disposable income. In the absence of MFIP, only 30 percent of welfare recipients in Minnesota are predicted to work sometime during the year after random assignment. They receive MFIP benefits without responding to the financial incentives of the program.[11]

Critics of earnings disregards, which were authorized in the 1967 amendments to the Social Security Act, argue that the disregards should apply only in calculation of payments, not in determining welfare eligibility. Inequity results: "Because of the necessity of establishing eligibility before receiving the benefit of the disregard, it was possible for some families to retain welfare eligibility once established even after earnings reached levels that would have precluded acceptance for public assistance if reported at the time of application." With earned income disregards, labor force participation would go up, but duration of stay on welfare would increase as well. However, because being active in the job market leads to on-the-job training and experience and eventually to higher productivity, higher wages and termination from the welfare rolls could also result.[12]

INCREASING RESOURCES OF WELFARE RECIPIENTS

INCREASING ASSET LIMITS Federal welfare policy has traditionally placed a limit on the resources recipients could possess, assuming that families should sell or use their resources to support themselves before taking welfare benefits. But many states, in an effort to help those families become self-sufficient, have sought waivers to permit recipients to have vehicles, savings accounts, and other resources that might assist them in becoming independent. States have taken different approaches to balancing the values of encouraging resource accumulation and requiring recipients to rely on their own resources before using public ones. California's "Work Pays Demonstration Project" permits recipients to have $2,000 in assets and $4,500 equity in a car.[13] Colorado's "Personal Responsibility and Employment Program" allows recipients to own a car regardless of its value or equity.[14] Connecticut's "A Fair Chance" program increased the resource limit to $3,000.[15] Georgia's "Work for Welfare Project" (WFW) proposed increasing the vehicle asset limit to $4,500, adjusted annually based on the new car component of the Consumer Price Index; the vehicle could be of any value as long as it was used to commute to work or school.[16] Iowa permits $2,000 in assets for applicants and $5,000 in assets for welfare families.[17] Maryland and Nebraska also raised the resource limit to $5,000.[18] South Carolina's "Self-Sufficiency and Personal Responsibility Program" raised the resource limits to $3,000 and exempted life insurance policies, one vehicle, and interest and dividend payments.[19] Other states have revised their vehicle asset limits: Wisconsin ($2,500); Iowa ($3,000), Maryland ($5,000), Oklahoma ($5,000), Michigan (one vehicle completely disregarded), Missouri (no dollar limit on one vehicle), New York (may exclude value of one vehicle if developing own business), and North Dakota (one vehicle, no dollar limit for commuting to work).[20]

ALLOWING FOR SPECIALIZED SAVINGS ACCOUNTS   Many states encourage recipients to save money in preparation for self-sufficiency. Arizona's "EMPOWER" program permits $100 a month in Individual Development Accounts, to a maximum of $9,000.[21] California's "Work Pays Demonstration Project" permits $2,000 in assets, up to $5,000 in savings accounts, for home purchase, starting a business, or educating children.[22] Iowa's Individual Development Accounts can also be used for education, training, home ownership, starting a business, or family emergencies.[23] Virginia allow savings of up to $5,000 for purchase of a home or for education.[24] Massachusetts' "Welfare Reform '95" permits employers to establish Individual Asset Accounts to help in the transition from subsidized to unsubsidized employment.[25] Mississippi's "Work First" program provides for Individual Development Accounts funded by employer contributions of $1 for each hour of work.[26] Oregon's JOBS Plus provides for Individual Education Accounts: Employers contribute $1 per hour of work; funds can be used for education or training (funds are available through the State Scholarship Commission after the participant is in a nonsubsidized job).[27] Pennsylvania's "Pathways to Independence" exempts retirement savings and education accounts.[28] The "Strengthening of South Dakota Families" allows children's savings account of up to $1,000.[29] Wisconsin's Special Resource Account Demonstration Project permits a special resource account of up to $10,000 for education and training.[30]

CASH AWARDS FOR WORK   Wisconsin's New Hope Project, in Milwaukee, seeks to increase employment through financial incentives. It is a volunteer program; low-income families and individuals, regardless of family structure or welfare status, are eligible. An alternative to welfare, New Hope provides benefits to participants who work at least thirty hours a week and guarantees jobs for those unable to meet the work requirement.[31]

COMBINATION OF FINANCIAL INCENTIVES   California's Work Pays Demonstration Project increases the resource limit to $2,000 and vehicle asset limit to $4,500; permits savings up to $5,000 in restricted accounts; creates an "Alternative Assistance Program" (CAAP), allowing welfare recipients with earned income to choose Medicaid and Child Care Assistance in lieu of a cash grant; and simplifies eligibility determinations for welfare and Food Stamps by making requirements compatible between the two programs.[32] Washington's Success Through Employment Program (STEP) eliminates the one hundred-hour rule.[33]

EVALUATING FINANCIAL INCENTIVES

Creating financial incentives for welfare recipients to earn income, save for education, buy houses, purchase vehicles to get to work, and raise money to start businesses are all important ways of encouraging self-sufficiency. These reforms are expected to produce a number of important benefits. They promise to increase the earnings and reduce benefit payments to welfare recipients who increase the number of hours they work. The reforms increase the welfare benefit payments of recipients who are already working or who would return to work in the absence of the program. Total transfer payments could "either decrease or increase, depending on whether the number of recipients who behaviorally respond to the program's incentives is larger or smaller than the number who receive windfall gains."[34]

The advantages of these reforms must be balanced against other objectives of the welfare system. Raising income returns by reducing benefits for those not working "compromises what is presumably the fundamental purpose of welfare: the alleviation of need."[35] Raising income returns by increasing earned income disregards may discourage recipients from leaving welfare completely and may keep them on the rolls longer. Some analysts and policy makers argue for "reduced emphasis of incorporation of work incentives within benefit calculations in favor of more suasion, work requirements, skills enhancement, and techniques for supplementing income over what is explicitly identified as a transitional period (of short duration) following employment."[36]

Certain studies have found some disincentive to full-time work. David H. Greenberg and others examined financial incentive programs in Minnesota, Florida, Vermont, New York, and Wisconsin. The goal of these programs was to increase earnings and reduce reliance on benefit payments through the use of work incentives. Because the incentives are benefit payments in and of themselves, financial incentive programs are successful only if some welfare payments continue to be received. To end their welfare dependency, recipients must earn enough wages that they are ineligible for transfer payments. Each of the programs studied increased incentives to work, but each also increased the incentive to work part time: "In each program, at high levels of work, the marginal tax rate for workers under the proposed programs is larger than the marginal tax rate for workers under the current system."[37]

The study concluded that the incentive programs would result in only small changes in employment among participants (an increase of 3 percent; full-time employment would decrease by 2 percent; and part-time

TABLE 8.2
REFORMS TO ENCOURAGE WORK BY PROVIDING SUPPORT SERVICES

Programs that profide subsidized services	States
Programs that provide more child care (during participation or during a transition to work)	Arizona, California, Connecticut, Delaware, Florida, Georgia, Indiana, Maine, Mississippi, Montana, Nebraska, New Jersey, New York, Ohio, Oklahoma, Oregon, Pennsylvania, South Carolina, Tennessee, Utah, Vermont, Virginia, West Virginia, Wisconsin
Programs that provide more health services (during participation or during a transition to work)	Arizona, Arkansas, Connecticut, Delaware, Florida, Georgia, Idaho, Indiana, Maine, Massachusetts, Mississippi, Montana, Nebraska, New Hampshire, Montana, Nebraska, New Hampshire, New Jersey, Oregon, Pennsylvania, South Carolina, Tennessee, Utah, Vermont, Virginia, Wisconsin
Programs that provide for additional travel expenses	California, Georgia, West Virginia

employment would increase by 5 percent). If states want to encourage full-time employment and eventual self-sufficiency, participants should be required to work full time before receiving extra benefits. More generous financial incentives have a greater impact on employment; however, in combination with other services, less generous programs could have a greater overall impact.[38]

TRANSITIONAL ASSISTANCE FOR CHILD CARE

Most states involved in welfare reform have recognized the importance of extending child-care benefits when recipients leave the welfare system (see Table 8.2). States typically offer transitional assistance of from twelve to twenty-four months: Arizona (twenty-four months), Delaware (additional twelve months), Nebraska (twenty-four months), New York (twelve months if employed recipients leave welfare because of child-support payments), Ohio (up to eighteen months), and Utah (twenty-four months). In a Virginia pilot program, those who become successfully employed may receive transitional benefits for up to 36 months.[39] California's "Incentives to Self-Sufficiency Project" provides transitional child care benefits to families that leave welfare because of marriage.[40] Connecticut's "A Fair Chance" extended transitional child care to twenty-four months; an additional waiver, "Reach for Jobs First," provides transitional child care to those who find employment within six months of losing welfare benefits (for any reason). Child care is provided until the family's income is more than 75 percent of the state median income.[41] South Carolina's "Self-Sufficiency and Personal Responsibility Program" reduced benefits for up to twelve months to recipients who would otherwise no longer be eligible for welfare because of employment. Families remain eligible for Medicaid and child care, and regular transitional Medicaid and child-care benefits begin at the end of the twelve months.[42] Some states have gone beyond the minimal federal child care program. Georgia's Positive Employment and Community Help (PEACH) program includes a partnership with businesses and community organizations to provide funds for some day care programs.[43]

HEALTH CARE

Some states have given priority to providing health care benefits to welfare families (see Table 8.2). Georgia's "Right From the Start" Medicaid health insurance provides health care for low-income pregnant women and small children. A case manager work with a woman from the beginning of her pregnancy until her baby's first birthday. The managers and nurses visit women in their homes, take them to clinic appointments, and show them how to care for their babies.[44]

Idaho Health Check is a free medical service for children on welfare. The service provides screening for any physical or developmental conditions that may endanger a child's life or well-being in the future. Services provided include health and developmental history, physical examination, record of shots, vision and hearing testing, laboratory services as needed, nutritional evaluation, and dental check. Corrective care for any problem found is provided free, such as dentistry, shots, or glasses. Recipients may choose their own doctor or receive care from the local health department. Transportation to all services is provided. Other social services provided include mental health services, adult and child development, child protective services, adoption services, child care licensing services, and information and referral services.

Since access to medical care through Medicaid is one reason why some workers leave low-paying jobs for welfare, providing transitional health-care benefits for families leaving welfare has become an important reform in encouraging work. States offer health benefits for varying lengths of time to those who leave welfare, usually from twelve to twenty-four months: Arizona (twenty-four months), Delaware (twelve months), Nebraska (twenty-four months if the recipient leaves welfare for work), Utah (twenty-four months). In a Virginia pilot program, those who become successfully employed may receive transitional benefits for up to thirty-six months.[45] Connecticut extends transitional Medicaid to twenty-four months; an additional waiver ("Reach for Jobs First") provides twenty-four months of transitional Medicaid to those who find employment within six months of losing welfare benefits (for any reason).[46] South Carolina's "Self-Sufficiency and Personal Responsibility Program" provides reduced benefits for up to twelve months to recipients who would otherwise no longer be eligible for welfare because of employment. Families remain eligible for Medicaid and child care during this phase-down period, and regular transitional Medicaid and child care benefits begin at the end of the twelve months.[47]

SUBSIDIZED TRANSPORTATION

Federal law requires states to provide payment or reimbursement for transportation and other work-related support services that they determine are necessary for an individual's participation in JOBS, but less attention has been given to this issue than to child care and health care (see Table 8.2). Lack of adequate transportation is a major barrier for many recipients.[48] In Arkansas, public transportation is unavailable to most participants, and the state provides reimbursement for gas money but not for mass-transit fares. As a result, some participants were forced to drop out of training programs.[49] A few states have gone beyond the federal minimum. West Virginia's "Joint Opportunities for Independence," for example, requires employers to pay individuals $1 an hour for work and travel expenses.[50]

THE ROLE OF SUPPORT SERVICES IN THE
WELFARE-TO-WORK TRANSITION

Extending support services during the transition from welfare to work is one of the most popular areas of welfare reform. Governors and congressional Democrats joined together to insist that the Republican welfare reform bills include larger child-care grants to states. As discussed in Chapter 1, the Family Support Act requires each state to guarantee child care if such is necessary for an individual's participation in education, training, or employment. Each state can provide child care directly, arrange care by use of contract or vouchers, provide cash or vouchers in advance to the caretaker relative, reimburse the caretaker relative, or adopt any other arrangement approved by the state agency. Regardless of the method, reimbursement for child care must at least equal the child-care amount disregarded in determining the welfare grant for which the family would otherwise be eligible. The reimbursement cannot exceed actual cost or applicable local market rates regardless of the method of child care chosen. States must provide up to twelve months of transitional child care (TCC) for clients moving into the labor force. In 1990, the law was amended to provide federal child-care funds for working families at risk for AFDC through the Child Care and Development Block Grant (CCDBG).

Studies of child care in state programs have demonstrated how important this kind of assistance is in making it possible for recipients to move from welfare to work. "Child care," defined in one study as "any care by an individual or facility other than the mother,"[51] differs across the states. Several financing mechanisms pay subsidies through a primarily private delivery system; this system encourages trade-offs among supply, cost, and quality. By neglecting to address these trade-offs, welfare reform policies raise but do not resolve "difficult dilemmas in service provision, state regulation, and consumer education." Preparation as a child-care consumer and success in securing suitable child care may have a substantial impact on a welfare recipient's transition from welfare to work.[52]

One study examined the child care provided in three California JOBS (GAIN) programs that all provide assistance through a vender/voucher system. They are also all mature JOBS programs: Unlike demonstrations with limited scope, these programs are permanent, county-wide programs that serve both mandatory and voluntary participants. The study sample was limited to JOBS clients who have young children (at least one under thirteen) and who actually participate in a program activity after orientation. Participants were recruited randomly at orientation; 74 percent volunteered, and the sample differed slightly from the GAIN population as a whole in that the clients had younger children. The study found that wide variation in the quality and convenience of child care used by program participants can be linked to mode of care, children's ages, and characteristics and behaviors of participants as consumers: "Welfare recipients entering job-training programs make substantial use of private child care, but the adequacy of these arrangements—given approaches to regulation and consumer education—is highly uncertain."[53]

The study proposed several measures of the adequacy of child care.

Structural features of care (small group sizes, adult–child ratio) determine child–caretaker interaction and affect child development (intellectual ability, language acquisition, social competence). The quality of adult–child interactions is most important and may be achieved in larger groups, but high staffing ratios and small group sizes generally contribute to quality relationships. Child-care decisions are "sensitive to price and convenience of location"; these factors figure prominently in child care selection and parental satisfaction. Parental satisfaction with child care arrangements is critical: Difficulty in arranging child care is a significant predictor of depression among employed mothers, and care compromises interfere with a child's adjustment to care.[54]

Child care involves important trade-offs: A "growing demand for services and constrained public and private resources intersect to create a three-way squeeze among availability, affordability, and quality." Child-care suppliers keep costs low by paying workers "near poverty-level wages." These low wages reduce worker training and increase worker turnover. "Compromises in staff quality and stability translate directly into lower quality" care.[55] The study rated two-thirds of the center-based classrooms at or below the minimally adequate level; 12 percent reached standards for good quality care: "almost half of children under three years of age are in care which is less than minimal quality."[56]

When federal social services block grant funds for subsidized child care were reduced in the 1980s, most states lowered licensing standards and cut back on monitoring. "A 1991 survey of state child-care regulating agencies found that thirty-two states had reduced budgets and staff for on-site monitoring that year"; 43 percent of all children in out-of-home care were in settings that do not meet "even minimal health and safety standards."[57] Even if providers are regulated, twenty states fail to conduct one unannounced on-site visit annually. Minimal regulation probably increases the overall supply of care, but it has a negative impact on quality. "States with more demanding licensing standards have been found to have fewer poor quality centers."[58]

Even if parents want quality programs, they have a hard time monitoring child care services because the services are largely unobservable. Studies have also shown that parents are "consistently less discriminatory in their evaluations" than are trained observers.[59] Lack of parental discrimination may reflect a need to balance convenience, cost, familiarity, and program quality. These limitations in discrimination are exacerbated because few child-care providers advertise (most consumers rely on informal referrals). Child-care resource and referral programs are improving consumer education; several states fund independent resource and referral agencies that provide information, referrals, and individualized counseling. Nationally, 9 percent of parents have used these services to secure child care. JOBS clients particularly may need consumer education and support because of their limited experience with market child care. However, the effect of consumer education "may be diluted by the exceptional transportation, time and income restraints facing low-income parents."[60] Constraints on program authority and capacity to evaluate or recommend alternatives may also lessen the value of referral services. Most provide information about location, fees and alternatives, but do not have the ability to assess or report adequacy of care.

Proponents of JOBS hope that both parents and children will be positively affected by the program; in reality, inadequate child care may hamper both child development and parental transitions to employment: "As recipients with younger and younger children are mandated to participate in job search, training and education programs, their need for substitute care may overwhelm the capacity of states to assure that minimally regulated, private care meets those thresholds."[61] The child care obtained by JOBS participants in the California study illustrates some of the challenges in making welfare to work a reality. Overall levels of satisfaction with care was lower than levels reported by those studying nationally representative samples, and many JOBS parents compromised either convenience or program quality. These compromises affect both child development and parental economic success.[62] The fact that participants had to compromise even while participating in "model" programs suggests "the limitations of current approaches to regulation and consumer education."[63] Referral services did help parents find better-quality care that was closer to GAIN activities; however, agencies are hampered by an inability to recommend good providers or warn participants about poor providers: "In the absence of stringent oversight by state licensing programs or by local resource and referral agencies, consumer education and referral assistance are important but insufficient solutions to maintaining minimum levels of child-care convenience and quality."[64]

A 1991 study by the Illinois Department of Public Aid emphasized that child care subsidies are vital if single parents are to leave welfare. However, at one point, only 20 percent of AFDC parents working or in school were using child care. The study summarized the challenges states face in ensuring that child care is available for parents who are leaving welfare for work. Most use informal child care from relatives, friends, or licensed-exempt homes of nonrelatives. Children under two were more likely to be at babysitters' homes, while children over two were more likely to be in a center; there was a dearth of spots for infants in centers.

The cost of care is major factor in care selection. Transportation problems, waiting lists, and scarcity of babysitters are significant barriers. Odd work hours make child care difficult, because most centers' hours parallel the traditional work week. Informal care that becomes the only option is often unreliable, making full-time work impossible. Low state reimbursement rates increase the likelihood of licensed-exempt care. Over 20 percent of children were placed with different care providers throughout the week; this can be debilitating for the development of young children. Having children with disabilities, the presence of infants and toddlers, the need to care for disabled adults, and having three or more children all inhibited mothers from entering school or work force. Problems with child care translate into work problems such as tardiness and absence.

The 1991 Illinois study offered a number of recommendations. Child care programs should be viewed in a broad context with education, training, employment assistance, housing, and other supports. States should:

Carefully inform welfare recipients of all child care programs, train caseworkers with accurate information, identify a child-care resource staff person, establish a unified child-care subsidy system, combine various existing programs, and educate parents to make good decisions for their families regarding care

Build the capacity of current child care programs, integrate Head Start with other programs for extended care of children, provide extended care for young children through early childhood programs based in the schools, and promote school- and community-based programs for school-age children whose parents work or are in education and training

Prevent welfare dependency by expanding funds for the transitional child care program, base eligibility and duration of assistance on need and income level rather than a fixed period of time, and view child care programs as part of a broader effort to help low income families become self-reliant

Enhance training and employment programs through at least additional coordination if not additional funding, target economic development toward depressed sections of the state, expand medical coverage for working families in poverty not covered by employer-sponsored health programs, and expand child care assistance for working families[65]

Restrictions on which day care providers can receive public funds pose a significant challenge to welfare parents. Most licensed, formal child-care givers operate during regular business hours, whereas welfare mothers may have to take evening classes, work at night jobs, and change their schedule frequently. Restrictions also run counter to the goal of welfare reform—to encourage recipients to take control of their lives. Making child care more difficult may reduce the number of mothers who work and also sends the signal that they cannot be trusted to make sure their children are well taken care of. Some states pay for any available day care, which seems to give mothers a much greater opportunity to get help with their children.

If, as some argue, licensing prevents child abuse and other problems, then perhaps all parents, and not just poor ones, should be prohibited from leaving their children with unlicensed care providers. Ideally, all child-care givers should be trained and operate in attractive, safe, and stimulating environments, but the child-care component of welfare reform needs a more modest goal. Governments can offer training programs for caregivers, offer low-interest loans for facilities, and even encourage some welfare recipients to become caregivers. Although that may perpetuate for some women the idea they can stay at home and fail to join the labor market, it is much better than current arrangements. As Paul Offner puts it, "a woman who gets off welfare by taking care of five neighborhood kids is surely setting a better example for her kids than one who sits at home and does nothing."[66]

ADMINISTRATIVE REFORMS

Integrating services can take a number of approaches: family services centers, electronic benefit transfer cards, automated tracking systems, and revision of benefit program rules. These are modest and relatively uncontroversial changes; nevertheless, obstacles to effective implementation do exist. Categorical funding "encourages agencies to draw a sharp line between those they will serve and those they will not."[67] Agencies prefer "specialists" instead of general case managers; historical mistrust between agencies reduces the prospects for cooperation. Proponents can be too flexible or too rigid in pursuing reform. Different funding sources, uncoordinated federal agencies, complicated congressional subcommittee structure, defensive agencies protecting their own turf, and strong support by special-interest groups are all part of the challenge.[68]

On the other hand, promising recommendations for integrating services include adopting a tight/loose approach, which gives a state a clear, firm, overall agenda but allows for flexibility in implementation; allowing for continuous monitoring and feedback; and giving flexibility and autonomy to individual actors in the process. Consolidating programs, filling gaps in service, offering flexibility to tailor programs to state needs, reducing administrative costs by eliminating duplicate programs, and focusing on outcomes rather than rules should all be part of the welfare reform agenda.[69] The most difficult administrative challenges involve making significant investments in case management and administrative procedures. Richard Nathan argues that we need to make "basic changes in the way we recruit, prepare, reward, and treat top managers in government so that good intentions by politicians become good results for citizens."[70]

One of the most important elements of welfare reform is to change the way in which the welfare system itself works. Options include providing alternative forms of assistance, improving the training of case workers, reorienting welfare agencies toward work, and integrating welfare with other programs. Table 8.3 outlines the main experiments in changing the structure of welfare programs; the discussion that follows summarizes some of the lessons we can draw from the states' experience in reforming welfare administration. Some of the programs are still in effect; others have been or will be phased out.

REVISING ELIGIBILITY RULES AND PROCEDURES

DIVERTING APPLICANTS: ONE-TIME CASH GRANTS AND "OPTING OUT" Several states permit recipients to opt out of welfare but still receive some services. California's "Work Pays Demonstration Project" permits recipients who work but who also have low welfare benefits to opt out of the program but still remain eligible for services such as Medi-Cal and child care, which are usually available only to welfare recipients.[71] Maryland's "Family Investment Program"[72] and Montana's "Families Achieving Independence"[73] initiative give families facing a short-term financial crisis a one-time payment equal to three months of benefits as an alternative to enrolling in welfare. Utah's "Single Parent Employment Demonstration" program also offers a one-time payment for emergency

TABLE 8.3
ADMINISTRATIVE REFORMS

Programs with revised application/ eligibility rules	States
Programs that provide a one-time cash grant in order to divert families from welfare	Maine, Maryland, Montana, New York, North Carolina, Texas, Utah, Virginia
Programs that waive the "one hundred-hour" rule for two-parent families	California, Florida, Indiana, Maryland, Michigan, Minnesota, Mississippi, Missouri, Montana, Ohio, Oklahoma, Oregon, Pennsylvania, South Carolina, Tennessee, Vermont, Utah, Washington, Wisconsin
Programs that emphasize paternity establishment as a condition of eligibility	Delaware, Illinois, Maine, Massachusetts, North Carolina, Ohio, South Carolina, Tennessee, Texas, Virginia

Programs with revised case management/benefit dispersal	States
Programs with more extensive case management and support (more caseworkers with better training; more intensive, personalized support)	Colorado, Delaware, Florida, Georgia, Illinois, Indiana, Kentucky, Michigan, Minnesota, Ohio, Oklahoma, Oregon, Pennsylvania, Utah, Virginia, Wisconsin
Programs with innovative automated tracking and benefit dispersal	California, Connecticut, Delaware, Minnesota, New Hampshire, Ohio, Rhode Island, South Carolina, Tennessee, Texas, Wyoming
Programs in which benefits can be "cashed out" (as a family grant or in order to subsidize employment)	Alabama, Arizona, Colorado, Indiana, Iowa, Maine, Massachusetts, Michigan, Minnesota, Mississippi, Missouri, Montana, Nebraska, North Carolina, North Dakota, Ohio, Oregon, Pennsylvania, Utah, Vermont, Virginia, Washington, Wisconsin
Programs in which measures are taken to reduce fraud	California, Connecticut, New York, Pennsylvania, Tennessee, Utah

Programs with administrative structural changes	States
Programs with increased interagency coordination (multiservice centers or partnerships between agencies)	Arkansas, Colorado, Connecticut, Delaware, Georgia, Illinois, Indiana, Iowa, Kentucky, Maryland, New Hampshire, New Mexico, Oklahoma, Oregon, Pennsylvania, South Carolina, Texas, Utah

TABLE 8.3
Administrative Reforms (*Continued*)

Programs with improved child support enforcement	Alabama, Arizona, Arkansas, California, Connecticut, Delaware, Florida, Georgia, Indiana, Maine, Maryland, Massachusetts, Michigan, Mississippi, Missouri, Montana, New York, New Jersey, North Dakota, Ohio, Oregon, Tennessee, Utah, Vermont, Virginia, Wisconsin, Wyoming
Programs that encourage or mandate noncustodial parent participation	Alabama, Florida, Georgia, Maryland, Massachusetts, Michigan, Minnesota, Mississippi, Missouri, New Hampshire, New Jersey, Ohio, Tennessee, Utah, Vermont,Virginia, Wyoming, Wisconsin
Programs that encourage community partnerships to provide program services	Arkansas, Colorado, Georgia, Illinois, Iowa, Kentucky, Minnesota, New Jersey, Tennessee

or special needs to keep families from having to go on welfare.[74] The "Virginia Independence Program" permits welfare applicants to receive one payment of up to 120 days of benefits; they are then ineligible for benefits for at least 160 days.[75] Similarly, New York's "Jobs First Strategy" offers a one-time cash grant, but it also permits welfare applicants to apply for child care or JOBS training.[76] Despite little research on the effects of this approach, it makes a great deal of sense to try to prevent welfare dependency by helping families survive short-term financial crises that might otherwise force them to enter the welfare system.

SIMPLIFYING RULES   Simplifying programs and making them more consistent enables welfare office staff to focus on case management rather than spending a great deal of time determining eligibility. Simplifying eligibility, however, is difficult because welfare, Food Stamps, Medicaid, and other programs are run by different federal agencies with different congressional overseers.[77] Nevertheless, states are experimenting with simplifying the application process by redefining eligibility requirements including alien status, child-support cooperation, residency requirements, unit definition, application for potential sources of income, and eligibility of strikers. States are also reevaluating verification and reporting requirements, vehicle and other resource exclusions, child care deductions, and restoration of benefits for underpayments.[78] California's welfare/Food Stamp Compatibility Project, for instance, seeks to simplify the eligibility process reduce errors by aligning the rules of the two programs. North Dakota's Training, Education, Employment and Management Project (TEEM) consolidates welfare, Food Stamps, and other programs into a single cash grant. Uniform, simplified eligibility rules set the gross income test at 50 percent of the base year poverty level; redefine countable income; increase earned income disregards; exempt one vehicle; eliminate the one hundred-hour rule; increase resource limits; exempt stepparent income for six months when determining the grant; and eliminate the $50 child-support pass-through.[79]

CASE MANAGEMENT

NEW ATTITUDES AND EMPHASIS OF CASEWORKERS   Kentucky requires that case managers of JOBS receive a week of special "New Roles Training," which provides an introduction to the knowledge, skills, and abilities necessary to be an effective case manager. The program focuses on helping case managers to be more sensitive to their clients, to develop interpersonal communication skills important to case managers' responsibilities, to develop problem-solving and confrontation skills that contribute to effective case management, and to develop other effective management skills.

MORE EXTENSIVE, INTENSIVE TRACKING   All states are required to implement a computerized tracking system for welfare, but some states have gone beyond federal requirements. Delaware's "Employment and Training Automated System" automates the referrals from the Financial Eligibility staff to First Step Case Managers; increases communication between welfare or Food Stamp eligibility staff and First Step contractor staff; maintains data containing work history, education, assessment data and dependent information on all participants; automates referrals to contractors and provides letters or notices regarding appointments, follow-up activities, and sanctions; and provides information for the staff to track activities via the system. Pennsylvania's "Pathways to Independence" extends case management counseling and referral services up to one year after a recipient leaves welfare.[80] Tennessee's conversion of family assistance case records to a new statewide computer system eliminated more than three hundred reports and forms.[81] Automation makes sense in improving agency efficiency and effectiveness, but increasing automation may still bump up against different eligibility rules for different programs.[82]

CONTRACTS   One of the most common welfare reforms is to require recipients to formulate and sign a contract or plan that outlines how they will eventually leave the welfare system and become self-sufficient. Wisconsin's "Pay for Performance" program, for example, includes three steps. First, an applicant meets with a "financial planning resource specialist" to discuss alternatives to welfare. Second, the applicant must complete sixty hours of JOBS activities prior to approval for welfare; thirty of those hours must include employer contact. Third, recipients who are approved for welfare benefits (after exploring alternatives and completing extensive job search) must work up to forty hours a week in JOBS. Sanctions are applied to those who do not participate: For each hour of nonparticipation, the welfare grant is reduced by an amount equal to the minimum wage; if the welfare grant is fully exhausted, the remaining sanction is applied to the Food Stamp allotment; if hours of participation fall below 25 percent of assigned hours without good cause, no welfare grant will be awarded and the Food Stamp amount will be reduced to $10.[83] There is only limited information on whether intensive case management leads to outcomes such as higher wage jobs, substantially more income, and greater long-term self-sufficiency.

ELECTRONIC BENEFIT PROGRAMS   Several states have shifted to distributing program benefits electronically as a way to speed delivery of services to recipients, reduce the stigma associated with using Food Stamps, improve administrative efficiency, save money, and reduce fraud and abuse.[84] Ohio has replaced paper Food Stamps with electronic cards in half of the state's counties.[85] In South Carolina, monthly benefits are credited to a debit card.[86] Wyoming's "Smartcard" delivers benefits via a microchip-embedded plastic card, which also serves as a portable family health record. The card is more convenient for benefit recipients, reduces transaction time and daily electronic payment for merchants, and improves efficiency and auditing capability for program managers.[87]

"CASHING OUT" BENEFITS   Alabama's "Avenues to Self-Sufficiency Through Employment and Training" (ASSETS) combines welfare, Food Stamps and Low-Income Home Energy Assistance programs into one cash assistance program.[88] Colorado's "Personal Responsibility and Employment Program" cashes out Food Stamps by adding the coupon value to the welfare grant.[89] Pennsylvania's "Pathways to Independence" permits recipients to cash out Food Stamps after two months of employment.[90] This option has permitted some states to close Food Stamp offices and save money on administrative costs.

MEASURES TO REDUCE FRAUD   Reducing fraud has been a perennial concern of welfare reform. California's "Incentives to Self-Sufficiency Project" increased penalties for specific types of fraud that are involved, according to a 1994 review, in about 4 percent of all California AFDC cases.[91] Several states fingerprint welfare applicants to weed out those who make multiple filings under different names. Pennsylvania has cracked down on welfare fraud through several efforts, including a ninety-day residency requirement on welfare recipients, raising age requirement for year-round cash assistance from forty-five to fifty-five years of age, and closing a loophole in state law that had allowed out-of-state residents to obtain cash benefits in Pennsylvania.[92]

INTERAGENCY CONSOLIDATION AND COORDINATION

Colorado's "Family Center Initiative" restructured the state's Department of Social Services, Department of Institutions, and Drug Abuse and Alcohol Division into the Department of Human Services run from comprehensive Family Centers that provide services in one location. The centers focus on early intervention and prevention, track client outcomes, help retrain workers, and provide services such as home visiting, child care, mental health services, screening for learning disabilities, basic education classes, access to other services through applications and monthly resource fairs, and outreach services for families with newborn children.[93]

Indiana's reforms share many of Colorado's goals and strategies. Indiana has developed a partnership among the Family and Social Services Administration's Division of Families and Children (DFC), Department of Employment and Training Services (DETS) (part of the Department of Workforce Development), and Department of Education (DOE) in order to operate IMPACT, its welfare reform program. This partnership was formed to serve customers more effectively and to avoid overlapping services. The program includes recipients in decision-making processes in order to help them become more self-sufficient, self-confident, and better able to function in their environments. IMPACT also works to build a sense of trust among program partners; provide the staff training necessary for the staff to better serve recipients; and streamline referral and reporting processes. The program seeks to help welfare and Food Stamp recipients to acquire essential skills and access the support systems they need to ensure self-sufficiency; provide the most efficient and cost-effective services possible; foster inter-agency and (inter-program) cooperation and share exemplary models throughout the state; stimulate innovative approaches and seek participant input; and encourage joint planning, funding, data sharing, and other cooperative initiatives.

In Delaware, interagency agreements have been established with the Department of Labor, Delaware Private Industry Council, Department of Public Instruction, and Division of Alcoholism, Drug Abuse and Mental Health. The state operates twelve multiservice centers where residents can apply for welfare, get Food Stamps, meet with counselors, and receive child and elderly care assistance.[94] Similarly, New Mexico has developed common locations for the field offices of the departments of labor, health, human services, education, and for other programs aimed at children, youth, and families.[95] Illinois' Humboldt Park Welfare-to-Work Demonstration Project also brings together a variety of services—health care, day care, Head Start, GED courses, parenting classes, and counseling for victims of rape, incest, domestic violence, and alcohol and drug abuse. The program costs about $6,000 per participant. One-fifth of all recipients who entered since February 1991 were employed and off welfare by 1994.[96]

Several additional states have emphasized agency and community coordination as part of their welfare reform initiatives. Georgia's PEACH (Positive Employment and Community Help) program was created in 1986 to move people from welfare to work. It is a cooperative effort among the Department of Human Resources Division of Family and Children Services, the Department of Labor, the Department of Education, the Department of Technical and Adult Education, the Job Training Partnership, and Community Action Agencies. Twenty-one Local Coordinating Councils, made up of community leaders and agency representatives, are responsible for developing additional local resources for the program and for ensuring cooperation between the varied agencies. Kentucky's welfare program partners include the Department for Social Insurance, Area Development Districts, the Workforce Development Cabinet, the Department of Employment Services, the Department of Social Services. The Kentucky programs also invites involvement from local merchants, religious organizations, nonprofit agencies, service groups, clubs, medical professionals, educators and a variety of other community-based individuals and organizations. Oklahoma has experimented with involving the Eastern Private Industry

Council and Oklahoma State University. The state provides welfare payments, recruitment and referrals of participants, Food Stamps and day care; EPIC provides tuition, books, fees and tools; and OSU provides housing, education and social services.[97]

CHILD SUPPORT COLLECTION

As discussed in Chapters 1 and 2, the lack of child support payments is a major cause of welfare dependency. The 1988 Family Support Act (FSA) establishes the requirements that make child support more enforceable. The Child Support Amendments of 1984 required states to develop suggested guidelines for judges and to provide expedited judicial or administrative procedures for hearing child support cases; the Family Support Act requires states to make these guidelines uniform. The act also requires states to withhold the wages of the absent parent who is not providing child support unless (1) a court finds good cause not to require income withholding or (2) both parents reach an agreement. According to the FSA, states may require each parent to furnish their Social Security numbers, to be placed on a newborn's birth certificate. Parents can then be located if it becomes necessary to withhold income for child support. States are also ordered to establish paternity of children born out of wedlock. Welfare recipients must cooperate with the state in this process.

Efforts by states to increase the level of child support paid to families has translated into decreased need for welfare. When states began to collect child support for welfare recipients, they usually kept the recovered funds in order to recoup welfare benefit payments. As welfare reform evolved, however, several states began to "pass through" a portion of collected child support to the family. These payments, often around $50, were disregarded by some states when determining benefit eligibility and counted as income by others. Currently, more states are experimenting with child support payment disregards, and some states are even returning all collected funds as cash grants to families. Child support payments are passed through to the family without affecting eligibility in Arizona, Mississippi, Montana, Oregon, and Wisconsin.[98] Connecticut's "A Fair Chance" requires the state to pay "the difference between the noncustodial parent's child support payments and a state-established minimum."[99] Virginia has experimented in one county with guaranteed child support "insurance" payments to welfare to assist welfare families in maintaining economic self-sufficiency when they leave welfare because of employment.[100]

Arizona's Child Support Enforcement Administration (CSEA) has several functions that are typical of state child support enforcement agencies: to locate absent, nonsupporting parents; to determine paternity; to establish and enforce support obligations; and to collect child support from absent parents. Originally, AFDC recipients turned alimony and child support from absent parents over to the State of Arizona; collected child support was used to repay the state and federal government for benefits paid to the families. Under that plan, when AFDC participation ended, child support paid for the current month was turned over to the family, but DES kept child support paid over and above the monthly support obligation until all AFDC payments were repaid. Arizona's most recent waiver, however, passes all child support collections through to the family without affecting the family's welfare eligibility. State services are also available to the general public to locate absent, nonsupporting parents and to establish paternity and collect child support.[101]

Indiana child-support enforcement agency officials make use of a number of tools including income withholding, liens on property, interception of state and federal income tax refunds, interception of unemployment compensation benefits, and interception of lottery winnings. Maine revokes the driver's and professional licenses of delinquents in child support payments. Minnesota requires welfare recipients to assign child-support rights to the local agency and to cooperate in finding absent parents. The state also excludes the first $50 of collected child support as income of the welfare recipient. New Jersey law requires probation departments to recruit private collection agencies to track down delinquent child-support payments.[102]

New York's "Child Assistance Program" (CAP), a fourteen-county demonstration project, is a volunteer program that encourages parents to establish paternity and obtain child support orders. It replaces welfare as an income support program by guaranteeing child support, providing intensive case management, allowing parents to keep more of their earned income while receiving benefits (in excess of 185 percent of the standard of need), and cashes out Food Stamps and child care assistance.[103] Under CAP, grant levels depend on the number of children covered by a court order for child support; families are eligible for welfare benefits until income reaches 150 percent of the poverty level. A 1992 evaluation found an average monthly earnings increase of 25 percent and a total family income that was 127 percent of poverty level, in comparison with 83 percent for welfare families. Most of that income comes from earnings, however, although one experimental group did receive 50 percent more in new child-support orders than the control group.[104] Another study found that CAP increased earnings by 27 percent, total income by 4 percent, and support orders by 25 percent. Earnings leveled off during the second year, and the government realized a small cost savings. But CAP had no impact on welfare receipt or on the amount received in support payments because new support orders weren't very substantial and absent fathers had low incomes.[105]

In addition to the JOBS requirement as a reform for single mothers and their children, some states have implemented child-support assurance programs, in which the states pay child support benefits whether or not they are collected from noncustodial parents. Wisconsin has a Child Support Assurance System (CSAS) that is often looked to as a model for other states. The system promises to increase income among single-parent families, decrease the welfare caseload, increase the work effort of current recipients, and decrease the pressure put on working single parents. It includes a uniform child-support standard, automatic income withholding, a minimum child-support benefit, and a wage subsidy for eligible families. Custodial parents must choose to participate either in the CSAS or in the welfare system. A 1992 study showed that the CSAS had the potential to reduce poverty and welfare caseloads significantly. In addition, if child support collections are increased by one-half of the difference between current collections and estimated ability to pay, CSAS will be less costly than welfare, even while decreasing poverty of single-parent households. Participation in this program increased the work effort of households previously receiving AFDC, and decreased the work effort of other participating households.[106] This finding is consistent with the idea that single heads of households should be expected to work, but only part time.[107] Child Support Assurance systems seem promising to the extent to which they offer women the opportunity to lift themselves and their children out of poverty. In current practice, they give work incentives to low-income women, but only women with a child-support order in place for all of their children can benefit from switching to CSAS from welfare.

Income withholding seems to be the most promising way to increase child-support payments, although its effects are still limited in comparison with the amount of benefits that could be paid. The withholding guidelines have also been useful in expediting matters, but states must be careful in choosing which guidelines to use, because they can result in very different outcomes. Ultimately, however, income withholding is effective only if parents are employed; children whose noncustodial fathers do not have paychecks can benefit only if their fathers begin to work. All states have been required by the federal government to implement the aforementioned reform in the area of child support receipt, but some states have gone even further. Part of the Family Support Act specifically encourages state government reforms, allowing states to take liberties that they previously could not under the welfare system. A requirement that those delinquent in payments participate in the JOBS program could help children of unmarried parents receive the support they need.

NONCUSTODIAL PARENT PROGRAMS

Many poor female-headed families have little possibility of receiving child support due to the perennial unemployment of their children's fathers. Many fathers lack the skills, education, and motivation to earn enough to meet their family obligations. Several states require noncustodial parents' participation in the JOBS program set up for welfare recipients. Dianne Wilkerson, a Massachusetts state senator and former AFDC recipient, emphasized the importance of efforts to reach these fathers: "We may push the young black males further out of the picture if we emphasize putting too many young mothers into jobs instead of fathers."[108] However, Chapter 6 indicates, JOBS programs have been widely criticized for rushing participants into substandard jobs with little training or education.

The Parents' Fair Share (PFS) demonstration project was designed to address challenges facing noncustodial parents. The program was implemented in nine sites in 1992 and 1993; its goals are to increase the earnings and living standard of poor noncustodial parents, increase child-support payments, improve the well-being of children, and reduce welfare participation. PFS targets underemployed or unemployed noncustodial parents of children on welfare and fathers who have not established paternity of their welfare children. The state provides job search assistance; education and skills training activities, especially on-the-job training; establishment of paternity; peer support groups and activities; conflict mediation services; and postplacement follow-up services. Participants are expected to attend activities at least three days a week; if they meet their obligations, child-support orders are temporarily reduced during PFS participation. The program is funded by the U.S. Department of Health and Human Services and several foundations, including the Pew Charitable Trusts and the Ford Foundation. Some four thousand parents enrolled in the PFS demonstration project. Two-thirds participated in program activities within four months of referral, a rate higher than participation in mandatory programs. Peer support activities were popular and productive. Increasing on-the-job training seemed to be the key step for participants to obtain jobs with increased wages.[109]

In Minnesota's program, a study of 70 of 191 PFS participants served between February 1992 and February 1994 showed that in the final six months surveyed, they paid 84 percent of their child support obligations. In contrast, during the six months before they had paid only 23 percent of their obligations.[110] An assessment of the Parents' Fair Share program in New York found that two-thirds of the four thousand delinquent parents—almost all of them fathers—who were ordered into the experimental program by courts actively participated in job-search workshops and remedial education classes. Most of the nonpaying fathers who did not participate either found jobs on their own or were referred back to the courts for further enforcement action. Only about 10 percent slipped through the system and evaded child support enforcement altogether. The pilot program had a much higher participation rate than usually achieved in experimental programs that require welfare recipients to undergo job training in order to continue receiving cash assistance. The program's pilot phase cost $5.6 million in private foundation and federal funds, an average of $1,400 for each parent.[111]

Other experiments aimed at noncustodial parents are promising. The Young Unwed Fathers Pilot Project is aimed at improving the earning capacity, parenting skills, and behavior of young fathers through education, counseling, training, and ongoing support for eighteen months; support services continue after job placement.[112] But attracting and enrolling young fathers, at least initially, has been difficult and expensive. Participants generally accept jobs before their job skills improve enough to have a positive affect on their long-term employment possibilities. Pressure to pay outstanding child support, lack of skills training options, and lack of in-program financial support contribute to premature job placement. Nevertheless, targeting young fathers has important positive results. Fathers in the program have significant relationships with their children and their children's mothers, and they are generally not responsible for multiple births. Fathers also report spending significant amounts of money on their children, often in addition to child-support payments.[113]

Florida's Project Independence includes a Child Support Enforcement Waiver, which permits staff members to recommend, "when appropriate" that noncustodial parents be required to participate in Project Independence and other employment and training programs.[114] Officials found that many of the absent parents referred to Project Independence were job ready and could be placed without intensive or costly intervention. In 1991, Florida applied for participation in the Parents' Fair Share federal demonstration project. The project basically followed the same plan Florida had been implementing in three counties for several years. Florida has also been serving noncustodial parents through New Chance, a project for young mothers and their children. This program has a Male Connection, which provides counseling and other appropriate services to partners of participants.[115]

Like many other programs, Michigan's noncustodial parent program involves immediate wage withholding and administrative streamlining. In addition, it encourages employers to cover all children under health insurance for their employees. It also requires hospitals to accept and record paternity establishments as part of birth registration. Michigan requires friends of the court to relay child-support obligations to consumer-reporting agencies as soon as an order is established. It also requires noncustodial parents not paying child support obligations to participate in schooling, community services, or job training. Mississippi courts may require unemployed, noncustodial fathers to participate in the JOBS program to meet child-support obligations.[116] Under the "Missouri Families—Mutual Responsibility Plan," noncustodial parents who volunteer for the state's JOBS program can receive credit against past-due child support.[117]

New Jersey has extended JOBS participation requirements beyond welfare recipients to General Assistance recipients (those who are not eligible for cash assistance, but who cannot or will not support themselves). Many of them are noncustodial parents. Each "family" or individual must develop a self-sufficiency plan. Family Resource Centers will help bring services to recipients. In addition to the General Assistance extension, New Jersey has implemented the Parents' Fair Share program.

Wisconsin's "Children First" program helps noncustodial, unemployed parents pay child support by helping them get jobs. The state bases its program on two principles: Both parents have a responsibility to support their children until they are eighteen, and children have a right to financial support from their parents.[118] Children First focuses on making noncustodial parents job ready through participation in the Community Work Experience Program (see Chapter 6). For the two counties involved, from 1987 to 1991, child support collections grew 87 percent. (As indicated above, Wisconsin has a much higher than average percentage of child support collection.) Under the Parental and Family Responsibility Initiative, Wisconsin also established a pilot parental education program in four counties that required all AFDC recipients under age 20 and their spouses or the noncustodial parents of their children to participate in classes on parenting, human growth and development, sex education, and independent living. Attendance was required for AFDC eligibility and for enrollment in the employment and training programs for noncustodial parents.[119] According to Wisconsin officials, "In 1993, 6,400 families got off welfare because fathers paid child support regularly."[120]

COMMUNITY PARTNERSHIPS

Several community partnership experiments have taken place in Illinois. The Peoria Integrated Employment Pilot Project coordinates the case management function and services that are provided by Public Aid, the Service District Area, local educational agencies and community college staff. The Near West Side Women's Self-Employment Project provides supportive services such as day care and transportation for clients. Project Match, managed by Northwestern University, is designed to help residents of Chicago's Cabrini Green housing development and the surrounding area obtain permanent employment, provides education, vocational training, intensified job search and other work-preparation activities. Project Match also offers extensive follow-up services to people who have been on public assistance for years and have never had a job.[121] The Young Parents Program in Chicago provides a wide range of programs, including education and training, parenting, child development, family planning, health nutrition, child support enforcement, and GED classes.[122] Three pilot programs that operated in Quincy, St. Clair (East St. Louis), and Chicago's West Side matched AFDC clients with volunteers to help them find employment and make a "successful transfer from welfare to work." Fifty percent of the fifty-eight participants obtained employment, 21 percent returned to college, 12 percent gained work experience, and 76 percent remained active in the program at least 12 months.[123]

Arkansas has tried to give community leaders more input in strategies to promote self-sufficiency. Local Planning Groups (LPGs) in each county include representatives from business groups, volunteer organizations, current and former recipients, and other community leaders and public agencies. LPGs are a forum in which to share information, showcase programs or initiatives, and develop resources needed to provide services. Minnesota's New Vista School demonstration project sponsors an apprenticeship project between Honeywell Corporation and the Minneapolis Public Schools that permits participants to qualify for $30 and increased earnings income disregards after completing the program.[124] Illinois' Community Partnership state grants are made to communities whose plans focus on the development of employability and that offer innovative education and training, family self-sufficiency, case management, and job development services. Other states have trained public aid clients to become child care workers, extended Head Start participation for children whose parents are working or in school, offered literacy and GED classes for parents of Head Start students, and sponsored job, health, and education and training fairs for low-income families.

THE IMPORTANCE OF IMPLEMENTATION

Richard Nathan, a prominent welfare policy scholar, has offered recommendations for reform of welfare or other public services that focus on implementation:

Creating momentum by acting quickly, while people are still excited about change and looking for leadership

Using organizational, personnel, and intergovernmental structures that can sustain reforms

Using a team approach to address focused, achievable goals and developing effective core management groups

Setting goals that can be used as the basis for rewards and punishments and developing positive reinforcement

Avoiding becoming mired in details and micromanaging subordinates

Cultivating good relationships with state legislative representatives

Not being afraid to take decisive action, even if it may occasionally create conflict[125] Perhaps the greatest challenge in welfare reform is to change the behavior of the welfare delivery structure. Reorienting welfare offices presents challenges, but they are not insurmountable. Clear incentives will change behavior; political support can help restructure agencies.

Administrative reform is critical to effective implementation. Once administrative reform is accomplished, however, states must face the greater challenge of changing the behavior of recipients and applicants. One of the dangers of welfare reform is that we may be tempted to stop with administrative reforms, when they are only a first step in a long process of change. We must also integrating welfare with a much broader policy agenda to promote stable families and reduce poverty. Even if we design and implement welfare reform programs perfectly, these efforts will not solve the problems that contribute to welfare dependency. Chapter 9 reviews the broader policy agenda of which welfare reform is only a part.

REFERENCES

[1] According to one estimate, by 1998, 1,700 more welfare parents would be working and earning an additional $4.3 million annually. HSA says that would multiply to as much as $17 million when money is spent on food, clothes, and so on. An additional $9 million would be added to the economy because of state and federal spending on child care, transportation, education, and training for a total benefit of $26 million. "Vermont Governor Supports Welfare Reform, Sees Economic Benefit," *The Outlook from the STATE CAPITALS* 47:33 (August 16, 1993).

[2] Sarah K. Gideonse and William R. Meyers, "Why the Family Support Act Will Fail," *Challenge* (September–October 1989): 33–39.

[3] "Vermont Governor Supports Welfare Reform."

[4] Gideonse and Meyers, "Why the Family Support Act Will Fail."

[5] U.S. Department of Health and Human Services, Administration for Children and Families, Office of Family Assistance, "State Welfare Demonstrations," *H.H.S. Fact Sheet* (Washington, D.C.: Government Printing Office, January 1996).

[6] Douglas J. Besharov, "The New Paternalism: Programs and Proposals" (prepared for the American Enterprise Institute for Public Policy Research, Washington, D.C., April 1993).

[7] U.S. Department of Health and Human Services, "State Welfare Demonstrations."

[8] Michelle Odom, "The Illinois, Virginia and Colorado Welfare Waivers," *W-Memo* (January–February 1994): 7–10.

[9] David H. Greenberg, Charles Michalopoulos, and Philip K. Robins, "Making Work Pay: Testing the Use of Financial Incentives to Reduce Welfare Dependency in the United States and Canada" (paper presented at the annual meetings of the Association for Public Policy and Management, Chicago, October 29, 1994).

[10] Ibid.

[11] Ibid., 20.

[12] Michael Wiseman, "New State Welfare Initiatives" (Madison: La Follette Institute of Public Affairs, University of Wisconsin–Madison, August 1992), 29.

[13] U.S. Department of Health and Human Services, "State Welfare Demonstrations."

[14] Ibid.

[15] Ibid.

[16] Ibid.

[17] Ibid.

[18] Ibid.

[19] Ibid.

[20] Ibid.

[21] Ibid.

[22] Ibid.

[23] Ibid.

[24] Ibid.

[25] Ibid.

[26] Ibid.

[27] Ibid.

[28] Ibid.

[29] Ibid.

[30] Jennifer A. Neisner, "State Welfare Initiatives," *CRS Report for Congress* (Washington D.C.: Congressional Research Service, January 24, 1995).

[31] Greenberg, Michalopoulos, and Robins, "Making Work Pay."

[32] Neisner, "State Welfare Initiatives."

[33] U.S. Department of Health and Human Services, "State Welfare Demonstrations."

[34] Greenberg, Michalopoulos, and Robins, "Making work pay," 7.

[35] Wiseman, "New State Welfare Initiatives," 13.

[36] Ibid., 14.

[37] Greenberg, Michalopoulos, and Robins, "Making work pay," 11.

[38] Ibid., 5.

[39] U.S. Department of Health and Human Services, "State Welfare Demonstrations."

[40] Ibid.

[41] Ibid.

[42] Ibid., 19–20.

[43] "Georgia Expanding Day Care for Welfare Recipients," *The Outlook from the STATE CAPITALS*, 47:41 (October 1993).

[44] Georgia Department of Human Resources, "Because People Matter . . . 1990 Annual Report" (1990): 5–6.

[45] U.S. Department of Health and Human Services, "State Welfare Demonstrations."

[46] Ibid.

[47] Ibid., 19–20.

[48] Laurie Udesky, "The Numbers Game," *Southern Exposure* (Summer 1991): 14–18, at 16.

[49] Gordon Young, "Rural Roulette: Workfare Got Its Start along the Back Roads of Arkansas, but Today the Program Punishes More Women Than It Employs," *Southern Exposure* (Summer 1991): 19–22, at 21.

[50] U.S. Department of Health and Human Services, "State Welfare Demonstrations."

[51] Marcia K. Meyers, "Child Care, Parental Choice and Consumer Education in JOBS Welfare-to-Work Programs" (Syracuse, N.Y.: Maxwell School of Citizenship and Public Affairs, Syracuse University, 1995).

[52] Ibid., 1.

[53] Ibid., 2.

[54] Ibid., 3.

[55] Ibid., 4.

[56] Ibid., 5.

[57] Ibid., 6.

[58] Ibid., 6.

[59] Ibid., 7.

[60] Ibid., 8.

[61] Ibid., 9.

[62] Ibid., 30.

[63] Ibid., 31.

[64] Ibid., 32.

[65] Institute of Applied Research, "Child Care and AFDC Recipients in Illinois: Patterns, Problems and Needs" (Illinois Department of Public Aid, Division of Family Support Services, 1991).

[66] Paul Offner, "Day Careless," *The New Republic* (April 18, 1994): 18–19.

[67] Jane Waldfogel, "Integrating Child and Family Services: Lessons from Arkansas, Colorado, and Maryland" (Cambridge, Mass.: Malcolm Wiener Center for Social Policy, Harvard University, October, 1994): 8.

[68] U.S. General Accounting Office, *Welfare Programs."*

[69] Ibid.

[70] Richard P. Nathan, *Turning Promises into Performance: The Management Challenge of Implementing Workfare* (New York: Columbia University Press, 1993), XV.

[71] U.S. Department of Health and Human Services, "State Welfare Demonstrations."

[72] Ibid., 12.

[73] Ibid.

[74] Ibid.

[75] Ibid.

[76] Ibid.

[77] Senate Appropriations Sub-Committee on Labor, Health and Human Services, and Education, *Utah Single Parent Employment Demonstration Program and National Welfare Reform*, testimony by Janet A. Hansen, April 11, 1994.

[78] Ibid.

[79] Neisner, "State Welfare Initiatives."

[80] U.S. Department of Health and Human Services, "State Welfare Demonstrations."

[81] Shelley Borysiewicz, "Governors Using Innovative Approaches to Reform Welfare," *Governors' Bulletin* (National Governors Association, October 11, 1993): 5.

[82] U.S. General Accounting Office, *Welfare Programs,"* 20.

[83] U.S. Department of Health and Human Services, "State Welfare Demonstrations."

[84] "Electronic Welfare Transfer Bill Introduced in Missouri," *The Outlook from the STATE CAPITALS* 46:15 (April 1992).

[85] B. G. Gregg, "Ohio a Leader in Welfare Reform," *The Cincinnati Enquirer*, March 25, 1995, p. A8.

[86] Borysiewicz, "Governors Using Innovative Approaches to Reform Welfare," 5.

[87] "Fifteen More Pacesetting Programs," *Governing* (October 1992): 44–45.

[88] Christina Klein, "Aid to Families with Dependent Children Self-Sufficiency Project" (Alaska: Department of Health and Social Services, Division of Public Assistance, February 1993).

[89] U.S. Department of Health and Human Services, "State Welfare Demonstrations."

[90] Ibid.

[91] U.S. General Accounting Office, *Welfare Programs*, 20.

[92] "Pennsylvania Senate Appropriations Committee Approves Welfare Reform Legislation," *PR Newswire* (May 6, 1992).

[93] Waldfogel, "Integrating Child and Family Services."

[94] Susan Kellam, "Welfare Experiments: Are States Leading the Way Toward National Reform?" *CQ Researcher* 4:34 (September 16, 1994): 795–815.

[95] Borysiewicz, "Governors Using Innovative Approaches to Reform Welfare," 5.

[96] William Claiborne, "On the Receiving End of Welfare Reform," *The Washington Post*, National Weekly Edition, April 18–24, 1994, p. 31.

[97] Oklahoma Department of Human Services, "Fiscal Year 1991 Annual Report" (1991).

[98] U.S. Department of Health and Human Services, "State Welfare Demonstrations."

[99] Ibid., 6.

[100] Ibid.

[101] U.S. Department of Health and Human Services, "State Welfare Demonstrations," 4. Arizona's EMPOWER (Employing and Moving People Off Welfare and Encouraging Responsibility) was approved May 22, 1995.

[102] Borysiewicz, "Governors Using Innovative Approaches to Reform Welfare."

[103] William L. Hamilton, Larry L. Orr, Stephen H. Bell, Nancy R. Burstein, and David J. Fein, "The Effects of Alternative Welfare-to-Work Strategies on AFDC Caseloads" (paper presented at the 16th Annual Research Conference of the Association for Public Policy Analysis and Management, October 1994): 7; Besharov, "The New Paternalism."

[104] Klein, "Aid to Families with Dependent Children Self-Sufficiency Project."

[105] Evelyn Ganzglass, "Research Findings on the Effectiveness of State Welfare-to-Work Programs" (Washington, D.C.: Employment and Social Services Policy Studies, Center for Policy Research, National Governors' Association, 1994).

[106] Irwin Garfinkel and Charles F. Manski, eds., *Evaluating Welfare and Training Programs* (Cambridge, Mass.: Harvard University Press, 1992), 18.

[107] David Ellwood, opening Statement to Working Group on Welfare Reform, Family Support and Independence, Washington, D.C., August 19, 1993.

[108] David Holstrom, "Bay State Plan Sparks Protests from Recipients," *The Christian Science Monitor*, December 8, 1993, p. 3.

[109] Dan Bloom and Kay Sherwood, "Matching Opportunities to Obligations: Lessons for Child Support Reform from the Parents' Fair Share Pilot Phase" (New York: Manpower Demonstration Research Corporation, April 1994).

[110] Charles Mahtesian, "Turning Deadbeats into Dads," *Governing* (October 1994): 37.

[111] William Claiborne, "Support Program Helps 'Deadbeat Dads' Find Jobs," *The Washington Post*, February 11, 1994, p. A3.

[112] Ganzglass, "Research Findings on the Effectiveness of State Welfare-to-Work Programs."

[113] Ibid.

[114] Florida Department of Health and Rehabilitative Services, *Project Independence Annual Management Report* (1988), 11.

[115] Ibid., 3.

[116] U.S. Department of Health and Human Services, "State Welfare Demonstrations," 13.

[117] Ibid., 14.

[118] Office of the Governor, "Welfare Reform in Wisconsin: A Summary" (September 1992): 5.

[119] Ibid., 4.

[120] Sondra J. Nixon, "States Experimenting with Ways to Help People Stay Off Welfare," *Congressional Quarterly*, 53:27 (July 1995): 2003.

[121] Illinois Department of Public Aid, "Project Chance: Annual Report Fiscal Year 1991," (1991): 30–32; Illinois Department of Public Aid, "Project Chance Annual Report 1992" (1992): 22, 80.

[122] Illinois Department of Public Aid, "Project Chance Annual Report 1992," 6.

[123] Ibid., 21.

[124] Neisner, "State Welfare Initiatives," *CRS Report for Congress*.

[125] Nathan, *Turning Promises into Performance*, 134–36.

9

Welfare Reform as
We May Come to Know It

The passage of the 1996 welfare reform law accelerates state reform, but since state initiatives are quite new and only limited assessments of them are available, the debate will now proceed in earnest in state capitols, legislatures, human service agencies, county governments, and in the public. The issues are, for the most part, the same issues that have been on the welfare reform agenda of the 1990s. This chapter summarizes the issues raised earlier in the book as welfare becomes a state responsibility. It concludes with a brief discussion of how the end of this round of the great American welfare reform debate might foster a new debate that deals with a much broader range of issues.

WELFARE REFORM IN THE STATES

The prospects for welfare reform in the states generate conflicting views. From one perspective, the abandonment of a national obligation to care for poor children is a major diminution of shared values and commitments. For others, it is the key to more effective welfare policy. Pessimists fear a "race to the bottom," as states abandon welfare programs in order to save money. Optimists argue that Justice Louis Brandeis was right when he wrote:

> It is one of the happy incidents of the federal system that a single courageous State may, if its citizens choose, serve as a laboratory; and try novel social and economic experiments without risk to the rest of the country.[1]

It is too early to tell which view most closely reflects what eventually happens. Welfare reforms have been driven by four primary goals: saving money, changing behavior, helping families become self-sufficient, and turning over more power to the states. These somewhat contradictory goals are so popular that states cannot easily pick and choose from among them. States such as Wisconsin, however, give some evidence that welfare spending need not decrease or could even increase modestly as long as welfare is working.

The experience of states in welfare reform, however brief, does provide some basis for drawing some conclusions. First, some states, usually led by entrepreneurial governors, have developed some innovative approaches to reforming the welfare system. Second, although states are not hotbeds of creativity and change, some interesting and promising experiments have been undertaken. Some states will do well—there are plenty of ideas out there about how to improve the welfare system. Those who are looking for ways to do so will find some alternatives to pursue.

It is striking that for a handful of governors and states, welfare reform has become a major political interest, garnering a great deal of attention and political capital. For most states, however, welfare is not a high priority. It is unpopular; solutions are difficult and might not work; and many state leaders are more involved in other issues. Governors and legislators have a strong incentive to be tough on welfare. They also have clear incentives to ensure they are not promoting socially dysfunctional behavior. Political rewards are few for investing time and energy in helping those who are most disadvantaged and in need of help. It seems hard to imagine a scenario in which there would *not* be a "race to the bottom" among some states during an economic downturn and when resources become more scarce.

Support for reforming welfare is widely felt and strongly held. One reason for this is that it is hard to be against "reforming" anything. Another is that welfare reform means so many different things that it may be almost impossible for anyone not to come up with a change in welfare they favor. Devolution to states is attractive for all of the reasons proponents have given—flexibility and tailoring of programs to recipients' needs and local conditions, experimentation and learning by experience. The federal government will still have a role: Block grants permit some redistribution to occur, and states that have high unemployment or are otherwise less well off than others will need more assistance. Some federal standards will still remain in areas such as maintenance of effort, so states will be obligated to continue to provide a minimum of support to welfare families, and some federal guidelines will require states to pursue at least a few common policy objectives. Devolution will largely eliminate the waiver process along with the time and energy states and the federal government were required to expend to gain those waivers, thereby encouraging even more experimentation and innovation. Welfare will be much more open to shifts in budgetary priorities and needs.

But the symbolic loss of welfare as a national entitlement is not insignificant. The national commitment to an entitlement for poor families was a small but visible component of a national ethic of fairness, justice, and common concern. Although welfare could and did promote undoubtedly pathological dependence in some recipients, it also could and did provide a bridge for families torn apart by death or divorce until they could become self-sufficient. It provided the opportunity for countless women to gain basic education, job training, and employment. It ensured an income for millions of children who might not have had other means of support. A national entitlement or a right to welfare, critics argue, is divisive and harmful to our polity. But rights and entitlements can also be viewed as manifestations of our common concerns, our commitment to each other. That welfare contributed to dependency, illegitimacy, and other problems does not mean that we should abandon our commitments to help those among us who are vulnerable to hunger and homelessness and often are least able to help themselves. We may be sacrificing a great deal in order to gain the advantages of devolution, and in an era when many decry the collapse of collective values and ideals, we take a risk when we reject one example of a collective commitment.

Welfare reform will most likely not end poverty. Some promising reforms have been initiated, but the ideological fervor that would-be reformers have brought to the debate has encouraged polarization and made progress difficult. Good policy analysis has been difficult and has been intertwined with political pressure, typical of any policy issue that is so politically charged. Welfare reform will always be driven more by ideology than analysis, but good analysis can help provide the basis for compromise when the political will is present. The challenge is to ensure that welfare reform meets the needs and problems of welfare recipients as well as of politicians.[2]

The experiments in states raise more questions than they answer. Bipartisan support for ending the current system does not keep a daunting list of issues from facing welfare reformers. States face tremendous challenges in transforming their welfare systems into job-training and placement agencies, in finding jobs for welfare recipients, in dealing with the consequences of changing eligibility requirements, and in devising support for welfare recipients as they move into the work force.

Table 9.1 outlines the actions required of states to implement the new welfare law during the first two years.

In 1996 some states were ill prepared for the responsibilities thrust on them by the new welfare law. Only a few states had statewide welfare-to-work programs in place. The new child support provisions alone are complicated enough to pose a challenge to most state legislatures, argued Sheri Steisel, staff member at the National Conference of State Legislatures. Many state legislatures meet infrequently, making quick legislation action impossible. Even such states as California, which had developed welfare-to-work programs based on pilot projects, have to scramble to extend the work requirements to 50 percent of recipients as the law requires.[3]

State welfare officials voiced their apprehension about how they would meet the new work requirements. Even the most successful state pilot projects have not been able to get the kind of success required by the new law—at least 25 percent of welfare recipients working at least 20 hours a week, and 50 percent within five years. In 1995, only 3.7 percent of women on welfare were working full time. The sanctions for failure to meet these goals are significant and can eventually cost states 21 percent of their block grant. Some observers of welfare policy in states described state officials as panicking; others feared states would simply cut people off welfare as a way to show compliance. Bill Biggs, former head of Utah's welfare-to-work program, said that to show compliance with the law, the state plans to count the number of people who are diverted from ever going on welfare through job placement assistance when they first go to a welfare office. Community service work will also be expanded, he said.[4]

But a provision added at the last minute gives states an out: Waivers that had been approved before the new law took effect will continue until they expire, even if they contradict provisions of the new law. Forty-three states have waivers; only Alaska, Idaho, Kansas, Kentucky, Nevada, New Mexico, Rhode Island, and the District of Columbia do not. Waivers are in place from five to eleven years. Time limits in many states apply only to adults, for example, and children can continue to receive benefits.[5] States such as Vermont, which emphasizes child care, health care, and training; Iowa, which includes postsecondary education; and Minnesota, which offers training and education programs, may continue those programs, but still have to meet the work percentage goals.[6] States that have work-related waivers are usually more stringent than the old law, but less demanding than the new law. Some states' waivers define work broadly to include educational activities that do not count

TABLE 9.1
THE TIMETABLE FOR IMPLEMENTING WELFARE REFORM

August 1996	Immigrants arriving in the United States were no longer eligible for most benefits provided by the federal government.
	Strict standards for determining SSI eligibility took effect.
August 1996	States began revising their welfare programs (to include time limits, work requirements and exemptions, child support sanctions, living arrangements for minor parents, school requirements for minor parents, limits on aid to noncitizens) and preparing to accept block grants. States could submit plans anytime before July 1, 1997; date of the submission of the plan became the effective date for the welfare provisions of the law, including the time limits.
	Noncitizens receiving SSI and food stamps became ineligible for these benefits as their cases are reviewed.
October 1, 1996	AFDC ended when the new fiscal year began; states could continue to offer AFDC benefits if they wished.
	New Food Stamp standards took effect, reducing benefits and tightening eligibility.
	States were eligible to apply for contingency funds for caseload or unemployment increases.
January 1, 1997	States could cut off cash assistance, Medicaid, and social services to noncitizens who were recipients of these programs when the law took effect in August 1996.
July 1, 1997	Most provisions of the new law took effect; states must submit their new welfare program to HHS; states with waivers could continue to operate under them after they expire even if the waivers are inconsistent with the new law.
October 1, 1997	States can apply for supplemental funds to help with rapid population growth.
October 1, 1998	States can apply for supplemental grants as rewards for high-quality programs.
	Supplemental funds will be available for the five states achieving the largest reductions in illegitimacy.

Sources: Jocelyn Guyer, Cindy Mann, and David A. Super, "The Timeline for Implementing the New Welfare Law," Washington D.C.: Center on Budget and Policy Priorities (August 15, 1996); Robert Pear, "Overhauling Welfare: A Look at the Year Ahead," *The New York Times*, August 7, 1996, p. P.7.

as work under the new law. Even with that expansive definition, only 14 percent of the adults on welfare are engaged in some kind of work, job training, or educational activity. Increasing the percentage and tightening the range of permissible activities will put stress on states.

The law also provides that states will gain credits from reducing their roles in meeting the work requirement: If a state's caseload falls by 10 percent, the work requirement is reduced by the same amount. The national caseload has dropped significantly since 1995, making it easy for now for many states to meet the work requirement. But this may create an incentive for states to cut their rolls, even if it does not lead recipients to work. As Mark H. Greenberg put it, "It's often cheaper simply to cut aid than to help someone find a job."[7]

Much of the attention has focused on the imposition of time limits on participation in the welfare system. Many states had already received waivers to impose time limits before the new law was passed. Some twenty states had, by 1997, imposed even tighter limits than the federal law provided. But for most recipients, those time limits are years away. More immediate are the sanctions that states can impose for failing to comply with new requirements. Most states have in place provisions that require recipients to participate in training or work programs or they will lose all or part of their benefits. And for those who find jobs, the challenge will be to keep them in the face of the cost of transportation, child care, and health care. There is considerable evidence that work requirements discourage some recipients from applying for welfare and nudge others off the rolls earlier than they otherwise would leave. However, we don't know what has happened and will happen to these families. Welfare reform will be tested when states try to move recipients who are least prepared to work off the rolls as their time limits approach and during the next economic downturn, when unemployment rises and it becomes more difficult to find jobs for people on welfare. The ultimate test of welfare reform is whether more families become self-sufficient and fewer children live in poverty, rather than what happens to welfare rolls, and studies that take place during the next few years will begin to answer these questions.

WELFARE AND THE BROADER SOCIAL POLICY AGENDA

The great American welfare reform debate is not over. It will continue as we examine what states do. But perhaps the most important consequence of the Personal Responsibility and Work Opportunity Act of 1996 is to permit a new debate to emerge that would focus on how to help the poor in America. Efforts to remedy the problems that plague welfare cannot be separated from broader efforts to rethink our commitment to the welfare state. I am convinced that our commitment to the welfare state is stronger than is often currently believed, and sturdier than the current attempts to undermine it. But the jury is still out on the future of the welfare state.

PROVIDING JOBS

American society has changed and no longer supports the idea of paying mothers to stay home and take care of children. Parents of all income levels are expected to work. AFDC is outmoded and should be replaced with a new commitment to make it possible for all Americans to work, to take care of their children, and to give additional help to low-income families.[8] At least two components have been left out of the welfare reform agenda. First, how can we ensure that everyone in America who can work has a job? Second, how can we improve the ability of Americans to compete in the global economy, that is, what are the most important educational and training efforts we can make to invest in human capital? The welfare reform debate drowned out these issues. Now that we can no longer blame welfare for the ills that plague us, and now that we agree on the importance of work, what do we need to do to encourage it and make it a reality for all Americans? Since one of the primary goals of welfare reform is employment, jobs need to be available. But welfare is not part of a strong public commitment to full employment, to ensuring that everyone who can work has the opportunity to do so. Without that commitment, welfare reform as we have come to know it is doomed. All of the key reforms—job training, time limits, transition support, and so on—assume that jobs are available and that most recipients will be hired. But where local economies are depressed, that will not happen. Welfare reform will have to be combined with a commitment to ensuring that everyone has the opportunity to work. This, in turn, will require states to take at least four kinds of actions.

First, they will need to find ways to ensure that local labor markets are open to women and people of color. Discrimination will need to be reduced. Affirmative actions or other interventions will be required to ensure that those barriers are broken down and that private employment opportunities are available. We need a renewed commitment to fighting employment discrimination, expanding opportunities, and reducing the problems women face in obtaining equal pay, fair compensation, and job opportunities.

The second challenge will be to find ways to expand private labor markets to make more jobs available. States will have to be even more aggressive in promoting jobs. They will have to balance efforts to entice new employers with those aimed at keeping the ones already located within their borders. States must ensure that tax breaks and other inducements to new businesses do not prevent the pursuit of other public policies, including offering subsidies to employers to hire welfare recipients.

A third challenge will be to ensure public-sector jobs as a final resort so that everyone will indeed have the chance to work. Again, the expenses for that commitment are considerable but unavoidable. The current welfare reform debate has largely failed to explore this broader agenda.

A fourth challenge is to strengthen those institutions of civil society that can work with government and business to improve community life, reduce crime, improve the physical infrastructure, and foster social capital so communities can mobilize to solve their problems. Because welfare recipients differ so greatly, solving the problems they face requires the efforts of many different groups, organizations, and individuals. For some, spiritual renewal will be part of their evolution toward self-sufficiency, and local churches will play a key role in welfare reform. For others, different kinds of support groups will help fill their needs.

FATHERHOOD AND FAMILIES

The welfare reform agenda has also failed to deal with the decline of fatherhood and families. There is no more effective way of preventing welfare dependency as well as promoting self-sufficiency for those on welfare than to encourage men to take responsibility for their children and families. We must encourage families to stay together and discourage divorce, without reverting to the situation of powerlessness many women feel when trapped in abusive or other dysfunctional families. We must find ways to promote marriage among those who produce children and to discourage from having children those who are not willing to provide for them. Much more vigorous and aggressive enforcement of child-support payments is also important. Those who resist that movement because of legitimate concerns about protecting their visitation rights ought to work with others to find ways to respond to those problems without sacrificing the overall principle that men and women need to be held accountable for the children they produce. No reform is more important than those aimed at fostering fatherhood, but few public goals seem to be less amendable to solution through some new governmental program than promoting responsible fatherhood.

The reform agenda has not addressed the problems women face, such as discrimination and domestic violence. Strengthening two-parent families must include ways to help women who find themselves in untenable family situations. The agenda must also include a commitment to helping poor children. Part of the challenge here is to avoid the intergenerational debate over whether we give too much to the elderly and not enough to children. Welfare needs to be part of a much broader system to ensure children have an adequate income.

Between 1960 and 1990, the percentage of children who lived apart from their biological fathers grew from 17 to 36 percent. During this time, the percentage of out-of-wedlock births exploded from 5 to 30 percent of all births. For African Americans, nearly 70 percent of births occur outside of marriage. The United States has the highest teenage pregnancy rate in the Western world. About 1 million teen pregnancies occur each year; 81 percent of first births to women aged 15 to 17 are out of wedlock.[9] The divorce rate has doubled over the past thirty years and has increased fourfold since 1900. At least 50 percent of new marriages in the United States will end in divorce, also the highest divorce rate in the Western world. Since 1974, more marriages have ended in divorce than with the death of one spouse.

More than 60 percent of divorced couples have at least one child. Divorce seriously disrupts fatherhood. Men tend to tie marriage and childrearing together so that if their marriage deteriorates, so does their responsibility as fathers. In contrast, most women continue to care for their children when their marriages collapse. Only about half of divorced fathers see their children more than several times a year.[10]

The marriage rate has fallen as nonmarital cohabitation has grown. The percent of unmarried adults cohabiting has quadrupled since 1970. More and more single women and lesbian couples are raising children, further evidence of a belief that fathers are not essential in raising children. In public opinion surveys, men and boys show much less interest than in the past in fatherhood and family responsibilities.[11]

David Popenoe's review of research on family structure, the presence of fathers, and children's well-being found compelling evidence that fathers play a critical role in the raising of children. As a result, society has a profound interest in promoting fatherhood. The "great social complexity of modern societies requires longer periods of socialization and dependency for children than ever before."[12] Research findings are clear. Children who are raised with only one biological parent are more likely to drop out of high school, become teenage mothers, and be out of school or out of work than those raised by both parents. About half of that effect is attributed to lower resources, since one-parent families are much poorer on average than two-parent families. The relationship between lack of fathers present and criminal activity of children is much stronger than any other factor such as race or low income. The problem is not just having one adult in the household: Children in stepfamilies or foster or adoptive families do not do significantly better than those raised by single women. Fatherly love cannot be easily transferred or learned by others. Fathers make unique contribution to the nurturing of children; they do not simply double the amount of parental attention, but are more likely to encourage competition, risk taking, and independence than the emotional security and relationships mothers so frequently engender. Men and women complement each other, in general; although some single parents are remarkably successful in assuming both roles, as a whole, families where both parents are actively engaged in and committed to their children provide an ideal environment for childrearing.[13]

Not only is fatherhood of great value to children, Popenoe argues, it is a boon to men themselves and to the broader society. Family life helps discipline men to control their passions, engage in regular work, and sacrifice some of their interests in behalf of others. Unattached men are more likely to be engaged in criminal activity than are married men. They are more likely to live self-aggrandizing, predatory lives than are married men. Married men live longer, have better health, and enjoy other benefits over nonmarried men. Even if fathers were not needed by their children, society would benefit greatly from ensuring that men are attached to families.[14]

Popenoe reviews the arguments made by those who believe that fathers are no longer needed, that they do not play an essential role in the family and in society: Women are now sufficiently independent economically that they no longer need to rely on men. Society provides protection through police, and for many women, the greatest threat to their physical well-being comes from abusive husbands. Traditional family life is inherently unequal. Women and children have suffered from male domination and selfishness; a commitment to equality requires a new kind of family. Men often desert their wives and children and it is better, in the long run, for those women and children never to become dependent on men. Men do not provide anything unique to a family and can be replaced by others. Single mothers and their children have been stigmatized by society, and that unfairness has been reduced as fatherless families become more accepted. Some women are able to raise children without a father present. But given the overall trends and general experience, we need to find ways to promote fatherhood so that children enjoy the advantages fathers offer to families without reverting to some of the dysfunctional consequences. As Popenoe puts it, "it is imperative for the well-being of children and society that we retain the nuclear family—but not the nuclear family as it has existed in recent centuries."[15]

If we choose as a society to give greater value to children, improve their well-being, and give priority to their careful nurturing and preparation for adulthood, one of the most important steps we can take is to promote fatherhood and two-parent families. Can we develop cultural norms and values that encourage men to care for their children, discourage sexual activity among unmarried teens and discourage women from having out-of-wedlock births, dissuade couples from divorcing, and promote two-parent marriage? Can we reshape our commitment to unbridled individualism with a balance of freedom and responsibility? The social and cultural trends that have produced the decline of fatherhood and marriage are strong and will not be easily reversed. There is, however, some hope for common ground. If we recognize that traditional families have been problematic for many women and children, we can find ways to strengthen families without naively calling for a return to the past. It is in everyone's interest to see that children are nurtured and prepared for productive adult lives; the cost to society of neglected children or those poorly prepared is so great that everyone ought to have an interest in making families work. This clearly requires men and women to sacrifice some of their self-interest; those who are not willing to make such sacrifices should be strongly discouraged from having children.

STRENGTHENING FAMILIES

Much of this is beyond the realm of public policy. The changes will have to come from elsewhere. Religious institutions, businesses, educators, social workers and other human-service professionals, marriage counselors and family therapists, physicians, entertainers, the media, and civic groups and leaders are in powerful positions to encourage changes that will ensure that children and families become more valued in our society.[16] Those institutions and forces that have the greatest impact on our culture and society have the greatest opportunity to reverse the trend that now means the children of this generation are worse off than those of the previous one.[17]

Government can play a role, however, in at least four areas. First, it can strengthen and expand public policies already in place to encourage businesses to provide work environments that are more conducive to family life, that provide parental leaves, and that encourage flexible work schedules and job sharing. If the cost of products and services produced by these companies increases, consumers can come to understand that they will gain tremendous social benefits that will come from a workplace more attuned to the needs of families and parenting. The Family Leave Act can be expanded to provide more flexibility for families and be extended to more employees. Government agencies can provide clear examples of family-friendly employment policy.

Second, although they only have limited impact, government programs can do more to emphasize sexual restraint and discourage sexual activity until adulthood. Responsibilities of parents can become a central part of the curriculum of public schools. Educational campaigns can actively promote the values essential to fatherhood and strong, stable, two-parent families.

Third, marriage laws can be changed to discourage divorce, especially when children are present; to create more vigorous enforcement of child support obligations; and to require careful planning to meet the needs of children when divorce does occur. One option is to create a two-tiered system of divorce: For married couples with no children, no-fault divorce could be maintained. For families with children, fault-based divorce could be reinstated along with a one-year waiting period before the divorce is completed, with court supervision to ensure that child support, visitation, other and parental responsibilities are provided for.[18] Governments should also require automatic deduction of alimony and child support from the noncustodial parent's paycheck, require that the primary caregiver of the children be given the family's house if applicable, and require parents who remarry to support the first set of children at the same living standard as the new family.[19] At minimum, if divorce is not made more difficult, governments can do more to protect the interests of children and ensure that parents meet the obligations they automatically assume when they bear children.

Fourth, more investment should be directed to health care, child care, and education for children. Governments can increase money available to parents for childrearing through grants and tax credits and deductions and can encourage marriage through the structure of the tax law.

A detailed discussion of these issues is beyond the scope of a book on welfare reform. But welfare reform will not solve the problems to which it is aimed unless the broader agenda is addressed. The debate over how to strengthen families should continue. Republicans and Democrats, liberals and conservatives, and many others have differing views about whether we should make divorce more difficult, whether we should restrict legally recognized marriage to heterosexual couples, and how we might promote fatherhood and parenthood.

It is not surprising, then, that Congress has been unsuccessful in legislating welfare policy. These are difficult issues and the politics of welfare policy is treacherous. The most promising changes seem to be those that require recipients who can work to move quickly into private sector jobs and that provide the support services necessary for recipients to be able to work or guarantee public-service jobs if other work is not available. Imposing these requirements and providing the jobs to make the mandates work costs more than simply providing a monthly check, and where welfare savings are the primary goal, the current welfare system, with all its flaws, will be perpetuated, simply at a lower price tag.

WELFARE AND ANTI-POVERTY POLICY

The debate over welfare reform has largely ignored the broader policy context in which welfare reform must take place in order to accomplish its overall goal of reducing poverty. Even if welfare reform moves recipients into the work force and discourages single young women from having children and starting up AFDC households, welfare recipients will still be battered by the host of problems that confront poor Americans.

One way to characterize the welfare reform debate is to argue that we have two broad policy choices to end welfare as we know it: cut back cash assistance dramatically or replace welfare with a commitment to finding a job for everyone who wants one. By eliminating welfare, we put the pressure on recipients to find ways to meet their needs. Exceptions could be made for those who are unable to work; we should continue to offer support through SSI and other programs that permits them to live lives of modest dignity. But since there are not presently enough jobs for welfare recipients who can work, let alone the millions of unemployed Americans, cutting welfare is inconsistent with American public values. More consistent with those values is a collective commitment to secure work opportunities for everyone who can work and to provide support for low-income workers for child care, health insurance, Food Stamps and other nutrition programs, and training. These commitments are challenging but not impossible. They can be achieved by state and local governments with the federal government facilitating information exchange and providing financial assistance.

More difficult are two remaining issues, as well as the broader context of poverty in America. First, in order to pay for the cost of a full employment policy, other transfer payments will have to be scaled back and means tested. Although the political challenges of this approach are significant, some progress has been made in softening opposition. Numerous proposals have been devised to reduce the entitlements of the well-to-do. That effort must continue; I believe it will ultimately be successful. Second, state and local governments and communities will need to provide minimal food and shelter for those who choose not to work. Children of parents who can but choose not to work after jobs are assured them need to have options such as residential schools where they can get an adequate education in a safe and nurturing environment. State and local governments and communities will need to realize more clearly that prevention of social problems is much superior to treating them. Prevention begins with helping children in families that cannot provide for their basic needs. Finally, the host of other collective tasks such as improving public safety, education, housing, transportation, and infrastructure as well as shifting to an economy that is ultimately more environmentally sustainable are also part of the solution to reducing poverty.

Welfare reform can only address a small slice of these broad problems. We need reasonable expectations about what it can and cannot accomplish. Welfare reform is more difficult than proponents of one position or another usually recognize, but solutions are not beyond our reach. Despite the limited scope of the welfare reform agenda, accomplishing the goal of truly reforming welfare would be a considerable achievement. Welfare reform efforts that are tough on work and require recipients to engage in constructive, contributing activities, may be able to help bridge the political chasm separating proponents and opponents of the welfare state.

Modest success in welfare policy may encourage us to take on some of the other issues that must be addressed if we are to seriously reduce the poverty and bleak prospects that plague so many of our citizens. Can we envision an alternative to current policies? Congress could keep a strong commitment to helping poor children, but encourage states to experiment.[20] Congress could, in the words of Rep. Dan Coats (R.-Ind.) "go beyond Government" to encourage and strengthen, nurture and expand those mediating institutions of family, community, volunteer associations of charity, of church, faith-based charities—those institutions that offer real solutions and real hope. We need to begin to look at transforming our society by transforming lives one at a time inside out. For the most part, this is work that cannot be done by institutions of government. Government can feed the body and help train the mind, but it cannot nurture the soul or renew the spirit. This is the work of institutions outside of government.[21]

WELFARE AND THE BROADER AGENDA OF ECONOMIC EQUALITY   The economic challenges facing the United States are starkly outlined in a few figures that demonstrate how much the world has changed in a half-century. In 1945, the United States produced 75 percent of the global GNP; in 1970, 50 percent; in 1995, 20 percent. Once, U.S. companies produced 90 percent of the cars sold in the world; in 1995, 55 percent. American workers must compete against people in less developed countries who work for 36 or 40 or 50 cents an hour.[22] What should the United States do to address these fundamental challenges to working Americans? Should we make a major investment in workers? How much should we spend? And what is a reasonable safety net for the poor?

A more equitable labor market, one that is more open to women and people of color, requires a commitment to some kind of affirmative action. Affirmative action need not be a zero sum game, but can be structured in ways that give women and minorities an even playing field and also free them to increase their numbers in high-level positions.[23]

Economic inequality in America has steadily worsened over the past quarter century. By 1994, the Census Bureau reported that the wealthiest 20 percent of Americans earned about 50 percent of the nation's total income, whereas the poorest 20 percent only earned about 5 percent. This level of inequality is not inevitable; it was in fact declining in the United States until the 1970s. Despite the rising inequality, Republicans in particular have argued that we have no choice, given global competitive pressures, but to reduce government regulations, cut back on the welfare state, and repeal the progressivity of the income tax.

There are two reasons why the Republican agenda should be resisted. First, it fails to recognize the importance of education, training, and other collective efforts to improve our competitive capability. Leaving workers and companies alone to face competitive pressures will allow some to do well, but many more will do poorly. Investments in education, infrastructure, research, and other public goods is an important part of helping Americans compete effectively in global markets. Second, the Republican agenda fails to recognize the role of equality in fostering liberal democracy, in encouraging political participation and civil society. A failure to cultivate political institutions makes the threat of populist demagoguery more likely. It exacerbates divisions in society: as Michael Walzer describes it, "the arrogance of the wealthy, the humbling of the poor." Demonizing welfare mothers is a manifestation of this trend. Inequality, Walzer fears, threatens the future of our economy, our constitutional protections for dissent, our voluntary associations and social movements, and our basically decent politics.[24]

What are the solutions to poverty? What is required to effectively treat the causes and not just the symptoms of poverty? One part of the solution is to reduce the number of out-of-wedlock births and fatherless families; second, a major investment in education; third, support for working families so they can better care for their children; fourth, a national commitment to full employment rather than fighting inflation. Lyn Hogan of the Democratic Leadership Council has proposed an alternative to welfare:

> Replacing welfare with an employment system abolishes welfare's perverse incentives. A work-based system will move people from dependence on government to self-sufficiency; replace the indignity of handouts with the dignity of work; reward initiative, not punish it; and make opportunity, responsibility, family and community the organizing principles of life for the nation's poor.[25]

POVERTY AND THE FUTURE OF WELFARE

The future of welfare and the welfare state is uncertain. But given the three decades of debate over welfare reform, what are the issues that lie ahead? To explore that debate we must find a language that reflects the key issues, concepts, and differences of opinion, while permitting the efficiency that comes from labels and shorthand abbreviations for complex positions. The traditional liberal-conservative dichotomy has been widely criticized as inadequate. Liberals who are expected to champion individual freedom somehow favor big national government and the attendant limits on freedom that necessarily entails. Conservatives who espouse stability and order somehow embrace the dynamism of market forces that may obliterate communities and uproot families. Bill Clinton as much as anyone seems to have found success in blurring those differences. He and other New Democrats appear to have been able to gain widespread support for moderate, middle-of-the road positions that fit neither the liberal or conservative mode. Nevertheless, conservatism and liberalism still dominate political communication, and with the addition of some adjectives, can provide a gross and oversimplified but nevertheless useful shorthand for comparing the primary competing political paradigms in America.

THE IDEA OF EQUAL OPPORTUNITY

Much of the debate can be captured within two competing paradigms, the conservative opportunity society and the egalitarian welfare state. The COS assumes that lower cuts, reduced government regulation, and spending cuts will free America's productive resources, stimulate economic growth, and provide opportunities for all Americans. A second plank of the agenda requires that the freedom unleashed by the scaling back of government be checked and bounded by moral values, the traditional family structure, organized religion, and the institutions of civil society. Economic liberalism and social conservatism combine to provide the underpinnings for economic opportunity and social stability.

The shift to a state-centered welfare system is consistent with the conservative opportunity society vision. Time limits and other restrictions on eligibility create incentives for self-reliance and discourage dependency. Targeting teenagers who bear children outside of marriage will reduce illegitimacy and promote families. Promoting work encourages welfare recipients to become integrated into the dominant institutions of American society and to gain the economic and psychological benefits that come from productive work. For those who need assistance, because they are not able-bodied or capable of self-support, or need more assistance to prepare themselves for meaningful work, local government and private organizations are better suited than national programs to provide that assistance. Local control can promote community involvement in solving problems and encourage the kind of committed volunteerism that is more likely to engage recipients in transforming their lives than traditional, bureaucratic schemes ever can.

This vision of welfare and the broader context of markets, economic freedom, and community institutions is attractive for several reasons. It could solve some of the most vexing problems surrounding poverty and welfare. It offers a broad array of efforts that together can help those who are economically inactive, psychologically discouraged, and physically isolated. It is rooted in values of work, family, self-sufficiency, and community responsibility that ring true to many Americans. But the vision also requires a leap of faith that the institutions of local government and civil society will be sufficiently energetic, capable, and sensitive to meet these heightened expectations. In some communities, no doubt such institutions exist or will arise. Some communities have the energy, resources, leadership, and good will to rally efforts on behalf of those who need help. But what about the communities that are so racked by crime, decay, discouragement, or economic decline that they seem to lack even the spark necessary to ignite such an effort? Perhaps the realization that there is no national safety net will stimulate the kind of volunteerism, community, and support that lay dormant while there were alternatives. It is no small irony that conservatives who are sometimes branded as pessimists about the human enterprise or skeptical of progress are the real optimists here, eager to place their faith in local government, community organizations, and the marketplace. Perhaps it is because most of them expect never to be in a situation of dependence, and have the educational, social, and psychological resources to be independent. But some advocates of the conservative opportunity society have themselves been poor and disadvantaged and are true believers in the potential of individual empowerment. Their faith is not blind but rooted in immediate, personal experience.

Advocates of a liberal egalitarian state are generally quite pessimistic about the likelihood that markets, local government, and private institutions will foster equal opportunity. Their skepticism is also rooted in personal experience. The struggle for civil rights, for equality for women, for fairness to homosexuals and other victims of intolerance, has produced a sober appreciation of the problems of community and the need for a commitment to national rights. They believe that the racism, sexism, parochialism, and lack of opportunity that have characterized many communities continue. Their natural skepticism of government has been replaced by a faith that only a strong, national government can counter prejudice, social intolerance, and the concentration of economic power, and ensure that opportunity is equally and fairly distributed.

A liberal egalitarian state is also an attractive public philosophy. It promises a minimum level of assistance to those who are needy. It promises a minimum level of consistency across states and regions so that people are not penalized because of where they live. The liberal egalitarian state takes that core American ideal of equality of opportunity so seriously that it seeks to ensure that ideal reaches everyone. It avoids the threat that some states will turn their backs on the most politically unpopular of their residents and use scarce resources for more fashionable constituencies. Perhaps most important, a liberal egalitarian state recognizes that participation in a global economy requires a national effort. The tremendous economic changes that buffet Americans require a strong national commitment to ensuring opportunities, especially in areas that are economically isolated and depressed.

Neither side has completely won or lost the debate over welfare reform. Liberals got continued federal spending on welfare, albeit through block grants; more spending on child care than was originally envisioned; continuation of the federal Food Stamp and Medicaid programs; and a requirement that states maintain most of their existing welfare commitment. But conservatives clearly won the battle. They achieved their goals of ending the federal welfare entitlement, imposing time limits on welfare, spending less on means-tested programs, and removing one highly visible element of big government. They had to retreat in important ways in their quest to change welfare, but they prevailed on most of their key concerns. The new welfare law made greater changes to the old system than anyone imagined possible only a few years earlier.

THE FUTURE OF THE WELFARE STATE

What are the implications of the welfare battle for the war on the welfare state? It is exceedingly difficult to attempt an objective answer to that question. Those who are looking for victory point to long-term indicators of a shift away from the Democrats' promise of a Great Society led by a strong, pervasive, interventionist federal government. The shift began with Ronald Reagan in 1981, continued even though a Democrat moved in the White House after the 1992 election, expanded in 1994 as one-party rule ended in the House of Representatives, and resulted in the end of one of the most visible and politically significant elements of the welfare state during the closing days of the 104th Congress in 1996. Welfare reform opened the floodgates unlocked by Reagan to devolve power from the national government to states. It will be followed by devolution of health care and other key elements that formerly made up a national safety net.

Those who are looking for evidence that a strong federal government is alive and well, that the national welfare state and its egalitarian commitment will continue, have much to cite. Welfare was a remarkably unpopular program. Its clash with powerful cultural values was so striking that reform was inevitable. But the many years it took to bring about change reflects support for even the most vulnerable of the welfare state's programs. The inability of Republicans to make changes in Medicaid and Medicare and the potency of the Democratic use of health programs in branding the Republican Congress as extremist provides much encouragement. The tenuousness of support in the nation for Republicans reflected in polling data produced in anticipation of the 1996 election is further evidence that the Republican agenda of 1994 has not yet garnered majority support.

Perhaps the truth is somewhere in the middle. The ending of a national commitment to helping poor children and families is tremendously significant. If that is no longer a fundamental national commitment, then much of the welfare state is susceptible to arguments for devolution—not that we should no longer have a social safety net, but that the net should be sewn by each state. But welfare had become so unpopular and criticisms of it so universal, that one could argue its devolution to states could be more of an aberration than a harbinger of things to come. It is difficult to overstate the potency of the frustration that working Americans felt as they saw their taxes go to people who were not required to do anything in exchange for cash benefits. The situation fed on fears of social unrest, poverty, and decay that result from children having children they cannot raise and the collapse of fatherhood and strong families.

Perhaps the future of the shape and location of the welfare state is more within the hands of the Democratic party than the Republican reformers. Bob Dole could legitimately claim, as he did throughout the 1996 presidential campaign, that the Republican party was the party of reform. But the debate over the welfare state is much more immediate and divisive in the Democratic party, split between those who demand a strong, national presence to combat poverty, discrimination, and the host of other social ills, and those who favor devolution, experimentation, community control, and other approaches. If the Democrats are able to find some common ground that, for example, encourages local innovation and experimentation while still providing some national minimum protection and benefits, then the national safety net will continue, no doubt somewhat looser, but intact. If, on the other hand, Democrats are not able to manage the difficult debate and they degenerate into two irreconcilable camps, they may provide the void for Republicans to fill. But Republicans are also strongly divided over some welfare issues.

For now, mainstream public sentiment in America seems to favor moderate, pragmatic, consensual solutions to problems. Americans' skepticism with political rhetoric and vitriolic and divisive debate has been well described. What made welfare reform so politically popular was the widespread perception of common ground: Welfare needed to be reformed. But people were optimistic that it could be done in ways that will provide help to those who need and deserve it, and create the kinds of incentives needed to move people from dependency to self-sufficiency.

Although there is growing agreement that Medicare and Social Security are unsustainable at current tax and payment rates, there is no emergent consensus over how to solve the problem. Until that emerges, "reforms" will be difficult. But the pace of reform can be accelerated. Despite the strong support for changing welfare, it still required Bill Clinton's 1992 promise to end welfare and pressure from the 1996 election to keep his word, as well as the determination of the Republican House and Senate leaders to put it high on the agenda. Given the strong public support for changing welfare, and the lack of powerful advocates for the existing system, this was not a major act of leadership. Congressional Democrats did have the chance to reform welfare, but they did not. The Reagan administration had the chance to at least push for major reform but did not. It was not until there was a change in leadership at both ends of Pennsylvania Avenue that fundamental change was possible.

WELFARE REFORM AND SOCIAL POLICY

Welfare reform must be integrated with economic and social policies that reduce poverty and strengthen families. We can try to do welfare reform on the cheap, but that will not prevent future problems. We can pay now or later. Prevention is much preferable because it can help children, parents, and families make something of their lives rather than require society to intervene. Thirty years ago, in his inaugural address, President John F. Kennedy called on his fellow citizens to "bear the burden of a long twilight struggle, year in and year out, 'rejoicing in hope, patient in tribulation'—a struggle against the common enemies of man: tyranny, poverty, disease and war itself."[26] Lyndon Johnson, in his 1964 State of the Union address, committed his administration to "unconditional war on poverty in America."[27] Not long after that war began, it was overwhelmed by Lyndon Johnson's other war in Southeast Asia. None of the five presidents who followed Johnson ever pursued the idea of a war on poverty. In reality, that war has never really been fought; the necessary resources and energy have never been committed. Most of the optimism and enthusiasm generated in the mid-1960s dissipated within a few years, and difficulty of the task and competing concerns discouraged all but the most ardent champions of a war on poverty.

Social policy is clearly a risky, uncertain enterprise, and failures are just as likely as successes. We have been so afraid that if women and children are given a decent income they will become so dependent on government assistance that they will never escape the need for it. As a consequence, we have permitted millions of children and women to suffer from poverty so that we would not run the risk of encouraging dependency. That risk is real, but the potential harm it represents must be balanced by the actual damage inflicted by poverty. Children deserve the opportunity to grow up in a reasonably safe, healthy, and sustainable environment. Providing sufficient resources to raise children in such an environment is a minimum obligation we have to each other. It is a moral imperative. It is a wise investment in the future. It will translate into money saved to treat social problems that are inevitable if no intervention is made. Even if assistance to these families does not have ideal policy attributes, it will nevertheless represent our commitment to decency, to reducing suffering, and to caring for each other.

Part of an agenda to reduce poverty could be to raise the level of cash benefits to provide an adequate, minimum income, and to ensure that all eligible families are served. The clearest way to reduce poverty among children is to provide more assistance to their parents. It would be ideal if that assistance can be combined with other efforts to promote self-sufficiency and self-improvement.

Welfare policy must be seen as part of a much broader commitment to social policy. There has never been a comprehensive, aggressive effort to reclaim urban areas from the violence, crime, and decay that afflict them. Housing policy, educational reform in urban schools, increased police protection, encouraging investments and job creation in economically depressed areas are all part of the policy agenda. Programs exist to address virtually all of the causes of poverty, but they have never been funded sufficiently to permit all those who qualify to participate.

Finally, the primary determinant of poverty is unemployment. Training and educational programs must be combined with a commitment to guarantee a job for every person who seeks one. Training programs that are not combined with guaranteed employment opportunities are destined to fuel frustration and discouragement. The full-employment legislation passed in the 1970s has never been taken very seriously, but the legislative framework is in place. Poor mothers who have educational and training programs, support services, adequate child care, and guaranteed opportunities to work may not all take advantage of these programs. Providing an opportunity for those who choose to take advantage of them would still be a great step forward for us as a society, and of incalculable benefit to those women and their children. Ensuring jobs would do much to reduce the reliance on welfare, and would help us begin to address the unmet needs in our urban areas, protect our natural resources, and address other pressing public concerns.

We do not lack ideas or precedents for reducing and even eliminating poverty among children and women in our society. Other countries, particularly those in Western Europe, have made much more progress than the United States in reducing poverty. Their progress has usually been steady, in contrast to the fits of progressivism and retrenchment that have characterized social policy in the United States. Others are not without serious social, economic, and political challenges in providing for poor families: crime, drugs, suicide, delinquency, divorce, and abortion are widespread. The economic, political, and cultural differences between the United States and these other nations are considerable. The welfare state is under attack in some European countries and is at least being reevaluated in others. But other countries seem to have the foresight and wisdom to make investments today that promise future benefits. We Americans seem to lack the patience to support effective solutions and demand, instead, immediate solutions to long-run problems.

We also lack the sense of responsibility for ensuring that all members of our society have access to a minimum level of resources even as we proclaim our commitment to equality of opportunity. The more resources individuals command, the more opportunity they enjoy. Equality of opportunity is a commitment to both freedom and equality, as all people have the opportunity to develop their talents and abilities and make something of their lives.

We rightly recognize the value of voluntary efforts to remedy social problems, but we fail to realize that volunteerism cannot replace ensuring that needs are met. Volunteerism is great for the volunteers, but when it falls short, women and children needlessly suffer. It is inexcusable, in a society as rich as ours, that we find so many real and imagined reasons to ignore the pain and misery that plague so many of our neighbors.

Much of the debate in the United States over "family policy" has failed to address the tremendous challenges facing women, children, and families. The current public fixation is with child care: Should child care be subsidized directly or through income tax credits? Should federal health and safety standards should be set for child care centers or left to the states? How much we should spend, the level of benefits to recipients, and eligibility for participation are all widely debated. But none of the proposals would go very far in eliminating poverty among

American children, nor would they provide much help for working mothers in addressing the challenges they face. If we are serious about encouraging families, we could pursue public policies that provide an allowance for every child living in a family at or below poverty levels. There would be some disadvantages to such an effort, some inefficiency and waste, some who would misuse the funds made available, but these costs are outweighed by the benefits realized.

Society has a primary interest in the health of the family. What goes on in families is of enormous importance for the rest of society: They are the most effective institution we have for preparing children to participate in our social, economic, and political processes and environments. Reducing poverty among children ought to be a compelling public purpose. Remedying the unfairness in the distribution of poverty is another such purpose. Welfare policy can only solve part of these problems. But the high stakes compel us to try and come up with policies that work.

WELFARE POLICY AND POLICY MAKING

One of the most serious threats to democratic government is the temptation of politicians to overpromise, to commit the nation to unrealistic goals. Government inevitably falls short, causing modest, reasonable progress to be discounted and skepticism to grow. Promises to end welfare, when we do not know how to do that, are a serious barrier to progress.[28]

Can we avoid the welfare policy trap, in which we promise to make major reforms and create high expectations, then enact reforms but only partially fund them, so that for most recipients there is little change? As one congressional staff member put it, "half-measures are, after all, the norm with this subject."[29] Despite the apparent support for comprehensive reform, adequate funding of such reforms is very unlikely. We need to explore modest changes. There are lots of candidates; being more modest and realistic in our reform efforts, and ensuring that those efforts are fully funded, may be more important than which initiative we pursue first.

The prospect for reforms that fundamentally improve the welfare system is uncertain. At one level, the issues are difficult but less complex than for some other policy areas. A key challenge is finding the additional money that is necessary to help recipients who are least prepared to take a job receive the training, counseling and other assistance they need and to ensure that jobs are available for everyone able to work.

At another level, welfare reform can only be a part of a much broader agenda to address the problems that lead to the need for welfare. But there is only limited political will for such an ambitious agenda, and we will need to pursue it through moderate improvements in policy that will contribute incrementally to the solutions we need. Perhaps more than anything else, the current round of welfare reform efforts will be successful if it does two things: (1) create reasonable expectations for modest improvements in the current system and meet those expectations; and (2) engender some confidence that federal and state governments can design and implement effective social policies so that the broader agenda of reducing poverty and expanding opportunity in America can be pursued.

Finally, can we protect welfare recipients and maintain our commitment to helping the most vulnerable among us even as we try to change their behavior? There is resentment and backlash against welfare recipients. Judging the poor seems inevitable. We make moral judgments about what causes their plight and what they ought to do to solve their problems. They ought to get a job, go to school, stop having babies. Perhaps the moralizing is unavoidable. We need to make hard choices about what actions we will encourage, tolerate, and reward. But perhaps our moralizing and our policy making can be informed by a little more compassion, a little less confidence about our own achievements and our own self-sufficiency. John Rawls's essay on justice argues that we cannot claim credit for our successful status in life; our advantageous circumstances, the support we find around us, even our own industry and self-determination cannot be claimed as earned.[30] Our religious traditions offer similar warnings about judging the poor, against claiming for ourselves that which belongs to God, and about failing to share the resources we have been given with those who lack them.

REFERENCES

[1] *New State Ice Co. v. Liebmann*, 285 U.S. 262, 311 (1932) (Justice Brandeis, dissenting).

[2] Donald F. Norris and Lyke Thompson, eds. *The Politics of Welfare Reform* (Thousand Oaks, Calif.: Sage Publications, 1995), 236–37.

[3] William Claiborne and Judith Havemann, "A Block Grant That's a Hot Potato," *The Washington Post*, National Weekly Edition, August 12–18, 1996, p. 30.

[4] Dana Milbank, "Welfare Law's Work Rules Worry States," *The Wall Street Journal*, August 5, 1996, p. A2.

[5] Robert Pear, "Changes in How Welfare Is Operated, While Sweeping, Will Be Taking Shape Slowly," *The New York Times*, August 6, 1996, p. A11.

[6] Milbank, "Welfare Law's Work Rules Worry States."

[7] Pear, "Changes in How Welfare Is Operated, While Sweeping, Will Be Taking Shape Slowly"; Jason DeParle, "U.S. Welfare System Dies As State Programs Emerge," *The New York Times*, June 30, 1997, p. A1.

[8] Theda Skocpol, "Welfare: Where Do We Go from Here? Bury It," *The New Republic* (August 12, 1996): 20–21.

[9] David Popenoe, *Life Without Father* (New York: The Free Press, 1996): 63–64.

[10] Ibid., 26–31.

[11] Ibid., 25–26, 41.

[12] Ibid., 5.

[13] Ibid., 11–12.

[14] Ibid., 12–13.

[15] Ibid., 7–8, quote at 15.

[16] See Council on Families in America, "Marriage in America: A Report to the Nation," summarized in Popenoe, *Life Without Father*, 199–201, for a discussion of suggestions for each of these groups.

[17] See, for example, Michael J. McManus, "The Marriage-Saving Movement," *The American Enterprise* (May/June 1996): 28–33.

[18] William A. Galston, "Braking Divorce for the Sake of Children," *The American Enterprise* (May/June 1996): 36.

[19] Rosin, "Separation Anxiety," 14–16.

[20] See comments of Senator Bill Bradley, 104 *Cong. Rec.*, S. 9366 (August 1, 1996).

[21] Ibid.

[22] Figures are from Sen. Bob Kerrey, 104 *Cong. Rec.*, S. 9339–40 (August 1, 1996).

[23] See Barbara Bergmann, *In Defense of Affirmative Action* (New York: Basic Books, 1996).

[24] Michael Walzer, "Gulf Crisis," *The New Republic* (August 5, 1996): 25.

[25] Quoted in William Raspberry, "Welfare Reform, Wisconsin Style," *The Washington Post*, July 15, 1996, p. A19.

[26] John F. Kennedy, *Public Papers of the Presidents of the United States: John F. Kennedy, 1961* (Washington, D.C.: U.S. Government Printing Office, 1962), 2.

[27] Lyndon B. Johnson, *Public Papers of the Presidents of the United States: Lyndon B. Johnson, 1963–64*, book 1 (Washington, D.C.: U.S. Government Printing Office, 1965), 114.

[28] Jacob Weisberg, "Leaner, Cleaner Liberals," *The New Republic* (April 1, 1996): 17–25, at 19.

[29] Offner, "Target the Kids," at 10.

[30] John Rawls, *A Theory of Justice* (Cambridge, Mass.: Harvard University Press, 1971).

Index